Introduction to Reliable and Secure Distributed Programming

Christian Cachin • Rachid Guerraoui
Luís Rodrigues

Introduction to

Reliable and Secure Distributed Programming

Second Edition

 Springer

Dr. Christian Cachin
IBM Research Zürich
Säumerstrasse 4
8803 Rüschlikon
Switzerland
cca@zurich.ibm.com

Prof. Luís Rodrigues
INESC-ID
Instituto Superior Técnico
Rua Alves Redol 9
1000-029 Lisboa
Portugal
ler@ist.utl.pt

Prof. Dr. Rachid Guerraoui
Ecole Polytechnique
Fédérale Lausanne (EPFL)
Fac. Informatique et Communications
Lab. Programmation Distribuée (LPD)
Station 14
1015 Lausanne
Bat. INR
Switzerland
Rachid.Guerraoui@epfl.ch

ISBN 978-3-642-42327-7   ISBN 978-3-642-15260-3 (eBook)
DOI 10.1007/978-3-642-15260-3
Springer Heidelberg Dordrecht London New York

ACM Computing Classification (1998): C.2, F.2, G.2

Cover design: KuenkelLopka GmbH

Printed on acid-free paper

Springer is part of Springer Science+Business Media (www.springer.com)

To Irene, Philippe and André.
To Maria and Sarah.
To Hugo and Sara.

Preface

This book provides an introduction to distributed programming abstractions and presents the fundamental algorithms that implement them in several distributed environments. The reader is given insight into the important problems of distributed computing and the main algorithmic techniques used to solve these problems. Through examples the reader can learn how these methods can be applied to building distributed applications. The central theme of the book is the tolerance to uncertainty and adversarial influence in a distributed system, which may arise from network delays, faults, or even malicious attacks.

Content

In modern computing, a program usually encompasses *multiple processes*. A process is simply an abstraction that may represent a physical computer or a virtual one, a processor within a computer, or a specific thread of execution in a concurrent system. The fundamental problem with devising such distributed programs is to have all processes *cooperate* on some *common* task. Of course, traditional centralized algorithmic issues still need to be dealt with for each process individually. Distributed environments, which may range from a single computer to a data center or even a global system available around the clock, pose additional challenges: how to achieve a robust form of cooperation despite process failures, disconnections of some of the processes, or even malicious attacks on some processes? Distributed algorithms should be dependable, offer reliability and security, and have predictable behavior even under negative influence from the environment.

If no cooperation were required, a distributed program would simply consist of a set of independent centralized programs, each running on a specific process, and little benefit could be obtained from the availability of several processes in a distributed environment. It was the need for cooperation that revealed many of the fascinating problems addressed by this book, problems that need to be solved to make distributed computing a reality. The book not only introduces the reader to these problem statements, it also presents ways to solve them in different contexts.

Not surprisingly, distributed programming can be significantly simplified if the difficulty of robust cooperation is encapsulated within specific *abstractions*. By encapsulating all the tricky algorithmic issues, such distributed programming abstractions bridge the gap between network communication layers, which are usually frugal in terms of dependability guarantees, and distributed application layers, which usually demand highly dependable primitives.

The book presents various distributed programming abstractions and describes algorithms that implement them. In a sense, we give the distributed application programmer a library of abstract interface specifications, and give the distributed system builder a library of algorithms that implement the specifications.

A significant amount of the preparation time for this book was devoted to formulating a collection of exercises and developing their solutions. We strongly encourage the reader to work out the exercises. We believe that no reasonable understanding can be achieved in a passive way. This is especially true in the field of distributed computing, where the human mind too often follows some attractive but misleading intuition. The book also includes the solutions for all exercises, to emphasize our intention to make them an integral part of the content. Many exercises are rather easy and can be discussed within an undergraduate teaching classroom. Other exercises are more difficult and need more time. These can typically be studied individually.

Presentation

The book as such is self-contained. This has been made possible because the field of distributed algorithms has reached a certain level of maturity, where distracting details can be abstracted away for reasoning about distributed algorithms. Such details include the behavior of the communication network, its various kinds of failures, as well as implementations of cryptographic primitives; all of them are treated in-depth by other works. Elementary knowledge about algorithms, first-order logic, programming languages, networking, security, and operating systems might be helpful. But we believe that most of our abstractions and algorithms can be understood with minimal knowledge about these notions.

The book follows an incremental approach and was primarily written as a textbook for teaching at the undergraduate or basic graduate level. It introduces the fundamental elements of distributed computing in an intuitive manner and builds sophisticated distributed programming abstractions from elementary ones in a modular way. Whenever we devise algorithms to implement a given abstraction, we consider a simple distributed-system model first, and then we revisit the algorithms in more challenging models. In other words, we first devise algorithms by making strong simplifying assumptions on the distributed environment, and then we discuss how to weaken those assumptions.

We have tried to balance intuition and presentation simplicity on the one hand with rigor on the other hand. Sometimes rigor was affected, and this might not have been always on purpose. The focus here is rather on abstraction specifications and algorithms, not on computability and complexity. Indeed, there is no theorem in this book. Correctness arguments are given with the aim of better understanding the algorithms: they are not formal correctness proofs per se.

Organization

The book has six chapters, grouped in two parts. The first part establishes the common ground:

- In Chapter 1, we *motivate* the need for distributed programming abstractions by discussing various applications that typically make use of such abstractions. The chapter also introduces the modular notation and the pseudo code used to describe the algorithms in the book.
- In Chapter 2, we present different kinds of *assumptions* about the underlying distributed environment. We introduce a family of distributed-system models for this purpose. Basically, a model describes the low-level abstractions on which more sophisticated ones are built. These include process and communication link abstractions. This chapter might be considered as a reference to other chapters.

The remaining four chapters make up the second part of the book. Each chapter is devoted to one problem, containing a broad class of related abstractions and various algorithms implementing them. We will go from the simpler abstractions to the more sophisticated ones:

- In Chapter 3, we introduce communication abstractions for distributed programming. They permit the *broadcasting* of a message to a group of processes and offer diverse reliability guarantees for delivering messages to the processes. For instance, we discuss how to make sure that a message delivered to one process is also delivered to all other processes, despite the crash of the original sender process.
- In Chapter 4, we discuss *shared memory* abstractions, which encapsulate simple forms of distributed storage objects, accessed by read and write operations. These could be files in a distributed storage system or registers in the memory of a multi-processor computer. We cover methods for reading and writing data values by clients, such that a value stored by a set of processes can later be retrieved, even if some of the processes crash, have erased the value, or report wrong data.
- In Chapter 5, we address the *consensus* abstraction through which a set of processes can decide on a common value, based on values that the processes initially propose. They must reach the same decision despite faulty processes, which may have crashed or may even actively try to prevent the others from reaching a common decision.
- In Chapter 6, we consider *variants of consensus*, which are obtained by extending or modifying the consensus abstraction according to the needs of important applications. This includes total-order broadcast, terminating reliable broadcast, (non-blocking) atomic commitment, group membership, and view-synchronous communication.

The distributed algorithms we study not only differ according to the actual abstraction they implement, but also according to the assumptions they make on the underlying distributed environment. We call the set of initial abstractions that an algorithm takes for granted a *distributed-system model*. Many aspects have a fundamental impact on how an algorithm is designed, such as the reliability of the links, the degree of synchrony of the system, the severity of the failures, and whether a deterministic or a randomized solution is sought.

In several places throughout the book, the same basic distributed programming primitive is implemented in multiple distributed-system models. The intention behind this is two-fold: first, to create insight into the specific problems encountered in a particular system model, and second, to illustrate how the choice of a model affects the implementation of a primitive.

A detailed study of all chapters and the associated exercises constitutes a rich and thorough introduction to the field. Focusing on each chapter solely for the specifications of the abstractions and their underlying algorithms in their simplest form, i.e., for the simplest system model with crash failures only, would constitute a shorter, more elementary course. Such a course could provide a nice companion to a more practice-oriented course on distributed programming.

Changes Made for the Second Edition

This edition is a thoroughly revised version of the first edition. Most parts of the book have been updated. But the biggest change was to expand the scope of the book to a new dimension, addressing the key concept of *security against malicious actions*. Abstractions and algorithms in a model of distributed computing that allows adversarial attacks have become known as *Byzantine fault-tolerance*.

The first edition of the book was titled "Introduction to Reliable Distributed Programming." By adding one word ("secure") to the title – and adding one co-author – the evolution of the book reflects the developments in the field of distributed systems and in the real world. Since the first edition was published in 2006, it has become clear that most practical distributed systems are threatened by intrusions and that insiders cannot be ruled out as the source of malicious attacks. Building dependable distributed systems nowadays requires an interdisciplinary effort, with inputs from distributed algorithms, security, and other domains.

On the technical level, the syntax for modules and the names of some events have changed, in order to add more structure for presenting the algorithms. A module may now exist in multiple instances at the same time within an algorithm, and every instance is named by a unique identifier for this purpose. We believe that this has simplified the presentation of several important algorithms.

The first edition of this book contained a companion set of running examples implemented in the Java programming language, using the *Appia* protocol composition framework. The implementation addresses systems subject to crash failures and is available from the book's online website.

Online Resources

More information about the book, including the implementation of many protocols from the first edition, tutorial presentation material, classroom slides, and errata, is available online on the book's website at:

```
http://distributedprogramming.net
```

References

We have been exploring the world of distributed programming abstractions for almost two decades now. The material of this book has been influenced by many researchers in the field of distributed computing. A special mention is due to Leslie Lamport and Nancy Lynch for having posed fascinating problems in distributed computing, and to the *Cornell school* of reliable distributed computing, including Özalp Babaoglu, Ken Birman, Keith Marzullo, Robbert van Rennesse, Rick Schlichting, Fred Schneider, and Sam Toueg.

Many other researchers have directly or indirectly inspired the material of this book. We did our best to reference their work throughout the text. All chapters end with notes that give context information and historical references; our intention behind them is to provide hints for further reading, to trace the history of the presented concepts, as well as to give credit to the people who invented and worked out the concepts. At the end of the book, we reference books on other aspects of distributed computing for further reading.

Acknowledgments

We would like to express our deepest gratitude to our undergraduate and graduate students from the École Polytechnique Fédérale de Lausanne (EPFL) and the University of Lisboa (UL), for serving as reviewers of preliminary drafts of this book. Indeed, they had no choice and needed to prepare for their exams anyway! But they were indulgent toward the bugs and typos that could be found in earlier versions of the book as well as associated slides, and they provided us with useful feedback.

Partha Dutta, Corine Hari, Michal Kapalka, Petr Kouznetsov, Ron Levy, Maxime Monod, Bastian Pochon, and Jesper Spring, graduate students from the School of Computer and Communication Sciences of EPFL, Filipe Araújo and Hugo Miranda, graduate students from the Distributed Algorithms and Network Protocol (DIALNP) group at the Departamento de Informática da Faculdade de Ciências da Universidade de Lisboa (UL), Leila Khalil and Robert Basmadjian, graduate students from the Lebanese University in Beirut, as well as Ali Ghodsi, graduate student from the Swedish Institute of Computer Science (SICS) in Stockholm, suggested many improvements to the algorithms presented in the book.

Several implementations for the "hands-on" part of the book were developed by, or with the help of, Alexandre Pinto, a key member of the *Appia* team, complemented with inputs from several DIALNP team members and students, including Nuno Carvalho, Maria João Monteiro, and Luís Sardinha.

Finally, we would like to thank all our colleagues who were kind enough to comment on earlier drafts of this book. These include Felix Gaertner, Benoit Garbinato, and Maarten van Steen.

Acknowledgments for the Second Edition

Work on the second edition of this book started while Christian Cachin was on sabbatical leave from IBM Research at EPFL in 2009. We are grateful for the support of EPFL and IBM Research.

We thank again the students at EPFL and the University of Lisboa, who worked with the book, for improving the first edition. We extend our gratitude to the students at the Instituto Superior Técnico (IST) of the Universidade Técnica de Lisboa, at ETH Zürich, and at EPFL, who were exposed to preliminary drafts of the additional material included in the second edition, for their helpful feedback.

We are grateful to many attentive readers of the first edition and to those who commented on earlier drafts of the second edition, for pointing out problems and suggesting improvements. In particular, we thank Zinaida Benenson, Alysson Bessani, Diego Biurrun, Filipe Cristóvão, Dan Dobre, Felix Freiling, Ali Ghodsi, Seif Haridi, Matúš Harvan, Rüdiger Kapitza, Nikola Knežević, Andreas Knobel, Mihai Letia, Thomas Locher, Hein Meling, Hugo Miranda, Luís Pina, Martin Schaub, and Marko Vukolić.

Christian Cachin
Rachid Guerraoui
Luís Rodrigues

Contents

1. Introduction

I am putting myself to the fullest possible use, which is all I think that any
conscious entity can ever hope to do.
(HAL 9000)

This chapter first motivates the need for distributed programming abstractions. Special attention is given to abstractions that capture the problems that underlie robust forms of cooperation between multiple processes in a distributed system, usually called *agreement* abstractions. The chapter then advocates a modular strategy for the development of distributed programs by making use of those abstractions through specific Application Programming Interfaces (APIs).

A simple, concrete example of an API is also given to illustrate the notation and event-based invocation scheme used throughout the book to describe the algorithms that implement our abstractions. The notation and invocation schemes are very close to those that are found in practical implementations of distributed algorithms.

1.1 Motivation

Distributed computing addresses algorithms for a set of processes that seek to achieve some form of cooperation. Besides executing concurrently, some of the processes of a distributed system might stop operating, for instance, by crashing or being disconnected, while others might stay alive and keep operating. This very notion of *partial failures* is a characteristic of a distributed system. In fact, this notion can be useful if one really feels the need to differentiate a distributed system from a concurrent system. It is in order to quote Leslie Lamport here:

> "A distributed system is one in which the failure of a computer you did not even know existed can render your own computer unusable."

When a subset of the processes have failed, or become disconnected, the challenge is usually for the processes that are still operating, or connected to the majority of

C. Cachin et al., *Introduction to Reliable and Secure Distributed Programming*,
DOI: 10.1007/978-3-642-15260-3_1,
© Springer-Verlag Berlin Heidelberg 2011

the processes, to synchronize their activities in a consistent way. In other words, the cooperation must be made robust to tolerate partial failures and sometimes also adversarial attacks. This makes distributed computing a hard, yet extremely stimulating problem. Due to the asynchrony of the processes, the possibility of failures in the communication infrastructure, and perhaps even malicious actions by faulty processes, it may be impossible to accurately detect process failures; in particular, there is often no way to distinguish a process failure from a network failure, as we will discuss in detail later in the book. Even worse, a process that is under the control of a malicious adversary may misbehave deliberately, in order to disturb the communication among the remaining processes. This makes the problem of ensuring consistent cooperation even more difficult. The challenge in distributed computing is precisely to devise algorithms that provide the processes that remain operating with enough consistent information so that they can cooperate correctly and solve common tasks.

In fact, many programs that we use today are distributed programs. Simple daily routines, such as reading e-mail or browsing the Web, involve some form of distributed computing. However, when using these applications, we are typically faced with the simplest form of distributed computing: *client–server* computing. In client–server computing, a centralized process, the *server*, provides a service to many remote *clients*. The clients and the server communicate by exchanging messages, usually following a request–reply form of interaction. For instance, in order to display a Web page to the user, a browser sends a request to the Web server and expects to obtain a response with the information to be displayed. The core difficulty of distributed computing, namely, achieving a consistent form of cooperation in the presence of partial failures, may pop up even by using this simple form of interaction. Going back to our browsing example, it is reasonable to expect that the user continues surfing the Web if the consulted Web server fails (but the user is automatically switched to another Web server), and even more reasonable that the server process keeps on providing information to the other client processes, even when some of them fail or get disconnected.

The problems above are already nontrivial when distributed computing is limited to the interaction between two parties, such as in the client–server case. However, there is more to distributed computing than handling client–server interactions. Quite often, not only two, but several processes need to cooperate and synchronize their actions to achieve a common goal. The existence of multiple processes complicates distributed computing even more. Sometimes we talk about *multiparty* interactions in this general case. In fact, both patterns may coexist in a quite natural manner. Actually, many distributed applications have parts following a client–server interaction pattern and other parts following a multiparty interaction pattern. This may even be a matter of perspective. For instance, when a client contacts a server to obtain a service, it may not be aware that, in order to provide that service, the server itself may need to request the assistance of several other servers, with whom it needs to coordinate to satisfy the client's request. Sometimes, the expression *peer-to-peer computing* is used to emphasize the absence of a central server.

1.2 Distributed Programming Abstractions

Just like the act of smiling, the act of abstracting is restricted to very few natural species. By capturing properties that are common to a large and significant range of systems, abstractions help distinguish the fundamental from the accessory, and prevent system designers and engineers from reinventing, over and over, the same solutions for slight variants of the very same problems.

From the Basics ... Reasoning about distributed systems should start by abstracting the underlying physical system: describing the relevant elements in an abstract way, identifying their intrinsic properties, and characterizing their interactions, lead us to define what is called a *system model*. In this book we will use mainly two abstractions to represent the underlying physical system: *processes* and *links*.

The processes of a distributed program abstract the active entities that perform computations. A process may represent a computer, a processor within a computer, or simply a specific thread of execution within a processor. In the context of network security, a process may also represent a trust domain, a principal, or one administrative unit. To cooperate on some common task, the processes may typically need to exchange messages using some communication network. Links abstract the physical and logical network that supports communication among processes. It is possible to represent multiple realizations of a distributed system by capturing different properties of processes and links, for instance, by describing how these elements may operate or fail under different environmental conditions.

Chapter 2 will provide a deeper discussion of the various distributed-system models that are used in this book.

... to the Advanced. Given a system model, the next step is to understand how to build abstractions that capture recurring interaction patterns in distributed applications. In this book we are interested in abstractions that capture robust cooperation problems among groups of processes, as these are important and rather challenging. The cooperation among processes can sometimes be modeled as a distributed *agreement* problem. For instance, the processes may need to agree on whether a certain event did (or did not) take place, to agree on a common sequence of actions to be performed (from a number of initial alternatives), or to agree on the order by which a set of inputs need to be processed. It is desirable to establish more sophisticated forms of agreement from solutions to simpler agreement problems, in an incremental manner. Consider, for instance, the following situations:

- In order for processes to be able to exchange information, they must initially agree on who they are (say, using IP addresses on the Internet) and on some common format for representing messages. They may also need to agree on some way of exchanging messages (say, to use a reliable data stream for communication, like TCP over the Internet).
- After exchanging some messages, the processes may be faced with several alternative plans of action. They may need to reach a *consensus* on a common plan, out of several alternatives, and each participating process may have initially its own plan, different from the plans of the other processes.

- In some cases, it may be acceptable for the cooperating processes to take a given step only if all other processes also agree that such a step should take place. If this condition is not met, all processes must agree that the step should *not* take place. This form of agreement is crucial in the processing of distributed transactions, where this problem is known as the *atomic commitment* problem.
- Processes may not only need to agree on which actions they should execute but also need to agree on the order in which these actions should be executed. This form of agreement is the basis of one of the most fundamental techniques to replicate computation in order to achieve fault tolerance, and it is called the *total-order broadcast* problem.

This book is about mastering the difficulty that underlies these problems, and devising *abstractions* that encapsulate such problems. The problems are hard because they require coordination among the processes; given that processes may fail or may even behave maliciously, such abstractions are powerful and sometimes not straightforward to build. In the following, we motivate the relevance of some of the abstractions covered in this book. We distinguish the case where the abstractions emerge from the natural distribution of the application on the one hand, and the case where these abstractions come out as artifacts of an engineering choice for distribution on the other hand.

1.2.1 Inherent Distribution

Applications that require sharing or dissemination of information among several participant processes are a fertile ground for the emergence of problems that required distributed programming abstractions. Examples of such applications are information dissemination engines, multiuser cooperative systems, distributed shared spaces, process control systems, cooperative editors, distributed databases, and distributed storage systems.

Information Dissemination. In distributed applications with information dissemination requirements, processes may play one of the following roles: information producers, also called *publishers*, or information consumers, also called *subscribers*. The resulting interaction paradigm is often called *publish–subscribe*.

Publishers produce information in the form of notifications. Subscribers register their interest in receiving certain notifications. Different variants of the publish–subscribe paradigm exist to match the information being produced with the subscribers' interests, including channel-based, subject-based, content-based, or type-based subscriptions. Independently of the subscription method, it is very likely that several subscribers are interested in the same notifications, which the system should broadcast to them. In this case, we are typically interested in having all subscribers of the same information receive the same set of messages. Otherwise the system will provide an unfair service, as some subscribers could have access to a lot more information than other subscribers.

Unless this reliability property is given for free by the underlying infrastructure (and this is usually not the case), the sender and the subscribers must coordinate to agree on which messages should be delivered. For instance, with the dissemination of an audio stream, processes are typically interested in receiving most of the information but are able to tolerate a bounded amount of message loss, especially if this allows the system to achieve a better throughput. The corresponding abstraction is typically called a *best-effort broadcast*.

The dissemination of some stock exchange information may require a more reliable form of broadcast, called *reliable broadcast*, as we would like all active processes to receive the same information. One might even require from a stock exchange infrastructure that information be disseminated in an ordered manner. In several publish–subscribe applications, producers and consumers interact indirectly, with the support of a group of intermediate cooperative brokers. In such cases, agreement abstractions may be useful for the cooperation among the brokers.

Process Control. Process control applications are those where several software processes have to control the execution of a physical activity. Basically, the processes might be controlling the dynamic location of an aircraft or a train. They might also be controlling the temperature of a nuclear installation or the automation of a car production plant.

Typically, every process is connected to some sensor. The processes might, for instance, need to exchange the values output by their assigned sensors and output some common value, say, print a single location of the aircraft on the pilot control screen, despite the fact that, due to the inaccuracy or failure of their local sensors, they may have observed slightly different input values. This cooperation should be achieved despite some sensors (or associated control processes) having crashed or not observed anything. This type of cooperation can be simplified if all processes agree on the same set of inputs for the control algorithm, a requirement captured by the *consensus* abstraction.

Cooperative Work. Users located on different nodes of a network may cooperate in building a common software or document, or simply in setting up a distributed dialogue, say, for an online chat or a virtual conference. A shared working space abstraction is very useful here to enable effective cooperation. Such a distributed shared memory abstraction is typically accessed through *read* and *write* operations by the users to store and exchange information. In its simplest form, a shared working space can be viewed as one virtual unstructured storage object. In more complex incarnations, shared working spaces may add a structure to create separate locations for its users to write, and range all the way from Wikis to complex multiuser distributed file systems. To maintain a consistent view of the shared space, the processes need to agree on the relative order among *write* and *read* operations on the space.

Distributed Databases. Databases constitute another class of applications where agreement abstractions can be helpful to ensure that all transaction managers obtain a consistent view of the running transactions and can make consistent decisions on how these transactions are serialized.

Additionally, such abstractions can be used to coordinate the transaction managers when deciding about the outcome of the transactions. That is, the database servers, on which a given distributed transaction has executed, need to coordinate their activities and decide whether to commit or abort the transaction. They might decide to abort the transaction if any database server detected a violation of the database integrity, a concurrency control inconsistency, a disk error, or simply the crash of some other database server. As we pointed out, the distributed programming abstraction of *atomic commit* (or commitment) provides such distributed cooperation.

Distributed Storage. A large-capacity storage system distributes data over many storage nodes, each one providing a small portion of the overall storage space. Accessing stored data usually involves contacting multiple nodes because even a single data item may be spread over multiple nodes. A data item may undergo complex transformations with error-detection codes or error-correction codes that access multiple nodes, to protect the storage system against the loss or corruption of some nodes. Such systems distribute data not only because of the limited capacity of each node but also for increasing the fault-tolerance of the overall system and for reducing the load on every individual node.

Conceptually, the storage system provides a shared memory abstraction that is accessed through *read* and *write* operations, like the shared working space mentioned before. But since it uses distribution also for the purpose of enhancing the overall resilience, it combines aspects of inherently distributed systems with aspects of artificially distributed systems, which are discussed next.

1.2.2 Distribution as an Artifact

Often applications that are not inherently distributed also use sophisticated abstractions from distributed programming. This need sometimes appears as an artifact of the engineering solution to satisfy some specific requirements such as *fault tolerance*, *load balancing*, or *fast sharing*.

We illustrate this idea through *state-machine replication*, which is a powerful way to achieve fault tolerance in distributed systems. Briefly, replication consists in making a centralized service highly available by executing several copies of it on different machines that are assumed to fail independently. This ensures the continuity of the service despite the failure of a subset of the machines. No specific hardware is needed: fault tolerance through replication is software-based. In fact, replication may also be used within an information system to improve the read access performance to data by placing it close to the processes where it is likely to be queried. For a service that is exposed to attacks over the Internet, for example, the same approach also tolerates malicious intrusions that subvert a limited number of the replicated nodes providing the service.

For replication to be effective, the different copies must be maintained in a consistent state. If the states of the replicas may diverge arbitrarily, it does not make sense to talk about replication. The illusion of *one* highly available service would fall apart and be replaced by that of several distributed services, each possibly failing independently. If replicas are deterministic, one of the simplest ways to guarantee full consistency is to ensure that all replicas receive the same set of requests in the same order. Typically, such guarantees are enforced by an abstraction called *total-order broadcast*: the processes need to agree here on the sequence of messages they deliver. Algorithms that implement such a primitive are nontrivial, and providing the programmer with an abstraction that encapsulates these algorithms makes the design of a replicated service easier. If the replicas are nondeterministic then ensuring their consistency requires different *ordering* abstractions, as we will see later in this book. The challenge in realizing these abstractions lies in tolerating the faults that may affect the replicas, which may range from a simple process crash to being under the control of a malicious adversary.

1.3 The End-to-End Argument

Distributed programming abstractions are useful but may sometimes be difficult or expensive to implement. In some cases, no simple algorithm is able to provide the desired abstraction and the algorithm that solves the problem can have a high complexity, e.g., in terms of the number of interprocess communication steps and messages. Therefore, depending on the system model, the network characteristics, and the required quality of service, the overhead of the abstraction can range from the negligible to the almost prohibitive.

Faced with performance constraints, the application designer may be driven to mix the relevant logic of the abstraction with the application logic, in an attempt to obtain an optimized integrated solution. The rationale is usually that such a solution should perform better than a solution obtained by the modular approach, where the abstraction is implemented as an independent service that can be accessed through a well-defined interface. The approach can be further supported by a superficial interpretation of the end-to-end argument: most complexity should be implemented at the higher levels of the communication stack. This argument could be applied to any form of (distributed) programming.

However, even if performance gains can be obtained by collapsing the application and the underlying layers in some cases, such a monolithic approach has many disadvantages. Most importantly, it is prone to errors. Some of the algorithms that will be presented in this book have a considerable amount of difficulty and exhibit subtle dependencies among their internal elements. An apparently obvious "optimization" may break the algorithm correctness. To quote Donald Knuth here:

> "Premature optimization is the root of all evil."

Even if the designer reaches the amount of expertise required to master the difficult task of embedding these algorithms in the application, there are several other reasons to keep both implementations independent. The most compelling one is that there is usually no single solution for a given distributed computing problem. This is particularly true because of the variety of distributed system models. Instead, different solutions can usually be proposed and none of these solutions may strictly be superior to the others: each may have its own advantages and disadvantages, performing better under different network or load conditions, making different trade-offs between network traffic and message latency, and so on. Relying on a modular approach allows the most suitable implementation to be selected when the application is deployed, or even allows choosing at runtime among different implementations in response to changes in the environment.

Encapsulating tricky issues of distributed interactions by abstractions with well-defined interfaces significantly helps us reason about the correctness of the application, and port it from one system to the other. We strongly believe that in many distributed applications, especially those that require many-to-many interaction, building preliminary prototypes of the distributed application using several abstraction layers can be very helpful.

Ultimately, one may indeed consider optimizing the performance of the final release of a distributed application and using some integrated prototype that implements several abstractions in one monolithic piece of code. However, full understanding of each of the enclosed abstractions in isolation is fundamental to ensure the correctness of the combined code.

1.4 Software Components

1.4.1 Composition Model

Notation. One of the biggest difficulties we had to face when thinking about describing distributed algorithms was to find an adequate way to represent these algorithms. When representing a centralized algorithm, one could decide to use a programming language, either by choosing an existing popular one or by inventing a new one with pedagogical purposes in mind.

Although there have indeed been several attempts to come up with distributed programming languages, these attempts have resulted in rather complicated notations that would not have been viable to describe general-purpose distributed algorithms in a pedagogical way. Trying to invent a distributed programming language was not an option. Even if we had the time to invent one successfully, at least one book would have been required to present the language itself.

Therefore, we have opted to use pseudo code to describe our algorithms. The pseudo code reflects a reactive computing model where components of the same process communicate by exchanging events: an algorithm is described as a set of event handlers. These react to incoming events and possibly trigger new events. In fact, the pseudo code is very close to the actual way we programmed the algorithms in our experimental framework. Basically, the algorithm description can be seen as actual code, from which we removed all implementation-related details that were more confusing than useful for understanding the algorithms. This approach hopefully simplifies the task of those who will be interested in building running prototypes from the descriptions found in this book.

A Simple Example. Abstractions are typically represented through an API. We will informally discuss here a simple example API for a distributed programming abstraction.

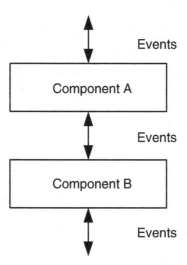

Figure 1.1: Composition model

Throughout the book, we shall describe APIs and algorithms using an *asynchronous event-based composition* model. Every process hosts a set of software *components*, called *modules* in our context. Each component is identified by a name, and characterized by a set of properties. The component provides an interface in the form of the events that the component accepts and produces in return. Distributed programming abstractions are typically made of a collection of components, at least one for every process, that are intended to satisfy some common properties.

Software Stacks. Components can be composed to build software stacks. At each process, a component represents a specific layer in the stack. The application layer is at the top of the stack, whereas the networking layer is usually at the bottom. The layers of the distributed programming abstractions we will consider are typically in the middle. Components within the same stack communicate through the exchange of *events*, as illustrated in Fig. 1.1. A given abstraction is typically materialized by a set of components, each running at a process.

According to this model, each component is constructed as a state-machine whose transitions are triggered by the reception of events. Events may carry information such as a data message, or group membership information, in one or more *attributes*. Events are denoted by ⟨ *EventType* | *Attributes*, ... ⟩. Often an event with the same name is used by more than one component. For events defined for component *co*, we, therefore, usually write:

⟨ *co, EventType* | *Attributes*, ... ⟩.

Each event is processed through a dedicated *handler* by the process (i.e., by the corresponding component). A handler is formulated in terms of a sequence of instructions introduced by *upon event*, which describes the event, followed by pseudo code with instructions to be executed. The processing of an event may result in new events being created and triggering the same or different components. Every event triggered by a component of the same process is eventually processed, if the process is correct (unless the destination module explicitly filters the event; see the *such that* clause ahead). Events from the same component are processed in the order in which they were triggered. This *first-in-first-out (FIFO) order* is only enforced on events exchanged among local components in a given stack. The messages among different processes may also need to be ordered according to some criteria, using mechanisms orthogonal to this one. We shall address this interprocess communication issue later in this book.

We assume that every process executes the code triggered by events in a mutually exclusive way. This means that the same process does not handle two events concurrently. Once the handling of an event is terminated, the process keeps on checking if any other event is triggered. This periodic checking is assumed to be fair, and is achieved in an implicit way: it is not visible in the pseudo code we describe.

The pseudo code of a sample component co_1 that consists of two event handlers looks like this:

---

upon event $\langle co_1, Event_1 \mid att_1^1, att_1^2, \dots \rangle$ **do**
    do something;
    trigger $\langle co_2, Event_2 \mid att_2^1, att_2^2, \dots \rangle$;   *// send some event*

upon event $\langle co_1, Event_3 \mid att_3^1, att_3^2, \dots \rangle$ **do**
    do something else;
    trigger $\langle co_2, Event_4 \mid att_4^1, att_4^2, \dots \rangle$;   *// send some other event*

Such a decoupled and asynchronous way of interacting among components matches very well the requirements of distributed applications: for instance, new processes may join or leave the distributed system at any moment and a process must be ready to handle both membership changes and reception of messages at any time. Hence, the order in which concurrent events will be observed cannot be defined a priori; this is precisely what we capture through our component model.

For writing complex algorithms, we sometimes use handlers that are triggered when some condition in the implementation becomes true, but do not respond to an external event originating from another module. The condition for an internal event is usually defined on local variables maintained by the algorithm. Such a handler consists of an *upon* statement followed by a condition; in a sample component *co*, it might look like this:

---

upon *condition* **do**   *// an internal event*
    do something;

An *upon event* statement triggered by an event from another module can also be qualified with a condition on local variables. This handler executes its instructions only when the external event has been triggered and the condition holds. Such a conditional event handler of a component *co* has the following form:

---

upon event $\langle$ *co, Event* | $att_1^1, att_1^2, \ldots \rangle$ **such that** *condition* **do**
    do something;

An algorithm that uses conditional event handlers relies on the run-time system to buffer external events until the condition on internal variables becomes satisfied. We use this convention because it simplifies the presentation of many algorithms, but the approach should not be taken as a recipe for actually implementing a practical system: such a run-time system might need to maintain unbounded buffers. But, it is not difficult to avoid conditional event handlers in an implementation. Every conditional event handler can be transformed into a combination of a (pure) event handler and two handlers for internal events in three steps: (1) introduce a local variable for storing the external event when it occurs and install an event handler triggered by the external event without any condition; (2) introduce a local variable for storing that the condition on the internal variables has become true; and (3) add a local event handler that responds to the internal event denoting that the external event has occurred and the internal condition has been satisfied.

1.4.2 Programming Interface

The APIs of our components include two types of events, *requests* and *indications*; their detailed semantics depend on the component at which they occur:

- *Request* events are used by a component to *invoke* a service at another component or to *signal* a condition to another component. For instance, the application layer might trigger a *request* event at a component in charge of broadcasting a message with some reliability guarantee to the processes in a group, or propose a value to be decided on by the group. A request may also carry signaling information, for example, when the component has previously output some data to the application layer and the request confirms that the application layer has processed the data. From the perspective of the component handling the event, request events are inputs.
- *Indication* events are used by a component to *deliver* information or to *signal* a condition to another component. Considering the broadcast example given earlier, at every process that is a destination of the message, the component in charge of implementing the actual broadcast primitive will typically perform some processing to ensure the corresponding reliability guarantee, and then use an *indication* event to deliver the message to the application layer. Similarly, the decision on a value will be indicated with such an event. An indication event may

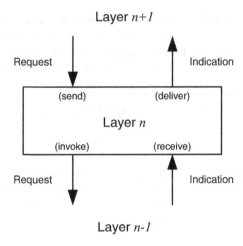

Figure 1.2: Layering

also take the role of a confirmation, for example, when the component responsible for broadcasting indicates to the application layer that the message was
indeed broadcast. From the perspective of the component triggering the event,
indication events are outputs.

A typical execution at a given layer consists of the following sequence of actions,
as illustrated in Fig. 1.2. We consider here a broadcast abstraction that ensures a
certain reliability condition, that is, a primitive where the processes need to agree
on whether or not to deliver a message broadcast by some process.

1. The procedure for *sending* a broadcast message is initiated by the reception of a
   request event from the layer above.
2. To ensure the properties of the broadcast abstraction, the layer will send one or
   more messages to its remote peers by *invoking* the services of the layer below
   (using request events of the lower layer).
3. Messages sent by the peer layers are also *received* using the services of the
   underlying layer (through indication events of the lower layer).
4. When a message is received, it may have to be stored temporarily until the adequate reliability property is satisfied, before being *delivered* to the layer above
   using an *indication* event.

Requests and indications do not always carry payload data; they may also indicate
conditions for synchronizing two layers with each other. For example, the broadcast
abstraction may confirm that its service has been concluded reliably by triggering
a specialized indication event for the layer above. In this way, a broadcast implementation can require that the application layer waits until a broadcast request is
confirmed before triggering the next broadcast request. An analogous mechanism
can be used to synchronize the delivery of broadcast messages to the application

layer above. When the application layer takes a long time to process a message, for example, the application may trigger a specialized request event for the broadcast abstraction to signal that the processing has completed and the application is now ready for the next broadcast message to be delivered.

1.4.3 Modules

Not surprisingly, most of the modules described in this book perform some interaction with the corresponding modules on peer processes; after all, this is a book about distributed computing. It is, however, also possible to have modules that perform only local actions. As there may exist multiple copies of a module in the runtime system of one process concurrently, every *instance* of a module is identified by a corresponding *identifier*.

To illustrate the notion of modules, we describe a simple abstract *job handler* module. An application may *submit* a job to the handler abstraction and the job handler *confirms* that it has taken the responsibility for processing the job. Module 1.1 describes its interface. The job handler confirms every submitted job. However, the interface explicitly leaves open whether or not the job has been processed at the time when the confirmation arrives.

Module 1.1: Interface and properties of a job handler

Module:

    Name: JobHandler, **instance** *jh*.

Events:

    Request: $\langle$ *jh, Submit* $\mid$ *job* $\rangle$: Requests a job to be processed.

    Indication: $\langle$ *jh, Confirm* $\mid$ *job* $\rangle$: Confirms that the given job has been (or will be) processed.

Properties:

    JH1: *Guaranteed response:* Every submitted job is eventually confirmed.

Algorithm 1.1 is a straightforward job-handler implementation, which confirms every job only after it has been processed. This implementation is *synchronous* because the application that submits a job learns when the job has been processed.

A second implementation of the job-handler abstraction is given in Algorithm 1.2. This implementation is *asynchronous* and confirms every submitted job immediately; it saves the job in an unbounded buffer and processes buffered jobs at its own speed in the background.

Algorithm 1.2 illustrates two special elements of our notation for algorithms: initialization events and internal events. To make the *initialization* of a component explicit, we assume that a special $\langle$ *Init* $\rangle$ event is generated automatically by the

---

Algorithm 1.1: Synchronous Job Handler

Implements:
    JobHandler, **instance** *jh*.

upon event ⟨ *jh*, *Submit* | *job* ⟩ **do**
    process(*job*);
    trigger ⟨ *jh*, *Confirm* | *job* ⟩;

---

runtime system when a component is created. This event may initialize some data
structures used by the component and perform some setup actions. For instance, in
the asynchronous job handler example, it is used to create an empty buffer. The last
upon statement of Algorithm 1.2 represents an event handler that responds to an
internal event, as introduced in the previous section.

Algorithm 1.2: Asynchronous Job Handler

Implements:
    JobHandler, **instance** *jh*.

upon event ⟨ *jh*, *Init* ⟩ **do**
    buffer := ∅;

upon event ⟨ *jh*, *Submit* | *job* ⟩ **do**
    buffer := *buffer* ∪ {*job*};
    trigger ⟨ *jh*, *Confirm* | *job* ⟩;

upon *buffer* ≠ ∅ **do**
    job := selectjob(*buffer*);
    process(*job*);
    buffer := *buffer* \ {*job*};

To demonstrate how modules are composed, we use the job-handler module and
extend it by a module that adds a layer on top; the layer may apply an arbitrary
transformation to a job before invoking the job handler on it. The composition of
the two modules is illustrated in Fig. 1.3.

The interface of the job transformation layer adds an ⟨ *Error* ⟩ event, which
occurs when the transformation fails, but not otherwise; the interface shown in
Module 1.2.

An example of a transformation is given in Algorithm 1.3. The layer implements
a bounded-length queue of jobs waiting to be processed. The jobs are stored in
an array *buffer* of length M, which is initialized to the M-vector of ⊥-values,
denoted by $[\bot]^M$. Two variables *top* and *bottom* point into *buffer* such that the
next arriving job is stored at index *top* and the next job to be removed is at index
bottom. To keep the code simple, these variables are unbounded integers and they
are reduced modulo M to access the array. The algorithm interacts synchronously

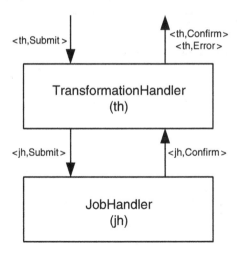

Figure 1.3: A stack of job-transformation and job-handler modules

---

Module 1.2: Interface and properties of a job transformation and processing abstraction

Module:

    Name: TransformationHandler, **instance** *th*.

Events:

    Request: ⟨ *th, Submit* | *job* ⟩: Submits a job for transformation and for processing.

    Indication:⟨ *th, Confirm* | *job* ⟩: Confirms that the given job has been (or will be) transformed and processed.

    Indication:⟨ *th, Error* | *job* ⟩: Indicates that the transformation of the given job failed.

Properties:

    TH1: *Guaranteed response:* Every submitted job is eventually confirmed or its transformation fails.

    TH2: *Soundness:* A submitted job whose transformation fails is not processed.

---

with the underlying job handler and waits before submitting the next job until the previously submitted job has been confirmed. When Algorithm 1.3 is combined with the synchronous job handler (Algorithm 1.1), the run-time system does not need any unbounded buffers.

Modules are usually instantiated statically; this happens only once and occurs implicitly when the implementation of another component includes the module among the list of its *used* modules. There is one static instance of every module, which may be shared by many modules. A protocol module can also be instantiated

---

Algorithm 1.3: Job-Transformation by Buffering

Implements:
   TransformationHandler, **instance** *th*.

Uses:
   JobHandler, **instance** *jh*.

upon event ⟨ *th, Init* ⟩ **do**
      $top := 1$;
      $bottom := 1$;
      $handling := \text{FALSE}$;
      $buffer := [\bot]^M$;

upon event ⟨ *th, Submit | job* ⟩ **do**
      if $bottom + M = top$ **then**
            trigger ⟨ *th, Error | job* ⟩;
      else
            $buffer[top \bmod M + 1] := job$;
            $top := top + 1$;
            trigger ⟨ *th, Confirm | job* ⟩;

upon $bottom < top \wedge handling = \text{FALSE}$ **do**
      $job := buffer[bottom \bmod M + 1]$;
      $bottom := bottom + 1$;
      $handling := \text{TRUE}$;
      trigger ⟨ *jh, Submit | job* ⟩;

upon event ⟨ *jh, Confirm | job* ⟩ **do**
      $handling := \text{FALSE}$;

---

dynamically with an a-priori unknown number of instances. The initializations of dynamic instances are mentioned explicitly in the code of the algorithm that calls them.

All module abstractions in this book are presented as isolated instances, in order to keep their descriptions simple. Every instance has an identifier. When a higher-level algorithm invokes multiple instances of a lower-level abstraction, we ensure that every instance is named by a unique identifier. Any application that uses the abstractions should respect the same rule.

1.5 Classes of Algorithms

As noted earlier, in order to provide a particular service, a layer at a given process may need to execute one or more rounds of message exchange with the peer layers at remote processes. The behavior of each peer, characterized by the set of messages that it is capable of producing and accepting, the format of each of these messages, and the legal sequences of messages, is sometimes called a *protocol*. The purpose of the protocol is to ensure the execution of some *distributed algorithm*, the concurrent execution of different sequences of steps that ensure the provision of the desired service. This book covers several of these distributed algorithms.

To give the reader an insight into how the failure assumptions, the environment, the system parameters, and other design choices affect the algorithm design, this book includes several different classes of algorithmic solutions to implement our distributed programming abstractions, namely:

1. *fail-stop* algorithms, designed under the assumption that processes can fail by crashing but the crashes can be reliably detected by all the other processes;
2. *fail-silent* algorithms, where process crashes can never be reliably detected;
3. *fail-noisy* algorithms, where processes can fail by crashing and the crashes can be detected, but not always in an accurate manner (accuracy is only eventual);
4. *fail-recovery* algorithms, where processes can crash and later recover and still participate in the algorithm;
5. *fail-arbitrary* algorithms, where processes can deviate arbitrarily from the protocol specification and act in malicious, adversarial ways; and
6. *randomized* algorithms, where in addition to the classes presented so far, processes may make probabilistic choices by using a source of randomness.

These classes are not disjoint, and it is important to notice that we do not give a solution from each class for every abstraction. First, there are cases where it is known that some abstraction cannot be implemented by an algorithm of a given class. For example, some of the coordination abstractions we consider in Chap. 6 do not have fail-noisy (and hence fail-silent) solutions and it is not clear how to devise meaningful randomized solutions to such abstractions. In other cases, such solutions may exist but devising them is still an active area of research.

Reasoning about distributed algorithms in general, and in particular about algorithms that implement distributed programming abstractions, first involves defining a clear model of the distributed system where these algorithms are supposed to operate. Put differently, we need to figure out what basic abstractions the processes assume in order to build more sophisticated ones. The basic abstractions we consider capture the allowable behavior of the processes and their communication links in the distributed system. Before delving into concrete algorithms to build sophisticated distributed programming abstractions, we, thus, need to understand such basic abstractions. This will be the topic of the next chapter.

1.6 Chapter Notes

- The idea of using multiple, replicated processes for tolerating faults of individual processes links together most algorithms presented in this book. This paradigm can be traced back to the work on the *Software-Implemented Fault Tolerance (SIFT)* project in 1978, which addressed the challenging problem of building a fault-tolerant computer for aircraft control (Wensley et al. 1978).

- The atomic commit problem was posed in the context of distributed databases by Gray (1978). Later Skeen (1981) introduced a variant of the problem that ensures also liveness. We describe the nonblocking atomic commit problem in Chap. 6.
- The end-to-end argument was developed by Saltzer, Reed, and Clark (1984).
- State-machine replication and its relation total-order broadcast are described in a survey of Schneider (1990). Chapter 6 treats these two topics in detail.

2. Basic Abstractions

These are my principles. If you don't like them, I have others.

(Groucho Marx)

Applications that are deployed in practical distributed systems usually execute on a myriad of different machines and communication infrastructures. Physical machines differ in the number of processors, type of processors, amount and speed of both volatile and persistent memory, and so on. Communication infrastructures differ in parameters such as latency, throughput, reliability, etc. On top of these machines and infrastructures, a huge variety of software components are sometimes needed to support one application: operating systems, file systems, middleware, communication protocols, with each component having its own specific features.

One might consider implementing distributed services that are tailored to specific combinations of the elements listed earlier. Such implementations would depend on one type of machine, one form of communication, one operating system, and so on. However, in this book, we are interested in abstractions and algorithms that are relevant for a wide range of distributed environments. In order to achieve this goal we need to capture the fundamental characteristics of various distributed systems in some basic abstractions, on top of which we can later define other more elaborate, and generic, distributed programming abstractions.

This chapter presents the basic abstractions we use to model a distributed system composed of active entities that perform computations and communicate by exchanging messages.

Two kinds of abstractions will be of primary importance: those representing *processes* and those representing communication *links*. Not surprisingly, it does not seem to be possible to model the huge diversity of physical networks and operational conditions with a single process abstraction and a single link abstraction. Therefore, we will define different instances for each kind of basic abstraction. For instance, we will distinguish process abstractions according to the types of faults that they may exhibit. Besides our process and link abstractions, we will also introduce a third

C. Cachin et al., *Introduction to Reliable and Secure Distributed Programming*,
DOI: 10.1007/978-3-642-15260-3_2,
© Springer-Verlag Berlin Heidelberg 2011

failure-detector abstraction, as a convenient way to capture reasonable assumptions about the timing behavior of processes and links.

Later in the chapter we will identify relevant combinations of our three categories of abstractions. Such a combination is what we call a *distributed-system model*.

This chapter also contains our first module descriptions, used to specify our basic abstractions, as well as our first algorithms, used to implement these abstractions. The specifications and the algorithms are rather simple and should help illustrate our notation, before proceeding in subsequent chapters to more sophisticated specifications and algorithms.

2.1 Distributed Computation

2.1.1 Processes and Messages

We abstract the units that are able to perform computations in a distributed system through the notion of a *process*. We consider that the system is composed of N different processes, named p, q, r, s, and so on. The set of processes in the system is denoted by Π. Unless stated otherwise, this set is static and does not change, and every process knows the identities of all processes. Sometimes, a function $rank : \Pi \rightarrow \{1, \ldots, N\}$ is used to associate every process with a unique index between 1 and N. In the description of an algorithm, the special process name *self* denotes the name of the process that executes the code. Typically, we will assume that all processes of the system run the same local algorithm. The sum of these copies constitutes the actual distributed algorithm.

We do not assume any particular mapping of our abstract notion of process to the actual processors or threads of a specific computer machine or operating system. The processes communicate by exchanging messages and the messages are uniquely identified, say, by their original sender process using a sequence number or a local clock, together with the process identifier. In other words, we assume that all messages that are ever exchanged by some distributed algorithm are unique. Messages are exchanged by the processes through communication *links*. We will capture the properties of the links that connect the processes through specific link abstractions, which we will discuss later.

2.1.2 Automata and Steps

A *distributed algorithm* consists of a distributed collection of automata, one per process. The automaton at a process regulates the way the process executes its computation steps, i.e., how it reacts to a message. Every process is implemented by the same automaton, as illustrated in Fig. 2.1; they interact through some means of communication that will be introduced later. The *execution* of a distributed algorithm is represented by a sequence of steps executed by the processes. The elements of the sequences are the steps executed by the processes involved in the algorithm. A partial execution of the algorithm is represented by a finite sequence of steps, an infinite execution by an infinite sequence of steps.

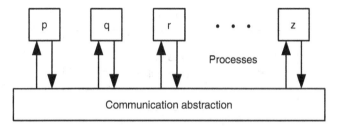

Figure 2.1: A distributed algorithm consisting of processes that are implemented by identical automata

It is convenient for presentation simplicity to assume the existence of a global clock, outside the control of the processes. This clock provides a global and linear notion of time that regulates the execution of the algorithms. The steps of the processes are executed according to ticks of the global clock: one step per clock tick. Even if two steps are executed at the same physical instant, we view them as if they were executed at two different times of our global clock. A *correct* process executes an infinite number of steps of its automaton, i.e., every such process has an infinite share of time units (we come back to this notion in the next section) and follows the specified algorithm. In a sense, there is some entity, sometimes called a global scheduler, that assigns time units to processes, though the very notion of time is outside the control of the processes.

A process step consists of *receiving* (sometimes we also say *delivering*) a message from another process (global event), *executing* a local computation (local event), and *sending* a message to some process (global event) (Fig. 2.2). The execution of the local computation and the sending of a message is determined by the process automaton, i.e., by the local algorithm. Local events are typically those exchanged between modules of the same process at different layers.

Sometimes a process has no message to receive or send, but has some local computation to perform; this is captured simply by assuming that messages can be *nil*, in the sense that the process receives or sends a special *nil* message. Of course, a process might not have any local computation to perform either, in which case it simply does not touch any of its local variables. In this case, the local computation is also *nil*.

It is important that the interaction between the components of one process is viewed as local computation and not as communication, although they look syntactically the same. When an event is exchanged between two modules of the same process, the algorithm performs a *computation step* that is local. In contrast, a *communication step* of the algorithm occurs when a process sends a message to another process, and the latter receives this message, through events occuring at different processes. The process is the unit of communication, just like it is the unit of failure, as we will discuss. As the transmission delay of a network is typically much larger than the local computation delay, the number of communication steps of an algorithm has a significant impact on the latency and the performance of a distributed

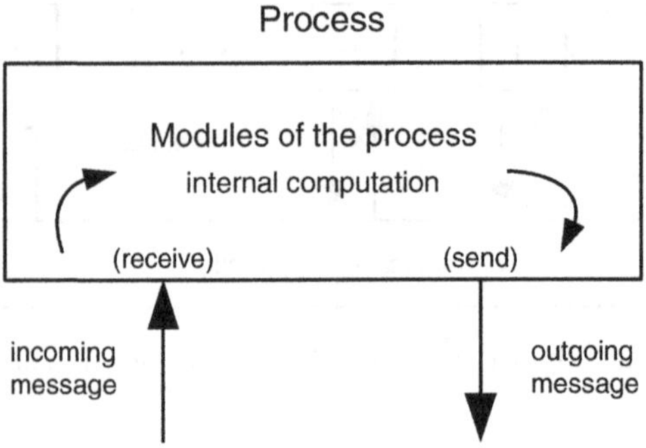

Process

Figure 2.2: Step of a process

algorithm. Needless to say, the number of computation steps may also affect the performance of the algorithm, especially when computationally expensive operations are involved, such as cryptographic operations.

An important parameter of the process abstraction is the restriction imposed on the speed at which local steps are performed and messages are exchanged. We will come back to this aspect when discussing timing assumptions later in this chapter.

Unless specified otherwise, we will consider *deterministic* algorithms. That is, for every step performed by any given process, the local computation executed by the process, the local state after the computation, and the message sent by this process are uniquely determined by the message received by the process and its local state prior to executing the step.

In specific situations, we will also discuss *randomized* (or *probabilistic*) algorithms, where every process may use a local *random source*. The output of the random source determines the choice of the local computation to perform or the next message to send, according to a probability distribution over the set of possible values output by the source.

2.1.3 Safety and Liveness

When we devise a distributed algorithm to implement a distributed programming abstraction, we seek to satisfy the properties of the abstraction in all possible executions of the algorithm, covering all possible sequences of steps executed by the processes according to the algorithm. The scheduling of these steps remains outside the control of the processes and depends on the global scheduler. The properties of the abstraction to be implemented needs to be satisfied for a large set of possible interleavings of these steps. These properties usually fall into two classes: *safety* and *liveness*. Having in mind the distinction between these classes usually helps to understand the two complementary faces of the abstraction and to devise an adequate algorithm for implementing it.

Safety. Basically, a *safety property* is a property of a distributed algorithm that can be violated at some time t and never be satisfied again after that time. Roughly speaking, safety properties state that the algorithm should not do anything wrong. To illustrate this, consider a property of perfect links (which we will discuss in more detail later in this chapter) stating that no process should receive a message unless this message was indeed sent. In other words, communication links should not invent messages out of thin air. To state that this property is violated in some execution of an algorithm, we need to determine a time t at which some process receives a message that was never sent. This observation helps devise a correctness argument (by contradiction) for an algorithm presumably satisfying the property.

More precisely, a safety property is a property such that, whenever it is violated in some execution E of an algorithm, there is a partial execution E' of E such that the property will be violated in any extension of E'. This means that safety properties prevent a set of unwanted execution prefixes from occurring.

Of course, safety properties are not enough. Sometimes, a good way of preventing bad things from happening consists in simply doing nothing. In many countries, some public administrations seem to understand this rule quite well and, hence, have an easy time ensuring safety.

Liveness. In order to define a useful abstraction, it is therefore necessary to add some *liveness properties*. They ensure that eventually something good happens. For instance, to define a meaningful notion of perfect links, we require that if a correct process sends a message to a correct destination process, then the destination process should eventually deliver the message (besides the safety property which stipulates that messages should not be invented out of thin air and only be delivered if priorly sent). To state that such a liveness property is violated in a given execution, we need to show that there is an infinite scheduling of the steps of the algorithm where the message is never delivered.

More precisely, a liveness property is a property of a distributed system execution such that, for any time t, there is some hope that the property can be satisfied at some time $t' \geq t$. It is a property for which, quoting Cicero, "while there is life there is hope."

Combining them. The challenge is to guarantee both liveness and safety. (The difficulty is not in *talking*, or *not lying*, but in *telling the truth*.) Indeed, useful distributed services are supposed to provide both liveness and safety properties. Formulating an abstraction with only one kind of property is usually a sign for a flawed specification.

Consider, for instance, the traditional interprocess communication service of a reliable, ordered data stream: it ensures that messages exchanged between two processes are neither lost nor duplicated, and are received in the order in which they were sent. As we pointed out, requiring that messages are not lost is a liveness property. Requiring that messages are not duplicated and that they are received in the order in which they were sent are safety properties.

As another example, the *soundness* property of the job handler abstraction in Module 1.2 from Sect. 1.4 represents a safety property. Moreover, Modules 1.1 and 1.2 in the same section both contain a *guaranteed response* property, which is a liveness property.

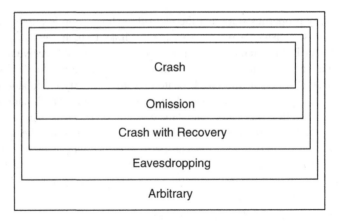

Figure 2.3: Types of process failures

It is usually better, for modularity purposes, to separate the safety and liveness properties of an abstraction specification into disjoint classes. However, we will sometimes for the sake of conciseness consider properties that are neither pure liveness nor pure safety properties, but rather a union of both.

2.2 Abstracting Processes

2.2.1 Process Failures

A process executes the distributed algorithm assigned to it through the set of components implementing the algorithm within that process. A *failure* occurs whenever the process does not behave according to the algorithm. Our unit of failure is the process. When the process fails, all its components fail at the same time.

Process abstractions differ according to the nature of the faults that cause them to fail. Possible failures range from a crash, where a process simply stops to execute any steps, over an omission to take some steps, a crash with subsequent recovery, to arbitrary and even adversarial behavior. We discuss these kinds of failures in the subsequent sections. Figure 2.3 summarizes the types of failures.

2.2.2 Crashes

The simplest way of failing for a process is when the process stops executing steps. The process executes its algorithm correctly, including the exchange of messages with other processes, until some time t, after which it stops executing any local computation and does not send any message to other processes. In other words, the process *crashes* at time t and never recovers after that time. We call this a *crash fault* (Fig. 2.3), and talk about a *crash-stop* process abstraction. With this abstraction, a process is said to be *faulty* if it crashes at some time during the execution. It is said to be *correct* if it never crashes and executes an infinite number of steps. We discuss two ramifications of the crash-stop abstraction.

It is usual to devise algorithms that implement a given distributed programming abstraction, say, some form of agreement, provided that only a limited number f of processes are faulty, which might be a minority of the processes or all processes up to one. Assuming a bound on the number of faulty processes in the form of a parameter f means that any number of processes up to f may fail, but not that f processes actually exhibit such faults in every execution. The relation between the number f of potentially faulty processes and the total number N of processes in the system is generally called *resilience*.

It is important to understand here that such an assumption does not mean that the hardware underlying these processes is supposed to operate correctly forever. In fact, the assumption means that in every execution of an algorithm that relies on that abstraction, it is very unlikely that more than f of processes crash during the lifetime of that very execution. An engineer picking such an algorithm for a given application should be confident that the chosen elements underlying the software and hardware architecture make that assumption plausible. In general, it is also a good practice, when devising algorithms that implement a given distributed abstraction under certain assumptions, to determine precisely which properties of the abstraction are preserved and which can be violated when a specific subset of the assumptions are not satisfied, e.g., when more than f processes crash.

By considering the crash-stop process abstraction, one assumes that a process executes its algorithm correctly, but may crash at some time; after a process has crashed, it never recovers. That is, once it has crashed, the process does not ever perform any step again. Obviously, in practice, processes that crash can be restarted and hence may recover. In fact, it is usually desirable that they do. But with the crash-stop abstraction, a recovered process is no longer part of the system.

It is also important to notice that, in practice, the crash-stop process abstraction neither precludes the possibility of recovery nor does it mean that recovery should be prevented for a given algorithm (assuming a crash-stop process abstraction) to behave correctly. It simply means that the algorithm should not rely on some of the processes to recover in order to pursue its execution. These processes might not recover, or might recover only after a long period encompassing the crash detection and then the restarting delay. In some sense, an algorithm that is not relying on crashed processes to recover would typically be faster than an algorithm relying on some of the processes to recover (we will discuss this issue in the next section). Nothing prevents recovered processes from getting informed about the outcome of the computation, however, and from participating again in subsequent instances of the distributed algorithm.

Unless explicitly stated otherwise, we will assume the crash-stop process abstraction throughout this book.

2.2.3 Omissions

A more general kind of fault is an *omission* fault (Fig. 2.3). An omission fault occurs when a process does not send (or receive) a message that it is supposed to send (or receive) according to its algorithm. In general, omission faults are due to buffer overflows or network congestion that cause messages to be lost. With an omission, the process deviates from the algorithm assigned to it by dropping some messages that should have been exchanged with other processes.

Omission faults are not discussed further in this book, except through the related notion of crash-recovery faults, introduced next.

2.2.4 Crashes with Recoveries

Sometimes, the assumption that particular processes never crash is simply not plausible for certain distributed environments. For instance, assuming that a majority of the processes do not crash might simply be too strong, even if this should not happen only during the period until an algorithm execution terminates.

An interesting alternative in this case is the *crash-recovery* process abstraction; we also talk about a *crash-recovery* fault (Fig. 2.3). In this case, we say that a process is faulty if either the process crashes and never recovers or the process keeps infinitely often crashing and recovering. Otherwise, the process is said to be correct. Basically, such a process is eventually always up and running (as far as the lifetime of the algorithm execution is concerned). A process that crashes and recovers a finite number of times is correct in this model.

According to the crash-recovery abstraction, a process can crash and stop to send messages, but might recover later. This can be viewed as an omission fault, with one exception, however: a process might suffer *amnesia* when it crashes and lose its internal state. This significantly complicates the design of algorithms because, upon recovery, the process might send new messages that contradict messages that the process might have sent prior to the crash. To cope with this issue, we sometimes assume that every process has, in addition to its regular volatile memory, a *stable storage* (also called a *log*), which can be accessed through *store* and *retrieve* operations.

Upon recovery, we assume that a process is aware that it has crashed and recovered. In particular, a specific ⟨ Recovery ⟩ event is assumed to be automatically generated by the runtime environment whenever the process recovers, in a similar manner to the ⟨ Init ⟩ event that is generated whenever a process starts executing some algorithm. The processing of the ⟨ Recovery ⟩ event should, for instance, retrieve the relevant state of the process from stable storage before the processing of other events is resumed. The process might, however, have lost all the remaining data that was preserved in volatile memory. This data should thus be properly reinitialized. The ⟨ Init ⟩ event is considered atomic with respect to recovery. More precisely, if a process crashes in the middle of its initialization procedure and recovers, say, without having finished the procedure properly, the process resumes again with processing the initialization procedure and then continues to process the ⟨ Recovery ⟩ event.

In some sense, a crash-recovery kind of failure matches an omission fault if we consider that every process stores every update to any of its variables in stable storage. This is not very practical because access to stable storage is usually expensive (as there is a significant delay in accessing it). Therefore, a crucial issue in devising algorithms with the crash-recovery abstraction is to minimize the access to stable storage.

One way to alleviate the need for accessing any form of stable storage is to assume that some of the processes never crash (during the lifetime of an algorithm execution). This might look contradictory with the actual motivation for introducing the crash-recovery process abstraction in the first place. In fact, there is no contradiction, as we explain later. As discussed earlier, with crash-stop faults, some distributed-programming abstractions can be implemented only under the assumption that a certain number of processes never crash, say, a majority of the processes participating in the computation, e.g., four out of seven processes. This assumption might be considered unrealistic in certain environments. Instead, one might consider it more reasonable to assume that at least two processes do not crash during the execution of an algorithm. (The rest of the processes would indeed crash and recover.) As we will discuss later in the book, such an assumption makes it sometimes possible to devise algorithms assuming the crash-recovery process abstraction without any access to a stable storage. In fact, the processes that do not crash implement a virtual stable storage abstraction, and the algorithm can exploit this without knowing in advance which of the processes will not crash in a given execution.

At first glance, one might believe that the crash-stop abstraction can also capture situations where processes crash and recover, by simply having the processes change their identities upon recovery. That is, a process that recovers after a crash, would behave with respect to the other processes as if it were a different process that was simply not performing any action. This could easily be implemented by a recovery procedure which initializes the process state as if it just started its execution and also changes the identity of the process. Of course, this process should be updated with any information it might have missed from others, as if it did not receive that information yet. Unfortunately, this view is misleading, as we explain later. Again, consider an algorithm devised using the crash-stop process abstraction, and assuming that a majority of the processes never crash, say at least four out of a total of seven processes composing the system. Consider, furthermore, a scenario where four processes do indeed crash, and one process recovers. Pretending that the latter process is a different one (upon recovery) would mean that the system is actually composed of eight processes, five of which should not crash. The same reasoning can then be made for this larger number of processes. However, a fundamental assumption that we build upon is that the set of processes involved in any given computation is static, and the processes know of each other in advance.

A tricky issue with the crash-recovery process abstraction is the interface between software modules. Assume that some module of a process, involved in the implementation of some specific distributed abstraction, delivers some message or decision to the upper layer (say, the application layer), and subsequently the process hosting the module crashes. Upon recovery, the module cannot determine if the upper layer (i.e., the application) has processed the message or decision before crashing or not. There are at least two ways to deal with this issue:

1. One solution is to change the interface between modules. Instead of delivering a message or a decision to the upper layer (e.g., the application layer), the module may instead store the message or the decision in stable storage, which can also be accessed by the upper layer. The upper layer should subsequently access the stable storage and consume the delivered information.
2. A different approach consists in having the module periodically deliver a message or a decision to the upper layer until the latter explicitly asks for the stopping of the delivery. That is, the distributed programming abstraction implemented by the module is responsible for making sure the application will make use of the delivered information. Of course, the application layer needs to filter out duplicates in this case.

For the algorithms in this book that address crash-recovery faults, we generally adopt the first solution (see the logged perfect links abstraction in Sect. 2.4.5 for an example).

2.2.5 Eavesdropping Faults

When a distributed system operates in an untrusted environment, some of its components may become exposed to an adversary or even fall under its control. A relatively benign form of adversarial action occurs when a process leaks information obtained in an algorithm to an outside entity. The outsider may *eavesdrop* on multiple processes in this way and correlate all leaked pieces of information with each other. Faults of this kind threaten the confidentiality of the data handled by an algorithm, such as the privacy of messages that are disseminated by a broadcast algorithm or the secrecy of data written to a storage abstraction. We call this an *eavesdropping fault* of a process.

As the example of attacks mounted by remote adversaries against machines connected to the Internet shows, such eavesdropping faults occur in practice. An eavesdropping fault cannot be detected by observing how an affected process behaves in an algorithm, as the process continues to perform all actions according to its instructions. The adversary merely reads the internal state of all faulty processes. In practice, however, the eavesdropper must run some code on the physical machine that hosts the faulty process, in order to mount the attack, and the presence of such code can be detected and will raise suspicion. Eavesdropping faults typically affect communication links before they affect the processes; hence, one usually assumes that if any process is susceptible to eavesdropping faults then all communication links are also affected by eavesdropping and leak all messages to the adversary.

Eavesdropping can be prevented by cryptography, in particular by encrypting communication messages and stored data. Data encryption is generally orthogonal to the problems considered in this book, and confidentiality plays no significant role in implementing our distributed programming abstractions. Therefore, we will not consider eavesdropping faults any further here, although confidentiality and privacy are important for many secure distributed programs in practice.

2.2.6 Arbitrary Faults

A process is said to fail in an *arbitrary* manner if it may deviate in any conceivable way from the algorithm assigned to it. The *arbitrary-fault* behavior is the most general one. When we use it, we make no assumptions on the behavior of faulty processes, which are allowed any kind of output and, therefore, can send any kind of message. Such failures are also called *Byzantine* for historical reasons (see the notes at the end of this chapter) or *malicious* failures. The terms "arbitrary faulty" and "Byzantine" are synonyms throughout this book. We model a process that may behave arbitrarily as an *arbitrary-fault* process abstraction or a *Byzantine* process abstraction.

Not surprisingly, arbitrary faults are the most expensive to tolerate, but this is the only acceptable option when unknown or unpredictable faults may occur. One also considers them when the system is vulnerable to attacks, where some of its processes may become controlled by malicious users that deliberately try to prevent correct system operation.

Similar to the case of eavesdropping faults, one can simplify reasoning about arbitrary faults by assuming the existence of one determined adversary that coordinates the actions of all faulty processes. Whenever we consider algorithms with Byzantine processes, we also allow this adversary to access the messages exchanged over any communication link, to read messages, modify them, and insert messages of its own. In practice, a remote attacker may take over control of the physical machine that hosts the faulty process and not only read the state of a process but also completely determine the process' behavior.

An arbitrary fault is not necessarily intentional and malicious: it can simply be caused by a bug in the implementation, the programming language, or the compiler. This bug can thus cause the process to deviate from the algorithm it was supposed to execute. Faults that are triggered by benign bugs can sometimes be detected, and their effects eliminated, by the process itself or by other processes, through double-checking of results and added redundancy. As arbitrary but nonmalicious events of this kind often appear to be random and follow a uniform distribution over all errors, verification of the data can use simple verification methods (such as cyclic redundancy checks). Against a determined adversary, these methods are completely ineffective, however. On the other hand, a system that protects against arbitrary faults with a malicious intention also defends against nonmalicious faults.

Throughout this book, we consider only arbitrary faults of intentional and malicious nature. This gives the algorithms where processes are subject to arbitrary faults a robust notion of protection, because the given guarantees do not depend on the nature of and the intention behind an arbitrary fault. The added protection usually relies on cryptographic primitives, whose security properties may not be broken even by a determined adversary. Cryptographic abstractions are introduced in the next section.

2.3 Cryptographic Abstractions

Algorithms that operate in untrusted environments, where messages may be exposed to a malicious adversary, rely on cryptographic methods for their protection. The basic cryptographic primitives considered here are: *hash functions*, *MACs*, and *digital signatures*.

The physical implementations of the cryptographic abstractions usually rely on some keys being present at all processes. Distributing the right keys to all participants in a distributed computation is the task of key management, which is outside the scope of this book (see also Sect. 2.7.2).

2.3.1 Hash Functions

A cryptographic *hash function* maps a bit string of arbitrary length to a short, unique representation. The functionality provides only a single operation H; its invocation takes a bit string x of arbitrary length as an input parameter and returns a value h, which is a short bit string of fixed length in practice. A hash function is collision-free in the sense that no process, not even one subject to arbitrary faults, can find two distinct values x and x' such that $H(x) = H(x')$.

Formally, one can imagine that the hash function is implemented by a distributed oracle accessible to every process, which maintains a list $\mathcal{L}$ of all inputs x that have been queried so far by any process. When a process invokes H on a value $x \in \mathcal{L}$, then H responds with the index of x in $\mathcal{L}$; otherwise, H appends x to $\mathcal{L}$ and returns its index. The index is represented in binary and padded to a fixed length, which must be large enough such that the space of indices is never exhausted in the execution of any algorithm using the hash function. This ideal implementation models the collision-resistance property of hash functions, but no other properties of real-world hash functions.

Hash functions are one of the most basic cryptographic abstractions; their implementations are very fast, also long inputs can be hashed in a short time on ordinary machines.

2.3.2 Message-Authentication Codes (MACs)

A *message-authentication code (MAC)* authenticates data between two entities. It is based on a shared symmetric key, which is known only to the sender and to the receiver of a message, but to nobody else. For a message of its choice the sender can compute an authenticator for the receiver. Given an authenticator and a message, the receiver can verify that the message has indeed been authenticated by the sender. It is infeasible for any other entity than the sender and the verifier to come up with a message that was never authenticated and to produce an authenticator that the receiver accepts as valid during verification.

When using message authentication in the algorithms of this book, every ordered pair of processes in $\Pi \times \Pi$ is associated with a separate MAC. More precisely, such a message-authentication scheme provides the following functionality: it is a distributed oracle with two operations, *authenticate* and *verifyauth*.

The oracle internally maintains a set $\mathcal{A}$, initially empty. The invocation of *authenticate* takes a sender process identifier p, a receiver process identifier q, and a bit string m as parameters and returns an authenticator a with the response; internally, it adds the tuple (p, q, m, a) to $\mathcal{A}$. The *verifyauth* operation takes an identifier q of a receiver process, an identifier p of a sender process, a bit string m, and a putative authenticator a as parameters; if $(p, q, m, a) \in \mathcal{A}$ then the operation returns the Boolean value TRUE; otherwise, the response of the operation is FALSE.

Only process p may invoke *authenticate*$(p, \cdot, \cdot)$, and only process q may invoke *verifyauth*$(q, \cdot, \cdot, \cdot)$.

In other words, the functionality satisfies that *verifyauth*(q, p, m, a) returns TRUE for all processes p and q and for all messages m if and only if process p has previously invoked *authenticate*(p, q, m) and obtained a as response; otherwise, the operation *verifyauth*(q, p, m, a) returns FALSE.

As MACs are based on fast symmetric cryptographic primitives in practice (such as hash functions, stream ciphers, or block ciphers), they can be computed and verified very fast.

2.3.3 Digital Signatures

A *digital signature scheme* provides data authentication in systems with multiple entities that need not share any information beforehand. Physical realizations of digital signatures associate a public-key/private-key pair with an entity. The private key is given to the entity and must remain secret; the public key is accessible to anyone. With the private key the entity can produce a signature for a statement of its choice. The public key is associated with the identity of an entity, and everyone with access to the public key can verify that the signature on the statement is valid.

It is infeasible for any entity that does not know the private key to come up with a statement that was never signed and to forge a valid signature on it.

For using digital signatures in this book, every process in Π can sign messages with its own identity and verify the signatures produced by the other processes. Formally, the functionality of digital signatures is captured by a distributed oracle with two operations: *sign* and *verifysig*. The invocation of *sign* takes a process identifier p and a bit string m as parameters and returns a signature s with the response. The *verifysig* operation takes an identifier q of a process, a bit string m, and a putative signature s as parameters and returns a Boolean value $b \in \{\text{FALSE}, \text{TRUE}\}$ with the response. Only process p may invoke *sign*$(p, \cdot)$. Every process (including the adversary) may invoke *verifysig* without restriction on the parameters.

The functionality satisfies that *verifysig*(q, m, s) returns TRUE for all processes q, and for all messages m, if and only if process q has previously invoked *sign*(q, m) and obtained s as response; otherwise, *verifysig*(q, m, s) returns FALSE.

Equivalently, one can imagine that the signature scheme oracle maintains a set $\mathcal{S}$ and implements an operation *sign*(p, m) that returns s by adding (p, m, s) to $\mathcal{S}$. The operation *verifysig*(q, m, s) is implemented by evaluating the condition $(q, m, s) \in \mathcal{S}$ and returning the result.

The text m to be signed and verified using a signature scheme must be represented as a bit string. Sometimes we will use structured texts that consist of multiple components. In order to avoid problems with the interpretation of a text made of k components $c_1, c_2, \ldots, c_k$, we use the notation $c_1 \| c_2 \| \ldots \| c_k$, where $\|$ is a special symbol that represents for the concatenation of bit strings.

A signature scheme is more powerful than a MAC in the sense that authenticated messages can be verified by all entities and relayed even by untrusted entities. In this sense, a MAC behaves like oral messages exchanged between people, whereas a digital signature scheme models the exchange unforgeable written messages.

For instance, when a MAC is used to authenticate a message from a sender to a receiver, and the receiver has verified that the message is authentic and has not been modified, the receiver cannot convince a third entity of this fact. This holds because the specification of the MAC does not permit the third entity to verify an authenticator intended for a separate entity. Hence, the third party must trust the receiver, but the receiver might be malicious and lie to the third party about the authenticity of the message. In this case, the third party could not tell whether the sender is correct and the message was authentic but the receiver lied, or whether the receiver is correct and the sender did not send a correctly authenticated message to the receiver. With a digital signature scheme, on the other hand, only the sender can authenticate information; thus, the third party could verify on its own if the sender's message is authentic, even if the message has been relayed by a faulty receiver.

Digital signatures are based on public-key cryptography (or asymmetric cryptography); because of their underlying mathematical structure, they add considerable computational overhead compared to the symmetric cryptographic primitives.

2.4 Abstracting Communication

The abstraction of a *link* is used to represent the network components of the distributed system. Every pair of processes is connected by a bidirectional link, a topology that provides full connectivity among the processes. In practice, different topologies may implement this abstraction, possibly using routing algorithms. Concrete examples of architectures that materialize the link abstraction, such as the ones illustrated in Fig. 2.4, include the use of (a) a fully connected mesh, (b) a broadcast medium (such as an Ethernet), (c) a ring, or (d) a mesh of links interconnected by bridges and routers (such as the Internet). Many algorithms refine the abstract network view to make use of the properties of the underlying topology.

Messages exchanged between processes over a link are unique. Every message includes enough information for the recipient of a message to uniquely identify its sender. When a link is used by crash-stop or crash-recovery process abstractions, this property can be implemented trivially. When the processes are exposed to more severe faults or arbitrary faults, the network may also exhibit these faults; it may cause a correct process to accept and deliver a message that was inserted by an adversary on the network, for example. Algorithms for this model rely on cryptographic methods to provide correct sender identification, which is robust despite attacks by the network or by faulty processes.

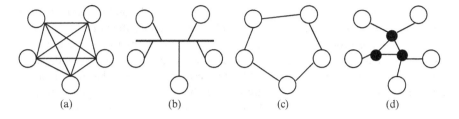

| (a) | (b) | (c) | (d) |

Figure 2.4: The link abstraction and different instances

When two processes exchange messages in a request–reply manner, they will usually have means to identify which reply message is a response to which request message. This can be achieved by having the processes generate timestamps or unique identifiers, based on sequence numbers, local clocks, or a source of randomness. This assumption alleviates the need for explicitly introducing such timestamps in the algorithm.

2.4.1 Link Failures

In a distributed system, it is possible for messages to be lost when transiting through the network. However, it is reasonable to assume that the probability for a message to reach its destination is nonzero because it is very unlikely that all messages exchanged among two processes are systematically lost unless there is a severe network failure (such as a network partition). A simple way to overcome the inherent unreliability of the network is to keep on retransmitting messages until they reach their destinations. Messages in a network may also be subject to attacks by an adversary, who may inspect or modify their content, or prevent that they are delivered. In this case, messages need to be additionally protected using cryptographic methods. Again, we assume that some messages reach their destination because preventing all communication among two processes is difficult.

In the following, we introduce five different link abstractions, three of them implemented by the crash-stop process abstraction, one for the crash-recovery abstraction, and one for a Byzantine process abstraction. Some are stronger than others in the sense that they provide more reliability guarantees. All are *point-to-point* links abstractions, i.e., they support communication between pairs of processes. (Broadcast communication abstractions for communicating from one to many processes are defined in the next chapter.)

We will first describe the abstraction of *fair-loss links*, which captures the basic idea that messages might be lost but the probability for a message not to be lost is nonzero. Then, we describe higher-level abstractions that could be implemented over fair-loss links using retransmission mechanisms to hide from the programmer part of the unreliability of the network. More precisely, we consider *stubborn* and *perfect links* abstractions, and show how they can be implemented on top of fair-loss links. These three abstractions assume a crash-fault process abstraction; a *logged perfect links* abstraction that deals with crash-recovery faults and an *authenticated links* abstraction that deals with arbitrary faults are presented afterward.

We define the properties of each of our link abstractions using two kinds of events: a ⟨ *Send* ⟩ request event to send a message and a ⟨ *Deliver* ⟩ indication event that delivers a message. We prefer the term *deliver* over the more general term *receive* to emphasize that we are talking about a specific link abstraction to be implemented over the network. A message is typically *received* at a given port of the network and stored within some buffer, and then some algorithm is executed to make sure the properties of the required link abstraction are satisfied, before the message is actually *delivered*. When there is no ambiguity, we alternatively use the term *receive* to mean *deliver*. On the other hand, when implementing a communication abstraction A over a communication abstraction B, we will sometimes use the term *deliver* for A and *receive* for B to disambiguate.

A process invokes the *send* request of a link abstraction to request the sending of a message using that abstraction. When the process invokes the request, we say that the process *sends* the message. It is then up to the link abstraction to transmit the message to the target process, according to the actual specification of the abstraction. The *deliver* indication is triggered by the algorithm implementing the abstraction on a destination process. When this event occurs on a process p for a message m, we say that p *delivers* m.

2.4.2 Fair-Loss Links

The *fair-loss links* abstraction is the weakest variant of the link abstractions considered here. Its interface is described by Module 2.1 and consists of two events: a request event, used to send messages, and an indication event, used to deliver the messages.

Module 2.1: Interface and properties of fair-loss point-to-point links

Module:

    Name: FairLossPointToPointLinks, **instance** *fll*.

Events:

    Request: ⟨ *fll, Send* | q, m ⟩: Requests to send message m to process q.

    Indication: ⟨ *fll, Deliver* | p, m ⟩: Delivers message m sent by process p.

Properties:

    FLL1: *Fair-loss:* If a correct process p infinitely often sends a message m to a correct process q, then q delivers m an infinite number of times.

    FLL2: *Finite duplication:* If a correct process p sends a message m a finite number of times to process q, then m cannot be delivered an infinite number of times by q.

    FLL3: *No creation:* If some process q delivers a message m with sender p, then m was previously sent to q by process p.

Fair-loss links are characterized by three properties. The *fair-loss* property guarantees that a link does not systematically drop every message. Therefore, if the sender process and the recipient process are both correct, and if the sender keeps retransmitting a message, the message is eventually delivered. The *finite duplication* property intuitively ensures that the network does not repeatedly perform more retransmissions than that performed by the sending process. Finally, the *no creation* property ensures that no message is created or corrupted by the network.

2.4.3 Stubborn Links

We define the abstraction of *stubborn links* in Module 2.2. This abstraction hides the lower-layer retransmission mechanisms used by the sender process, when using actual fair-loss links, to make sure its messages are eventually delivered by the destination process.

The *stubborn delivery* property causes every message sent over the link to be delivered at the receiver an unbounded number of times. The *no creation* property is the same as before and prevents the link from inventing messages.

Module 2.2: Interface and properties of stubborn point-to-point links

Module:

    Name: StubbornPointToPointLinks, **instance** *sl*.

Events:

    Request: $\langle$ *sl, Send* $\mid q, m$ $\rangle$: Requests to send message m to process q.

    Indication: $\langle$ *sl, Deliver* $\mid p, m$ $\rangle$: Delivers message m sent by process p.

Properties:

    SL1: *Stubborn delivery:* If a correct process p sends a message m once to a correct process q, then q delivers m an infinite number of times.

    SL2: *No creation:* If some process q delivers a message m with sender p, then m was previously sent to q by process p.

Algorithm: Retransmit Forever. Algorithm 2.1, called "Retransmit Forever," describes a very simple implementation of a stubborn link over a fair-loss link. As the name implies, the algorithm simply keeps on retransmitting all messages sent. This overcomes possible omissions in the links. Note that we assume here the availability of a *timeout* service that can be invoked using the *starttimer* function and which triggers a $\langle$ *Timeout* $\rangle$ event after a specified delay Δ. The timeout is triggered again only after the next call of *starttimer*. This is a purely local mechanism, i.e., it can be implemented by a local counter and does not rely on any global synchronization mechanism.

We discuss, in the following, the correctness of the algorithm for a stubborn link instance *sl*, as well as its performance.

Algorithm 2.1: Retransmit Forever

Implements:
  StubbornPointToPointLinks, **instance** *sl*.

Uses:
  FairLossPointToPointLinks, **instance** *fll*.

upon event ⟨ *sl, Init* ⟩ **do**
    sent := ∅;
    starttimer(Δ);

upon event ⟨ *Timeout* ⟩ **do**
    forall $(q, m) \in sent$ **do**
        trigger ⟨ *fll, Send* | *q, m* ⟩;
    starttimer(Δ);

upon event ⟨ *sl, Send* | *q, m* ⟩ **do**
    trigger ⟨ *fll, Send* | *q, m* ⟩;
    sent := *sent* ∪ {(*q, m*)};

upon event ⟨ *fll, Deliver* | *p, m* ⟩ **do**
    trigger ⟨ *sl, Deliver* | *p, m* ⟩;

Correctness. The *fair-loss* property of the underlying fair-loss links instance *fll* guarantees that, if the target process is correct, then every message that is *sl*-sent by every correct process will indeed be *fll*-delivered infinitely often by the target process. This is because the algorithm makes sure the sender process keeps *fll*-sending those messages infinitely often, unless the sender process itself crashes. The *no creation* property is simply preserved by the underlying links.

Performance. The algorithm is clearly not efficient and its purpose is primarily pedagogical. It is pretty clear that, within a practical application, it does not make much sense for a process to keep on, and at every step, retransmitting previously sent messages infinitely often. There are at least two complementary ways to prevent that effect and, hence, to make the algorithm more practical. First, it is important to remember that the very notions of infinity and infinitely often are context-dependent: they basically depend on the algorithm making use of stubborn links. After the algorithm making use of those links has ended its execution, there is no need to keep on sending messages. Second, an acknowledgment mechanism can be added to notify a sender that it does not need to keep on sending a given set of messages any more. This mechanism can be performed whenever a target process has delivered (i.e., properly consumed) those messages, or has delivered messages that semantically subsume the previous ones, e.g., in stock exchange applications when new values might subsume old ones. Such a mechanism should however be viewed as an external algorithm, and cannot be integrated within our algorithm implementing stubborn links. Otherwise, the algorithm might not be implementing the stubborn link abstraction anymore, for the subsume notion is not a part of the abstraction.

2.4.4 Perfect Links

With the stubborn links abstraction, it is up to the target process to check whether a given message has already been delivered or not. Adding mechanisms for detecting and suppressing message duplicates, in addition to mechanisms for message retransmission, allows us to build an even higher-level primitive: the *perfect links* abstraction, sometimes also called the *reliable links* abstraction. The perfect links abstraction specification is captured by Module 2.3. The interface of this module also consists of the same two events as the link abstractions introduced before: a request event (for sending messages) and an indication event (for delivering messages).

Perfect links are characterized by three properties. The *reliable delivery* property together with the *no duplication* property ensures that every message sent by a correct process is delivered by the receiver exactly once, if the receiver is also correct. The third property, *no creation*, is the same as in the other link abstractions.

Module 2.3: Interface and properties of perfect point-to-point links

Module:

   Name: PerfectPointToPointLinks, **instance** *pl.*

Events:

   Request: $\langle pl, Send \mid q, m \rangle$: Requests to send message m to process q.

   Indication: $\langle pl, Deliver \mid p, m \rangle$: Delivers message m sent by process p.

Properties:

   PL1: *Reliable delivery:* If a correct process p sends a message m to a correct process q, then q eventually delivers m.

   PL2: *No duplication:* No message is delivered by a process more than once.

   PL3: *No creation:* If some process q delivers a message m with sender p, then m was previously sent to q by process p.

Algorithm: Eliminate Duplicates. Algorithm 2.2 ("Eliminate Duplicates") conveys a very simple implementation of perfect links over stubborn ones. It simply keeps a record of all messages that have been delivered in the past; when a message is received, it is delivered only if it is not a duplicate. In the following, we discuss the correctness of the algorithm for a perfect point-to-point links instance *pl*, as well as its performance.

Correctness. Consider the *reliable delivery* property of perfect links. Let m be any message *pl*-sent by some process p to some process q, and assume that these two processes are correct. According to the algorithm, process p *sl*-sends m to q

---

Algorithm 2.2: Eliminate Duplicates

Implements:
    PerfectPointToPointLinks, **instance** *pl*.

Uses:
    StubbornPointToPointLinks, **instance** *sl*.

upon event ⟨ *pl, Init* ⟩ **do**
    delivered := ∅;

upon event ⟨ *pl, Send* | *q, m* ⟩ **do**
    trigger ⟨ *sl, Send* | *q, m* ⟩;

upon event ⟨ *sl, Deliver* | *p, m* ⟩ **do**
    if *m* ∉ *delivered* **then**
        delivered := *delivered* ∪ {*m*};
        trigger ⟨ *pl, Deliver* | *p, m* ⟩;

---

using the underlying stubborn links abstraction *sl*. Because of the *stubborn delivery* property of that primitive, *q* eventually *sl*-delivers *m*, at least once, and hence *pl*-delivers *m*. The *no duplication* property follows from the test performed by the algorithm whenever a message is *sl*-delivered and before *pl*-delivering that message. The *no creation* property simply follows from the *no creation* property of the underlying stubborn links.

Performance. Besides the performance considerations we discussed for our stubborn links implementation, i.e., Algorithm 2.1 ("Retransmit Forever"), and which clearly apply to the perfect links implementation of Algorithm 2.2 ("Eliminate Duplicates"), there is an additional concern related to maintaining the ever growing set of messages *delivered* at every process, given actual physical memory limitations.

At first glance, one might think of a simple way to circumvent this issue by having the target process acknowledge messages periodically and the sender process acknowledge having received such acknowledgments and promise not to send those messages anymore. There is no guarantee, however, that such messages are no longer in transit and will reach the target process afterward. The latter process might deliver the message again in this case, violating the *no creation* property. Additional mechanisms based on timestamps could be used, however, to recognize such old messages and to circumvent this problem.

2.4.5 Logged Perfect Links

With a crash-recovery process abstraction, the "Eliminate Duplicates" algorithm presented earlier is unsuitable for implementing the perfect links abstraction. The problem with the algorithm is its internal state to detect duplicates, which is maintained in volatile memory. If a process crashes, the state is lost. Upon recovery, the process will no longer remember which messages have already been delivered and might deliver the same message twice. To avoid this problem, the crash-recovery process abstraction may use stable storage, which is accessed through *store* and *retrieve* operations.

As discussed in Sect. 2.2, an important difference between the crash-stop and crash-recovery process abstractions lies in the way that a module sends its output to another module in a higher layer. Recall that the unit of failures is the process and, hence, the crash of a process affects all its modules. When an algorithm simply triggers an event to deliver a message, the process may crash immediately after triggering the event, before the output can be processed by the higher layer, for instance. We need an alternative way for delivering an output in the crash-recovery model; it consists of logging the output in stable storage.

We redefine the interface of all communication abstractions in the context of crash-recovery faults, and in particular the interface of the point-to-point links abstraction, as follows. Instead of triggering an event to deliver a message, the module writes the message to a local log, implemented by a variable in stable storage. This variable can also be accessed by the modules in the layer above, through a *retrieve* operation. To notify the layer above of the delivery, the module triggers an event ⟨ *Deliver* | *identifier* ⟩ that contains only the name *identifier* of the logging variable in stable storage.

For the link abstraction in the crash-recovery model, we use a variable *delivered* that contains a set of tuples of the form (s, m), where s denotes the sender process of a message m. We say that a message m is *log-delivered* from sender s whenever the process adds (s, m) to *delivered* and subsequently triggers a ⟨ *Deliver* ⟩ event with the name of *delivered* for the first time. In other words, a message message m is log-delivered from sender s at the time when an event ⟨ *Deliver* | *delivered* ⟩ occurs for a variable *delivered* in stable storage, such that *delivered* contains (s, m) but did not contain (s, m) at any time when ⟨ *Deliver* | *delivered* ⟩ occurred previously. For exploiting this notion correctly, the layer above this module must remember which messages it has already log-delivered.

Specification. The *logged perfect links* abstraction in Module 2.4 implements an interface according to this description. The logged perfect links abstraction maintains a set of sender/message pairs in a variable *delivered* in stable storage and triggers ⟨ *Deliver* | *delivered* ⟩ events. The properties of the abstraction in terms of log-delivered messages are almost the same as those of perfect point-to-point links (Module 2.3) in terms of delivered messages.

There is a subtle difference in the statement of the *reliable delivery* property, however. The perfect point-to-point links abstraction uses crash-stop processes, where a process may crash only once and a correct process never crashes. But the crash-recovery process abstraction, as used by logged perfect links, may crash a finite number of times and is still called *correct* if it always recovers from a crash. But even a correct crash-recovery process abstraction may lose its state; when it crashes immediately after executing a ⟨ *Send* ⟩ event with a message m and before taking any other steps, then it is not possible that the process remembers anything about m when it recovers, or that any other process in the system ever

---

Module 2.4: Interface and properties of logged perfect point-to-point links

Module:

    Name: LoggedPerfectPointToPointLinks, **instance** *lpl*.

Events:

    Request: $\langle$ *lpl, Send* $\mid q, m$ $\rangle$: Requests to send message m to process q.

    Indication: $\langle$ *lpl, Deliver* $\mid$ *delivered* $\rangle$: Notifies the upper layer of potential updates to variable *delivered* in stable storage (which log-delivers messages according to the text).

Properties:

    LPL1: *Reliable delivery:* If a process that never crashes sends a message m to a correct process q, then q eventually log-delivers m.

    LPL2: *No duplication:* No message is log-delivered by a process more than once.

    LPL3: *No creation:* If some process q log-delivers a message m with sender p, then m was previously sent to q by process p.

---

log-delivers m. For this reason, the *reliable delivery* property requires only that a message is eventually log-delivered if the sender *never* crashes (and not if the sender is merely correct, as for link abstractions with processes subject to crash faults).

Algorithm: Log Delivered. Algorithm 2.3 ("Log Delivered") is the direct adaptation of the "Eliminate Duplicates" algorithm that implements perfect point-to-point links from stubborn links. It simply keeps a record of all messages that have been log-delivered in the past; however, here it stores this record in stable storage and exposes it also to the upper layer.

Correctness. The correctness argument is the same as that for the "Eliminate Duplicates" algorithm, except for the fact that delivering here means logging the message in stable storage.

Performance. In terms of messages, the performance of the "Log Delivered" algorithm is similar to that of the "Eliminate Duplicates" algorithm. However, algorithm "Log Delivered" requires one log operation every time a new message is received.

2.4.6 Authenticated Perfect Links

This section considers messages communicated in a network with Byzantine process abstractions. Recall that in this model, the communication links themselves may also behave arbitrarily. In principle, a link abstraction subject to arbitrary faults might simply not allow *any* communication. However, we assume that such denial-of-service attacks cannot prevent all communication between correct processes in a distributed system.

Algorithm 2.3: Log Delivered

Implements:
   LoggedPerfectPointToPointLinks, **instance** *lpl*.

Uses:
   StubbornPointToPointLinks, **instance** *sl*.

upon event $\langle$ *lpl*, *Init* $\rangle$ **do**
   delivered := $\emptyset$;
   store(*delivered*);

upon event $\langle$ *lpl*, *Recovery* $\rangle$ **do**
   retrieve(*delivered*);
   trigger $\langle$ *lpl*, *Deliver* | *delivered* $\rangle$;

upon event $\langle$ *lpl*, *Send* | q, m $\rangle$ **do**
   trigger $\langle$ *sl*, *Send* | q, m $\rangle$;

upon event $\langle$ *sl*, *Deliver* | p, m $\rangle$ **do**
   if not exists $(p', m') \in$ *delivered* such that $m' = m$ **then**
      delivered := *delivered* $\cup$ $\{(p, m)\}$;
      store(*delivered*);
      trigger $\langle$ *lpl*, *Deliver* | *delivered* $\rangle$;

In the following, we assume that the processes may communicate with each other using a fair-loss point-to-point links abstraction according to Module 2.1. Note that its *fair-loss* property is sound with respect to a Byzantine process abstraction; but, its *finite duplication* and *no creation* properties permit that if there is only one faulty process, a correct process may deliver any legal message an unbounded number of times and without any correct process previously having sent it. This is simply because the Byzantine process may insert the message infinitely often and pretend that it originates from an arbitrary sender process.

Furthermore, the fair-loss links abstraction can be extended to a stubborn links abstraction (Module 2.2) in the presence of Byzantine processes, by repeatedly sending a broadcast message over the fair-loss links as in the "Retransmit Forever" algorithm. But, the *no creation* property of stubborn links cannot be ensured either.

A fair-loss links abstraction or a stubborn links abstraction alone is thus not very useful with a Byzantine process abstraction. But cryptographic authentication can turn them into a more useful *authenticated perfect links* primitive, which eliminates the forgery of messages on the links between two correct processes. This abstraction is specified in Module 2.5. It uses the same interface as the other point-to-point links abstractions. The *reliable delivery* and *no duplication* properties of authenticated links are the same as for perfect links. Only the *authenticity* property for Byzantine processes is stronger than the corresponding *no creation* property for crash-stop processes.

Module 2.5: Interface and properties of authenticated perfect point-to-point links

Module:

    Name: AuthPerfectPointToPointLinks, **instance** *al*.

Events:

    Request: ⟨ *al*, *Send* | *q*, *m* ⟩: Requests to send message *m* to process *q*.

    Indication: ⟨ *al*, *Deliver* | *p*, *m* ⟩: Delivers message *m* sent by process *p*.

Properties:

    AL1: *Reliable delivery:* If a correct process sends a message *m* to a correct process *q*, then *q* eventually delivers *m*.

    AL2: *No duplication:* No message is delivered by a correct process more than once.

    AL3: *Authenticity:* If some correct process *q* delivers a message *m* with sender *p* and process *p* is correct, then *m* was previously sent to *q* by *p*.

Algorithm 2.4: Authenticate and Filter

Implements:
    AuthPerfectPointToPointLinks, **instance** *al*.

Uses:
    StubbornPointToPointLinks, **instance** *sl*.

upon event ⟨ *al*, *Init* ⟩ **do**
    delivered := ∅;

upon event ⟨ *al*, *Send* | *q*, *m* ⟩ **do**
    a := *authenticate*(*self*, *q*, *m*);
    trigger ⟨ *sl*, *Send* | *q*, [*m*, *a*] ⟩;

upon event ⟨ *sl*, *Deliver* | *p*, [*m*, *a*] ⟩ **do**
    if *verifyauth*(*self*, *p*, *m*, *a*) ∧ *m* ∉ *delivered* **then**
        delivered := *delivered* ∪ {*m*};
        trigger ⟨ *al*, *Deliver* | *p*, *m* ⟩;

Algorithm: Authenticate and Filter. Algorithm 2.5 ("Authenticate and Filter") uses a MAC to implement authenticated perfect point-to-point links over a stubborn links abstraction. An instance *al* uses the MAC to compute an authenticator over the message, the sender identifier, and the recipient identifiers for every *al*-sent message. It *sl*-sends the message together with the authenticator. When a message and an authenticator are *sl*-delivered, the algorithm verifies that the message contents as well as the indicated sender and recipient identifiers are valid using the MAC. Note that the recipient is the process itself, which is denoted by *self*. When the authenticator is valid, the process *al*-delivers the message.

Correctness. As the algorithm only extends Algorithm 2.2 ("Eliminate Dupli-cates") with the statements that implement cryptographic authentication, the *reliable delivery* and *no duplication* properties follow from the same argument as for Algorithm 2.2. For the *authenticity* property, consider a *sl*-delivered tuple (p, m, a) that causes message m to be *al*-delivered with sender p. The MAC only accepts the authenticator a as valid when it was computed by process p with receiver pro-cess *self* and message m. Hence, the authenticator a was computed by process p and m was indeed *al*-sent by p.

Performance. As the implementation uses the same steps as Algorithm 2.2, the same issue arises for the set *delivered* that grows without bound. Cryptographic authentication adds a modest computational overhead.

2.4.7 On the Link Abstractions

Throughout this book, we will mainly assume perfect links in the context of crash-stop process abstractions or their logged and authenticated variants in the context of crash-recovery and Byzantine process abstractions, respectively. It may seem un-realistic to assume that links are perfect when it is known that physical links may lose, duplicate, or modify messages. This assumption only captures the fact that these problems can be addressed by some lower-level protocol. As long as the net-work remains connected and processes do not commit an unbounded number of omission failures, link crashes may be masked by routing. The loss of messages can be masked through retransmission, as we have just explained through various algo-rithms. This functionality is often found in standard transport-level protocols such as TCP. These protocols are typically supported by the operating system and need not be reimplemented.

The details of how the perfect links abstraction is implemented are not relevant for understanding the fundamental principles of many distributed algorithms. On the other hand, when developing actual distributed applications, these details become relevant. For instance, it may happen that some distributed algorithm requires the use of sequence numbers and message retransmissions, even assuming perfect links. In this case, in order to avoid the redundant use of similar mechanisms at differ-ent layers, it may be more effective to rely just on weaker links, such as fair-loss or stubborn links. The algorithms implementing logged and authenticated perfect point-to-point links in the previous section already demonstrated this.

Indeed, as we have observed in the crash-recovery model, delivery is imple-mented by exposing a log maintained in stable storage. The upper layer is, therefore, required to keep its own record of which messages in the log it has already pro-cessed. Thus, the upper layer will generally have the ability to eliminate duplicates and can often operate using the weaker abstraction of stubborn links, avoiding the use of more expensive logged perfect links.

More generally, many networking issues should be considered when moving to concrete implementations. Among others they include:

- *Network topology.* Many optimizations can be achieved if the network topology is exposed to the upper layers. For instance, communication in a local-area network (LAN) exhibits a much lower latency than communication over wide-area links. Such facts should be taken into account by any practical algorithm.
- *Flow control.* In a practical system, the resources of a process are bounded. This means that a process can handle only a limited number of messages per unit of time. If a sender exceeds the receiver's capacity, messages are lost. Practical systems must include feedback mechanisms to allow the senders to adjust their sending rate to the capacity of receivers.
- *Heterogeneity.* In a real system, not all processes are equal. In fact, it may happen that some processes run on faster processors, have more memory, can access more bandwidth, or are better connected than others. This heterogeneity may be exploited by an algorithm such that more demanding tasks are assigned to the most powerful and best-connected processes first.

2.5 Timing Assumptions

An important part in the characterization of a distributed system is the behavior of its processes and links with respect to the passage of time. In short, determining whether we can make any assumption about time bounds on communication delays and (relative) process speeds is of primary importance for every distributed-system model. We introduce time-related models in this section and consider the *failure-detector* abstraction as a particularly useful way to abstract timing assumptions in the next section.

2.5.1 Asynchronous System

Assuming an *asynchronous* distributed system comes down to not making any timing assumption about processes and links. This is precisely the approach taken so far for defining process and link abstractions. That is, we did not assume that processes have access to any sort of physical clock, nor did we assume any bounds on processing or communication delays.

Even without access to physical clocks, it is still possible to measure the passage of time based on the transmission and delivery of messages, such that time is defined with respect to communication. Time measured in this way is called *logical time*, and the resulting notion of a clock is called a *logical clock*.

The following algorithm can be used to measure logical time in an asynchronous distributed system:

1. Each process p keeps an integer called *logical clock* l_p, initially 0.
2. Whenever an event occurs at process p, the logical clock l_p is incremented by one unit.
3. When a process sends a message, it adds a timestamp to the message with the value of its logical clock at the moment the message is sent. The timestamp of an event e is denoted by $t(e)$.

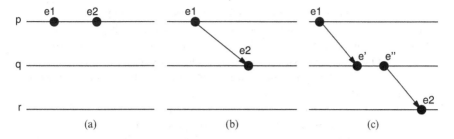

Figure 2.5: The *happened-before* relation

4. When a process p receives a message m with timestamp t_m, process p increments its logical clock in the following way: $l_p := \max\{l_p, t_m\} + 1$.

An interesting aspect of logical clocks is the fact that they capture cause–effect relations in systems where the processes can only interact through message exchanges. We say that an event e_1 may have *potentially caused* another event e_2, denoted as $e_1 \to e_2$, when the following condition applies:

(a) e_1 and e_2 occurred at the same process p and e_1 occurred before e_2;
(b) e_1 corresponds to the transmission of a message m at a process p and e_2 to the reception of m at some other process q; or
(c) there exists some event e', such that $e_1 \to e'$ and $e' \to e_2$.

The relation defining the potential causality condition is called the *happened-before* relation, and it is illustrated in Fig. 2.5. It can be shown that if the events are timestamped with logical clocks then $e_1 \to e_2 \Rightarrow t(e_1) < t(e_2)$. Note that the opposite implication is not true.

As we discuss in the next chapters, even in the absence of any physical timing assumption, and using only a logical notion of time, we can implement some useful distributed programming abstractions. Many abstractions do, however, need some physical timing assumptions. In fact, even a very simple form of agreement, namely, *consensus*, is impossible to solve in an asynchronous system even if only one process fails, and it can only do so by crashing (see the historical note at the end of this chapter). In the consensus problem, which we will address later in this book, the processes each start with an initial value, and have to agree on a common final value among the initial values. The consequence of the consensus impossibility is immediate for the impossibility of deriving algorithms for many agreement abstractions, including group membership or totally ordered group communication.

2.5.2 Synchronous System

Although assuming an *asynchronous* system comes down to not making any physical timing assumption on processes and links, assuming a *synchronous* system comes down to assuming the following properties:

1. *Synchronous computation.* There is a known upper bound on processing delays. That is, the time taken by any process to execute a step is always less than this bound. Remember that a step gathers the delivery of a message (possibly *nil*) sent by some other process, a local computation (possibly involving interaction among several layers of the same process), and the sending of a message to some other process (possibly omitted).
2. *Synchronous communication.* There is a known upper bound on message transmission delays. That is, the time period between the instant at which a message is sent and the instant at which the message is delivered by the destination process is smaller than this bound.

A real-time clock provides an alternative way for synchronization among multiple processes, and a synchronous system is alternatively characterized as follows:

3. *Synchronous physical clocks.* Every process is equipped with a local physical clock. There is a known upper bound on the rate at which the local physical clock deviates from a global real-time clock.

Note that such a global clock exists also in our universe, but merely as a fictional device to simplify the reasoning about steps taken by processes. This clock is not accessible to the processes and no algorithm can rely on it.

In a synchronous distributed system, several useful services can be provided. We enumerate some of them:

- *Timed failure detection.* Every crash of a process may be detected within bounded time: whenever a process p crashes, all processes that did not crash detect the crash of p within a known bounded time. This can be achieved, for instance, using a heartbeat mechanism, where processes periodically exchange messages and detect, within a limited time period, the crashes.
- *Measure of transit delays.* It is possible to get a good approximation of the delays of messages in the communication links and, from there, infer which nodes are more distant or connected by slower or overloaded links.
- *Coordination based on time.* One can implement a *lease* abstraction that provides the right to execute some action during a fixed time period, e.g., for manipulating a specific file. The right expires automatically at the end of the time period.
- *Worst-case performance.* By assuming a bound on the number of faults and on the load of the system, it is possible to derive *worst-case response times* for any given algorithm. This allows a process to know when a message that it has sent is received by the destination process (provided that the latter is correct). This can be achieved even if we assume that processes commit omission faults without crashing, as long as we bound the number of these omission faults.
- *Synchronized clocks.* A synchronous system makes it possible to synchronize the clocks of the different processes in such a way that they are never apart by more than some known constant δ, called the clock synchronization precision. Synchronized clocks allow processes to coordinate their actions and ultimately execute synchronized global steps. Using synchronized clocks makes it possible to timestamp events using the value of the local clock at the instant they occur.

These timestamps can be used to order events in the system. If there was a system where all delays were constant, it would be possible to achieve perfectly synchronized clocks (i.e., where δ would be 0). Unfortunately, such a system cannot be built. In practice, δ is always greater than zero and events within δ cannot be ordered.

Not surprisingly, the major limitation of assuming a synchronous system model is the *coverage* of the model, i.e., the difficulty of building a system where the timing assumptions hold with high probability. This typically requires careful analysis of the network and processing load and the use of appropriate processor and network scheduling algorithms. Although this is appropriate for some LANs, it may not be feasible, or not even desirable, in large-scale systems such as the Internet. On the Internet, for example, there are periods where messages can take a very long time to arrive at their destination. One should consider very large values to capture the processing and communication bounds. This would mean, however, to consider worst-case values which are typically much higher than average values. These worst-case values are usually so high that any application based on them would be very slow.

2.5.3 Partial Synchrony

Generally, distributed systems appear to be synchronous. More precisely, for *most* systems that we know of, it is relatively easy to define physical time bounds that are respected *most of the time*. There are, however, periods where the timing assumptions do not hold, i.e., periods during which the system is asynchronous. These are periods where the network is overloaded, for instance, or some process has a shortage of memory that slows it down. Typically, the buffer that a process uses to store incoming and outgoing messages may overflow, and messages may thus get lost, violating the time bound on the delivery. The retransmission of the messages may help ensure the reliability of the communication links but introduce unpredictable delays. In this sense, practical systems are *partially synchronous*.

One way to capture partial synchrony is to assume that the timing assumptions only hold eventually, without stating when exactly. This means that there is a time after which these assumptions hold forever, but this time is not known. In a way, instead of assuming a synchronous system, we assume a system that is *eventually synchronous*. It is important to notice that in practice, making such assumptions neither means that (1) there is a time after which the underlying system (consisting of application, hardware, and networking components) is synchronous forever nor does it mean that (2) the system needs to be initially asynchronous, and then only after some (long) period becomes synchronous. The assumption simply captures the very fact that the system may not always be synchronous, and there is no bound on the period during which it is asynchronous. However, we expect that there are periods during which the system is synchronous, and some of these periods are long enough for an algorithm to do something useful or to terminate its execution.

2.6 Abstracting Time

2.6.1 Failure Detection

So far we have discussed the asynchronous system assumption, which is simple but inherently limited, the synchronous system assumption, which is powerful but has limited coverage in practice, and the intermediate partially synchronous system assumption. Each of these assumptions makes sense for specific environments and is plausible for reasoning about general-purpose implementations of high-level distributed programming abstractions.

An asynchronous system contains no timing assumptions, and our process and link abstractions directly capture that. But, these abstractions are not sufficient for defining synchronous and partially synchronous systems. One way to add timing assumptions could be to augment our process and link abstractions with timing guarantees to encompass synchronous and partially synchronous systems. This would lead to overly complicated specifications. Instead, we consider a separate notion to encapsulate their capabilities related to synchrony. We introduce the abstraction of a *failure detector* that provides information about which processes have crashed and which are correct, and allow that this information is not necessarily accurate. In particular, we will consider failure detectors that encapsulate the timing assumptions of a synchronous system and failure detectors that encapsulate the timing assumptions of a partially synchronous system. Not surprisingly, the information provided by the first kind of failure detectors about crashed processes will be more accurate than the information provided by those of the second kind. Clearly, the stronger the timing assumptions we make on the distributed system (to implement the failure detector) the more accurate is that information.

There are at least two advantages of the failure-detector abstraction over an approach where we would directly make timing assumptions on processes and links. First, the failure-detector abstraction alleviates the need for extending the process and link abstractions introduced earlier in this chapter with timing assumptions. As a consequence, the simplicity of those abstractions is preserved. Second, and as we will see in the following, we can reason about the behavior of a failure detector using axiomatic properties with no explicit references to physical time. Such references are usually prone to error. In practice, except for specific applications like process control, timing assumptions are indeed mainly used to detect process failures, in other words, to implement failure detectors.

Arbitrary-faulty Processes. In our discussion of timing assumptions, we have only considered crash faults and crash-recovery faults so far, but not arbitrary or Byzantine faults. In principle, a failure-detection abstraction can also be formulated for the Byzantine process abstraction; however, Byzantine processes make it inherently difficult to implement them.

As we will see, a failure detector that should give information about remote processes that may merely crash can be realized by asking the remote processes to periodically perform some actions. Assume for a moment that the communication between an observer process and the remote processes is fault-free and synchronous.

If crashes are the only kinds of faults that may occur, the following holds. When the observer ever notices that a remote process stops performing these actions, it can safely conclude that the remote process has failed. The remote process will also have stopped participating in any algorithm that it might have run, and the algorithm can properly react to the failure. Furthermore, when a remote process crashes while executing an algorithm, the observer is also guaranteed that the failure detector eventually detects that failure. Summarizing, a failure detector for crash faults provides an accurate failure signal about a remote process if and only if the process stops behaving properly in an algorithm.

Such a correspondence is not given with the arbitrary-fault process abstraction. Especially, when the source of the fault is a malicious attack, the adversary behind the attack wants to evade being detected and will take great care to make the process behave properly in any algorithm that it runs. The attacked process will only deviate from the algorithm once it can catch its prey and do the harm. The faulty process may easily pretend to behave correctly for all remote observers in the context of the failure detector, and at the same time badly violate its specification in the algorithm. In the face of Byzantine faults, a failure-detector abstraction is difficult to implement and its output may not be very useful. Therefore, we do not consider failure detectors with Byzantine process abstractions; but we will later discuss a realistic leader-detector abstraction that relies crucially on algorithm-specific information about the proper performance of a remote process.

2.6.2 Perfect Failure Detection

In synchronous systems, and assuming a crash-stop process abstraction, crashes can be accurately detected using *timeouts*. For instance, assume that a process sends a message to another process and awaits a response. If the recipient process does not crash then the response is guaranteed to arrive within a time period equal to the worst-case processing delay plus two times the worst-case message transmission delay (ignoring the clock drifts). Using its own clock, a sender process can measure the worst-case delay required to obtain a response and detect a crash when no such reply arrives within the timeout period; the crash detection will usually trigger a corrective procedure. We encapsulate such a way of detecting failures for synchronous systems in a *perfect failure-detector* abstraction.

Specification. The perfect failure detector is also denoted by $\mathcal{P}$ (as an abbreviation of "perfect"), and it outputs, at every process, the identities of the processes that it detects to have crashed; we simply say that it *detects* a process. To detect the crash of a process p, the failure detector triggers an event $\langle\, Crash \mid p \,\rangle$ with argument p. The perfect failure detector never changes its mind and detections are permanent; in other words, once a process p is detected (to have crashed) by some process q, the process p remains detected by q forever.

A perfect failure detector is characterized by the properties of Module 2.6. A perfect failure detector eventually detects all crashed processes (the *strong completeness* property) and never outputs false detections, i.e., never detects a noncrashed process (the *strong accuracy* property).

Module 2.6: Interface and properties of the perfect failure detector

Module:

    Name: PerfectFailureDetector, **instance** $\mathcal{P}$.

Events:

    Indication: $\langle\ \mathcal{P},\ Crash\ |\ p\ \rangle$: Detects that process p has crashed.

Properties:

    PFD1: *Strong completeness:* Eventually, every process that crashes is permanently detected by every correct process.

    PFD2: *Strong accuracy:* If a process p is detected by any process, then p has crashed.

Algorithm: Exclude on Timeout. Algorithm 2.5, which we call "Exclude on Timeout," implements a perfect failure detector assuming a synchronous system. The perfect communication links do not lose messages sent among correct processes, and the transmission period of every message is bounded by some known constant, in comparison to which the local processing time of a process, as well as the clock drifts, are negligible. The algorithm exchanges heartbeat messages among all processes and uses a specific timeout mechanism initialized with a delay Δ. The delay is chosen large enough such that every process has enough time to send a heartbeat message to all, every heartbeat message has enough time to be delivered, the correct destination processes have enough time to process the heartbeat and to send a reply message, and the replies have enough time to reach the original sender and to be processed. Whenever the timeout period expires, a $\langle\ Timeout\ \rangle$ event is triggered and all processes from which no reply has been received are declared to have crashed. Furthermore, a new exchange of heartbeat and reply messages is started.

The algorithm keeps track of the processes that did not return the reply in time in a variable *detected* and triggers one event $\langle\ Crash\ |\ p\ \rangle$ for every process p that it adds to *detected*.

Correctness. Consider the *strong completeness* property of a perfect failure detector. If a process p crashes, it stops replying to heartbeat messages, and no process will deliver its messages: remember that perfect links ensure that no message is delivered unless it was sent. Every correct process will thus detect the crash of p.

Consider now the *strong accuracy* property of a perfect failure detector. The crash of a process p is detected by some other process q only if q does not deliver a message from p before the timeout period. This can happen only if p has indeed crashed because the algorithm makes sure p must have sent a message otherwise, and the synchrony assumption implies that the message should have been delivered before the timeout period.

Algorithm 2.5: Exclude on Timeout

Implements:
    PerfectFailureDetector, **instance** $\mathcal{P}$.

Uses:
    PerfectPointToPointLinks, **instance** *pl*.

upon event $\langle\ \mathcal{P},\ Init\ \rangle$ **do**
    alive := Π;
    detected := $\emptyset$;
    starttimer(Δ);

upon event $\langle\ Timeout\ \rangle$ **do**
    forall $p \in \Pi$ **do**
        if $(p \notin alive) \wedge (p \notin detected)$ **then**
            detected := *detected* $\cup \{p\}$;
            trigger $\langle\ \mathcal{P},\ Crash\ |\ p\ \rangle$;
        trigger $\langle\ pl,\ Send\ |\ p,\ [\textsc{HeartbeatRequest}]\ \rangle$;
    alive := $\emptyset$;
    starttimer(Δ);

upon event $\langle\ pl,\ Deliver\ |\ q,\ [\textsc{HeartbeatRequest}]\ \rangle$ **do**
    trigger $\langle\ pl,\ Send\ |\ q,\ [\textsc{HeartbeatReply}]\ \rangle$;

upon event $\langle\ pl,\ Deliver\ |\ p,\ [\textsc{HeartbeatReply}]\ \rangle$ **do**
    alive := *alive* $\cup \{p\}$;

Performance. For presentation simplicity, we omitted a simple optimization which consists in not sending any heartbeat messages to processes that were detected to have crashed.

It is important to notice that the time to detect a failure depends on the timeout delay. A large timeout, say ten times the expected delay needed to send a message and deliver it to all processes, would reasonably cope with situations where the delay would be slightly extended. However, one would want to detect and react to failures earlier, with a shorter timeout. The risk here is that the probability to falsely detect a crash is higher. One way to cope with such a trade-off is to assume an imperfect failure detector, as we will discuss later.

2.6.3 Leader Election

Often one may not need to detect which processes have failed, but rather need to identify one process that has *not* failed. This process may then act as the *leader* that coordinates some steps of a distributed algorithm, and in a sense it is *trusted* by the other processes to act as their leader. The *leader election* abstraction introduced here provides such support. It can also be viewed as a failure detector in the sense that its properties do not depend on the actual computation of the processes but rather on their failures. Indeed, the leader-election abstraction can be implemented in a straightforward way from a perfect failure detector.

Module 2.7: Interface and properties of leader election

Module:

    Name: LeaderElection, **instance** *le*.

Events:

    Indication: $\langle$ *le, Leader* $\mid p$ $\rangle$: Indicates that process p is elected as leader.

Properties:

    LE1: *Eventual detection:* Either there is no correct process, or some correct process is eventually elected as the leader.

    LE2: *Accuracy:* If a process is leader, then all previously elected leaders have crashed.

We consider the leader-election abstraction only for crash-stop process abstractions; it cannot be formulated for crash-recovery and arbitrary-fault process abstractions.

More generally, the leader-election abstraction consists in choosing one process to be selected as a unique representative of the group of processes in the system. For this abstraction to be useful in a distributed setting, a new leader should be elected if the current leader crashes. The abstraction is particularly useful in a primary-backup replication scheme, for instance. Following this scheme, a set of replica processes coordinate their activities to provide the illusion of a unique highly available service that tolerates faults of some processes. Among the set of replica processes, one is chosen as the leader. This leader process, sometimes called the *primary*, treats the requests submitted by the client processes on behalf of the other replicas, called *backups*. Before the leader returns a reply to a given client, it updates the backups. If the leader crashes, one of the backups is elected as the new leader. We will study algorithms of this type for implementing consensus in Chap. 5.

Specification. We define the leader-election abstraction in terms of a specific $\langle$ *Leader* $\mid p$ $\rangle$ indication event. When triggered with a parameter p at some given time, it means that process p is elected as leader from that time on until it crashes. The properties of the abstraction are given in Module 2.7.

The *eventual detection* property ensures the eventual presence of a correct leader. Clearly, it may be the case that, at some point in time, no process is the leader. It may also be the case that no leader is running. However, the property ensures that, unless there is no correct process, some correct process is eventually elected as the leader. The *accuracy* property ensures the stability of the leader. In other words, it ensures that the leader may only change when the past leader has crashed. Indirectly, this property precludes the possibility for two processes to be leader at the same time.

Algorithm: Monarchical Leader Election. Algorithm 2.6 implements the leader-election abstraction assuming a perfect failure detector. The algorithm exploits the a-priori ranking among the processes (see Sect. 2.1). A process can become

---

Algorithm 2.6: Monarchical Leader Election

Implements:
    LeaderElection, **instance** *le*.

Uses:
    PerfectFailureDetector, **instance** $\mathcal{P}$.

upon event $\langle$ *le, Init* $\rangle$ **do**
    suspected := $\emptyset$;
    leader := $\perp$;

upon event $\langle$ $\mathcal{P}$, *Crash* $\mid p$ $\rangle$ **do**
    suspected := *suspected* $\cup$ $\{p\}$;

upon *leader* $\neq$ *maxrank*($\Pi \setminus$ *suspected*) **do**
    leader := *maxrank*($\Pi \setminus$ *suspected*);
    trigger $\langle$ *le, Leader* $\mid$ *leader* $\rangle$;

---

leader only if all processes with a higher rank have crashed. Imagine that the rank represents the royal ordering in a monarchy. The queen has the highest rank, the prince the second highest, and so on. The prince becomes leader if and only if the queen dies. If the prince dies, maybe his younger sister is the next in the list, and so on.

The algorithm expresses this order with a function *maxrank*(S), which selects the process with the highest rank from a set of processes S. In other words, $maxrank(S) = \arg\max_{p \in S}\{rank(p)\}$.

Correctness. The *eventual detection* property follows from the *strong completeness* property of $\mathcal{P}$, whereas the *accuracy* property follows from the *strong accuracy* property of $\mathcal{P}$.

Performance. The process of becoming a leader is a local operation. The time to react to a failure and become the new leader directly depends on the latency of the failure detector.

2.6.4 Eventually Perfect Failure Detection

Just like we can encapsulate timing assumptions of a synchronous system in a *perfect failure-detector* abstraction, we can similarly encapsulate timing assumptions of a partially synchronous system within an *eventually perfect failure detector* abstraction.

Specification. An eventually perfect failure-detector abstraction detects crashes accurately after some a priori unknown point in time, but may make mistakes before that time. This captures the intuition that, most of the time, timeout delays can be adjusted so they can lead to accurately detecting crashes. However, there are periods where the asynchrony of the underlying system prevents failure detection to be

---

Module 2.8: Interface and properties of the eventually perfect failure detector

Module:

    Name: EventuallyPerfectFailureDetector, **instance** $\diamond\mathcal{P}$.

Events:

    Indication: $\langle\,\diamond\mathcal{P},\,Suspect\mid p\,\rangle$: Notifies that process p is suspected to have crashed.

    Indication: $\langle\,\diamond\mathcal{P},\,Restore\mid p\,\rangle$: Notifies that process p is not suspected anymore.

Properties:

    EPFD1: *Strong completeness:* Eventually, every process that crashes is permanently suspected by every correct process.

    EPFD2: *Eventual strong accuracy:* Eventually, no correct process is suspected by any correct process.

---

accurate and leads to false suspicions. In this case, we talk about failure *suspicion* instead of failure detection.

More precisely, to implement an eventually perfect failure detector abstraction, the idea is to also use a timeout, and to suspect processes that did not send heartbeat messages within a timeout delay. The original timeout might be set to a short duration if the goal is to react quickly to failures. Obviously, a suspicion may be wrong in a partially synchronous system. A process p may suspect a process q, even if q has not crashed, simply because the timeout delay chosen by p to suspect the crash of q was too short. In this case, p's suspicion about q is false. When p receives a message from q, p revises its judgment and stops suspecting q. Process p also increases its timeout delay; this is because p does not know what the bound on communication delay will eventually be; it only knows there will be one. Clearly, if q now crashes, p will eventually suspect q and will never revise its judgment. If q does not crash then there is a time after which p will stop suspecting q, i.e., the timeout delay used by p to suspect q will eventually be large enough because p keeps increasing it whenever it commits a false suspicion. This is because we assume that there is a time after which the system is synchronous.

An eventually perfect failure detector is denoted by $\diamond\mathcal{P}$ (where $\diamond$ stands for "eventually") and defined by $\langle\,Suspect\,\rangle$ and $\langle\,Restore\,\rangle$ events. A process p is said to be *suspected* by process q after q has triggered the event $\langle\,Suspect\mid p\,\rangle$ and until it triggers the event $\langle\,Restore\mid p\,\rangle$, which is said to *restore p*. Module 2.8 describes the properties of the abstraction, which consist of a *strong completeness* property and an *eventual strong accuracy* property. Note that even though the *strong completeness* property reads almost the same as the corresponding property of the perfect failure detector, it means something different because the eventually perfect failure detector can restore a suspected process.

Algorithm: Increasing Timeout. Algorithm 2.7, called "Increasing Timeout," implements an eventually perfect failure detector assuming a partially synchronous

---

Algorithm 2.7: Increasing Timeout

Implements:
    EventuallyPerfectFailureDetector, **instance** $\Diamond\mathcal{P}$.

Uses:
    PerfectPointToPointLinks, **instance** *pl*.

upon event $\langle\,\Diamond\mathcal{P},\,Init\,\rangle$ **do**
    alive := Π;
    suspected := $\emptyset$;
    delay := Δ;
    starttimer(*delay*);

upon event $\langle\,Timeout\,\rangle$ **do**
    if *alive* $\cap$ *suspected* $\neq \emptyset$ **then**
        delay := *delay* + Δ;
    forall $p \in \Pi$ **do**
        if $(p \notin$ *alive*$) \wedge (p \notin$ *suspected*$)$ **then**
            suspected := *suspected* $\cup \{p\}$;
            trigger $\langle\,\Diamond\mathcal{P},\,Suspect\,|\,p\,\rangle$;
        else if $(p \in$ *alive*$) \wedge (p \in$ *suspected*$)$ **then**
            suspected := *suspected* $\setminus \{p\}$;
            trigger $\langle\,\Diamond\mathcal{P},\,Restore\,|\,p\,\rangle$;
        trigger $\langle\,pl,\,Send\,|\,p,\,[\text{HEARTBEATREQUEST}]\,\rangle$;
    alive := $\emptyset$;
    starttimer(*delay*);

upon event $\langle\,pl,\,Deliver\,|\,q,\,[\text{HEARTBEATREQUEST}]\,\rangle$ **do**
    trigger $\langle\,pl,\,Send\,|\,q,\,[\text{HEARTBEATREPLY}]\,\rangle$;

upon event $\langle\,pl,\,Deliver\,|\,p,\,[\text{HEARTBEATREPLY}]\,\rangle$ **do**
    alive := *alive* $\cup \{p\}$;

---

system. As for Algorithm 2.5 ("Exclude on Timeout"), we make use of a specific timeout mechanism initialized with a delay Δ. In Algorithm 2.7, a process that is suspected does not remain suspected forever as in Algorithm 2.5; instead, when a message arrives from a suspected process after the timeout has expired, a $\langle\,Restore\,\rangle$ event is triggered for the process and the timeout value is increased.

Correctness. The *strong completeness* property is satisfied as for Algorithm 2.5 ("Exclude on Timeout"). If a process crashes, it will stop sending messages and will be suspected by every correct process; no process will ever revise its judgment about that suspicion.

For the *eventual strong accuracy* property, consider the point in time after which the system becomes synchronous and the timeout delay becomes larger than twice the message transmission delay (plus the clock drifts and the local processing times). After this point in time, for any heartbeat message sent by a correct process to a correct process, a heartbeat reply message is received within the timeout delay. Hence, any correct process that was wrongly suspecting some correct process will revise its suspicion, and no correct process will ever be suspected by a correct process.

Performance. Analogously to the perfect failure detector, the time to detect a failure depends on the timeout delay. The difference here is that the initial timeout can be set more aggressively so that $\Diamond \mathcal{P}$ reacts faster to failures than $\mathcal{P}$. This may lead to false suspicions, but as the specification of $\Diamond \mathcal{P}$ permits them, they do no harm, unlike in the case of $\mathcal{P}$.

2.6.5 Eventual Leader Election

As we discussed earlier, instead of focusing on faulty processes, it may be better to look at correct ones. In particular, it is sometimes convenient to elect a correct process that will perform certain computations on behalf of the others. With a perfect failure detector, one could implement a perfect leader-election abstraction with the properties of Module 2.7. This is impossible with an eventually perfect failure detector (see the exercises at the end of the chapter). Instead, we can implement a weaker notion of leader election, which ensures the uniqueness of the leader only *eventually*. As we will see later in the book, this abstraction is useful within consensus algorithms. An eventual leader-election abstraction can also be implemented with crash-recovery and arbitrary-fault process abstractions. In this section, we consider only crash-stop and crash-recover process abstractions; the next section describes leader election with Byzantine processes.

Specification. The *eventual leader-detector* abstraction, with the *eventual accuracy* and *eventual agreement* properties stated in Module 2.9, and denoted by Ω, encapsulates a leader-election primitive which ensures that *eventually* the correct processes will elect the same correct process as their leader. Nothing precludes the possibility for leaders to change in an arbitrary manner and for an arbitrary period of time. Moreover, many leaders might be elected during the same period of time without having crashed. Once a unique leader is determined, and does not change

---

Module 2.9: Interface and properties of the eventual leader detector

Module:

    Name: EventualLeaderDetector, **instance** Ω.

Events:

    Indication: $\langle\, \Omega,\ \textit{Trust} \mid p \,\rangle$: Indicates that process p is trusted to be leader.

Properties:

    ELD1: *Eventual accuracy:* There is a time after which every correct process trusts some correct process.

    ELD2: *Eventual agreement:* There is a time after which no two correct processes trust different correct processes.

---

again, we say that the leader has *stabilized*. Such a stabilization is guaranteed by the specification of Module 2.9. The abstraction is defined in terms of a single indication event $\langle$ *Trust* $\mid p$ $\rangle$, which carries the identity of the leader process. Process p is said to be *trusted* afterward until an indication event with another leader process occurs.

Algorithm: Monarchical Eventual Leader Detection. With a crash-stop process abstraction, an eventual leader detector can be obtained directly from $\Diamond\mathcal{P}$. Algorithm 2.8, called "Monarchical Eventual Leader Detection," implements Ω using the same approach as used in Algorithm 2.6 ("Monarchical Leader Election"), with the only difference that deaths in the royal family are not final. The algorithm maintains the set of processes that are suspected by $\Diamond\mathcal{P}$ and declares the nonsuspected process with the highest rank to be the leader. Eventually, and provided at least one process is correct, the same correct process will be trusted by all correct processes.

Algorithm 2.8: Monarchical Eventual Leader Detection

Implements:
    EventualLeaderDetector, **instance** Ω.

Uses:
    EventuallyPerfectFailureDetector, **instance** $\Diamond\mathcal{P}$.

upon event $\langle$ Ω, *Init* $\rangle$ **do**
    suspected := $\emptyset$;
    leader := $\bot$;

upon event $\langle$ $\Diamond\mathcal{P}$, *Suspect* $\mid p$ $\rangle$ **do**
    suspected := *suspected* $\cup$ $\{p\}$;

upon event $\langle$ $\Diamond\mathcal{P}$, *Restore* $\mid p$ $\rangle$ **do**
    suspected := *suspected* $\setminus$ $\{p\}$;

upon *leader* $\neq$ maxrank($\Pi \setminus$ *suspected*) **do**
    leader := maxrank($\Pi \setminus$ *suspected*);
    trigger $\langle$ Ω, *Trust* $\mid$ *leader* $\rangle$;

Correctness. The *eventual accuracy* property of the eventual leader detector follows from the *strong completeness* property of $\Diamond\mathcal{P}$ because a process does not trust a process that it suspects and because there is a time after which a process permanently suspects every process that crashes. Together with the *eventual strong accuracy* property of $\Diamond\mathcal{P}$, this implies also the *eventual agreement* property because every correct process eventually suspects exactly the set of crashed processes.

Performance. The algorithm uses only local operations and is therefore immediate. The time to react to a failure and become the new leader directly depends on the latency of the failure detector in the same way as for Algorithm 2.6.

Algorithm: Elect Lower Epoch. The eventual leader detector Ω can also be implemented with the crash-recovery process abstraction. Algorithm 2.9 ("Elect Lower

---

Algorithm 2.9: Elect Lower Epoch

Implements:
    EventualLeaderDetector, **instance** Ω.

Uses:
    FairLossPointToPointLinks, **instance** fll.

upon event $\langle\ \Omega,\ Init\ \rangle$ **do**
    $epoch := 0$;
    $store(epoch)$;
    $candidates := \emptyset$;
    trigger $\langle\ \Omega,\ Recovery\ \rangle$;   // recovery procedure completes the initialization

upon event $\langle\ \Omega,\ Recovery\ \rangle$ **do**
    $leader := maxrank(\Pi)$;
    trigger $\langle\ \Omega,\ Trust\ |\ leader\ \rangle$;
    $delay := \Delta$;
    $retrieve(epoch)$;
    $epoch := epoch + 1$;
    $store(epoch)$;
    forall $p \in \Pi$ **do**
        trigger $\langle\ fll,\ Send\ |\ p,\ [\text{HEARTBEAT}, epoch]\ \rangle$;
    $candidates := \emptyset$;
    $starttimer(delay)$;

upon event $\langle\ Timeout\ \rangle$ **do**
    $newleader := select(candidates)$;
    if $newleader \neq leader$ **then**
        $delay := delay + \Delta$;
        $leader := newleader$;
        trigger $\langle\ \Omega,\ Trust\ |\ leader\ \rangle$;
    forall $p \in \Pi$ **do**
        trigger $\langle\ fll,\ Send\ |\ p,\ [\text{HEARTBEAT}, epoch]\ \rangle$;
    $candidates := \emptyset$;
    $starttimer(delay)$;

upon event $\langle\ fll,\ Deliver\ |\ q,\ [\text{HEARTBEAT}, ep]\ \rangle$ **do**
    if exists $(s, e) \in candidates$ such that $s = q \wedge e < ep$ **then**
        $candidates := candidates \setminus \{(q, e)\}$;
    $candidates := candidates \cup (q, ep)$;

Epoch") presented here implements Ω directly, without relying on a failure-detector abstraction. It works with crash-stop and with crash-recovery process abstractions, assumes partial synchrony, and relies on at least one process to be correct. Remember that this implies, with a process crash-recovery abstraction, that at least one process in every execution either does not ever crash or eventually recovers and never crashes again.

In the algorithm, every process maintains an *epoch number* that keeps track of how many times the process crashed and recovered. It stores the epoch number in an integer variable *epoch*; whenever the process recovers from a crash, it retrieves *epoch* from stable storage, increments it, and stores it again in stable storage. The goal of the algorithm is to elect the active process with the lowest epoch number as a leader, i.e., the one that has crashed and recovered the least often.

, A process periodically sends a *heartbeat* message to all processes, containing its current epoch number. Besides, every process keeps a variable *candidates* that determines the potential leader processes. The variable *candidates* is initially empty and is emptied again when the process sends a heartbeat message. Whenever the process receives a heartbeat message from process q containing epoch number ep, the process adds the pair (q, ep) to *candidates*.

Initially, the leader for all processes is the process with the highest rank among all, i.e., process $maxrank(\Pi)$. After every timeout delay, a process checks whether the current leader may continue to be the leader. The test uses a deterministic function *select*$(\cdot)$ that picks one process from *candidates* according to the following rule: it considers the process/epoch pairs in *candidates* with the lowest epoch number, selects the corresponding processes, and returns the process with the highest rank among them. This choice guarantees that when a process p is elected leader, but keeps on crashing and recovering forever, then p will eventually be replaced by a correct process. By definition, the epoch number of a correct process will eventually stop growing.

A process increases its timeout delay whenever it selects a new leader. This guarantees that if leaders keep changing because the timeout delay is too short with respect to communication delays, the delay will continue to increase, until it eventually becomes large enough for the leader to stabilize when the system becomes synchronous.

Correctness. Consider the *eventual accuracy* property and assume by contradiction that there is a time after which a correct process p permanently trusts the same faulty process q. There are two cases to consider (remember that we consider a crash-recovery process abstraction): (1) process q eventually crashes and never recovers again or (2) process q keeps crashing and recovering forever.

Consider case (1). As q crashes and does not ever recover again, q will send its *heartbeat* messages to p only a finite number of times. Because of the *no creation* and *finite duplication* properties of the underlying fair-loss links, there is a time after which p stops delivering such messages from q. Eventually, q will be excluded from *candidate* and p will elect a new leader different from q, a contradiction.

Consider now case (2). As q keeps crashing and recovering forever, its epoch number will continue to increase forever. For any correct process r, there is a time after which its epoch number will be lower than that of q. After this time, either (2.1) process p will stop delivering messages from q, and this can happen if q crashes and recovers so quickly that it does not have the time to send enough messages to p (remember that, with fair-loss links, a message is guaranteed to be delivered by its target only if it is sent infinitely often), or (2.2) process p delivers messages from q but with higher epoch numbers than those of r. In both cases, p will stop trusting q, which contradicts the assumption. Hence, process p eventually trusts some correct process.

Consider now the *eventual agreement* property. We need to explain why there is a time after which no two distinct correct processes are trusted by two other correct processes. Let $C \subseteq \Pi$ be the subset of correct processes in a given execution. Consider, furthermore, the time after which (1) the system becomes synchronous, (2) the processes in C never crash again, (3) the epoch numbers stop increasing at every correct process, and (4) for every process $p \in C$ and every faulty process q, process p either stops delivering messages from q or q's epoch number at p is strictly larger than the largest epoch number of any process in C at p. Because of the assumptions of a partially synchronous system, the properties of the underlying fair-loss links, and the algorithm itself, such a time will eventually be reached. After it is reached, every correct process trusts a process in C, and C is a subset of the processes in variable *candidates* at every correct process whenever the ⟨ *Timeout* ⟩ event occurs. Because of the function *select*($\cdot$), all correct processes trust the same process from C.

2.6.6 Byzantine Leader Election

We now introduce an eventual leader-detector abstraction with Byzantine processes. As mentioned before in the context of failure detectors, one cannot rely on the time-liness of simple responses for detecting arbitrary faults. We must exploit another way to determine remotely whether a process is faulty or performs correctly as a leader. Our approach is best described as "trust, but verify." Every newly chosen leader gets a chance to perform well. But the other processes monitor its actions, and should the leader not have achieved the desired goal after some time, they replace it with a new leader. Electing political leaders uses the same approach in many countries.

More specifically, we assume that the leader should perform some actions according to an algorithm, within some time bounds. If the leader performs wrongly or exceeds the allocated time before reaching this goal then other processes detect this and report it as a failure to the leader detector. In an eventually synchronous system, every process always behaves according the algorithm and eventually all remote processes also observe this; if such correct behavior cannot be observed from a process then the process must be faulty. To make this work in an eventually synchronous system, every elected leader is given progressively more time than its predecessors to achieve its goal.

It is important that this notion of good performance depends on the specific algorithm executed by the processes, which relies on the output from the leader-detection module. Therefore, eventual leader election with Byzantine process abstractions is not an isolated low-level abstraction, as with crash-stop processes, but requires some input from the higher-level algorithm. For expressing this input, we introduce a ⟨ *Complain* | p ⟩ event. Every process may *complain* against the current leader p by triggering this event. We assume that every correct process successively increases the time between issuing complaints.

The *Byzantine leader-detector* abstraction is obtained from Module 2.9 by augmenting its interface with the ⟨ *Complain* | p ⟩ request. The *eventual accuracy* property, which required every process to trust a correct process eventually, is

---

Module 2.10: Interface and properties of the Byzantine eventual leader detector

Module:

    Name: ByzantineLeaderDetector, **instance** *bld*.

Events:

    Indication: $\langle$ *bld, Trust* $\mid p$ $\rangle$: Indicates that process p is trusted to be leader.

    Request: $\langle$ *bld, Complain* $\mid p$ $\rangle$: Receives a complaint about process p.

Properties:

    BLD1: *Eventual succession:* If more than f correct processes that trust some process p complain about p, then every correct process eventually trusts a different process than p.

    BLD2: *Putsch resistance:* A correct process does not trust a new leader unless at least one correct process has complained against the previous leader.

    BLD3: *Eventual agreement:* There is a time after which no two correct processes trust different processes.

---

replaced by two new conditions. The *eventual succession* property ensures that the primitive eventually elects a new leader after more than f correct processes have complained against the current leader. Furthermore, the *putsch resistance* property ensures that no leader is removed from power, unless at least one *correct* process has complained against the leader. Taken together, these conditions imply that every correct process eventually trust some process that appears to perform its task in the higher-level algorithm. Module 2.10 summarizes the specification. In contrast to Module 2.9, one cannot require that every correct process eventually trusts a *correct* process because a Byzantine process may behave just like a correct process.

Algorithm: Rotating Byzantine Leader Detection. Algorithm 2.10, called "Rotating Byzantine Leader Detection," implements a Byzantine eventual leader-detector abstraction, assuming that $N > 3f$. The algorithm maintains a continuously increasing round number and deterministically derives the leader from it. Recall that N denotes the number of processes in the system (i.e., the size of Π). The leader of a round r is simply the process p whose rank is $r \bmod N$. Because there is no process with rank 0, the leader is the process with rank N if $r \bmod N = 0$. This derivation is given by the function

$$leader(r) \;=\; \begin{cases} p & \text{where } p \text{ satisfies } rank(p) = r \bmod N, \text{ if } r \bmod N \neq 0 \\ q & \text{such that } rank(q) = N, \text{ otherwise.} \end{cases}$$

A process broadcasts a COMPLAINT message when the higher-level algorithm triggers a $\langle$ *Complain* $\mid p$ $\rangle$ event and p is the current leader. Whenever a process receives more than $2f$ COMPLAINT messages against the current leader, it switches

---

Algorithm 2.10: Rotating Byzantine Leader Detection

Implements:
    ByzantineLeaderDetector, **instance** *bld*.

Uses:
    AuthPerfectPointToPointLinks, **instance** *al*.

upon event ⟨ *bld, Init* ⟩ **do**
        round := 1;
        complainlist := $[\perp]^N$;
        complained := FALSE;
        trigger ⟨ *bld, Trust | leader(round)* ⟩;

upon event ⟨ *bld, Complain | p* ⟩ **such that** $p = leader(round)$ **and**
            complained = FALSE **do**
        complained := TRUE;
        forall $q \in \Pi$ **do**
            trigger ⟨ *al, Send | q,* [COMPLAINT, *round*] ⟩;

upon event ⟨ *al, Deliver | p,* [COMPLAINT, *r*] ⟩ **such that** $r = round$ **and**
            complainlist[*p*] = $\perp$ **do**
        complainlist[*p*] := COMPLAINT;
        if $\#(complainlist) > f \wedge complained =$ FALSE **then**
            complained := TRUE;
            forall $q \in \Pi$ **do**
                    trigger ⟨ *al, Send | q,* [COMPLAINT, *round*] ⟩;
        else if $\#(complainlist) > 2f$ **then**
            round := *round* + 1;
            complainlist := $[\perp]^N$;
            complained := FALSE;
            trigger ⟨ *bld, Trust | leader(round)* ⟩;

---

to the next round. Furthermore, when a process receives more than f COMPLAINT
messages but has not sent a COMPLAINT message itself in the current round, it joins
the complaining processes and also sends a COMPLAINT message. This mechanism
serves two goals: first, it ensures that the Byzantine processes alone cannot provoke
a leader change; second, it guarantees that once a correct process switches to the
next round, every other correct process eventually also switches to that round.

In Algorithm 2.10, the function $\#(S)$ for a set S or for a list S denotes the
number of elements in set S or the number of non-$\perp$ entries in list S, respectively.
It is used throughout this book to obtain the cardinality of a data structure.

In the pseudo code, the notation $[x]^N$ for any symbol x denotes the N-vector
$[x, \ldots, x]$; vectors may be indexed by processes or by numbers.

Correctness. The *eventual succession* property follows directly from the algorithm
because every complaining correct process broadcasts a COMPLAINT message.
These messages cause the remaining correct processes to chime in, so that every

correct process eventually receives $N - f > 2f$ COMPLAINT messages and replaces the current leader.

Because there are only f Byzantine processes, the *putsch resistance* property follows trivially. For the *eventual agreement* property, note that the correct processes eventually cease to complain against a correct leader because they wait long enough for the leader to achieve its goal. When all COMPLAINT messages have been received subsequently, every correct process is in the same round and trusts the same process.

2.7 Distributed-System Models

A combination of (1) a process abstraction, (2) a link abstraction, and possibly (3) a failure-detector abstraction defines a *distributed-system model*. In the following, we discuss several models that will be considered throughout this book to reason about distributed-programming abstractions and the algorithms used to implement them. We also discuss important properties of abstraction specifications and algorithms that will be useful reasoning tools for the following chapters.

2.7.1 Combining Abstractions

Clearly, we will not consider all possible combinations of basic abstractions. On the other hand, it is interesting to discuss more than one possible combination to get an insight into how certain assumptions affect the design of an algorithm. We have selected six specific combinations to define several different models studied in this book.

- **Fail-stop.** We consider the crash-stop process abstraction, where the processes execute the deterministic algorithms assigned to them, unless they possibly crash, in which case they do not recover. Links are supposed to be perfect (Module 2.3). Finally, we assume the existence of a perfect failure detector ($\mathcal{P}$) of Module 2.6. As the reader will have the opportunity to observe, when comparing algorithms in this model with algorithms in other models discussed later, these assumptions substantially simplify the design of distributed algorithms.
- **Fail-noisy.** We consider the crash-stop process abstraction together with perfect links (Module 2.3). In addition, we assume here the existence of the eventually perfect failure detector ($\diamond\mathcal{P}$) of Module 2.8 or the eventual leader detector (Ω) of Module 2.9. This model represents an intermediate case between the fail-stop model and the fail-silent model (introduced next).
- **Fail-silent.** We consider the crash-stop process abstraction together with perfect links (Module 2.3) only. This model does not assume any failure-detection or leader-election abstractions. That is, processes have no means to get any information about other processes having crashed.
- **Fail-recovery.** This model uses the crash-recovery process abstraction, according to which processes may crash and later recover and still participate in the

algorithm. Algorithms devised for this model have to cope with consequences of amnesia, i.e., that a process may forget what it did prior to crashing, but may use stable storage for this. Links are assumed to be stubborn (Module 2.2) and algorithms may rely on the eventual leader detector (Ω) of Module 2.9.

- **Fail-arbitrary.** This is the most general of our distributed-system models and uses the fail-arbitrary (or Byzantine) process abstraction and the authenticated perfect links abstraction in Module 2.5. This model could also be called the *fail-silent-arbitrary* model.

  When Byzantine process abstractions are considered together with authenticated perfect links and in combination with the Byzantine eventual leader-detector abstraction (Module 2.10), we call it the *fail-noisy-arbitrary* model.

- **Randomized.** The randomized model is of a different nature than the other distributed-system models, and can be thought of being orthogonal to all of them. We use it for more general process abstractions than otherwise. Algorithms in the randomized system model are not necessarily deterministic; the processes may use a random source to choose among several steps to execute. Typically, the corresponding algorithms implement a given abstraction with some (hopefully high) probability. Randomization is sometimes the only way to solve a problem or to circumvent inherent inefficiencies of deterministic algorithms.

It is important to note that many abstractions in the book will be specified only for the three models with crash-stop processes, that is, for the fail-stop, fail-noisy, and fail-silent models. In other distributed system models, especially in the fail-recovery and the fail-arbitrary models, they must be formulated differently and represent a different abstraction, strictly speaking.

Moreover, many abstractions we study cannot be implemented in all models. For example, some abstractions that we will consider in Chap. 6 do not have fail-silent solutions or fail-arbitrary implementations, and it is not clear how to devise meaningful randomized solutions to such abstractions. For other abstractions, such solutions may exist but devising them is still an active area of research. This is, for instance, the case for randomized solutions to the shared memory abstractions we consider in Chap. 4.

2.7.2 Setup

In all system models considered here, the identities of all processes are defined before the execution begins and must be known globally. In practice, they are either configured though a manual process by an administrator or installed automatically by a membership service, which itself must be initialized.

The cryptographic abstractions also require keys to be distributed according to the identities of all processes. For instance, a MAC requires one shared symmetric key for every pair of processes; a digital signature scheme requires one public/private key pair for every process such that only the process itself knows its private key and all processes know the public keys of all others. Key distribution occurs outside the system model. In practice, a trusted agent distributes the necessary keys during system setup, typically at the same time when the identities of the processes in the system are defined.

2.7.3 Quorums

A recurring tool for designing fault-tolerant algorithms for a set of N processes are *quorums*. A quorum is a set of processes with special properties.

A *quorum* in a system with N crash-fault process abstractions (according to the fail-stop, fail-noisy, fail-silent, or fail-recovery system model) is any *majority* of processes, i.e., any set of *more than* $N/2$ processes (equivalently, any set of $\lceil \frac{N+1}{2} \rceil$ or more processes). Several algorithms rely on quorums and exploit the fact that every two quorums overlap in at least one process. Note that even if $f < N/2$ processes fail by crashing, there is always at least one quorum of noncrashed processes in such systems.

In a system consisting of arbitrary-fault process abstractions, two majority quorums may not intersect in a correct process. A *Byzantine quorum* tolerating f faults is a set of *more than* $(N + f)/2$ processes (equivalently, any set of $\lceil \frac{N+f+1}{2} \rceil$ or more processes). Two Byzantine quorums always overlap in at least one *correct* process. To see why this is the case, note that in any Byzantine quorum, there might be f Byzantine processes. Every Byzantine quorum contains, thus, more than

$$\frac{N+f}{2} - f = \frac{N-f}{2}$$

correct processes. Two disjoint Byzantine quorums together would have *more than*

$$\frac{N-f}{2} + \frac{N-f}{2} = N - f$$

correct members. But there are only $N - f$ correct processes; hence, one correct process must occur in both Byzantine quorums.

Algorithms that rely on Byzantine quorums often need to make progress after obtaining some message from a Byzantine quorum of processes. Because up to f faulty processes may not respond, there must exist at least a Byzantine quorum of correct processes in the system, from which the desired response eventually arrives. This condition is satisfied only when

$$N - f > \frac{N+f}{2},$$

or equivalently when $N > 3f$, as simple manipulation shows. Therefore, algorithms tolerating Byzantine faults usually require that only $f < N/3$ processes may fail.

2.7.4 Measuring Performance

When we present a distributed algorithm that implements a given abstraction, we analyze its cost mainly using two metrics: (1) the number of messages required to terminate an operation of the abstraction, and (2) the number of communication steps required to terminate such an operation. For some algorithms, we evaluate also (3) its total communication size, which is the sum of the lengths of all messages sent by an algorithm. It is measured in bits. When evaluating the performance of algorithms in a crash-recovery model, besides the number of communication steps and the number of messages, we also consider (4) the number of accesses to stable storage (or the "logging operations").

In general, we count the messages, communication steps, and disk accesses in specific executions of the algorithm, especially in failure-free executions. Such executions are more likely to happen in practice and are those for which the algorithms are optimized. It makes sense to plan for the worst, by providing means in the algorithms to tolerate failures, and hope for the best, by optimizing the algorithms for the case where failures do not occur. Algorithms that have their performance go proportionally down when the number of failures increases are sometimes called *gracefully degrading* algorithms.

Performance measurements are often stated in *Big-O Notation*, which provides only an upper bound on the asymptotic behavior of the function when its argument grows larger; usually the argument is N, the number of processes in the system. More precisely, when a metric satisfies $O(g(N))$ for a function g, it means that for all N bigger than some value N_0, the measure is at most a constant times $g(N)$ in absolute value. In this case, the metric is said to be "on the order of $g(N)$." For instance, a complexity of $O(N)$ is also called *linear* in N, and a complexity of $O(N^2)$ is called *quadratic* in N.

Precise performance studies help select the most suitable algorithm for a given abstraction in a specific environment and conduct *real-time* analysis. Consider, for instance, an algorithm that implements the abstraction of perfect communication links, and hence ensures that every message sent by a correct process to a correct process is eventually delivered by the latter. Note the implications of this property on the timing guarantees: for every execution of the algorithm, and every message sent in that execution, there is a time delay within which the message is eventually delivered. The time delay is, however, defined a posteriori. In practice one would require that messages be delivered within some time delay defined a priori, for every execution and possibly every message. To determine whether a given algorithm provides this guarantee in a given environment, a careful performance study needs to be conducted on the algorithm, taking into account various aspects of the environment, such as the operating system, the scheduler, and the network. Such studies are out of the scope of this book. We present algorithms that are applicable to a wide range of distributed systems, where bounded delays cannot be enforced, and where specific infrastructure-related properties, such as real-time demands, are not strictly required.

2.8 Exercises

Exercise 2.1: *Explain under which assumptions the fail-recovery and the fail-silent models are similar in (note that in both models any process can commit omission faults).*

Exercise 2.2: *The perfect point-to-point links abstraction allows messages from one sender to arrive at a receiver in a different order than they were sent. Some applications rely on* first-in first-out *(FIFO) order communication, however. Specify a FIFO-order perfect point-to-point links abstraction which ensures, in addition to the guarantees of perfect point-to-point links, that messages are not reordered.*

Exercise 2.3: *Provide an implementation of FIFO-order perfect point-to-point links (Exercise 2.2) on top of perfect point-to-point links using sequence numbers.*

Exercise 2.4: *Does the following statement satisfy the synchronous-computation assumption?* On my server, no request ever takes more than 1 week to be processed.

Exercise 2.5: *Can we implement the perfect failure-detector abstraction in a model where the processes may commit omission faults and where we cannot bound the number of such faults? What if this number is bounded but unknown? What if processes that can commit omission faults commit a limited and known number of such faults and then crash?*

Exercise 2.6: *In a fail-stop model, can we determine a priori a time period such that, whenever a process crashes, all correct processes suspect this process to have crashed after this period?*

Exercise 2.7: *In a fail-stop model, which of the following properties are safety properties?*

1. *every process that crashes is eventually detected;*
2. *no process is detected before it crashes;*
3. *no two processes decide differently;*
4. *no two correct processes decide differently;*
5. *every correct process decides before t time units;*
6. *if some correct process decides then every correct process decides.*

Exercise 2.8: *Suppose an algorithm A implements a distributed programming abstraction M using a failure detector D that is assumed to be eventually perfect. Can A violate a safety property of M if D is not eventually perfect, for example, when D permanently outputs the empty set?*

Exercise 2.9: *Specify a distributed programming abstraction M and an algorithm A implementing M using a failure detector D that is supposed to satisfy a set of properties, such that the liveness of M is violated if D does not satisfy its properties.*

Exercise 2.10: *Is there an algorithm that implements the leader-election abstraction with the eventually perfect failure detector?*

2.9 Solutions

Solution 2.1: When processes crash, they lose the content of their volatile memory and they commit omissions. If we assume (1) that processes do have stable storage and store every update of their state in stable storage and (2) that processes are not aware they have crashed and recovered then the two models are similar.

Solution 2.2: A specification of *FIFO-order perfect point-to-point links* is shown in Module 2.11.

Module 2.11: Interface and properties of FIFO-order perfect point-to-point links

Module:

> **Name:** FIFOPerfectPointToPointLinks, **instance** *fpl*.

Events:

> **Request:** $\langle$ *fpl, Send* $\mid q, m$ $\rangle$: Requests to send message m to process q.
>
> **Indication:** $\langle$ *fpl, Deliver* $\mid p, m$ $\rangle$: Delivers message m sent by process p.

Properties:

> **FPL1–FPL3:** Same as properties PL1–PL3 of perfect point-to-point links (Module 2.3).
>
> **FPL4:** *FIFO delivery:* If some process sends message m_1 before it sends message m_2, then no correct process delivers m_2 unless it has already delivered m_1.

Solution 2.3: Algorithm 2.11, "Sequence Number," implements FIFO-order perfect point-to-point links on top of perfect point-to-point links.

Solution 2.4: The answer is yes. This is because the time it takes for the server to process a request is bounded and known, 1 week.

Solution 2.5: It is impossible to implement a perfect failure-detector abstraction if the number of omissions faults is unknown. Indeed, to guarantee the *strong completeness* property of the failure detector, a process p must detect the crash of another process q after some timeout delay. No matter how this delay is chosen, it can exceed the transmission delay times the number of omissions that q commits. This causes a violation of the *strong accuracy* property of the failure detector. If the number of possible omissions is known in a synchronous system, we can use it to calibrate the timeout delay of the processes to accurately detect failures. If the delay exceeds the maximum time during which a process can commit omission faults, without having actually crashed, it can safely detect the process as having crashed.

Algorithm 2.11: Sequence Number

Implements:
    FIFOPerfectPointToPointLinks, **instance** *fpl*.

Uses:
    PerfectPointToPointLinks, **instance** *pl*.

upon event ⟨ *fpl*, *Init* ⟩ **do**
        forall $p \in \Pi$ **do**
            $lsn[p] := 0;$
            $next[p] := 1;$

upon event ⟨ *fpl*, *Send* | q, m ⟩ **do**
        $lsn[q] := lsn[q] + 1;$
        trigger ⟨ *pl*, *Send* | $q, (m, lsn[q])$ ⟩;

upon event ⟨ *pl*, *Deliver* | $p, (m, sn)$ ⟩ **do**
        $pending := pending \cup \{(p, m, sn)\};$
        while exists $(q, n, sn') \in pending$ such that $sn' = next[q]$ **do**
            $next[q] := next[q] + 1;$
            $pending := pending \setminus \{(q, n, sn')\};$
            trigger ⟨ *fpl*, *Deliver* | q, n ⟩;

Solution 2.6: The answer is no, because the perfect failure detector only ensures that processes that crash are eventually detected, but there is no bound on the time it takes for these crashes to be detected. This demonstrates a fundamental difference between algorithms assuming a synchronous system and algorithms assuming a perfect failure detector (fail-stop model). In a precise sense, a synchronous model is strictly stronger.

Solution 2.7: We discuss each property separately.

1. *Every process that crashes is eventually detected.* This is a liveness property; we can never exhibit a time t in some execution and state that the property is violated. There is always the hope that eventually the failure detector detects the crashes.
2. *No process is detected before it crashes.* This is a safety property. If a process is detected at time t before it has crashed then the property is violated at time t.
3. *No two processes decide differently.* This is also a safety property, because it can be violated at some time t and never be satisfied again.
4. *No two correct processes decide differently.* Since a *correct* process is a process that never crashes and executes an infinite number of steps, the set of correct processes is known a priori. Therefore, this property is also a safety property: once two correct processes have decided differently in some partial execution, no matter how we extend the execution, the property would not be satisfied.
5. *Every correct process decides before t time units.* This is a safety property: it can be violated at some time during an execution, where all correct processes have

executed t of their own steps. If violated at that time, there is no hope that it will
be satisfied again.

6. *If some correct process decides then every correct process decides.* This is a
   liveness property: there is always the hope that the property is satisfied. It is
   interesting to note that the property can actually be satisfied by having the processes not do anything. Hence, the intuition that a safety property is one that is
   satisfied by doing nothing may be misleading.

The conclusion in the last property is often stated more explicitly as ... *then every
correct process eventually decides.* The presence of the word "eventually" usually
allows one to identify liveness properties.

Solution 2.8: The answer is no. Intuitively, the reason is that the eventually perfect
failure-detector abstraction may make mistakes before some arbitrary, but unknown
time t. If algorithm A were to violate a safety property before t, this violation could
not be corrected later.

More precisely, assume by contradiction that A violates some safety property
of M if D does not satisfy its properties. Because of the very nature of a safety
property, there is a time t and an execution R of the system such that the property
is violated at time t in R. Consider now a run R' of A that is similar to R up to
time t, but the properties of the eventually perfect failure detector hold at some time
later than t. This is possible because D satisfies *eventual accuracy* and *eventual
agreement* conditions. Then A would also violate the same safety property of M in
R', even if the failure detector is eventually perfect.

Solution 2.9: An example of such abstraction is simply the eventually perfect
failure detector itself. Note that such abstraction has no safety property.

Solution 2.10: Recall that the leader-election abstraction is defined with the following properties: (1) either there is no correct process or some correct process is
eventually the leader; and (2) if a process is leader then all previously elected leaders have crashed. It is not possible to implement this abstraction with the eventually
perfect failure detector, as we discuss later.

Consider an execution R_1 where no process fails; let p be the first process elected
leader, and let t be the time at which p first declares itself leader. Consider an
execution R_2, similar to R_1 until time t, but where p crashes right after time t. Due
to the first property of the leader-election abstraction, another process is eventually
elected. Denote that process by q, and let $t' > t$ be the time at which q first declares
itself leader. With an eventually perfect failure detector, and until time t', there is
no way to distinguish such execution from one, which we denote by R_3, where p is
actually correct (but whose messages got delayed until after t'). This execution R_3
violates the specification of the leader-election abstraction (i.e., its second property).

2.10 Chapter Notes

- The notions of safety and liveness were singled out by Alpern and Schneider (1985). It was shown that any property of a distributed system execution can be viewed as a composition of a liveness and a safety property.
- The term *fault* is sometimes reserved for the known or suspected cause of a *failure*; similarly, a *failure* may mean only the observable deviation of an abstraction from its specification. Because we do not further analyze the inside of process failures, we adopt a loose interpretation of these terms here and often use the two interchangeably.
- Lamport (1978) introduced the notions of causality and logical time; this is probably the most influential work in the area of distributed computing.
- Pease, Shostak, and Lamport (1980) formulated the problem of agreement in the presence of faults, as a way to abstract the underlying problems encountered during the design of SIFT. A related but different abstraction for agreement was presented later by Lamport, Shostak, and Pease (1982), assuming that processes are subject to arbitrary faults. To motivate the question, the agreement problem was formulated in terms of a Byzantine army, commanded by multiple generals that communicated only by couriers, and where some limited number of generals might be conspiring with the enemy. The term "Byzantine" has been used ever since to denote faulty processes that deviate from their assigned program in malicious and adversarial ways.
- Algorithms that assume processes can only fail by crashing and that every process has accurate information about which processes have crashed have been considered by Schneider, Gries, and Schlichting (1984). They called such processes "fail-stop." In later works, this system model has been formulated using the notion of a perfect failure detector.
- Fischer, Lynch, and Paterson (1985) established the fundamental result that no deterministic algorithm solves the consensus problem in an asynchronous system, even if only one process fails and it can only do so by crashing.
- Dwork, Lynch, and Stockmeyer (1988) introduced intermediate timing models that lie between the synchronous and the asynchronous model and showed how to solve consensus under these assumptions. Systems with such timing assumption have been called "partially synchronous."
- The use of synchrony assumptions to build leasing mechanisms was explored by Gray and Cheriton (1989).
- In two influential papers whose roots date back to 1991, it was observed that for solving various problems, and in particular consensus, timing assumptions were mainly used to detect process crashes (Chandra and Toueg 1996; Chandra, Hadzilacos, and Toueg 1996). This observation led to the definition a failure-detector abstraction that encapsulates timing assumptions. For instance, the very fact that consensus can be solved in partially synchronous systems (Dwork, Lynch, and Stockmeyer 1988) can be formulated in the terminology of failure detectors by stating that consensus can be solved with unreliable failure detectors

(i.e., with the eventually perfect failure detector). The eventual leader-detector abstraction (Ω) also originates from this work.

- The idea of stubborn communication links was proposed by Guerraoui, Oliveria, and Schiper (1998), as a pragmatic variant of perfect links for the fail-recovery model, yet at a higher level than fair-loss links (Lynch 1996).
- The notion of an unreliable failure detector was precisely defined by Guerraoui (2000). Algorithms that rely on such failure detectors have been called "indulgent" (Guerraoui 2000; Dutta and Guerraoui 2005; Guerraoui and Raynal 2004).
- Aguilera, Chen, and Toueg (2000) extended the notion of failure detectors to the fail-recovery model.
- As pointed out, for systems with fail-arbitrary processes, it is not possible to define failure detectors independently of the algorithms that rely on them. In contrast to fail-stop processes, such failures are not context-free (Doudou, Garbinato, and Guerraoui 2005).
- Public-key cryptography and the concept of digital signatures were invented by Diffie and Hellman (1976). The first practical implementation of digital signatures and the most widely used one until today is the RSA algorithm, discovered shortly afterward (Rivest, Shamir, and Adleman 1978).
- Comprehensive information on implementing cryptographic primitives is given in the classic book of Menezes, van Oorschot, and Vanstone (1997). Modern cryptography is formalized using notions from complexity theory. Goldreich (2004) presents a thorough mathematical treatment of the field.
- In practice, the authenticated perfect links abstraction can be implemented by the TLS protocol on the Internet or by using so-called tunnels constructed with the secure shell (SSH) protocol. These protocols protect the confidentiality and integrity of transported messages; for providing authenticated links, encryption is not needed and might be turned off to improve performance.
- This book uses only idealized abstract cryptographic primitives, as first formulated by Dolev and Yao (1983). A model using only abstractions of cryptography to reason about algorithms in distributed systems is often called a "Dolev-Yao model." Recent work has started to bridge the gap between Dolev-Yao models and complexity-based formal models (Abadi and Rogaway 2002).
- Quorums have first been formalized to ensure consistency among the processes in a distributed system by Thomas (1979) and by Gifford (1979). Byzantine quorums were introduced by Malkhi and Reiter (1998).
- Apart from the majority quorums considered here, there exist many other quorum-system constructions, which also ensure that every two quorums overlap in at least one process. They can replace the majority quorums in the algorithms in this book and sometimes also improve the performance of these algorithms (Naor and Wool 1998).

3. Reliable Broadcast

He said: "I could have been someone";
She replied: "So could anyone."
(The Pogues)

This chapter covers *broadcast communication* abstractions. These are used to disseminate information among a set of processes and differ according to the reliability of the dissemination. For instance, *best-effort broadcast* guarantees that all correct processes deliver the same set of messages if the senders are correct. Stronger forms of reliable broadcast guarantee this property even if the senders crash while broadcasting their messages. Even stronger broadcast abstractions are appropriate for the arbitrary-fault model and ensure consistency with Byzantine process abstractions.

We will consider several related abstractions for processes subject to crash faults: *best-effort broadcast, (regular) reliable broadcast, uniform reliable broadcast, stubborn broadcast, probabilistic broadcast*, and *causal broadcast*. For processes in the crash-recovery model, we describe *stubborn broadcast, logged best-effort broadcast*, and *logged uniform reliable broadcast*. Finally, for Byzantine processes, we introduce *Byzantine consistent broadcast* and *Byzantine reliable broadcast*. For each of these abstractions, we will provide one or more algorithms implementing it, and these will cover the different models addressed in this book.

3.1 Motivation

3.1.1 Client–Server Computing

In traditional distributed applications, interactions are often established between two processes. Probably the most representative of this sort of interaction is the now classic *client–server* scheme. According to this model, a *server* process exports an interface to several *clients*. Clients use the interface by sending a request to the server and by later collecting a reply. Such interaction is supported by *point-to-point* communication protocols. It is extremely useful for the application if such a protocol

C. Cachin et al., *Introduction to Reliable and Secure Distributed Programming*,
DOI: 10.1007/978-3-642-15260-3_3,
© Springer-Verlag Berlin Heidelberg 2011

is *reliable*. Reliability in this context usually means that, under some assumptions (which are, by the way, often not completely understood by most system designers), messages exchanged between the two processes are not lost or duplicated, and are delivered in the order in which they were sent. Typical implementations of this abstraction are reliable transport protocols such as TCP on the Internet. By using a reliable point-to-point communication protocol, the application is free from dealing explicitly with issues such as acknowledgments, timeouts, message retransmissions, flow control, and a number of other issues that are encapsulated by the protocol interface.

3.1.2 Multiparticipant Systems

As distributed applications become bigger and more complex, interactions are no longer limited to bilateral relationships. There are many cases where more than two processes need to operate in a coordinated manner. Consider, for instance, a multiuser virtual environment where several users interact in a virtual space. These users may be located at different physical places, and they can either directly interact by exchanging multimedia information, or indirectly by modifying the environment.

It is convenient to rely here on *broadcast* abstractions. These allow a process to send a message within a *group* of processes, and make sure that the processes agree on the messages they deliver. A naive transposition of the reliability requirement from point-to-point protocols would require that no message sent to the group be lost or duplicated, i.e., the processes agree to deliver every message broadcast to them. However, the definition of agreement for a broadcast primitive is not a simple task. The existence of multiple senders and multiple recipients in a group introduces degrees of freedom that do not exist in point-to-point communication. Consider, for instance, the case where the sender of a message fails by crashing. It may happen that some recipients deliver the last message sent while others do not. This may lead to an inconsistent view of the system state by different group members. When the sender of a message exhibits arbitrary-faulty behavior, assuring that the recipients deliver one and the same message is an even bigger challenge.

The broadcast abstractions in this book provide a multitude of reliability guarantees. For crash-stop processes they range, roughly speaking, from *best-effort*, which only ensures delivery among all correct processes if the sender does not fail, through *reliable*, which, in addition, ensures *all-or-nothing* delivery semantics, even if the sender fails, to *totally ordered*, which furthermore ensures that the delivery of messages follow the same global order, and *terminating*, which ensures that the processes either deliver a message or are eventually aware that they should never deliver the message.

For arbitrary-faulty processes, a similar range of broadcast abstractions exists. The simplest one among them guarantees a form of *consistency*, which is not even an issue for crash-stop processes, namely, to ensure that two correct processes, if they deliver a messages at all, deliver the same message. The reliable broadcast abstractions and total-order broadcast abstractions among arbitrary-faulty processes additionally provide all-or-nothing delivery semantics and totally ordered delivery, respectively.

In this chapter, we will focus on best-effort and reliable broadcast abstractions. Stronger forms of broadcast will be considered in later chapters. The next three sections present broadcast abstractions with crash-stop process abstractions. More general process failures are considered afterward.

3.2 Best-Effort Broadcast

A broadcast abstraction enables a process to send a message, in a one-shot operation, to all processes in a system, including itself. We give here the specification and an algorithm for a broadcast communication primitive with a weak form of reliability, called *best-effort broadcast*.

3.2.1 Specification

With best-effort broadcast, the burden of ensuring reliability is only on the sender. Therefore, the remaining processes do not have to be concerned with enforcing the reliability of received messages. On the other hand, no delivery guarantees are offered in case the sender fails. Best-effort broadcast is characterized by the following three properties depicted in Module 3.1: *validity* is a liveness property, whereas the *no duplication* property and the *no creation* property are safety properties. They descend directly from the corresponding properties of perfect point-to-point links. Note that broadcast messages are implicitly addressed to all processes. Remember also that messages are unique, that is, no process ever broadcasts the same message twice and furthermore, no two processes ever broadcast the same message.

Module 3.1: Interface and properties of best-effort broadcast

Module:

    Name: BestEffortBroadcast, **instance** *beb*.

Events:

    Request: $\langle$ *beb, Broadcast* $\mid m$ $\rangle$: Broadcasts a message m to all processes.

    Indication: $\langle$ *beb, Deliver* $\mid p, m$ $\rangle$: Delivers a message m broadcast by process p.

Properties:

    BEB1: *Validity:* If a correct process broadcasts a message m, then every correct process eventually delivers m.

    BEB2: *No duplication:* No message is delivered more than once.

    BEB3: *No creation:* If a process delivers a message m with sender s, then m was previously broadcast by process s.

Algorithm 3.1: Basic Broadcast

Implements:
    BestEffortBroadcast, **instance** *beb*.

Uses:
    PerfectPointToPointLinks, **instance** *pl*.

upon event $\langle$ *beb, Broadcast* $\mid m \rangle$ **do**
    forall $q \in \Pi$ **do**
        trigger $\langle$ *pl, Send* $\mid q, m \rangle$;

upon event $\langle$ *pl, Deliver* $\mid p, m \rangle$ **do**
    trigger $\langle$ *beb, Deliver* $\mid p, m \rangle$;

3.2.2 Fail-Silent Algorithm: Basic Broadcast

We provide here algorithm "Basic Broadcast" (Algorithm 3.1) that implements best-effort broadcast using perfect links. This algorithm does not make any assumption on failure detection: it is a fail-silent algorithm. The algorithm is straightforward. Broadcasting a message simply consists of sending the message to every process in the system using perfect point-to-point links, as illustrated by Fig. 3.1 (in the figure, white arrowheads represent request/indication events at the module interface and black arrowheads represent message exchanges). The algorithm works because the properties of perfect links ensure that all correct processes eventually deliver the message, as long as the sender of a message does not crash.

Correctness. The properties of best-effort broadcast are trivially derived from the properties of the underlying perfect point-to-point links. The *no creation* property follows directly from the corresponding property of perfect links. The same applies to *no duplication*, which relies in addition on the assumption that messages broadcast by different processes are unique. *Validity* is derived from the *reliable delivery* property and the fact that the sender sends the message to every other process in the system.

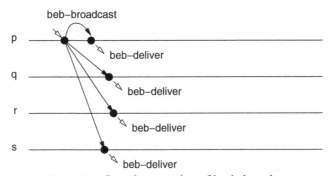

Figure 3.1: Sample execution of basic broadcast

Performance. For every message that is broadcast, the algorithm requires a single communication step and exchanges $O(N)$ messages.

3.3 Regular Reliable Broadcast

Best-effort broadcast ensures the delivery of messages as long as the sender does not fail. If the sender fails, some processes might deliver the message and others might not deliver it. In other words, they do not *agree* on the delivery of the message. Actually, even if the process sends a message to all processes before crashing, the delivery is not ensured because perfect links do not enforce the delivery when the sender fails. Ensuring agreement even when the sender fails is an important property for many practical applications that rely on broadcast. The abstraction of *(regular) reliable broadcast* provides exactly this stronger notion of reliability.

3.3.1 Specification

Intuitively, the semantics of a reliable broadcast algorithm ensure that the correct processes agree on the set of messages they deliver, even when the senders of these messages crash during the transmission. It should be noted that a sender may crash before being able to transmit the message, in which case no process will deliver it. The specification of reliable broadcast in Module 3.2 extends the properties of the best-effort broadcast abstraction (Module 3.1) with a new liveness property called *agreement*. The other properties remain unchanged (but are repeated here for completeness). The very fact that *agreement* is a liveness property might seem

---

Module 3.2: Interface and properties of (regular) reliable broadcast

Module:

    Name: ReliableBroadcast, **instance** *rb*.

Events:

    Request: $\langle$ *rb, Broadcast* $\mid m$ $\rangle$: Broadcasts a message m to all processes.

    Indication: $\langle$ *rb, Deliver* $\mid p, m$ $\rangle$: Delivers a message m broadcast by process p.

Properties:

    RB1: *Validity:* If a correct process p broadcasts a message m, then p eventually delivers m.

    RB2: *No duplication:* No message is delivered more than once.

    RB3: *No creation:* If a process delivers a message m with sender s, then m was previously broadcast by process s.

    RB4: *Agreement:* If a message m is delivered by some correct process, then m is eventually delivered by every correct process.

---

counterintuitive, as the property can be achieved by not having any process ever deliver any message. Strictly speaking, it is, however, a liveness property as it can always be ensured in extensions of finite executions. We will see other forms of *agreement* that are safety properties later in the book.

3.3.2 Fail-Stop Algorithm: Lazy Reliable Broadcast

We now show how to implement regular reliable broadcast in a fail-stop model. In our algorithm, depicted in Algorithm 3.2, which we have called "Lazy Reliable Broadcast," we make use of the best-effort broadcast abstraction described in the previous section, as well as the perfect failure detector abstraction $\mathcal{P}$ introduced earlier.

Algorithm 3.2: Lazy Reliable Broadcast

Implements:
　　ReliableBroadcast, **instance** *rb*.

Uses:
　　BestEffortBroadcast, **instance** *beb*;
　　PerfectFailureDetector, **instance** $\mathcal{P}$.

upon event $\langle$ *rb*, *Init* $\rangle$ **do**
　　correct := Π;
　　from[*p*] := $[\emptyset]^N$;

upon event $\langle$ *rb*, *Broadcast* | *m* $\rangle$ **do**
　　trigger $\langle$ *beb*, *Broadcast* | [DATA, *self*, *m*] $\rangle$;

upon event $\langle$ *beb*, *Deliver* | *p*, [DATA, *s*, *m*] $\rangle$ **do**
　　if $m \notin from[s]$ **then**
　　　　trigger $\langle$ *rb*, *Deliver* | *s*, *m* $\rangle$;
　　　　from[*s*] := *from*[*s*] $\cup \{m\}$;
　　　　if $s \notin correct$ **then**
　　　　　　trigger $\langle$ *beb*, *Broadcast* | [DATA, *s*, *m*] $\rangle$;

upon event $\langle$ $\mathcal{P}$, *Crash* | *p* $\rangle$ **do**
　　correct := *correct* $\setminus \{p\}$;
　　forall $m \in from[p]$ **do**
　　　　trigger $\langle$ *beb*, *Broadcast* | [DATA, *p*, *m*] $\rangle$;

To *rb*-broadcast a message, a process uses the best-effort broadcast primitive to disseminate the message to all. The algorithm adds some implementation-specific parameters to the exchanged messages. In particular, its adds a message descriptor (DATA) and the original source of the message (process *s*) in the *message header*. The result is denoted by [DATA, *s*, *m*] in the algorithm. A process that receives the message (when it *beb*-delivers the message) strips off the message header and *rb*-delivers it immediately. If the sender does not crash, then the message will be *rb*-delivered by all correct processes. The problem is that the sender might crash. In this case, the process that delivers the message from some other process detects that crash and relays the message to all others. We note that this is a language abuse: in fact, the process relays a copy of the message (and not the message itself).

At the same time, the process also maintains a variable *correct*, denoting the set of processes that have not been detected to crash by $\mathcal{P}$. Our algorithm is said to be *lazy* in the sense that it retransmits a message only if the original sender has been detected to have crashed. The variable *from* is an array of sets, indexed by the processes in Π, in which every entry s contains the messages from sender s that have been *rb*-delivered.

It is important to notice that, strictly speaking, two kinds of events can force a process to retransmit a message. First, when the process detects the crash of the source, and, second, when the process *beb*-delivers a message and realizes that the source has already been detected to have crashed (i.e., the source is not anymore in *correct*). This might lead to duplicate retransmissions when a process *beb*-delivers a message from a source that fails, as we explain later. It is easy to see that a process that detects the crash of a source needs to retransmit the messages that have already been *beb*-delivered from that source. On the other hand, a process might *beb*-deliver a message from a source after it detected the crash of that source: it is, thus, necessary to check for the retransmission even when no new crash is detected.

Correctness. The *no creation* (respectively *validity*) property of our reliable broadcast algorithm follows from the *no creation* (respectively *validity*) property of the underlying best-effort broadcast primitive. The *no duplication* property of reliable broadcast follows from our use of a variable *from* that keeps track of the messages that have been *rb*-delivered at every process and from the assumption of unique messages across all senders. *Agreement* follows here from the *validity* property of the underlying best-effort broadcast primitive, from the fact that every process relays every message that it *rb*-delivers when it detects the sender, and from the use of a perfect failure detector.

Performance. If the initial sender does not crash then the algorithm requires a single communication step and $O(N)$ messages to *rb*-deliver a message to all processes. Otherwise, it may take $O(N)$ steps and $O(N^2)$ messages in the worst case (if the processes crash in sequence).

3.3.3 Fail-Silent Algorithm: Eager Reliable Broadcast

In the "Lazy Reliable Broadcast" algorithm (Algorithm 3.2), when the *accuracy* property of the failure detector is not satisfied, the processes might relay messages unnecessarily. This wastes resources but does not impact correctness. On the other hand, we rely on the *completeness* property of the failure detector to ensure the broadcast *agreement*. If the failure detector does not ensure *completeness* then the processes might omit to relay messages that they should be relaying (e.g., messages broadcast by processes that crashed), and hence might violate *agreement*.

Algorithm 3.3: Eager Reliable Broadcast

Implements:
    ReliableBroadcast, **instance** *rb*.

Uses:
    BestEffortBroadcast, **instance** *beb*.

upon event ⟨ *rb, Init* ⟩ **do**
    delivered := ∅;

upon event ⟨ *rb, Broadcast* | *m* ⟩ **do**
    trigger ⟨ *beb, Broadcast* | [DATA, *self, m*] ⟩;

upon event ⟨ *beb, Deliver* | *p*, [DATA, *s, m*] ⟩ **do**
    if *m* ∉ *delivered* **then**
        delivered := *delivered* ∪ {*m*};
        trigger ⟨ *rb, Deliver* | *s, m* ⟩;
        trigger ⟨ *beb, Broadcast* | [DATA, *s, m*] ⟩;

In fact, we can circumvent the need for a failure detector (i.e., the need for its *completeness* property) by adopting an *eager* scheme: every process that gets a message relays it immediately. That is, we consider the worst case, where the sender process might have crashed, and we relay every message. This relaying phase is exactly what guarantees the *agreement* property of reliable broadcast. The resulting algorithm (Algorithm 3.3) is called "Eager Reliable Broadcast."

The algorithm assumes a fail-silent model and does not use any failure detector: it relies only on the best-effort broadcast primitive described in Sect. 3.2. In Fig. 3.2, we illustrate how the algorithm ensures *agreement* even if the sender crashes: process *p* crashes and its message is not *beb*-delivered by processes *r* and by *s*. However, as process *q* retransmits the message, i.e., *beb*-broadcasts it, the remaining processes also *beb*-deliver it and subsequently *rb*-deliver it. In our "Lazy

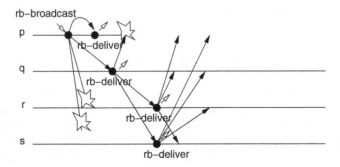

Figure 3.2: Sample execution of reliable broadcast with faulty sender

Reliable Broadcast" algorithm, process q will be relaying the message only after it has detected the crash of p.

Correctness. All properties, except *agreement*, are ensured as in the "Lazy Reliable Broadcast." The *agreement* property follows from the *validity* property of the underlying best-effort broadcast primitive and from the fact that every correct process immediately relays every message it *rb*-delivers.

Performance. In the best case, the algorithm requires a single communication step and $O(N^2)$ messages to *rb*-deliver a message to all processes. In the worst case, should the processes crash in sequence, the algorithm may incur $O(N)$ steps and $O(N^2)$ messages.

3.4 Uniform Reliable Broadcast

With regular reliable broadcast, the semantics just require the *correct* processes to deliver the same set of messages, regardless of what messages have been delivered by faulty processes. In particular, a process that *rb*-broadcasts a message might *rb*-deliver it and then crash, before the best-effort broadcast abstraction can even *beb*-deliver the message to any other process. Indeed, this scenario may occur in both reliable broadcast algorithms that we presented (eager and lazy). It is thus possible that no other process, including correct ones, ever *rb*-delivers that message. There are cases where such behavior causes problems because even a process that *rb*-delivers a message and later crashes may bring the application into a inconsistent state.

We now introduce a stronger definition of reliable broadcast, called *uniform reliable broadcast*. This definition is stronger in the sense that it guarantees that the set of messages delivered by *faulty* processes is always a *subset* of the messages delivered by correct processes. Many other abstractions also have such *uniform* variants.

3.4.1 Specification

Uniform reliable broadcast differs from reliable broadcast by the formulation of its *agreement* property. The specification is given in Module 3.3.

Uniformity is typically important if the processes interact with the external world, e.g., print something on a screen, authorize the delivery of money through a bank machine, or trigger the launch of a rocket. In this case, the fact that a process has delivered a message is important, even if the process has crashed afterward. This is because the process, before crashing, could have communicated with the external world after having delivered the message. The processes that did not crash should also be aware of that message having been delivered, and of the possible external action having been performed.

Figure 3.3 depicts an execution of a reliable broadcast algorithm that is not uniform. Both processes p and q *rb*-deliver the message as soon as they *beb*-deliver

---

Module 3.3: Interface and properties of uniform reliable broadcast

Module:

    Name: UniformReliableBroadcast, **instance** *urb*.

Events:

    Request: $\langle$ *urb, Broadcast* $\mid m$ $\rangle$: Broadcasts a message m to all processes.

    Indication: $\langle$ *urb, Deliver* $\mid p, m$ $\rangle$: Delivers a message m broadcast by process p.

Properties:

    URB1–URB3: Same as properties RB1–RB3 in (regular) reliable broadcast (Module 3.2).

    URB4: *Uniform agreement:* If a message m is delivered by some process (whether correct or faulty), then m is eventually delivered by every correct process.

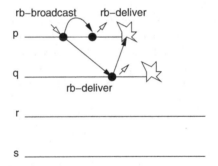

Figure 3.3: Nonuniform reliable broadcast

it, but crash before they are able to relay the message to the remaining processes. Still, processes r and s are consistent among themselves (neither has *rb*-delivered the message).

3.4.2 Fail-Stop Algorithm: All-Ack Uniform Reliable Broadcast

Basically, our "Lazy Reliable Broadcast" and "Eager Reliable Broadcast" algorithms do not ensure *uniform agreement* because a process may *rb*-deliver a message and then crash. Even if this process has relayed its message to all processes (through a best-effort broadcast primitive), the message might not reach any of the remaining processes. Note that even if we considered the same algorithms and replaced the best-effort broadcast abstraction with a reliable broadcast one, we would still not implement a uniform broadcast abstraction. This is because a process may deliver a message before relaying it to all processes.

Algorithm 3.4, named "All-Ack Uniform Reliable Broadcast," implements uniform reliable broadcast in the fail-stop model. Basically, in this algorithm, a process

---

Algorithm 3.4: All-Ack Uniform Reliable Broadcast

Implements:
UniformReliableBroadcast, **instance** *urb*.

Uses:
BestEffortBroadcast, **instance** *beb*.
PerfectFailureDetector, **instance** $\mathcal{P}$.

upon event ⟨ *urb, Init* ⟩ **do**
    delivered := ∅;
    pending := ∅;
    correct := Π;
    forall m **do** $ack[m]$:= ∅;

upon event ⟨ *urb, Broadcast | m* ⟩ **do**
    pending := *pending* ∪ {(*self, m*)};
    trigger ⟨ *beb, Broadcast |* [DATA, *self, m*] ⟩;

upon event ⟨ *beb, Deliver | p,* [DATA, *s, m*] ⟩ **do**
    $ack[m]$:= $ack[m]$ ∪ {p};
    if (*s, m*) ∉ *pending* **then**
        pending := *pending* ∪ {(*s, m*)};
        trigger ⟨ *beb, Broadcast |* [DATA, *s, m*] ⟩;

upon event ⟨ $\mathcal{P}$, *Crash | p* ⟩ **do**
    correct := *correct* \ {p};

function *candeliver*(m) **returns** Boolean **is**
    return (*correct* ⊆ $ack[m]$);

upon exists (*s, m*) ∈ *pending* such that *candeliver*(m) ∧ m ∉ *delivered* **do**
    delivered := *delivered* ∪ {m};
    trigger ⟨ *urb, Deliver | s, m* ⟩;

---

delivers a message only when it knows that the message has been *beb*-delivered and thereby *seen* by all correct processes. All processes relay the message once, after they have seen it. Each process keeps a record of processes from which it has already received a message (either because the process originally sent the message or because the process relayed it). When all correct processes have retransmitted the message, all correct processes are guaranteed to deliver the message, as illustrated in Fig. 3.4.

The algorithm uses a variable *delivered* for filtering out duplicate messages and a variable *pending*, used to collect the messages that have been *beb*-delivered and seen, but that still need to be *urb*-delivered.

The algorithm also uses an array *ack* with sets of processes, indexed by all possible messages. The entry $ack[m]$ gathers the set of processes that the process knows have seen m. Of course, the array can be implemented with a finite amount of

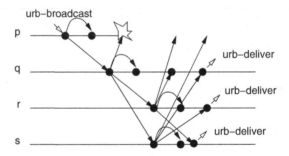

Figure 3.4: Sample execution of all-ack uniform reliable broadcast

memory by using a sparse representation. Note that the last *upon* statement of the algorithm is triggered by an internal event defined on the state of the algorithm.

Correctness. The *validity* property follows from the *completeness* property of the failure detector and from the *validity* property of the underlying best-effort broadcast. The *no duplication* property relies on the *delivered* variable to filter out duplicates. *No creation* is derived from the *no creation* property of the underlying best-effort broadcast. *Uniform agreement* is ensured by having each process wait to *urb*-deliver a message until all correct processes have seen and relayed the message. This mechanism relies on the *accuracy* property of the perfect failure detector.

Performance. When considering the number of communication steps, in the best case, the algorithm requires two communication steps to *urb*-deliver a message to all processes. In such scenario, in the first step it sends N messages and in the second step $N(N-1)$ messages, for a total of N^2 messages. In the worst case, if the processes crash in sequence, $N + 1$ steps are required. Therefore, uniform reliable broadcast requires one step more to deliver a message than its regular counterpart.

3.4.3 Fail-Silent Algorithm: Majority-Ack Uniform Reliable Broadcast

The "All-Ack Uniform Reliable Broadcast" algorithm of Sect. 3.4.2 (Algorithm 3.4) is not correct if the failure detector is not perfect. *Uniform agreement* would be violated if *accuracy* is not satisfied and *validity* would be violated if *completeness* is not satisfied.

We now give a uniform reliable broadcast algorithm that does not rely on a perfect failure detector but assumes a majority of correct processes, i.e., $N > 2f$ if we assume that up to f processes may crash. We leave it as an exercise to show why the majority assumption is needed in the fail-silent model, without any failure detector. Algorithm 3.5, called "Majority-Ack Uniform Reliable Broadcast," is similar to Algorithm 3.4 ("All-Ack Uniform Reliable Broadcast") in the fail-silent model, except that processes do not wait until all correct processes have seen a message, but only until a majority quorum has seen and retransmitted the message. Hence, the algorithm can be obtained by a small modification from the previous one, affecting only the condition under which a message is delivered.

Algorithm 3.5: Majority-Ack Uniform Reliable Broadcast

Implements:
    UniformReliableBroadcast, **instance** *urb*.

Uses:
    BestEffortBroadcast, **instance** *beb*.

// Except for the function *candeliver*(·) below and for the absence of ⟨ *Crash* ⟩ events
// triggered by the perfect failure detector, it is the same as Algorithm 3.4.

function *candeliver*(m) **returns** Boolean **is**
    return $\#(ack[m]) > N/2$;

Correctness. The algorithm provides uniform reliable broadcast if $N > 2f$. The *no duplication* property follows directly from the use of the variable *delivered*. The *no creation* property follows from the *no creation* property of best-effort broadcast.

To argue for the *uniform agreement* and *validity* properties, we first observe that if a correct process p *beb*-delivers some message m then p eventually *urb*-delivers m. Indeed, if p is correct, and given that p *beb*-broadcasts m according to the algorithm, then every correct process *beb*-delivers and hence *beb*-broadcasts m. As we assume a majority of the processes to be correct, p eventually *beb*-delivers m from more than $N/2$ processes and *urb*-delivers it.

Consider now the *validity* property. If a correct process p *urb*-broadcasts a message m then p *beb*-broadcasts m, and hence p *beb*-delivers m eventually; according to the above observation, p eventually also *urb*-delivers m. Consider now *uniform agreement*, and let q be any process that *urb*-delivers m. To do so, q must have *beb*-delivered m from a majority of the processes. Because of the assumption of a correct majority, at least one correct process must have *beb*-broadcast m. Hence, all correct processes eventually *beb*-deliver m by the *validity* property of best-effort broadcast, which implies that all correct processes also *urb*-deliver m eventually according to the observation made earlier.

Performance. The performance of the algorithm is similar to the performance of the "All-Ack Uniform Reliable Broadcast" algorithm.

3.5 Stubborn Broadcast

This section presents a *stubborn broadcast* abstraction that works with crash-stop process abstractions in the fail-silent system model, as well as with crash-recovery process abstractions in the fail-recovery model.

3.5.1 Specification

The stubborn broadcast abstraction hides a retransmission mechanism and delivers every message that is broadcast by a correct process an infinite number of times,

---

Module 3.4: Interface and properties of stubborn best-effort broadcast

---

Module:

    Name: StubbornBestEffortBroadcast, **instance** *sbeb.*

Events:

    Request: $\langle$ *sbeb, Broadcast* $\mid m \rangle$: Broadcasts a message m to all processes.

    Indication: $\langle$ *sbeb, Deliver* $\mid p, m \rangle$: Delivers a message m broadcast by process p.

Properties:

    SBEB1: *Best-effort validity:* If a process that never crashes broadcasts a message m, then every correct process delivers m an infinite number of times.

    SBEB2: *No creation:* If a process delivers a message m with sender s, then m was previously broadcast by process s.

---

similar to its point-to-point communication counterpart. The specification of *best-effort stubborn broadcast* is given in Module 3.4. The key difference to the best-effort broadcast abstraction (Module 3.1) defined for fail-no-recovery settings lies in the stubborn and perpetual delivery of every message broadcast by a process that does not crash. As a direct consequence, the *no duplication* property of best-effort broadcast is not ensured.

Stubborn broadcast is the first broadcast abstraction in the fail-recovery model considered in this chapter (more will be introduced in the next two sections). As the discussion of logged perfect links in Chap. 2 has shown, communication abstractions in the fail-recovery model usually rely on logging their output to variables in stable storage. For stubborn broadcast, however, logging is not necessary because every delivered message is delivered infinitely often; no process that crashes and recovers finitely many times can, therefore, miss such a message.

The very fact that processes now have to deal with multiple deliveries is the price to pay for saving expensive logging operations. We discuss a *logged best-effort broadcast* in the next section, which eliminates multiple deliveries, but adds at the cost of logging the messages.

The stubborn best-effort broadcast abstraction also serves as an example for stronger stubborn broadcast abstractions, implementing reliable and uniform reliable stubborn broadcast variants, for instance. These could be defined and implemented accordingly.

3.5.2 Fail-Recovery Algorithm: Basic Stubborn Broadcast

Algorithm 3.6 implements stubborn best-effort broadcast using underlying stubborn communication links.

Correctness. The properties of stubborn broadcast are derived directly from the properties of the stubborn links abstraction used by the algorithm. In particular,

---

Algorithm 3.6: Basic Stubborn Broadcast

Implements:
    StubbornBestEffortBroadcast, **instance** *sbeb*.

Uses:
    StubbornPointToPointLinks, **instance** *sl*.

upon event ⟨ *sbeb, Recovery* ⟩ **do**
    // do nothing

upon event ⟨ *sbeb, Broadcast* | *m* ⟩ **do**
    forall $q \in \Pi$ **do**
        trigger ⟨ *sl, Send* | *q, m* ⟩;

upon event ⟨ *sl, Deliver* | *p, m* ⟩ **do**
    trigger ⟨ *sbeb, Deliver* | *p, m* ⟩;

---

validity follows from the fact that the sender sends the message to every process in the system.

Performance. The algorithm requires a single communication step for a process to deliver a message, and exchanges at least N messages. Of course, the stubborn links may retransmit the same message several times and, in practice, an optimization mechanism is needed to acknowledge the messages and stop the retransmission.

3.6 Logged Best-Effort Broadcast

This section and the next one consider broadcast abstractions in the *fail-recovery model* that rely on logging. We first discuss how fail-recovery broadcast algorithms use stable storage for logging and then present a best-effort broadcast abstraction and its implementation.

3.6.1 Overview

Most broadcast specifications we have considered for the fail-stop and fail-silent models are not adequate for the fail-recovery model. As explained next, even the strongest one of our specifications, uniform reliable broadcast, does not provide useful semantics in a setting where processes that crash can later recover and participate in the computation.

For instance, suppose a message m is broadcast by some process p. Consider another process q, which should eventually deliver m. But q crashes at some instant, recovers, and never crashes again; in the fail-recovery model, q is a *correct* process. For a broadcast abstraction, however, it might happen that process q delivers m and crashes immediately afterward, without having processed m, that is, before the application had time to react to the delivery of m. When the process recovers later, it

---

Module 3.5: Interface and properties of logged best-effort broadcast

Module:

    Name: LoggedBestEffortBroadcast, **instance** *lbeb*.

Events:

    Request: ⟨ *lbeb, Broadcast* | *m* ⟩: Broadcasts a message m to all processes.

    Indication: ⟨ *lbeb, Deliver* | *delivered* ⟩: Notifies the upper layer of potential updates to variable *delivered* in stable storage (which log-delivers messages according to the text).

Properties:

    LBEB1: *Validity:* If a process that never crashes broadcasts a message m, then every correct process eventually log-delivers m.

    LBEB2: *No duplication:* No message is log-delivered more than once.

    LBEB3: *No creation:* If a process log-delivers a message m with sender s, then m was previously broadcast by process s.

---

has no memory of m, because the delivery of m occurred asynchronously and could not be anticipated. There should be some way for process q to find out about m upon recovery, and for the application to react to the delivery of m. We have already encountered this problem with the definition of logged perfect links in Sect. 2.4.5.

We adopt the same solution as for logged perfect links: the module maintains a variable *delivered* in stable storage, stores every delivered messages in the variable, and the higher-level modules retrieve the variable from stable storage to determine the delivered messages. To notify the layer above about the delivery, the broadcast abstraction triggers an event ⟨ *Deliver* | *delivered* ⟩. We say that a message m is *log-delivered* from sender s whenever an event ⟨ *Deliver* | *delivered* ⟩ occurs such that *delivered* contains a pair (s, m) for the first time. With this implementation, a process that log-delivers a message m, subsequently crashes, and recovers again will still be able to retrieve m from stable storage and to react to m.

3.6.2 Specification

The abstraction we consider here is called *logged best-effort broadcast* to emphasize that it log-delivers messages by "logging" them to local stable storage. Its specification is given in Module 3.5. The logged best-effort broadcast abstraction has the same interface and properties as best-effort broadcast with crash-stop faults (Module 3.1), except that messages are log-delivered instead of delivered. As we discuss later, stronger logged broadcast abstractions (regular and uniform) can be designed and implemented on top of logged best-effort broadcast.

Algorithm 3.7: Logged Basic Broadcast

Implements:
    LoggedBestEffortBroadcast, **instance** *lbeb*.

Uses:
    StubbornPointToPointLinks, **instance** *sl*.

upon event ⟨ *lbeb*, *Init* ⟩ **do**
    delivered := ∅;
    store(*delivered*);

upon event ⟨ *lbeb*, *Recovery* ⟩ **do**
    retrieve(*delivered*);
    trigger ⟨ *lbeb*, *Deliver* | *delivered* ⟩;

upon event ⟨ *lbeb*, *Broadcast* | *m* ⟩ **do**
    forall $q \in \Pi$ **do**
        trigger ⟨ *sl*, *Send* | *q*, *m* ⟩;

upon event ⟨ *sl*, *Deliver* | *p*, *m* ⟩ **do**
    if $(p, m) \notin delivered$ **then**
        delivered := *delivered* ∪ {(*p*, *m*)};
        store(*delivered*);
        trigger ⟨ *lbeb*, *Deliver* | *delivered* ⟩;

3.6.3 Fail-Recovery Algorithm: Logged Basic Broadcast

Algorithm 3.7, called "Logged Basic Broadcast," implements logged best-effort broadcast. Its structure is similar to Algorithm 3.1 ("Basic Broadcast"). The main differences are the following:

1. The "Logged Basic Broadcast" algorithm uses stubborn best-effort links between every pair of processes for communication. They ensure that every message that is sent by a process that does not crash to a correct recipient will be delivered by its recipient an infinite number of times.
2. The "Logged Basic Broadcast" algorithm maintains a log of all delivered messages. When a new message is received for the first time, it is added to the log, and the upper layer is notified that the log has changed. If the process crashes and later recovers, the upper layer is also notified (as it may have missed a notification triggered just before the crash).

Correctness. The *no creation* property is derived from that of the underlying stubborn links, whereas *no duplication* is derived from the fact that the delivery log is checked before delivering new messages. The *validity* property follows from the fact that the sender sends the message to every other process in the system.

Performance. The algorithm requires a single communication step for a process to deliver a message, and exchanges at least N messages. Of course, stubborn links may retransmit the same message several times and, in practice, an optimization mechanism is needed to acknowledge the messages and stop the retransmission. Additionally, the algorithm requires a log operation for each delivered message.

3.7 Logged Uniform Reliable Broadcast

In a manner similar to the crash-no-recovery case, it is possible to define both reliable and uniform variants of best-effort broadcast for the fail-recovery setting.

3.7.1 Specification

Module 3.6 defines a *logged uniform reliable broadcast* abstraction, which is appropriate for the fail-recovery model. In this variant, if a process (either correct or not) log-delivers a message (that is, stores the variable *delivered* containing the message in stable storage), all correct processes should eventually log-deliver that message. The interface is similar to that of logged best-effort broadcast and its properties directly correspond to those of uniform reliable broadcast with crash-stop processes (Module 3.3).

Module 3.6: Interface and properties of logged uniform reliable broadcast

Module:

   Name: LoggedUniformReliableBroadcast, **instance** *lurb*.

Events:

   Request: $\langle$ *lurb*, *Broadcast* | m $\rangle$: Broadcasts a message m to all processes.

   Indication: $\langle$ *lurb*, *Deliver* | *delivered* $\rangle$: Notifies the upper layer of potential updates to variable *delivered* in stable storage (which log-delivers messages according to the text).

Properties:

   LURB1–LURB3: Same as properties LBEB1–LBEB3 in logged best-effort broadcast (Module 3.5).

   LURB4: *Uniform agreement:* If a message m is log-delivered by some process (whether correct or faulty), then m is eventually log-delivered by every correct process.

3.7.2 Fail-Recovery Algorithm: Logged Majority-Ack Uniform Reliable Broadcast

Algorithm 3.8, called "Logged Majority-Ack Uniform Reliable Broadcast," implements logged uniform broadcast, assuming that a majority of the processes

Algorithm 3.8: Logged Majority-Ack Uniform Reliable Broadcast

Implements:
    LoggedUniformReliableBroadcast, **instance** *lurb*.

Uses:
    StubbornBestEffortBroadcast, **instance** *sbeb*.

upon event ⟨ *lurb, Init* ⟩ **do**
    delivered := ∅;
    pending := ∅;
    forall *m* **do** *ack*[*m*] := ∅;
    store(*pending, delivered*);

upon event ⟨ *lurb, Recovery* ⟩ **do**
    retrieve(*pending, delivered*);
    trigger ⟨ *lurb, Deliver* | *delivered* ⟩;
    forall (*s, m*) ∈ *pending* **do**
        trigger ⟨ *sbeb, Broadcast* | [DATA, *s, m*] ⟩;

upon event ⟨ *lurb, Broadcast* | *m* ⟩ **do**
    pending := *pending* ∪ {(*self, m*)};
    store(*pending*);
    trigger ⟨ *sbeb, Broadcast* | [DATA, *self, m*] ⟩;

upon event ⟨ *sbeb, Deliver* | *p*, [DATA, *s, m*] ⟩ **do**
    if (*s, m*) ∉ *pending* **then**
        pending := *pending* ∪ {(*s, m*)};
        store(*pending*);
        trigger ⟨ *sbeb, Broadcast* | [DATA, *s, m*] ⟩;
    if *p* ∉ *ack*[*m*] **then**
        ack[*m*] := *ack*[*m*] ∪ {*p*};
        if #(*ack*[*m*]) > *N*/2 ∧ (*s, m*) ∉ *delivered* **then**
            delivered := *delivered* ∪ {(*s, m*)};
            store(*delivered*);
            trigger ⟨ *lurb, Deliver* | *delivered* ⟩;

is correct. It log-delivers a message m from sender s by adding (s, m) to the *delivered* variable in stable storage. Apart from *delivered*, the algorithm uses two other variables, a set *pending* and an array *ack*, with the same functions as in "All-Ack Uniform Reliable Broadcast" (Algorithm 3.4). Variable *pending* denotes the messages that the process has seen but not yet *lurb*-delivered, and is logged. Variable *ack* is not logged because it will be reconstructed upon recovery. When a message has been retransmitted by a majority of the processes, it is log-delivered. Together with the assumption of a correct majority, this ensures that at least one correct process has logged the message, and this will ensure the retransmission to all correct processes.

Correctness. Consider the *agreement* property and assume that some correct process p log-delivers a message m. To do so, a majority of the processes must have retransmitted the message. As we assume a majority of the processes is correct, at least one correct process must have logged the message (in its variable *pending*). This process will ensure that the message is eventually *sbeb*-broadcast to all correct processes; all correct processes will hence *sbeb*-deliver the message and acknowledge it. Hence, every correct process will log-deliver m. To establish the *validity* property, assume some process p *lurb*-broadcasts a message m and does not crash. Eventually, the message will be seen by all correct processes. As a majority of processes is correct, these processes will retransmit the message and p will eventually *lurb*-deliver m. The *no duplication* property is trivially ensured by the definition of log-delivery (the check that $(s, m) \notin delivered$ before adding (s, m) to *delivered* only serves to avoid unnecessary work). The *no creation* property is ensured by the underlying links.

Performance. Suppose that some process *lurb*-broadcasts a message m. All correct processes log-deliver m after two communication steps and two causally related logging operations (the variable *pending* can be logged in parallel to broadcasting the DATA message).

3.8 Probabilistic Broadcast

This section considers randomized broadcast algorithms, whose behavior is partially determined by a controlled random experiment. These algorithms do not provide deterministic broadcast guarantees but, instead, only make *probabilistic* claims about such guarantees.

Of course, this approach can only be used for applications that do not require full reliability. On the other hand, full reliability often induces a cost that is too high, especially for large-scale systems or systems exposed to attacks. As we will see, it is often possible to build scalable probabilistic algorithms that exploit randomization and provide good reliability guarantees.

Moreover, the abstractions considered in this book can almost never be mapped to physical systems in real deployments that match the model completely; some uncertainty often remains. A system designer must also take into account a small probability that the deployment fails due to such a mismatch. Even if the probabilistic guarantees of an abstraction leave room for error, the designer might accept this error because other sources of failure are more significant.

3.8.1 The Scalability of Reliable Broadcast

As we have seen throughout this chapter, in order to ensure the reliability of broadcast in the presence of faulty processes (and/or links with omission failures), a process needs to *send messages* to all other processes and needs to collect some form of *acknowledgment*. However, given limited bandwidth, memory, and processor resources, there will always be a limit to the number of messages that each process can send and to the acknowledgments it is able to collect in due time. If the

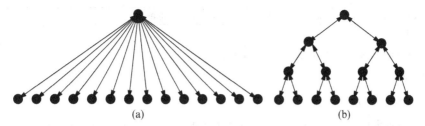

Figure 3.5: Direct vs. hierarchical communication for sending messages and receiving acknowledgments

group of processes becomes very large (say, thousands or even millions of members in the group), a process sending out messages and collecting acknowledgments becomes overwhelmed by that task (see Fig. 3.5a). Such algorithms inherently do not *scale*. Sometimes an efficient hardware-supported broadcast mechanism is available, and then the problem of collecting acknowledgments, also known as the *ack implosion* problem, is the worse problem of the two.

There are several ways to make algorithms more scalable. One way is to use some form of hierarchical scheme to send messages and to collect acknowledgments, for instance, by arranging the processes in a binary tree, as illustrated in Fig. 3.5b. Hierarchies can reduce the load of each process but increase the latency of the communication protocol. Additionally, hierarchies need to be reconfigured when faults occur (which may not be a trivial task), and even with this sort of hierarchies, the obligation to send and receive information, directly or indirectly, to and from every other process remains a fundamental scalability problem of reliable broadcast. In the next section we discuss how randomized approaches can circumvent this limitation.

3.8.2 Epidemic Dissemination

Nature gives us several examples of how a randomized approach can implement a fast and efficient broadcast primitive. Consider how an epidemic spreads through a population. Initially, a single individual is infected; every infected individual will in turn infect some other individuals; after some period, the whole population is infected. Rumor spreading or gossiping uses exactly the same mechanism and has proved to be a very effective way to disseminate information.

A number of broadcast algorithms have been designed based on this principle and, not surprisingly, these are often called *epidemic*, *rumor mongering*, *gossip*, or *probabilistic broadcast* algorithms. Before giving more details on these algorithms, we first define the abstraction that they implement, which we call *probabilistic broadcast*. To illustrate how algorithms can implement the abstraction, we assume a model where processes can only fail by crashing.

Module 3.7: Interface and properties of probabilistic broadcast
Module:

> **Name:** ProbabilisticBroadcast, **instance** *pb*.

Events:

> **Request:** ⟨ *pb, Broadcast* | *m* ⟩: Broadcasts a message *m* to all processes.

> **Indication:** ⟨ *pb, Deliver* | *p, m* ⟩: Delivers a message *m* broadcast by process *p*.

Properties:

> **PB1:** *Probabilistic validity:* There is a positive value ε such that when a correct process broadcasts a message *m*, the probability that every correct process eventually delivers *m* is at least $1 - \varepsilon$.

> **PB2:** *No duplication:* No message is delivered more than once.

> **PB3:** *No creation:* If a process delivers a message *m* with sender *s*, then *m* was previously broadcast by process *s*.

3.8.3 Specification

The probabilistic broadcast abstraction is depicted in Module 3.7. Its interface is the same as for best-effort broadcast (Module 3.1), and also two of its three properties, *no duplication* and *no creation*, are the same. Only the *probabilistic validity* property is weaker than the ordinary *validity* property and accounts for a failure probability ε, which is typically small.

As for previous communication abstractions introduced in this chapter, we assume that messages are implicitly addressed to all processes in the system, i.e., the goal of the sender is to have its message delivered to all processes of a given group, constituting what we call the system.

3.8.4 Randomized Algorithm: Eager Probabilistic Broadcast

Algorithm 3.9, called "Eager Probabilistic Broadcast," implements probabilistic broadcast. The sender selects *k* processes at random and sends them the message. In turn, each of these processes selects another *k* processes at random and forwards the message to those processes, and so on. The parameter *k* is called the *fanout* of a gossip algorithm. The algorithm may cause a process to send the message back to the same process from which it originally received the message, or to send it to another process that has already received the message.

Each step consisting of receiving a message and resending it is called a *round* of *gossiping*. The algorithm performs up to *R* rounds of gossiping for each message.

The description of the algorithm uses a function *picktargets*(*k*), which takes the fanout *k* as input and outputs a set of processes. It returns *k* random samples chosen from $\Pi \setminus \{self\}$ according to the uniform distribution without replacement. The

---

Algorithm 3.9: Eager Probabilistic Broadcast

Implements:
  ProbabilisticBroadcast, **instance** *pb*.

Uses:
  FairLossPointToPointLinks, **instance** *fll*.

upon event ⟨ *pb, Init* ⟩ **do**
  delivered := ∅;

procedure *gossip(msg)* **is**
  forall $t \in picktargets(k)$ **do trigger** ⟨ *fll, Send* | *t, msg* ⟩;

upon event ⟨ *pb, Broadcast* | *m* ⟩ **do**
  delivered := *delivered* ∪ {*m*};
  trigger ⟨ *pb, Deliver* | *self, m* ⟩;
  gossip([GOSSIP, *self, m, R*]);

upon event ⟨ *fll, Deliver* | *p*, [GOSSIP, *s, m, r*] ⟩ **do**
  if $m \notin delivered$ **then**
    delivered := *delivered* ∪ {*m*};
    trigger ⟨ *pb, Deliver* | *s, m* ⟩;
  if $r > 1$ **then** *gossip*([GOSSIP, *s, m, r* − 1]);

---

function *random(S)* implements the random choice of an element from a set S for this purpose. The pseudo code looks like this:

---

function *picktargets(k)* **returns** set of processes **is**
  targets := ∅;
  while #(*targets*) < *k* **do**
    candidate := random($\Pi \setminus \{self\}$);
    if $candidate \notin targets$ **then**
      targets := *targets* ∪ {*candidate*};
  return *targets*;

The fanout is a fundamental parameter of the algorithm. Its choice directly impacts the performance of the algorithm and the probability of successful reliable delivery (in the *probabilistic validity* property of probabilistic broadcast). A higher fanout not only increases the probability of having the entire population infected but also decreases the number of rounds required to achieve this. Note also that the algorithm induces a significant amount of redundancy in the message exchanges: any given process may receive the same message many times. A three-round execution of the algorithm with fanout three is illustrated in Fig. 3.6 for a system consisting of nine processes.

However, increasing the fanout is costly. The higher the fanout, the higher the load imposed on each process and the amount of redundant information exchanged

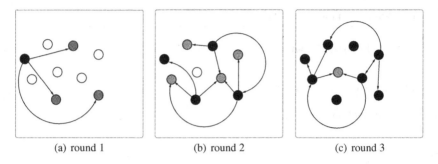

| (a) round 1 | (b) round 2 | (c) round 3 |

Figure 3.6: Epidemic dissemination or gossip (with fanout 3)

over the network. Therefore, to select the appropriate fanout value is of particular importance. Note that there are runs of the algorithm where a transmitted message may not be delivered to all correct processes. For instance, all processes that receive the message directly from the sender may select exactly the same set of k target processes and forward the message only to them, and the algorithm may stop there. In such a case, if k is much smaller than N, not all processes will deliver the message. As another example, there might be one process that is simply never selected by any process and never receives the message. This translates into the fact that reliable delivery is not guaranteed, that is, the probability that some process never delivers the message is nonzero. But by choosing large enough values of k and R in relation to N, this probability can be made arbitrarily small.

Correctness. The *no creation* and *no duplication* properties are immediate from the underlying point-to-point links and from the use of the variable *delivered*.

For the *probabilistic validity* property, the probability that for a particular broadcast message, all correct processes become infected and deliver the message depends on the fanout k and on the maximum number of rounds R.

We now derive a simple estimate of the probability that a particular correct process delivers a message. Suppose that the underlying fair-loss links deliver every message sent by the first infected correct process (i.e., the original sender) but no further message; in other words, only the sender disseminates the broadcast message. In every round, a fraction of $\gamma = k/N$ processes become infected like this (some may have been infected before). The probability that a given correct process remains uninfected is at most $1 - \gamma$. Hence, the probability that this process is infected after R rounds is at least about $E_1 = 1 - (1 - \gamma)^R$.

Toward a second, more accurate estimate, we eliminate the simplification that only one process infects others in a round. Suppose a fraction of $d = (N - f)/N$ processes are correct; assume further that in every round, the number of *actually* infected processes is equal to their *expected* number. Denote the expected number of infected and correct processes after round r by I_r. Initially, only the sender is infected and $I_0 = 1$. After round r for $r > 0$, we observe that I_{r-1} correct processes stay infected. Among the remaining $N - I_{r-1}$ processes, we expect that a fraction of d is correct and a fraction of γ of them becomes infected:

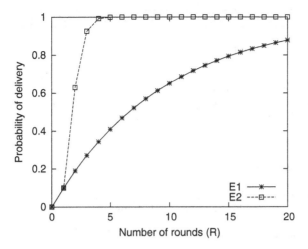

Figure 3.7: Illustration of gossip delivery probability to one correct process using the "Eager Probabilistic Broadcast" algorithm with $R = 1, \ldots, 20$ rounds, in terms of estimates E_1 and E_2 from the text

$$I_r = I_{r-1} + d\gamma(N - I_{r-1}).$$

As all I_r processes infect others in round $r + 1$, the infections in round $r + 1$ spread about as fast as if one process would have infected the others during additional I_r rounds. Summing this up over all R rounds, we obtain our second estimate: the probability of some correct process being infected after R rounds is about

$$E_2 = 1 - (1 - \gamma)^{\sum_{r=0}^{R-1} I_r}.$$

The two estimates E_1 and E_2 of the delivery probability for one process are plotted in Fig. 3.7 for a system of $N = 100$ processes, assuming that $f = 25$ faulty processes crash initially, and fanout $k = 10$.

Performance. The number of rounds needed for a message to be delivered by all correct processes also depends on the fanout. Every round involves one communication step. The algorithm may send $O(N)$ messages in every round and $O(N^R)$ messages in total, after running for R rounds; generally, the number of messages sent by the algorithm is dominated by the messages of the last round.

3.8.5 Randomized Algorithm: Lazy Probabilistic Broadcast

The "Eager Probabilistic Broadcast" algorithm described earlier uses only gossiping to disseminate messages, where infected processes *push* messages to other processes. A major disadvantage of this approach is that it consumes considerable resources and causes many redundant transmissions, in order to achieve reliable delivery with high probability. A way to overcome this limitation is to rely on epidemic push-style broadcast only in a first phase, until many processes are infected,

---

Algorithm 3.10: Lazy Probabilistic Broadcast (part 1, data dissemination)

Implements:
    ProbabilisticBroadcast, **instance** pb.

Uses:
    FairLossPointToPointLinks, **instance** fll;
    ProbabilisticBroadcast, **instance** upb.   // an *unreliable* implementation

upon event $\langle\,pb,\,Init\,\rangle$ **do**
    $next := [1]^N$;
    $lsn := 0$;
    $pending := \emptyset$; $stored := \emptyset$;

procedure $gossip(msg)$ **is**
    forall $t \in picktargets(k)$ **do trigger** $\langle\,fll,\,Send \mid t, msg\,\rangle$;

upon event $\langle\,pb,\,Broadcast \mid m\,\rangle$ **do**
    $lsn := lsn + 1$;
    trigger $\langle\,upb,\,Broadcast \mid [\textsc{Data},\,self,\,m,\,lsn]\,\rangle$;

upon event $\langle\,upb,\,Deliver \mid p,\,[\textsc{Data},\,s,\,m,\,sn]\,\rangle$ **do**
    if $random([0,1]) > \alpha$ **then**
        $stored := stored \cup \{[\textsc{Data},\,s,\,m,\,sn]\}$;
    if $sn = next[s]$ **then**
        $next[s] := next[s] + 1$;
        trigger $\langle\,pb,\,Deliver \mid s,\,m\,\rangle$;
    else if $sn > next[s]$ **then**
        $pending := pending \cup \{[\textsc{Data},\,s,\,m,\,sn]\}$;
        forall $missing \in [next[s],\ldots,sn - 1]$ **do**
            if no m' exists such that $[\textsc{Data},\,s,\,m',\,missing] \in pending$ **then**
                $gossip([\textsc{Request},\,self,\,s,\,missing,\,R - 1])$;
        $starttimer(\Delta,\,s,\,sn)$;

---

and to switch to a *pulling* mechanism in a second phase afterward. Gossiping until, say, half of the processes are infected is efficient. The pulling phase serves a backup to inform the processes that missed the message in the first phase. The second phase uses again gossip, but only to disseminate messages about which processes have missed a message in the first phase. This idea works for scenarios where every sender broadcasts multiple messages in sequence.

For describing an implementation of this idea in a compact way, we assume here that the first phase is realized by an *unreliable* probabilistic broadcast abstraction, as defined by Module 3.7, with a large probability ε that reliable delivery fails, in its *probabilistic validity* property. Concretely, we expect that a constant fraction of the processes, say, half of them, obtains the message after the first phase. The primitive could typically be implemented on top of fair-loss links (as the "Eager Probabilistic Broadcast" algorithm) and should work efficiently, that is, not cause an excessive amount of redundant message transmissions.

Algorithm 3.10–3.11, called "Lazy Probabilistic Broadcast," realizes probabilistic broadcast in two phases, with push-style gossiping followed by pulling. The

---

Algorithm 3.11: Lazy Probabilistic Broadcast (part 2, recovery)

---

upon event ⟨ *fll, Deliver* | p, [REQUEST, q, s, sn, r] ⟩ **do**
    if exists m such that [DATA, s, m, sn] ∈ *stored* **then**
        trigger ⟨ *fll, Send* | q, [DATA, s, m, sn] ⟩;
    else if $r > 0$ **then**
        gossip([REQUEST, q, s, sn, $r - 1$]);

upon event ⟨ *fll, Deliver* | p, [DATA, s, m, sn] ⟩ **do**
    pending := *pending* ∪ {[DATA, s, m, sn]};

upon exists [DATA, s, x, sn] ∈ *pending* such that $sn = next[s]$ **do**
    $next[s] := next[s] + 1$;
    pending := *pending* \ {[DATA, s, x, sn]};
    trigger ⟨ *pb, Deliver* | s, x ⟩;

upon event ⟨ *Timeout* | s, sn ⟩ **do**
    if $sn > next[s]$ **then**
        $next[s] := sn + 1$;

---

algorithm assumes that each sender is transmitting a stream of numbered messages. Message omissions are detected based on gaps in the sequence numbers of received messages. Each message is disseminated using an instance *upb* of unreliable probabilistic broadcast. Each message that is retained by a randomly selected set of receivers for future retransmission. More precisely, every process that *upb*-delivers a message stores a copy of the message with probability α during some maximum amount of time. The purpose of this approach is to distribute the load of storing messages for future retransmission among all processes.

Omissions can be detected using sequence numbers associated with messages. The array variable *next* contains an entry for every process p with the sequence number of the next message to be *pb*-delivered from sender p. The process detects that it has missed one or more messages from p when the process receives a message from p with a larger sequence number than what it expects according to *next*[p]. When a process detects an omission, it uses the gossip algorithm to disseminate a retransmission request. If the request is received by one of the processes that has stored a copy of the message then this process retransmits the message. Note that, in this case, the gossip algorithm does not have to ensure that the retransmission request reaches *all* processes with high probability: it is enough that the request reaches, with high probability, one of the processes that has stored a copy of the missing message. With small probability, recovery will fail. In this case, after a timeout with delay Δ has expired, a process simply jumps ahead and skips the missed messages, such that subsequent messages from the same sender can be delivered.

The pseudo code of Algorithm 3.10–3.11 uses again the function *picktargets*(k) from the previous section. The function *random*([0, 1]) used by the algorithm returns a random real number from the interval [0, 1]. The algorithm may invoke multiple timers, where operation *starttimer*(Δ, *parameters*) starts a timer instance identified by *parameters* with delay Δ.

Garbage collection of the stored message copies is omitted in the pseudo code for simplicity. Note also that when a timeout for some sender s and sequence number sn occurs, the pseudo code may skip some messages with sender s in *pending* that have arrived meanwhile (be it through retransmissions or delayed messages from s) and that should be processed; a more complete implementation would deliver these messages and remove them from *pending*.

Correctness. The *no creation* and *no duplication* properties follow from the underlying point-to-point links and the use of sequence numbers.

The probability of delivering a message to all correct processes depends here on the fanout (as in the "Eager Probabilistic Broadcast" algorithm) and on the reliability of the underlying dissemination primitive. For instance, if half of the processes *upb*-deliver a particular message and all of them were to store it (by setting $\alpha = 0$) then the first retransmission request to reach one of these processes will be successful, and the message will be retransmitted. This means that the probability of successful retransmission behaves like the probability of successful delivery in the "Eager Probabilistic Broadcast" algorithm.

Performance. Assuming an efficient underlying dissemination primitive, the broadcasting of a message is clearly much more efficient than in the "Eager Probabilistic Broadcast" algorithm.

It is expected that, in most cases, the retransmission request message is much smaller that the original data message. Therefore, this algorithm is also much more resource-effective than the "Eager Probabilistic Broadcast" algorithm.

Practical algorithms based on this principle make a significant effort to optimize the number of processes that store copies of each broadcast message. Not surprisingly, the best results can be obtained if the physical network topology is taken into account: for instance, in a wide-area system with processes in multiple LANs, an omission in a link connecting a LAN with the rest of the system affects all processes in that LAN. Thus, it is desirable to have a copy of the message in each LAN (to recover from local omissions) and a copy outside the LAN (to recover from the omission in the link to the LAN). Similarly, the retransmission procedure, instead of being completely random, may search first for a copy in the local LAN and only afterward at more distant processes.

3.9 FIFO and Causal Broadcast

So far, we have not considered any ordering guarantee among messages delivered by different processes. In particular, when we consider a reliable broadcast abstraction, messages can be delivered in any order by distinct processes.

In this section, we introduce reliable broadcast abstractions that deliver messages according to *first-in first-out (FIFO) order* and according to *causal order*. FIFO order ensures that messages broadcast by the same sender process are delivered in the order in which they were sent. Causal order is a generalization of FIFO order that additionally preserves the potential causality among messages from multiple senders. These orderings are orthogonal to the reliability guarantees.

3.9.1 Overview

Consider the case of a distributed message board that manages two types of information: proposals and comments on previous proposals. To make the interface user-friendly, comments are depicted attached to the proposal they are referring to. In order to make it highly available, it is natural to implement the board application by replicating all the information to all participants. This can be achieved through the use of a reliable broadcast primitive to disseminate both proposals and comments.

With reliable broadcast, however, the following sequence of events is possible: participant p broadcasts a message m_1 containing a new proposal; then p changes its mind and broadcasts a message m_2 with a modification to its previous proposal; because of message delays, another participant q delivers m_2 before m_1. It may be difficult for participant q to understand m_2 without the context of m_1. Imposing a *FIFO order* on the delivery of messages solves this problem because it requires q delivers m_1 before m_2 as they are from the same sender. FIFO order can be implemented by delaying the delivery of a message m from a given sender until all messages that the sender has broadcast before m have been delivered.

Even when reliable broadcast implements FIFO order, the following execution is still possible: participant p broadcasts a message m_1 containing its new proposal; participant q delivers m_1 and disseminates a comment on m_1 in message m_2; because of message delays, another participant r delivers m_2 before m_1. When participant r delivers m_2, it lacks the context of message m_1 to properly interpret m_2. Message delivery in *causal order* prevents this. It could be implemented by delaying the delivery of a message m_2 until every message m_1 that may have potentially caused m_2 (i.e., where $m_1 \rightarrow m_2$) has been delivered.

3.9.2 FIFO-Order Specification

The specification of reliable broadcast does not state anything about the order in which multiple messages are delivered. A FIFO-order is one of the simplest possible orderings and guarantees that messages from the same sender are delivered in the same sequence as they were broadcast by the sender. Note, this does not affect messages from different senders.

The *FIFO-order (reliable) broadcast* abstraction shown in Module 3.8 is obtained from the (regular) reliable broadcast abstraction (Module 3.2) by extending it with the *FIFO delivery* property. A uniform variation of FIFO-order (reliable) broadcast with causal order can be obtained in the same way. For brevity, we usually skip the term "reliable" refer to a *FIFO-order broadcast* abstraction.

3.9.3 Fail-Silent Algorithm: Broadcast with Sequence Number

Algorithm 3.12, "Broadcast with Sequence Number," implements FIFO-order reliable broadcast. Every process maintains a sequence number lsn for the *frb*-broadcast messages, and *rb*-broadcasts the value lsn together with the message. The process

Module 3.8: Interface and properties of FIFO-order (reliable) broadcast

Module:

Name: FIFOReliableBroadcast, **instance** *frb*.

Events:

Request: ⟨ *frb*, *Broadcast* | *m* ⟩: Broadcasts a message *m* to all processes.

Indication: ⟨ *frb*, *Deliver* | *p*, *m* ⟩: Delivers a message *m* broadcast by process *p*.

Properties:

FRB1–FRB4: Same as properties RB1–RB4 in (regular) reliable broadcast (Module 3.2).

FRB5: *FIFO delivery:* If some process broadcasts message m_1 before it broadcasts message m_2, then no correct process delivers m_2 unless it has already delivered m_1.

Algorithm 3.12: Broadcast with Sequence Number

Implements:
   FIFOReliableBroadcast, **instance** *frb*.

Uses:
   ReliableBroadcast, **instance** *rb*.

upon event ⟨ *frb*, *Init* ⟩ **do**
   lsn := 0;
   pending := ∅;
   next := $[1]^N$;

upon event ⟨ *frb*, *Broadcast* | *m* ⟩ **do**
   lsn := *lsn* + 1;
   trigger ⟨ *rb*, *Broadcast* | [DATA, *self*, *m*, *lsn*] ⟩;

upon event ⟨ *rb*, *Deliver* | *p*, [DATA, *s*, *m*, *sn*] ⟩ **do**
   pending := *pending* ∪ {(*s*, *m*, *sn*)};
   while exists (*s*, *m'*, *sn'*) ∈ *pending* such that *sn'* = *next*[*s*] **do**
      next[*s*] := *next*[*s*] + 1;
      pending := *pending* \ {(*s*, *m'*, *sn'*)};
      trigger ⟨ *frb*, *Deliver* | *s*, *m'* ⟩;

---

also maintains an array *next*, which contains an entry for every process *p* with the sequence number of the next message to be *frb*-delivered from sender *p*. The process buffers all messages received via the reliable broadcast primitive in a set *pending* and *frb*-delivers them according to the sequence number assigned per the sender. (The same mechanism is also found in the "Lazy Probabilistic Broadcast" algorithm.)

Correctness. Because the FIFO-order broadcast abstraction is an extension of reliable broadcast, and because the algorithm uses a reliable broadcast primitive directly, the algorithm satisfies the four basic properties (FRB1–FRB4) that also define reliable broadcast.

The *FIFO delivery* property follows directly from the assignment of sequence numbers to messages by every sender and from way that receivers buffer and *frb-deliver* messages according to the sequence number assigned by the sender.

Performance. The algorithm does not add any messages to the reliable broadcast primitive and only increases the message size by a marginal amount.

3.9.4 Causal-Order Specification

The *causal order* property for a broadcast abstraction ensures that messages are delivered such that they respect all cause–effect relations. The *happened-before* relation described earlier in this book (Sect. 2.5.1) expresses all such dependencies. This relation is also called the *causal order* relation, when applied to messages exchanged among processes and expressed by broadcast and delivery events. In this case, we say that a message m_1 may have *potentially caused* another message m_2, denoted as $m_1 \rightarrow m_2$, if any of the following relations apply (see Fig. 3.8):

(a) some process p broadcasts m_1 before it broadcasts m_2;
(b) some process p delivers m_1 and subsequently broadcasts m_2; or
(c) there exists some message m' such that $m_1 \rightarrow m'$ and $m' \rightarrow m_2$.

Using the causal order relation, one can define a broadcast abstraction with a *causal delivery* property, which states that all messages delivered by the broadcast abstraction are delivered according to the causal order relation. There must be no "holes" in the causal past, such that when a message is delivered, all messages that causally precede it have already been delivered.

The *causal-order (reliable) broadcast* abstraction shown in Module 3.9 is obtained from the (regular) reliable broadcast abstraction (Module 3.2) by extending it with a *causal delivery* property. A uniform variation of reliable broadcast with causal order can be stated analogously. The *causal-order uniform (reliable) broadcast* abstraction is shown in Module 3.10 and extends the uniform reliable broadcast abstraction (Module 3.3) with the *causal delivery* property. For brevity, we usually

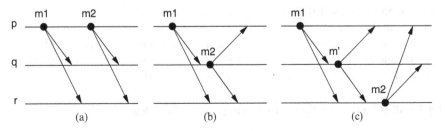

Figure 3.8: Causal order of messages

Module 3.9: Interface and properties of causal-order (reliable) broadcast

Module:

    Name: CausalOrderReliableBroadcast, **instance** *crb*.

Events:

    Request: $\langle$ *crb, Broadcast* $\mid m$ $\rangle$: Broadcasts a message m to all processes.

    Indication: $\langle$ *crb, Deliver* $\mid p, m$ $\rangle$: Delivers a message m broadcast by process p.

Properties:

    CRB1–CRB4: Same as properties RB1–RB4 in (regular) reliable broadcast (Module 3.2).

    CRB5: *Causal delivery:* For any message m_1 that potentially caused a message m_2, i.e., $m_1 \rightarrow m_2$, no process delivers m_2 unless it has already delivered m_1.

Module 3.10: Interface and properties of causal-order uniform (reliable) broadcast

Module:

    Name: CausalOrderUniformReliableBroadcast, **instance** *curb*.

Events:

    Request: $\langle$ *curb, Broadcast* $\mid m$ $\rangle$: Broadcasts a message m to all processes.

    Indication: $\langle$ *curb, Deliver* $\mid p, m$ $\rangle$: Delivers a message m broadcast by process p.

Properties:

    CURB1–CURB4: Same as properties URB1–URB4 in uniform reliable broadcast (Module 3.3).

    CURB5: Same as property CRB5 in causal-order broadcast (Module 3.9).

---

skip the term "reliable" and call the first one *causal-order broadcast* and the second one *causal-order uniform broadcast*.

As is evident from the first condition of causal order, the *causal delivery* property implies the *FIFO order* property in Module 3.8. Hence, a causal-order broadcast primitive provides also FIFO-order reliable broadcast.

The reader might wonder at this point whether it also makes sense to consider a *causal-order best-effort broadcast* abstraction, combining the properties of best-effort broadcast with the *causal delivery* property. As we show through an exercise at the end of the chapter, this would inherently be also reliable.

3.9.5 Fail-Silent Algorithm: No-Waiting Causal Broadcast

Algorithm 3.13, called "No-Waiting Causal Broadcast," uses an underlying reliable broadcast communication abstraction *rb*, accessed through an *rb*-broadcast request

---

Algorithm 3.13: No-Waiting Causal Broadcast

Implements:
    CausalOrderReliableBroadcast, **instance** *crb*.

Uses:
    ReliableBroadcast, **instance** *rb*.

upon event ⟨ *crb*, *Init* ⟩ **do**
    delivered := ∅;
    past := [];

upon event ⟨ *crb*, *Broadcast* | *m* ⟩ **do**
    trigger ⟨ *rb*, *Broadcast* | [DATA, *past*, *m*] ⟩;
    append(*past*, (*self*, *m*));

upon event ⟨ *rb*, *Deliver* | *p*, [DATA, *mpast*, *m*] ⟩ **do**
    if $m \notin delivered$ **then**
        forall $(s, n) \in mpast$ **do**   // by the order in the list
            if $n \notin delivered$ **then**
                trigger ⟨ *crb*, *Deliver* | *s*, *n* ⟩;
                delivered := *delivered* ∪ {*n*};
                if $(s, n) \notin past$ **then**
                    append(*past*, (*s*, *n*));
        trigger ⟨ *crb*, *Deliver* | *p*, *m* ⟩;
        delivered := *delivered* ∪ {*m*};
        if $(p, m) \notin past$ **then**
            append(*past*, (*p*, *m*));

---

and an *rb*-deliver indication. The same algorithm could be used to implement a uniform causal broadcast abstraction, simply by replacing the underlying reliable broadcast module by a uniform reliable broadcast module.

We call the algorithm *no-waiting* in the following sense: whenever a process *rb*-delivers a message *m*, it *crb*-delivers *m* without waiting for further messages to be *rb*-delivered. Each message *m* arrives as part of a DATA message together with a control field *mpast*, containing a list of all messages that causally precede *m* in the order these messages were delivered by the sender of *m*. When a pair (*mpast*, *m*) is *rb*-delivered, the receiver first inspects *mpast* and *crb*-delivers all messages in *mpast* that have not yet been *crb*-delivered; only afterward it *crb*-delivers *m*. In order to disseminate its own causal past, each process *p* stores all the messages it has *crb*-broadcast or *crb*-delivered in a local variable *past*, and *rb*-broadcasts *past* together with every *crb*-broadcast message.

Variables *past* and *mpast* in the algorithm are lists of process/message tuples. An empty list is denoted by [], the operation *append*(*L*, *x*) adds an element *x* at the end of list *L*, and the operation *remove*(*L*, *x*) removes element *x* from *L*. The guard that appears before each *append* operation after the process *rb*-delivers a DATA message prevents that a message occurs multiple times in *past*.

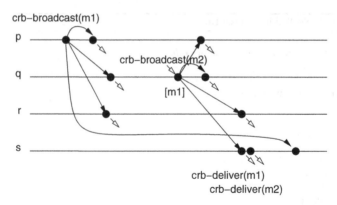

Figure 3.9: Sample execution of no-waiting causal broadcast

An important feature of Algorithm 3.13 is that the *crb*-delivery of a message is never delayed in order to enforce causal order. Figure 3.9 illustrates this behavior. Consider, for instance, process s that *rb*-delivers message m_2. As m_2 carries m_1 in its variable *mpast*, messages m_1 and m_2 are *crb*-delivered immediately, in causal order. Finally, when s *rb*-delivers m_1 from p, then m_1 is discarded.

Correctness. The first four properties (CRB1–CRB4), which are also properties of reliable broadcast, follow directly from the use of an underlying reliable broadcast primitive in the implementation of the algorithm, which *crb*-delivers a message immediately upon *rb*-delivering it. The *causal delivery* property is enforced by having every message carry its causal past and every process making sure that it *crb*-delivers the causal past of a message before *crb*-delivering the message itself.

Performance. The algorithm does not add additional communication steps or send extra messages with respect to the underlying reliable broadcast algorithm. However, the size of the messages grows linearly with time. In particular, the list *past* may become extremely large in long-running executions, because it includes the complete causal past of the process.

In the next subsection, we present a simple scheme to reduce the size of *past*. In the exercises, we describe an alternative implementation based on FIFO-broadcast with shorter causal past lists. We will later discuss an algorithm ("Waiting Causal Broadcast") that completely eliminates the need for exchanging past messages.

3.9.6 Fail-Stop Algorithm: Garbage-Collection of Causal Past

We now present a very simple optimization of the "No-Waiting Causal Broadcast" algorithm, depicted in Algorithm 3.14, to delete messages from the *past* variable. Algorithm 3.14 assumes a fail-stop model: it uses a perfect failure detector. The algorithm uses a distributed garbage-collection scheme and works as follows: when a process *rb*-delivers a message m, the process *rb*-broadcasts an ACK message to all processes; when an ACK message for message m has been *rb*-delivered from all correct processes, then m is purged from *past*.

Algorithm 3.14: Garbage-Collection of Causal Past (extends Algorithm 3.13)

Implements:
    CausalOrderReliableBroadcast, **instance** *crb*.

Uses:
    ReliableBroadcast, **instance** *rb*;
    PerfectFailureDetector, **instance** $\mathcal{P}$.

// Except for its ⟨ *Init* ⟩ event handler, the pseudo code of Algorithm 3.13 is also
// part of this algorithm.

upon event ⟨ *crb, Init* ⟩ **do**
    delivered := ∅;
    past := [];
    correct := Π;
    forall *m* **do** *ack*[*m*] := ∅;

upon event ⟨ $\mathcal{P}$, *Crash* | *p* ⟩ **do**
    correct := *correct* \ {*p*};

upon exists *m* ∈ *delivered* such that *self* ∉ *ack*[*m*] **do**
    ack[*m*] := *ack*[*m*] ∪ {*self*};
    trigger ⟨ *rb, Broadcast* | [ACK, *m*] ⟩;

upon event ⟨ *rb, Deliver* | *p*, [ACK, *m*] ⟩ **do**
    ack[*m*] := *ack*[*m*] ∪ {*p*};

upon *correct* ⊆ *ack*[*m*] **do**
    forall (*s'*, *m'*) ∈ *past* such that *m'* = *m* **do**
        remove(*past*, (*s'*, *m*));

This distributed garbage-collection scheme does not affect the correctness of the "No-Waiting Causal Broadcast" algorithm, provided the *strong accuracy* property of the failure detector holds. The algorithm purges a message only if this message has been *rb*-delivered by all correct processes. If the *completeness* property of the failure detector is violated then the only risk is to keep messages around that could have been purged, but correctness is not affected.

In terms of performance, every acknowledgment message disseminated through reliable broadcast adds $O(N^2)$ point-to-point messages to the network traffic. However, such acknowledgments can be grouped and disseminated in batch mode; as they are not in main path of *crb*-delivering a message, the acknowledgments do not slow down the causal-order broadcast algorithm.

Even with this optimization, the no-waiting approach might be considered too expensive in terms of bandwidth. In the following, we present an approach that tackles the problem at the expense of waiting.

Algorithm 3.15: Waiting Causal Broadcast

Implements:
    CausalOrderReliableBroadcast, **instance** *crb*.

Uses:
    ReliableBroadcast, **instance** *rb*.

upon event ⟨ *crb, Init* ⟩ **do**
    $V := [0]^N$;
    $lsn := 0$;
    $pending := \emptyset$;

upon event ⟨ *crb, Broadcast* | *m* ⟩ **do**
    $W := V$;
    $W[rank(self)] := lsn$;
    $lsn := lsn + 1$;
    trigger ⟨ *rb, Broadcast* | [DATA, W, m] ⟩;

upon event ⟨ *rb, Deliver* | *p*, [DATA, W, m] ⟩ **do**
    $pending := pending \cup \{(p, W, m)\}$;
    while exists $(p', W', m') \in pending$ such that $W' \leq V$ **do**
        $pending := pending \setminus \{(p', W', m')\}$;
        $V[rank(p')] := V[rank(p')] + 1$;
        trigger ⟨ *crb, Deliver* | p', m' ⟩;

3.9.7 Fail-Silent Algorithm: Waiting Causal Broadcast

Algorithm 3.15, called "Waiting Causal Broadcast," implements causal-order broad-cast without storing and disseminating any extra, causally related messages. Like Algorithm 3.13 ("No-Waiting Causal Broadcast"), it relies on an underlying reliable broadcast abstraction *rb* for communication, accessed through an *rb*-broadcast request and an *rb*-deliver indication.

An instance *crb* of Algorithm 3.15 does not keep a record of all past messages as in Algorithm 3.13. Instead, it represents the past with a vector of *sequence numbers*, more precisely, with an array V of N integers called a *vector clock*. The vector captures the causal precedence between messages. In particular, entry $V[rank(q)]$ corresponds to process q, using the *rank*() function from Sect. 2.1 that maps the processes to the integers between 1 and N.

Every process p maintains a vector clock V such that entry $V[rank(q)]$ repre-sents the number of messages that p has *crb*-delivered from process q; additionally, it maintains a local sequence number *lsn*, denoting the number of messages that p has itself *crb*-broadcast. Process p then adds V, with $V[rank(p)]$ replaced by *lsn*, to every *crb*-broadcast message m. When a process q *rb*-delivers some vector W and message m, where m was sent by process s, it compares W to its own vec-tor clock. The difference at index *rank*(s) between the vectors tells process p how

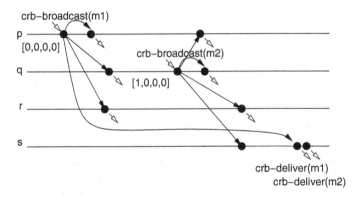

Figure 3.10: Sample execution of waiting causal broadcast

many messages are missing from process s. Process p needs to *crb*-deliver all these messages before it can *crb*-deliver m.

As the name "Waiting Causal Broadcast" indicates a process may have to wait sometimes before *crb*-delivering a message that it has already *rb*-delivered. This is the price to pay for limiting the size of the messages. Using the above description, it is indeed possible that process p cannot immediately *crb*-deliver message m after it is *rb*-delivered because $W[rank(p')] > V[rank(p')]$ for some process p' (which might be s, if *rb*-delivered messages from s were reordered). Hence, process p waits until the messages from p' that precede m in causal order have been *rb*-delivered and *crb*-delivered. On the other hand, it is possible that the *rb*-delivery of a single message triggers the *crb*-delivery of several messages that were already waiting to be *crb*-delivered.

As before, we use the notation $[x]^N$ for any symbol x as an abbreviation for the N-vector $[x, \ldots, x]$. For comparing two N-vectors of integers v and w, we say that $v \leq w$ whenever it holds for every $i = 1, \ldots, N$ that $v[i] \leq w[i]$.

Figure 3.10 shows an example of how a process has to wait. Process s *rb*-delivers message m_2 before it *rb*-delivers message m_1. But, it cannot *crb*-deliver m_2 immediately and has to wait until m_1 is *rb*-delivered. Messages m_1 and m_2 are only then *crb*-delivered in causal order. The figure shows the vector clock values broadcast together with the message.

Correctness. For the *validity* property, consider a message m that is *crb*-broadcast by some correct process p. According to the validity property of the underlying reliable broadcast, p directly *rb*-delivers m. Consider the vector V' that is *rb*-delivered together with m, which is taken from the vector clock V of p when it has *rb*-broadcast m. Since V may only have increased meanwhile, it holds $V \geq V'$ and m is *crb*-delivered immediately.

The *no duplication* and *no creation* properties follow directly from the underlying reliable broadcast abstraction.

To show *agreement*, consider a message m that is *crb*-delivered by some correct process p. Because of the *agreement* property of the underlying reliable broadcast, every correct process eventually *rb*-delivers m. According to the algorithm, and again relying on the *agreement* property of the reliable broadcast, every correct process also eventually *rb*-delivers every message that causally precedes m. Hence, every correct process eventually *crb*-delivers m.

Consider now the *causal order* property. Recall that the vector clock V at a process p stores the number of *crb*-delivered messages with sender q in entry $V[rank(q)]$. Furthermore, process p assigns a sequence number (starting at 0) to every message that it *rb*-broadcast in entry $rank(p)$ of the attached vector. When p *rb*-broadcasts a message m with attached vector W computed like this, then $W[rank(q)]$ messages from sender q causally precede m. But every receiver of m also counts the number of messages that it has *crb*-delivered from sender q and waits until $V[rank(q)]$ such messages have been *crb*-delivered before *crb*-delivering m.

Performance. The algorithm does not add any additional communication steps or messages to the underlying reliable broadcast algorithm. The size of the message header is linear in the number of processes in the system.

Variant. Algorithm "Waiting Causal Broadcast" also implements causal-order uniform broadcast, when the underlying reliable broadcast primitive is replaced by a uniform reliable broadcast primitive.

3.10 Byzantine Consistent Broadcast

For the first time in this book, we now consider an algorithm in the fail-arbitrary system model, where processes are subject to Byzantine faults. This introduces a number of complications for implementing the broadcast abstractions, but their specifications remain similar.

3.10.1 Motivation

As Byzantine processes may deviate arbitrarily from the instructions that an algorithm assigns to them, they may act as if they were deliberately preventing the algorithm from reaching its goals. An algorithm must be prepared to tolerate such behavior. For instance, all algorithms given earlier in this chapter for reliable broadcast fail when a Byzantine process participates. A faulty sender may interfere with the low-level best-effort broadcast primitive and cause the other processes to deliver different messages, which violates the *agreement* or *no duplication* property of reliable broadcast.

Most algorithms that realize primitives in the fail-arbitrary model rely on cryptographic mechanisms, at least to implement the authenticated perfect links abstraction that is used by all of them. But, cryptography alone is seldom the solution for tolerating Byzantine processes; often such algorithms are inherently more involved. Note that in the above example of an arbitrary-faulty sender, asking the sender to digitally sign every broadcast message does not help at all. As if the sender is faulty, it may simply sign the two different messages.

Like in the other system models, we distinguish between *faulty* and *correct* processes in the fail-arbitrary model. The separation is static, in the sense that even if a process is correct during some time when it participates in a distributed algorithm and fails only much later, it is considered *faulty*. As one cannot make any statements about the behavior of a Byzantine process, this distinction is also justified in the fail-arbitrary system model.

As the discussion of uniform reliable broadcast has shown, it is sometimes useful to take into account actions of faulty processes when only crash-stop or crash-recovery process abstractions are concerned. But a Byzantine process abstraction may act arbitrarily and no mechanism can guarantee anything that relates to its actions. Consequently, we do not define any "uniform" variants of primitives in the fail-arbitrary model.

A new issue arises with processes subject to arbitrary faults, however. Consider a "reliable broadcast" primitive. In the system models that only contain crash-stop process abstractions, a typical *agreement* property states "if some correct process delivers m, then every correct process eventually delivers m." Because reliable broadcast does not guarantee that messages are delivered in a specific order, this property is already useful for an application, because it can interpret a message by its sender and from its content. Even if multiple messages are delivered from the same sender, the application can distinguish them by adding appropriate tags to the messages when it broadcasts them. But in the fail-arbitrary model, a faulty sender is not bound to properly tag the application messages and it may even pretend to have broadcast *any* message. Hence, the notion of agreement for a reliable broadcast primitive in the fail-arbitrary model has to be defined differently.

The approach taken here identifies every single *instance* of a reliable broadcast in the fail-arbitrary model as an abstraction of its own. One instance only serves to reach agreement on a single delivered message. We consider two broadcast-instance primitives of this form, called *Byzantine consistent broadcast* and *Byzantine reliable broadcast*. Every such instance has a unique identifier and requires an a-priori agreement on the sender.

Multiple broadcast instances can be combined to the higher-level notion of a "reliable broadcast" with Byzantine faults, which we call *Byzantine broadcast channel*. We discuss a *consistent* and a *reliable* variant of Byzantine broadcast channels in subsequent sections. As with other primitives in this book, when a high-level algorithm invokes multiple instances of a low-level primitive, the implementation-level messages generated by a primitive must be tagged by a suitable identifier and sometimes the identifier must also be included in the cryptographic operations.

In practice, many algorithms implemented in the fail-arbitrary model collapse the notions of instances and channels again, and distinguish multiple instances simply by a sequence number and by their sender process.

3.10.2 Specification

A *Byzantine consistent broadcast* primitive solves one of the most basic agreement problems in the fail-arbitrary model. Every instance of consistent broadcast has a

---

Module 3.11: Interface and properties of Byzantine consistent broadcast

---

Module:

Name: ByzantineConsistentBroadcast, **instance** *bcb*, with sender *s*.

Events:

Request: ⟨ *bcb, Broadcast* | *m* ⟩: Broadcasts a message *m* to all processes. Executed only by process *s*.

Indication: ⟨ *bcb, Deliver* | *p, m* ⟩: Delivers a message *m* broadcast by process *p*.

Properties:

BCB1: *Validity:* If a correct process *p* broadcasts a message *m*, then every correct process eventually delivers *m*.

BCB2: *No duplication:* Every correct process delivers at most one message.

BCB3: *Integrity:* If some correct process delivers a message *m* with sender *p* and process *p* is correct, then *m* was previously broadcast by *p*.

BCB4: *Consistency:* If some correct process delivers a message *m* and another correct process delivers a message m', then $m = m'$.

---

designated sender process *s*, who broadcasts a message *m*. If the sender *s* is correct then every correct process should later deliver *m*. If *s* is faulty then the primitive ensures that every correct process delivers the same message, if it delivers one at all. In other words, with a faulty sender, some correct processes may deliver a message and others may not, but if two correct processes deliver a message, it is unique. This property is called *consistency*. The Byzantine consistent broadcast abstraction is shown in Module 3.13.

Note that *consistency* is a safety property; it is related to the *agreement* property of reliable broadcast abstractions with crash-stop processes, but *consistency* addresses a problem that does not arise with crash-stop processes, which always follow their algorithm. We will see in Sect. 3.11 how to complement *consistency* with a liveness property, such that the two properties together imply the equivalent of an *agreement* property in the fail-arbitrary model.

It has been shown that implementing the Byzantine consistent broadcast abstraction (as well as most other abstractions in the fail-arbitrary model presented in this book) requires that the number of faulty processes satisfies $f < N/3$.

3.10.3 Fail-Arbitrary Algorithm: Authenticated Echo Broadcast

This section presents the "Authenticated Echo Broadcast" algorithm shown in Algorithm 3.16, a first implementation of Byzantine consistent broadcast. It relies only on authenticated perfect links and exploits *Byzantine quorums* for guaranteeing consistency; it, therefore, requires $N > 3f$.

Algorithm 3.16: Authenticated Echo Broadcast

Implements:
    ByzantineConsistentBroadcast, **instance** bcb, with sender s.

Uses:
    AuthPerfectPointToPointLinks, **instance** al.

upon event ⟨ bcb, $Init$ ⟩ **do**
    $sentecho$:= FALSE;
    $delivered$:= FALSE;
    $echos$:= $[\bot]^N$;

upon event ⟨ bcb, $Broadcast$ | m ⟩ **do**   // only process s
    forall $q \in \Pi$ **do**
        trigger ⟨ al, $Send$ | q, [SEND, m] ⟩;

upon event ⟨ al, $Deliver$ | p, [SEND, m] ⟩ **such that** $p = s$ **and** $sentecho = $ FALSE **do**
    $sentecho$:= TRUE;
    forall $q \in \Pi$ **do**
        trigger ⟨ al, $Send$ | q, [ECHO, m] ⟩;

upon event ⟨ al, $Deliver$ | p, [ECHO, m] ⟩ **do**
    if $echos[p] = \bot$ **then**
        $echos[p]$:= m;

upon exists $m \neq \bot$ **such that** $\#(\{p \in \Pi \,|\, echos[p] = m\}) > \frac{N+f}{2}$
        and $delivered = $ FALSE **do**
    $delivered$:= TRUE;
    trigger ⟨ bcb, $Deliver$ | s, m ⟩;

Specifically, an instance bcb of the algorithm uses two rounds of message exchanges. In the first round, the sender s that bcb-broadcasts a message m disseminates m to all processes. In the second round, every process acts as a witness for the message m that it has received from the sender and resends m in an ECHO message to all others. When a process receives more than $(N + f)/2$ such ECHO messages containing the same message m, it bcb-delivers m. This round of echos authenticates a message m that was bcb-broadcast by s in the sense that the Byzantine processes cannot cause a correct process to bcb-deliver a message $m' \neq m$.

As an example of how the algorithm works, consider the following execution with $N = 4$ processes, shown in Fig. 3.11. The sender process p is faulty, i.e., Byzantine, and al-sends a SEND message containing some m to two correct processes q and s, but not to process r, the remaining process in the system. As processes q and s are correct, they al-send an ECHO message with m that they both al-deliver. Process p al-sends an ECHO message with m to q and s, and an ECHO message with $m' \neq m$ to process r. Processes q and r receive enough ECHO messages and both bcb-deliver m, but process r does not bcb-deliver any message. No matter what p sends to r, it will not bcb-deliver m' or any other message different

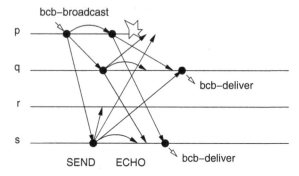

Figure 3.11: Sample execution of authenticated echo broadcast with faulty sender p

from m because that would require three ECHO messages with a content different from m. But this is impossible, since processes q and s sent an ECHO message containing m. Because process p is faulty, we ignore whether it *bcb*-delivers any message.

Correctness. Algorithm 3.16 implements a Byzantine consistent broadcast abstraction for $N > 3f$. The *validity* property follows from the algorithm because if the sender is correct, then every correct process *al*-sends an ECHO message and every correct process *al*-delivers at least $N - f$ of them. Because $N - f > (N + f)/2$ under the assumption that $N > 3f$, every correct process also *bcb*-delivers the message m contained in the ECHO messages.

The *no duplication* and *integrity* properties are straightforward to verify from the algorithm.

The *consistency* property follows from the observation that in order for a correct process p to *bcb*-deliver some m, it needs to receive (i.e., to *al*-deliver) more than $(N + f)/2$ ECHO messages containing m. A set of more than $(N + f)/2$ processes corresponds to a Byzantine quorum of processes (Sect. 2.7.3). Recall that every two Byzantine quorums overlap in at least one correct process. Consider a different correct process p' that *bcb*-delivers some m'. As p' has received a Byzantine quorum of ECHO messages containing m', and because the correct process in the intersection of the two Byzantine quorums sent the same ECHO message to p and to p', it follows that $m = m'$.

Performance. The algorithm requires two communication steps to *bcb*-deliver a message to all processes. Because the second step involves all-to-all communication, the algorithm uses $O(N^2)$ messages. Every low-level message on the authenticated perfect links contains essentially only the broadcast message itself.

3.10.4 Fail-Arbitrary Algorithm: Signed Echo Broadcast

A second implementation of Byzantine consistent broadcast that we call "Signed Echo Broadcast" is shown in Algorithm 3.17. It uses an authenticated perfect links abstraction and a cryptographic digital signature scheme (Sect. 2.3.3).

Algorithm 3.17: Signed Echo Broadcast

Implements:
 ByzantineConsistentBroadcast, **instance** *bcb*, with sender *s*.

Uses:
 AuthPerfectPointToPointLinks, **instance** *al*.

upon event ⟨ *bcb, Init* ⟩ **do**
  sentecho := FALSE;
  sentfinal := FALSE;
  delivered := FALSE;
  echos := $[\bot]^N$; Σ := $[\bot]^N$;

upon event ⟨ *bcb, Broadcast* | *m* ⟩ **do**   // only process *s*
  forall $q \in \Pi$ **do**
    trigger ⟨ *al, Send* | *q*, [SEND, *m*] ⟩;

upon event ⟨ *al, Deliver* | *p*, [SEND, *m*] ⟩ **such that** $p = s$ **and** *sentecho* = FALSE **do**
  sentecho := TRUE;
  σ := *sign*(*self, bcb*‖*self*‖ECHO‖*m*);
  trigger ⟨ *al, Send* | *s*, [ECHO, *m*, σ] ⟩;

upon event ⟨ *al, Deliver* | *p*, [ECHO, *m*, σ] ⟩ **do**   // only process *s*
  if *echos*[*p*] = $\bot$ $\wedge$ *verifysig*(*p, bcb*‖*p*‖ECHO‖*m*, σ) **then**
    echos[*p*] := *m*; Σ[*p*] := σ;

upon exists $m \neq \bot$ **such that** $\#(\{p \in \Pi \mid echos[p] = m\}) > \frac{N+f}{2}$
    and *sentfinal* = FALSE **do**
  sentfinal := TRUE;
  forall $q \in \Pi$ **do**
    trigger ⟨ *al, Send* | *q*, [FINAL, *m*, Σ] ⟩;

upon event ⟨ *al, Deliver* | *p*, [FINAL, *m*, Σ] ⟩ **do**
  if $\#(\{p \in \Pi \mid \Sigma[p] \neq \bot \wedge verifysig(p, bcb\|p\|\text{ECHO}\|m, \Sigma[p])\}) > \frac{N+f}{2}$
      and *delivered* = FALSE **do**
    delivered := TRUE;
    trigger ⟨ *bcb, Deliver* | *s*, *m* ⟩;

Compared to the "Authenticated Echo Broadcast" algorithm of the previous section, it uses digital signatures and sends fewer messages over the underlying authenticated links abstraction: only a linear number of messages instead of a quadratic number (in N). The basic idea is the same, however, in that the sender s first disseminates a message m to all processes and expects a Byzantine quorum of processes to witness for the act of broadcasting m. In contrast to Algorithm 3.16, the witnesses authenticate a request not by sending an ECHO message to all processes but by signing a statement to this effect, which they return to the sender s. Process s then collects a Byzantine quorum of these signed statements and relays them in a third communication step to all processes.

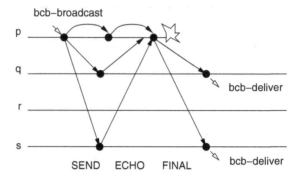

Figure 3.12: Sample execution of signed echo broadcast with faulty sender p

A sample execution of "Authenticated Echo Broadcast" with a faulty sender p is shown in Fig. 3.12. Processes q and s sign a statement that they "echo" the message m received from p in instance bcb, and return the signature to p. Again, processes q and s bcb-deliver the same message, and process r does not bcb-deliver any message.

It is important to include the identifier bcb of the algorithm instance in the argument to the digital signature scheme; otherwise, a Byzantine process might transport a signature issued by a correct process to a different context and subvert the guarantees of the algorithm there. Recall that the symbol ‖ stands for concatenating two bit strings.

Correctness. Given a digital signature scheme and an authenticated perfect links abstraction, Algorithm 3.17 implements a Byzantine consistent broadcast abstraction for $N > 3f$. The only difference to Algorithm 3.16 lies in replacing the ECHO message that a process sends directly to all others by a digital signature that conveys the same information indirectly and is transmitted via the sender. When one replaces the necessary Byzantine quorum of valid signatures in the verification of the FINAL message by a Byzantine quorum of *al*-delivered ECHO messages, the *consistency* property follows from the same argument as in Algorithm 3.16. The other three properties of Byzantine consistent broadcast are easily verified in the same way.

Performance. The "Signed Echo Broadcast" algorithm involves three communication steps to deliver a message m from the sender to all processes, which is one more than the "Authenticated Echo Broadcast" algorithm uses. But, the number of messages sent over the point-to-point links is only $O(N)$ instead of $O(N^2)$.

3.11 Byzantine Reliable Broadcast

This section presents the second broadcast primitive in the fail-arbitrary system model, called *Byzantine reliable broadcast*. An instance of the primitive only deals with broadcasting one message. It can be seen as the fail-arbitrary equivalent of the reliable broadcast abstraction defined in Sect. 3.3 for crash-stop processes, when the latter is restricted to one message. Implementing this primitive in a fail-arbitrary system model with N processes requires that $N > 3f$.

3.11.1 Specification

The Byzantine consistent broadcast primitive introduced in the previous section does not ensure agreement in the sense that a correct process delivers a message if and only if every other correct process delivers a message. The *Byzantine reliable broadcast* abstraction introduced here adds this guarantee by extending Byzantine consistent broadcast with a *totality* property. The resulting specification is given in Module 3.12. The interface of Byzantine reliable broadcast and its other properties are the same as in Module 3.11.

Module 3.12: Interface and properties of Byzantine reliable broadcast

Module:

    Name: ByzantineReliableBroadcast, **instance** *brb*, with sender *s*.

Events:

    Request: ⟨ *brb, Broadcast* | *m* ⟩: Broadcasts a message *m* to all processes. Executed only by process *s*.

    Indication: ⟨ *brb, Deliver* | *p, m* ⟩: Delivers a message *m* broadcast by process *p*.

Properties:

    BRB1–BRB4: Same as properties BCB1–BCB4 in Byzantine consistent broadcast (Module 3.11).

    BRB5: *Totality:* If some message is delivered by any correct process, every correct process eventually delivers a message.

Combining the *consistency* property (BRB4) and the *totality* property (BRB5) into one yields an *agreement* property for a Byzantine broadcast primitive. It requires exactly the same as the *agreement* property (RB4) of a (regular) reliable broadcast abstraction.

3.11.2 Fail-Arbitrary Algorithm: Authenticated Double-Echo Broadcast

Not surprisingly, an algorithm implementing Byzantine reliable broadcast requires more steps than an algorithm for Byzantine consistent broadcast. The "Authenticated Double-Echo Broadcast" algorithm presented here is a direct extension of the "Authenticated Echo Broadcast" algorithm that implements Byzantine consistent broadcast; the pseudo code is shown in Algorithm 3.18.

Algorithm 3.18: Authenticated Double-Echo Broadcast

Implements:
    ByzantineReliableBroadcast, **instance** *brb*, with sender *s*.

Uses:
    AuthPerfectPointToPointLinks, **instance** *al*.

upon event ⟨ *brb, Init* ⟩ **do**
    sentecho := FALSE;
    sentready := FALSE;
    delivered := FALSE;
    echos := $[\bot]^N$;
    readys := $[\bot]^N$;

upon event ⟨ *brb, Broadcast* | *m* ⟩ **do**   // only process *s*
    forall *q* ∈ *Π* **do**
        trigger ⟨ *al, Send* | *q*, [SEND, *m*] ⟩;

upon event ⟨ *al, Deliver* | *p*, [SEND, *m*] ⟩ **such that** *p* = *s* **and** *sentecho* = FALSE **do**
    sentecho := TRUE;
    forall *q* ∈ *Π* **do**
        trigger ⟨ *al, Send* | *q*, [ECHO, *m*] ⟩;

upon event ⟨ *al, Deliver* | *p*, [ECHO, *m*] ⟩ **do**
    if *echos*[*p*] = ⊥ **then**
        echos[*p*] := *m*;

upon exists *m* ≠ ⊥ such that $\#(\{p \in \Pi \mid echos[p] = m\}) > \frac{N+f}{2}$
            and *sentready* = FALSE **do**
    sentready := TRUE;
    forall *q* ∈ *Π* **do**
        trigger ⟨ *al, Send* | *q*, [READY, *m*] ⟩;

upon event ⟨ *al, Deliver* | *p*, [READY, *m*] ⟩ **do**
    if *readys*[*p*] = ⊥ **then**
        readys[*p*] := *m*;

upon exists *m* ≠ ⊥ such that $\#(\{p \in \Pi \mid readys[p] = m\}) > f$
            and *sentready* = FALSE **do**
    sentready := TRUE;
    forall *q* ∈ *Π* **do**
        trigger ⟨ *al, Send* | *q*, [READY, *m*] ⟩;

upon exists *m* ≠ ⊥ such that $\#(\{p \in \Pi \mid readys[p] = m\}) > 2f$
            and *delivered* = FALSE **do**
    delivered := TRUE;
    trigger ⟨ *brb, Deliver* | *s, m* ⟩;

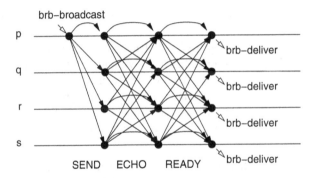

Figure 3.13: Failure-free execution of authenticated double-echo broadcast

The algorithm starts in the same way as "Authenticated Echo Broadcast" and adds a second round of "echoing," as its name already reveals. More precisely, the sender first disseminates a message to all processes. Every process echoes the message to all after receiving it from the sender. When a process has received a Byzantine quorum of such echoes, it sends a READY message to all processes that indicates its willingness to *brb*-deliver the message, given that enough other processes are also willing. Once a process receives a total of $2f + 1$ such indications in READY messages, it actually *brb*-delivers the message.

The algorithm contains one more mechanism: when a process receives only $f + 1$ READY messages but has not sent a READY message yet, it also sends a READY message. This step implements an amplification of the READY messages and is crucial for the *totality* property.

Figure 3.13 shows a failure-free execution of "Authenticated Double-Echo Broadcast" with a correct sender p. All processes *brb*-deliver the same message.

To see how the amplification step works, consider again the example execution of the "Authenticated Echo Broadcast" algorithm from Sect. 3.10.3. Suppose that process p is the only correct process that *al*-sends a READY message containing m, but correct process r somehow *bcr*-delivers m in the "Authenticated Double-Echo Broadcast" algorithm. As r must have received three READY messages with m, at least process p and one other correct process must have *al*-sent a READY message with m. These two processes are correct, thus, their READY messages are also *al*-delivered by the third correct process, which then *al*-sends a READY message according to the amplification step. Consequently, every correct process *bcr*-delivers m because three correct processes have sent a READY message containing m.

Correctness. Algorithm 3.18 implements a Byzantine reliable broadcast abstraction whenever $N > 3f$. The *validity*, *no duplication*, and *integrity* properties follow from the same arguments as in "Authenticated Echo Broadcast" (Algorithm 3.16).

For arguing about the *consistency* property, note that the *consistency* property of Algorithm 3.16 implies that if some of the correct processes *al*-send a READY message, they all do that with same contained message m. It is not possible that the faulty processes introduce enough READY messages with a content different from m.

Finally, the amplification step from $f + 1$ to $2f + 1$ READY messages ensures the *totality* property, as the example has already indicated. If some correct process *bcr*-delivers some m, then at least $f + 1$ correct processes must have *al*-sent a READY message containing m. As these processes are correct, every correct process eventually *al*-sends a READY message with m by the amplification step or after receiving enough ECHO messages. In either case, every correct process eventually *bcr*-delivers m.

Performance. The algorithm incurs three communication steps, and two of them are all-to-all message exchanges. In total, it uses $O(N^2)$ point-to-point messages for broadcasting one message. Note that the algorithm uses only the authenticated links abstraction that can be implemented with a MAC, but no computationally expensive digital signatures.

3.12 Byzantine Broadcast Channels

The broadcast abstractions for the fail-arbitrary model introduced in the previous sections only deliver at most one message. On the other hand, the broadcast abstractions for crash-stop processes considered earlier support an arbitrary number of messages. The abstraction of *Byzantine broadcast channels* introduced next also delivers multiple messages and provides an equivalent to the reliable broadcast abstractions for crash-stop processes.

3.12.1 Specifications

A Byzantine broadcast channel allows every process to broadcast messages by triggering ⟨ *Broadcast* ⟩ events. Like its equivalent for crash-stop processes, the abstraction supplies the name of the sender process p together with every delivered message. In addition to that, it also outputs a *label* ℓ that an application may use to distinguish multiple roles that a message may play. We say that the channel *delivers* a message m when it generates a ⟨ *Deliver* | p, ℓ, m ⟩ event. The label is an arbitrary bit string that can be determined by the implementation, under the only condition that the labels of all messages delivered on a channel for a particular sender are unique. One can think of it as a per-sender sequence number.

We introduce two forms of Byzantine broadcast channels, a *Byzantine consistent (broadcast) channel* and a *Byzantine reliable (broadcast) channel*, corresponding to the consistent and reliable variations of single-message Byzantine broadcast primitives. They are defined in Modules 3.13 and 3.14, respectively.

The properties in these two modules are extensions of the conditions for (single-message) Byzantine consistent broadcast and Byzantine reliable broadcast, respectively (Modules 3.11 and 3.12). In particular, the *validity* properties (BCCH1 and BRCH1) are the same, and the *no duplication*, *integrity*, and *consistency* properties

---

Module 3.13: Interface and properties of Byzantine consistent channel

Module:

    Name: ByzantineConsistentBroadcastChannel, **instance** *bcch*.

Events:

    Request: $\langle$ *bcch, Broadcast* $\mid m$ $\rangle$: Broadcasts a message m to all processes.

    Indication: $\langle$ *bcch, Deliver* $\mid p, \ell, m$ $\rangle$: Delivers a message m with label ℓ broadcast by process p.

Properties:

    BCCH1: *Validity:* If a correct process p broadcasts a message m, then every correct process eventually delivers m.

    BCCH2: *No duplication:* For every process p and label ℓ, every correct process delivers at most one message with label ℓ and sender p.

    BCCH3: *Integrity:* If some correct process delivers a message m with sender p and process p is correct, then m was previously broadcast by p.

    BCCH4: *Consistency:* If some correct process delivers a message m with label ℓ and sender s, and another correct process delivers a message m' with label ℓ and sender s, then $m = m'$.

Module 3.14: Interface and properties of Byzantine reliable channel

Module:

    Name: ByzantineReliableBroadcastChannel, **instance** *brch*.

Events:

    Request: $\langle$ *brch, Broadcast* $\mid m$ $\rangle$: Broadcasts a message m to all processes.

    Indication: $\langle$ *brch, Deliver* $\mid p, \ell, m$ $\rangle$: Delivers a message m with label ℓ broadcast by process p.

Properties:

    BRCH1–BRCH3: Same as properties BCCH1–BCCH3 of Byzantine consistent channel (Module 3.13).

    BRCH4: *Agreement:* If some correct process delivers a message m with label ℓ and sender s, then every correct process eventually delivers message m with label ℓ and sender s.

(BCCH2–BCCH4) of a Byzantine consistent channel require the same for every particular label as the corresponding properties of the single-message abstraction (BCB2–BCB4). The same applies to the *no duplication* and *integrity* properties (BRCH2 and BRCH3) of a Byzantine reliable channel, and its *agreement* property

(BRCH4) combines the *consistency* and *totality* properties of the single-message abstraction (BRB4 and BRB5).

3.12.2 Fail-Arbitrary Algorithm: Byzantine Consistent Channel

Implementing a Byzantine broadcast channel is straightforward, given the corresponding Byzantine broadcast primitive. Algorithm 3.19, called "Byzantine Consistent Channel," invokes a sequence of broadcast primitives for every sender such that exactly one is active at every instant. Recall that our module abstractions can exist in multiple instances, which may also be initialized dynamically by an algorithm. Algorithm 3.19 exploits that: it maintains a sequence number for every sender and creates a sequence of instances of the Byzantine broadcast primitive for every sender, identified by the sender and by the sequence number. As soon as a broadcast primitive instance delivers a message, the algorithm advances the sequence number and initializes the next instance.

This algorithm ignores the issue of cleaning up the used broadcast primitive instances; this matters in practice and actual implementations have to take care of this.

Correctness. It is easy to see that Algorithm 3.19 is correct because most of its properties follow directly from the properties of the underlying Byzantine consistent broadcast primitives. Using per-sender sequence numbers ensures the *no duplication consistency* properties for every sender and every label.

Algorithm 3.19: Byzantine Consistent Channel

Implements:
> ByzantineConsistentBroadcastChannel, **instance** *bcch*.

Uses:
> ByzantineConsistentBroadcast (multiple instances).

upon event ⟨ *bcch, Init* ⟩ **do**
> $n := [0]^N$;
> *ready* := TRUE;
> **forall** $p \in \Pi$ **do**
>> Initialize a new instance *bcb.p.n[p]* of ByzantineConsistentBroadcast
>> with sender p;

upon event ⟨ *bcch, Broadcast* | m ⟩ **such that** *ready* = TRUE **do**
> **trigger** ⟨ *bcb.self.n[self], Broadcast* | m ⟩;
> *ready* := FALSE;

upon event ⟨ *bcb.p.n[p], Deliver* | p, m ⟩ **do**
> **trigger** ⟨ *bcch, Deliver* | $p, n[p], m$ ⟩;
> $n[p] := n[p] + 1$;
> Initialize a new instance *bcb.p.n[p]* of ByzantineConsistentBroadcast with sender p;
> **if** $p = self$ **then**
>> *ready* := TRUE;

3.12.3 Fail-Arbitrary Algorithm: Byzantine Reliable Channel

Algorithm 3.20, called "Byzantine Reliable Channel," implements a Byzantine reliable channel abstraction with the same approach as Algorithm 3.19, simply by replacing Byzantine consistent broadcast with Byzantine reliable broadcast.

Algorithm 3.20: Byzantine Reliable Channel

Implements:
    ByzantineReliableBroadcastChannel, **instance** *brch.*

Uses:
    ByzantineReliableBroadcast (multiple instances).

// The algorithm is the same as Algorithm 3.19, with the only difference that it uses
// instances of ByzantineReliableBroadcast and not ByzantineConsistentBroadcast.

3.13 Exercises

Exercise 3.1: *Consider a process p that rb-broadcasts a message m in the "Lazy Reliable Broadcast" algorithm (Algorithm 3.2). Does the algorithm allow that p rb-delivers m before beb-broadcasting it? If not, modify the algorithm such that it is possible.*

Exercise 3.2: *Modify the "Lazy Reliable Broadcast" algorithm (Algorithm 3.2) to reduce the number of messages sent in case of failures, by assuming that some node(s) fail less often than others.*

Exercise 3.3: *Some of the algorithms given in this chapter have the processes continuously fill their different message buffers without emptying them. Modify them to remove unnecessary messages from the following variables:*

1. *variable from[p] in the "Lazy Reliable Broadcast" algorithm (Algorithm 3.2);*
2. *variable delivered in all reliable broadcast algorithms;*
3. *variable pending in the "All-Ack Uniform Reliable Broadcast" algorithm (Algorithm 3.4).*

Exercise 3.4: *What do we gain if we replace the underlying best-effort broadcast primitive with a reliable broadcast primitive in the "Majority-Ack Uniform Reliable Broadcast" algorithm (Algorithm 3.5)?*

Exercise 3.5: *Consider the "All-Ack Uniform Reliable Broadcast" algorithm (Algorithm 3.4). What happens if the* strong accuracy *property of the perfect failure detector is violated? What if its* strong completeness *property is violated?*

Exercise 3.6: *The "All-Ack Uniform Reliable Broadcast" algorithm in the fail-stop model (Algorithm 3.4) can be viewed as an extension of the "Eager Reliable Broadcast" algorithm (Algorithm 3.3). Would we gain anything by devising a uniform reliable broadcast algorithm that is an extension of the "Lazy Reliable Broadcast" algorithm (Algorithm 3.2), i.e., can we have the processes not relay messages unless they suspect the sender?*

Exercise 3.7: *Can we devise a uniform reliable broadcast algorithm with an eventually perfect failure detector but without assuming a majority of correct processes?*

Exercise 3.8: *The "All-Ack Uniform Reliable Broadcast" (Algorithm 3.4) and the "Majority-Ack Uniform Reliable Broadcast" (Algorithm 3.5) require a process to receive an acknowledgment from all nonfaulty or from a majority of the processes, respectively, before they can deliver a message. The acknowledgment is needed because when a process invokes the underlying best-effort broadcast and then crashes, all components of the process are affected and stop (including the best-effort broadcast module and any further underlying modules, such as the modules that may implement perfect links). The unit of failure is a process, as discussed in Sect. 2.2.*

For this exercise only, consider an idealized *and nonrealistic system model, where some component may invoke infallible lower-level components. In this model, the unit of failure is not a process but a module. Describe an implementation of uniform reliable broadcast that uses an* infallible *perfect point-to-point links abstraction in this idealized model.*

Exercise 3.9: *Give the specification of a logged reliable broadcast abstraction in the* fail-recovery *model (i.e., a weaker variant of Module 3.6) and an algorithm that implements it (i.e., a simpler variant of "Logged Majority-Ack Uniform Reliable Broadcast," Algorithm 3.8).*

Exercise 3.10: *The "Eager Probabilistic Broadcast" algorithm (Algorithm 3.9) assumes that the connectivity is the same among every pair of processes. In practice, it may happen that some processes are at shorter distances from each other and connected by more reliable links than others. For instance, the underlying network topology could be a set of local-area networks connected by long-haul links. Propose methods to exploit the topology in gossip algorithms.*

Exercise 3.11: *Compare the* causal delivery *property of Module 3.9 with the following property: "If a process delivers messages m_1 and m_2, and $m_1 \rightarrow m_2$, then the process must deliver m_1 before m_2."*

Exercise 3.12: *Can we devise a best-effort broadcast algorithm that satisfies the* causal delivery *property without being a causal broadcast algorithm, i.e., without satisfying the* agreement *property of a reliable broadcast?*

Exercise 3.13: *Can we devise a broadcast algorithm that does not ensure the* causal delivery *property but only its nonuniform variant: "no correct process p delivers a message m_2 unless p has already delivered every message m_1 such that $m_1 \rightarrow m_2$?"*

Exercise 3.14: *Suggest a modification of the garbage collection scheme for causal broadcast to collect messages sooner than in the "Garbage-Collection of Causal Past" algorithm (Algorithm 3.14).*

Exercise 3.15: *Design a "no-waiting" algorithm for causal broadcast, in which the transmitted messages do not grow as large as in the "No-Waiting Causal Broadcast" algorithm (Algorithm 3.13), by using a FIFO-order broadcast abstraction.*

Exercise 3.16: *The Byzantine consistent broadcast abstraction has been implemented twice: first, by Algorithm 3.16 "Authenticated Echo Broadcast" with $O(N^2)$ messages and using authenticated point-to-point links and an underlying MAC and second, by Algorithm 3.17 "Signed Echo Broadcast" with $O(N)$ messages and using a digital signature scheme. Construct an algorithm for Byzantine consistent broadcast that needs only $O(N)$ messages and relies on a MAC, but not on digital signatures. It should only assume that $N > 5f$. What is its performance?*

Exercise 3.17: *Recall that communication size measures the lengths of all messages communicated by an algorithm. Compare the communication sizes of the three Byzantine broadcast algorithms (Algorithms 3.16–3.18).*

3.14 Solutions

Solution 3.1: In the "Lazy Reliable Broadcast" algorithm also the sender process *beb*-broadcasts a message and subsequently *beb*-delivers the message before *rb*-delivering it. The following simple modification changes this. Let a process *rb*-deliver the messages as soon as it *rb*-broadcasts it, and make sure it adds the *rb*-delivered message to the *delivered* set. The necessary change to the "Lazy Reliable Broadcast" algorithm is shown in Algorithm 3.21.

Algorithm 3.21: Simple Optimization of Lazy Reliable Broadcast

---

upon event ⟨ *rb, Broadcast* | *m* ⟩ **do**
    delivered := *delivered* ∪ {*m*};
    trigger ⟨ *rb, Deliver* | *self, m* ⟩;
    trigger ⟨ *beb, Broadcast* | [DATA, *self, m*] ⟩;

Solution 3.2: In the "Lazy Reliable Broadcast" algorithm, if a process p *rb*-broadcasts a message and then crashes, $O(N^2)$ messages are relayed by the remaining processes to retransmit the message of process p. This is because a process that *beb*-delivers the message of p does not know whether the other processes have *beb*-delivered this message or not. However, it would be sufficient in this case if only one process relays the message of p.

To reduce the number of messages, one may rely on a specific process, called the leader process ℓ, which does not fail often and is more likely to *beb*-deliver messages. The links to and from this process are usually fast and very reliable, and the process runs on a reliable computer. A process p then forwards its messages to the leader ℓ, which coordinates the broadcast to every other process. If the leader is correct, every process will eventually *beb*-deliver and *rb*-deliver every message. Otherwise, the algorithm reverts to the previous approach, and every process is responsible for *beb*-broadcasting the messages that it *beb*-delivered.

Solution 3.3: We discuss each of the three message-buffer variables in the following.

1. Consider the variable *from*[p] in the "Lazy Reliable Broadcast" algorithm. The array *from* is used exclusively to store messages that are retransmitted in the case that their sender has failed. Such messages can be removed as soon as they have been retransmitted once. If the process q that retransmits them is correct, they will eventually be *beb*-delivered. Otherwise, if q is faulty, it does not matter that the other processes might not *beb*-deliver them.

2. Consider the variable *delivered* in all reliable broadcast algorithms. Messages cannot be removed from it. If a process crashes and its messages are retransmitted by two different processes then a process might *rb*-deliver the same message twice if it empties the *delivered* buffer in the meantime. This would violate the *no duplication* property.

   On the other hand, in practice the contents of *delivered* may be represented in a more compact form if the sender assigns a local sequence number to all messages that it *rb*-broadcasts, and every receiver additionally stores, for every sender *s*, a maximal contiguous sequence number *max[s]*, computed as follows. The receiver inspects the sequence number of any message that it *rb*-delivers from *s*. Once that all messages from *s* with a sequence number smaller than some bound *b* have been *rb*-delivered, the process sets *max[s]* to *b* and purges all messages sent by *s* with lower sequence numbers from *delivered*.

3. Consider the variable *pending* in the "All-Ack Uniform Reliable" broadcast algorithm. Messages can actually be removed from it as soon as they have been *urb*-delivered.

Solution 3.4: We gain nothing, because the "Majority-Ack Uniform Reliable Broadcast" algorithm does not assume and, hence, never uses the *agreement* property that is guaranteed by the reliable broadcast primitive.

Consider the following scenario, which illustrates the difference between using best-effort broadcast and using reliable broadcast. A process *p* *urb*-broadcasts a message and crashes. Suppose only one correct process *q* *beb*-delivers the message. With a reliable broadcast primitive instead, all correct processes would deliver the message. In the uniform reliable broadcast algorithm, *q* adds the message to its variable *pending* and then *beb*-broadcasts it. Since *q* is correct, all correct processes will deliver it, and thus, we have at least the same guarantee as if the original transmission used a reliable broadcast primitive.

Solution 3.5: Consider a system of three processes: *p*, *q*, and *r*. Suppose that *p* *urb*-broadcasts a message *m*. If *strong completeness* is not satisfied then *p* might never *urb*-deliver *m* if either of *q* and *r* crashes and *p* never detects their crash or *beb*-delivers *m* from them. Process *p* might wait indefinitely for them to relay *m* and the algorithm may violate the *validity* property.

Assume now that *strong accuracy* is violated and *p* falsely suspects *q* and *r* to have crashed. Process *p* eventually *urb*-delivers *m*. Assume that *p* crashes afterward. It might be the case that *q* and *r* have never *beb*-delivered *m* and have no way of knowing about *m*. Hence, they will not *urb*-deliver *m*, violating the *uniform agreement* property.

Solution 3.6: The advantage of the lazy scheme is that processes do not need to relay messages to ensure *agreement* if they do not suspect the sender to have crashed. In a failure-free scenario, only *N* messages are needed for all the processes to deliver a message. In the case of uniform reliable broadcast (without a majority), a process can only deliver a message when it knows that all correct processes have seen that message. Hence, the process needs some confirmation from all other processes that they have seen the message. A lazy scheme would be of no benefit here.

Solution 3.7: No, a majority of correct processes is necessary. We explain why this is the case, using a system of four processes $\{p, q, r, s\}$ by giving a so-called *partitioning* argument. Suppose it could indeed be implemented in this system when two out of the four processes may fail.

Consider an execution where process p *urb*-broadcasts a message m and assume that r and s crash in that execution without receiving any message either from p or from q. Because of the *validity* property of uniform reliable broadcast, there must be a time t at which p *urb*-delivers message m.

Consider now an execution that is similar to this one except that p and q crash right after time t, but r and s are correct. However, r and s have been falsely suspected by the failure detector at p and q, which is possible because the failure detector is only eventually perfect. In this execution, p has *urb*-delivered a message m whereas r and s have no way of knowing about the existence of m and they never *urb*-deliver it. This violates the *uniform agreement* property and shows that a majority of correct processes is necessary.

Solution 3.8: Suppose an "IdealPerfectPointToPointLinks" module is available in this idealized system model. The solution, shown in Algorithm 3.22, is almost the same as the "Eager Reliable Broadcast" (Algorithm 3.3), which implements only (regular) reliable broadcast. The sender sends the broadcast message to itself over the ideal perfect links; upon delivering a message m over the ideal perfect links that has not been delivered yet, it resends m to all processes and *urb*-delivers it.

Algorithm 3.22: Ideal Uniform Reliable Broadcast

Implements:
    ReliableBroadcast, **instance** *rb*.

Uses:
    IdealPerfectPointToPointLinks, **instance** *idealpl*.

upon event ⟨ *urb, Init* ⟩ **do**
    delivered := ∅;

upon event ⟨ *urb, Broadcast* | *m* ⟩ **do**
    trigger ⟨ *idealpl, Send* | *self*, [DATA, *self*, *m*] ⟩;

upon event ⟨ *idealpl, Deliver* | *p*, [DATA, *s*, *m*] ⟩ **do**
    if *m* ∉ *delivered* **then**
        delivered := *delivered* ∪ {*m*};
        forall *q* ∈ *Π* **do**
            trigger ⟨ *idealpl, Send* | *q*, [DATA, *s*, *m*] ⟩;
        trigger ⟨ *urb, Deliver* | *s*, *m* ⟩;

The *uniform agreement* property holds because every process sends m with the infallible point-to-point links primitive *before* it *urb*-delivers m. The infallible underlying module does not crash in this idealized model. If a process crashes, only the broadcast module crashes. Any *urb*-delivered message will never be forgotten by the ideal link module and will consequently be *urb*-delivered by every correct process.

Solution 3.9: Module 3.15 defines a logged reliable broadcast abstraction. In this variant, if a correct process log-delivers a message (i.e., stores the variable *delivered* with the message in it), all correct processes should eventually log-deliver that message. The only difference to Module 3.6 lies in the restriction of the fourth property (*agreement*) so that it needs to hold only for *correct* processes.

Module 3.15: Interface and properties of logged reliable broadcast

Module:

    Name: LoggedReliableBroadcast, **instance** *lrb*.

Events:

    Request: ⟨ *lrb, Broadcast* | m ⟩: Broadcasts a message m to all processes.

    Indication: ⟨ *lrb, Deliver* | *delivered* ⟩: Notifies the upper layer of potential updates to variable *delivered* in stable storage (which log-delivers messages according to the text).

Properties:

    LRB1–LRB3: Same as properties LBEB1–LBEB3 in logged best-effort broadcast (Module 3.5).

    LRB4: *Agreement:* If a message m is log-delivered by some correct process, then m is eventually log-delivered by every correct process.

Algorithm 3.23 implements logged reliable broadcast using an instance *sbeb* of stubborn best-effort broadcast. To broadcast a message, a process simply *sbeb*-broadcasts it; recall that this transmits the message to all processes over stubborn links. When a message is *sbeb*-delivered for the first time, it is *lrb*-delivered and *sbeb*-broadcast again to all processes. Upon recovery, a process retrieves the messages it has *lrb*-delivered and sends them to all other processes using stubborn best-effort broadcast.

Correctness. Consider the *agreement* property and assume some correct process p *lrb*-delivers a message m. If it does not crash then p *sbeb*-broadcasts the message and all correct processes will *sbeb*-deliver the message, based on the properties of the stubborn best-effort broadcast. If process p crashes, there is a time after which p recovers and does not crash again, such that it retrieves m and *sbeb*-broadcasts m to all processes. Again, all correct processes will *sbeb*-deliver the message based on the properties of the stubborn best-effort broadcast. The *validity* property follows

---

Algorithm 3.23: Logged Eager Reliable Broadcast

Implements:
    ReliableBroadcast, **instance** *lrb*.

Uses:
    StubbornBestEffortBroadcast, **instance** *sbeb*.

upon event ⟨ *lrb, Init* ⟩ **do**
    delivered := ∅;
    store(*delivered*);

upon event ⟨ *lrb, Recovery* ⟩ **do**
    retrieve(*delivered*);
    trigger ⟨ *lrb, Deliver | delivered* ⟩;
    forall $(s, m) \in delivered$ **do**
        trigger ⟨ *sbeb, Broadcast* | [DATA, s, m] ⟩;

upon event ⟨ *lrb, Broadcast | m* ⟩ **do**
    trigger ⟨ *sbeb, Broadcast* | [DATA, *self*, m] ⟩;

upon event ⟨ *sbeb, Deliver | p*, [DATA, s, m] ⟩ **do**
    if $m \notin delivered$ **then**
        delivered := *delivered* ∪ {m};
        store(*delivered*);
        trigger ⟨ *lrb, Deliver | delivered* ⟩;
        trigger ⟨ *sbeb, Broadcast* | [DATA, s, m] ⟩;

---

directly from the stubborn best-effort broadcast. The *no duplication* property is trivially ensured by the algorithm, whereas the *no creation* property is ensured by the underlying broadcast abstraction.

Performance. Let m be any message that is *lrb*-broadcast by some process p. All processes *lrb*-deliver m after one communication step. (If the stubborn link from p to p short-cuts the network then p *lrb*-delivers m immediately, without any communication step.)

Solution 3.10: One approach consists in assigning weights to the links connecting processes. Weights reflect the reliability of the links. We could easily adapt our algorithm to avoid excessive redundant transmission by gossiping through more reliable links with lower probability. An alternative approach consists in organizing the nodes in a hierarchy that reflects the network topology in order to reduce the traffic across domain boundaries.

Solution 3.11: We need to compare the two following properties:

1. If a process delivers a message m_2 then it must have delivered every message m_1 such that $m_1 \rightarrow m_2$ (Module 3.9).
2. If a process delivers messages m_1 and m_2, and $m_1 \rightarrow m_2$, then the process must deliver m_1 before m_2 (Exercise 3.11).

Property 1 says that *any* message m_1 that causally precedes m_2 must be delivered before m_2 if m_2 is delivered. Property 2 says that *any delivered* message m_1 that causally precedes m_2 must only be delivered before m_2 if m_2 is delivered.

Both properties are safety properties. In the first case, a process that delivers a message m without having delivered a message that causally precedes m violates the property and this is irremediable. In the second case, a process that delivers both messages without respecting the causal precedence might violate the property and this is also irremediable. The first property is, however, strictly stronger than the second one. If the first property is satisfied then the second one is. However, it can be the case that the second property is satisfied whereas the first one is not: a process delivers a message m_2 without ever delivering a message m_1 that causally precedes m_1 (for instance, if m_1 never reaches the process). Thus, the second property does not satisfy the potential causality relation.

Solution 3.12: The answer is no. Assume by contradiction that some broadcast algorithm ensures the *causal delivery* property and is not reliable but best-effort; define an instance *co* of the corresponding abstraction, where processes *co*-broadcast and *co*-deliver messages.

The only possibility for an algorithm to ensure the properties of best-effort broadcast but not those of reliable broadcast is to violate the *agreement* property: there must be some execution of the algorithm where some correct process p *co*-delivers a message m that some other process q does not ever *co*-deliver. Because the algorithm is best-effort, this can only happen if the process s that *co*-broadcasts the message is faulty.

Assume now that after *co*-delivering m, process p *co*-broadcasts a message m'. Given that p is correct and that the broadcast is best-effort, all correct processes, including q, will *co*-deliver m'. Given that m precedes m' in causal order, q must have *co*-delivered m as well, a contradiction. Hence, any best-effort broadcast that satisfies the *causal delivery* property satisfies *agreement* and is, thus, also a reliable broadcast.

Solution 3.13: The answer is no. Assume by contradiction that some algorithm does not ensure the *causal delivery* property but ensures its nonuniform variant. This means that the algorithm has some execution where some process p delivers some message m without delivering a message m' that causally precedes m. Given that we assume a model where processes do not self-destruct, p might very well be correct, in which case it violates even the nonuniform variant.

Solution 3.14: When removing a message m from the variable *past*, we can also remove all the messages that causally precede this message, and then recursively those that causally precede these. This means that a message stored in *past* must be stored with its own, distinct "past." This idea is similar to the approach taken by the algorithm of Exercise 3.15, but the resulting algorithm is still different from Algorithm 3.24 described there.

Solution 3.15: Algorithm 3.24, called "No-Waiting Causal Broadcast using FIFO Broadcast," implements causal-order broadcast with shorter messages than Algorithm 3.13. The idea is that, instead of adding the complete causal past to every message that is disseminated, it only adds the causal past collected since the last disseminated message and uses FIFO-order reliable broadcast to disseminate them.

The algorithm also maintains a list of messages that have been *crb*-delivered in a variable *list*. But in contrast to the variable *past* of Algorithm 3.13, *list* does not grow forever and is reset to the empty list every time when a message m is *crb*-broadcast. To simplify the notation, the algorithm appends also m to *list* and then *frb*-broadcasts only *list*. When a process receives such a list through *frb*-delivery, it inspects the list from the start to the end and *crb*-delivers every message that it has not yet *crb*-delivered (which is at least m, at the end of the list).

Because the variable *list* that maintains the causal past of a message is reset after every *crb*-broadcast message, the algorithm uses considerably shorter messages than Algorithm 3.13 in long runs. However, its *causal delivery* property only holds because the underlying reliable broadcast abstraction provides *FIFO delivery*.

Algorithm 3.24: No-Waiting Causal Broadcast using FIFO Broadcast

---

Implements:
    CausalOrderReliableBroadcast, **instance** *crb*.

Uses:
    FIFOReliableBroadcast, **instance** *frb*.

upon event ⟨ *crb, Init* ⟩ **do**
    delivered := ∅;
    list := [];

upon event ⟨ *crb, Broadcast* | m ⟩ **do**
    append(*list*, (*self*, m));
    trigger ⟨ *frb, Broadcast* | [DATA, *list*] ⟩;
    list := [];

upon event ⟨ *frb, Deliver* | p, [DATA, *mlist*] ⟩ **do**
    forall $(s, n) \in$ *mlist* **do**   // by the order in the list
        if $n \notin$ *delivered* **then**
            trigger ⟨ *crb, Deliver* | s, n ⟩;
            delivered := *delivered* ∪ {n};
            if $(s, n) \notin$ *list* **then**
                append(*list*, (s, n));

Solution 3.16: The solution uses the same communication pattern as the "Signed Echo Broadcast" algorithm, in order to retain its total cost of $O(N)$ messages. But, every signature from a process is replaced by a vector of MACs, one for every other process. More precisely, whenever a process p is asked to issue a signature σ on a bit string x, then it actually uses the MAC and calls *authenticate*(p, q, x) for every process $q \in \Pi$, saves the returned authenticators in an array μ, and uses μ instead of σ. Furthermore, whenever a process q is asked to verify a signature σ on some x, then q accesses its authenticator $\mu[q]$ in the vector of MACs and calls *verifyauth*$(p, q, x, \mu[q])$ instead. After this change, the algorithm still uses the same messages, but the ECHO and FINAL messages grow in length proportional to N. Hence, the communication size of the algorithm grows by a factor of N.

The only difference between a signature and such a vector of MACs occurs for authentication values generated by a Byzantine process: with digital signatures, every correct process computes the validity in the same way and either accepts a signature or not; but with a MAC vector μ generated by an arbitrary-faulty process, some correct process may consider μ to be valid, and for another correct process, the verification of μ may fail.

This drawback affects the liveness of the modified "Signed Echo Broadcast" algorithm. With the stronger assumption of $N > 5f$, however, this issue has no consequences. Specifically, it may be that a correct sender s sends a FINAL message with more than $(N + f)/2$ authenticator vectors that are valid for s, but some of these (up to f) turn out to be invalid at another correct process q. Hence, q would not deliver the message and violate *validity*. To cope with this case, the sender receives $N - f$ properly authenticated ECHO messages and relays them to all processes in the final step. Every process still accepts the FINAL message when it contains more than $(N + f)/2$ valid authenticators and delivers its content.

This modified algorithm satisfies the *validity* property because a correct sender has verified $N - f$ authenticators, of which at least $N - 2f$ must be from correct processes. Hence, every other correct process obtains

$$N - 2f > \frac{N + f}{2}$$

valid authenticators as well. The *consistency* property still follows from the same argument as with the original "Signed Echo Broadcast," because it only refers to authenticators computed by correct processes.

Solution 3.17: In Algorithm 3.16, every message sent via the authenticated perfect links essentially contains only the input message m. Therefore, the algorithm communicates a total of $O(N^2|m|)$ bits, where $|m|$ denotes the length of m.

Algorithm 3.17 uses more communication steps but fewer messages overall than Algorithm 3.16, namely only $O(N)$ messages. But as the FINAL message contains $O(N)$ signatures, its total communication size is $O(N|m| + N^2k)$ bits, where k denotes the length of a digital signature. This is comparable to Algorithm 3.16.

The total communication size of Algorithm 3.18 for broadcasting a message m is $O(N^2|m|)$ bits. All three algorithms require quadratic communication size in N.

3.15 Chapter Notes

- Requirements for a reliable broadcast communication abstraction can already be found in the work on SIFT (Wensley et al. 1978). An early work that formalizes a reliable broadcast abstraction and implements it in the fail-stop model was presented by Schneider, Gries, and Schlichting (1984).
- The use of reliable broadcast for distributed programming was popularized by the ISIS system (Birman and Joseph 1987), which was used in a variety of commercial applications.
- The ISIS system also included a causal broadcast abstraction, following the notion of causality initially introduced by Lamport (1978). Our "No-Waiting Causal Broadcast" algorithm was inspired by one of the earliest implementations of causal broadcast included in ISIS. The "Waiting Causal Broadcast" algorithm is based on the notion of vector clocks, which were introduced around 1988 (Fidge 1988; Ladin, Liskov, and Shrira 1990; Schwarz and Mattern 1994). The most detailed description of the algorithm to Our Knowledge, including a detailed proof of correctness, is given by Attiya and Welch (2004).
- The comprehensive survey of Hadzilacos and Toueg (1993) presents reliable broadcast, FIFO broadcast, and causal broadcast abstractions and corresponding implementations in a modular way. The algorithm in Exercise 3.15, which implements causal broadcast from FIFO broadcast, is based on this work.
- The problem of the uniformity of a reliable broadcast primitive was discussed by Hadzilacos (1984) and, then, further explored by Neiger and Toueg (1993).
- In this chapter, we presented algorithms that implement broadcast abstractions where all messages are broadcast to all processes in the system. So-called "multicast" abstractions have also been considered, where a message is only delivered to an arbitrary subset of the processes. This recipient group may be determined dynamically.

  It is also possible to ensure causal-order delivery for multicast abstractions, but such algorithms require a significantly larger amount of control information than those for global broadcast. These issues were addressed by Raynal, Schiper, and Toueg (1991).
- The idea of applying epidemic dissemination to implementing probabilistically reliable broadcast algorithms have been explored since 1992 (Golding and Long 1992; Birman et al. 1999). A precise specification of a probabilistic broadcast abstraction was suggested by Eugster, Guerraoui, and Kouznetsov (2004).

  Kermarrec, Massoulié, and Ganesh (2003) investigate trade-offs between the fanout and the reliability of the dissemination and give much a more detailed analysis of the probability of delivery than in the text.
- The topic of Exercise 3.10, to exploit topological features for probabilistic broadcast algorithms through a mechanism that assigns weights to links between processes, was proposed and discussed by Lin and Marzullo (1999). A similar idea, but using a hierarchy instead of weights, was proposed later to reduce the traffic across domain boundaries (Gupta, Kermarrec, and Ganesh 2006).

- The first probabilistic broadcast algorithm that did not depend on any global membership was given by Eugster et al. (2003). The idea has been refined since then (Voulgaris, Jelasity, and van Steen 2003; Jelasity, Guerraoui, Kermarrec, and van Steen 2004).

- The notion of message ages in probabilistic broadcast was introduced for purging messages and ensuring the scalability of process buffers by Kouznetsov, Guerraoui, Handurukande, and Kermarrec (2001). This approach was later refined to balance buffering among processes (Koldehofe 2003). Buffering was also discussed by Xiao, Birman, and van Renesse (2002). Techniques for flow control in probabilistic broadcast have also been developed, starting with the work of Rodrigues et al. (2003) and Garbinato, Pedone, and Schmidt (2004).

- Broadcast algorithms in the fail-arbitrary model have first been formulated as building blocks to implement Byzantine agreement. The Byzantine consistent broadcast abstraction is implicit in early papers on this topic (Toueg 1984; Bracha and Toueg 1985; Bracha 1987).

- Our "Authenticated Echo Broadcast" algorithm implementing Byzantine consistent broadcast was introduced by Srikanth and Toueg (1987). The idea behind our "Signed Echo Broadcast" algorithm can be traced back to the work of Dolev and Strong (1983); the presented algorithm was formulated as a broadcast primitive with digital signatures by Reiter (1994).

- The "Authenticated Double-Echo Broadcast" algorithm, which implements a Byzantine reliable broadcast abstraction, is attributed to Bracha (1987); previous versions of this algorithm have appeared as early as 1984. This algorithm is an important building block and has found many applications for implementing more complex tasks.

- The Byzantine broadcast channel abstraction and its implementations have been used in the SINTRA system (Cachin and Poritz 2002).

4. Shared Memory

> *I always tell the truth, even when I lie.*
> (Tony Montana – Scarface)

This chapter presents abstractions of shared memory. They represent distributed programming abstractions, which are shared among processes and encapsulate data storage functionality accessible by read and write operations. The memory abstractions are called *registers* because they resemble those provided by multiprocessor machines at the hardware level, though in many cases, including in this chapter, they are implemented over processes that communicate by exchanging messages over a network and do not share any physical storage device. A register abstraction also resembles a disk device accessed over a storage-area network, a file in a distributed file system, or a shared working space in a collaborative editing environment. Therefore, understanding how to implement register abstractions helps us understand how to implement such distributed storage systems.

We study here different variants of register abstractions. These differ in the number of processes that are allowed to read from and write to them, as well as in the semantics of their read operations in the face of concurrency and failures. We distinguish three kinds of semantics: *safe*, *regular*, and *atomic*.

We first consider the $(1, N)$ *regular* register abstraction. The notation $(1, N)$ means that one specific process can write and all N processes in the system can read. Then we consider the $(1, N)$ *atomic* register and the (N, N) atomic register abstractions. We specify and implement regular and atomic register abstractions in four of the distributed system models identified in Chap. 2: the fail-stop, fail-silent, fail-recovery, and fail-arbitrary models.

The $(1, N)$ *safe* register abstraction is the simplest one among the three; we skip it first and treat it only in the fail-arbitrary model toward the end of the chapter.

C. Cachin et al., *Introduction to Reliable and Secure Distributed Programming*,
DOI: 10.1007/978-3-642-15260-3_4,
© Springer-Verlag Berlin Heidelberg 2011

4.1 Introduction

4.1.1 Shared Storage in a Distributed System

In a multiprocessor machine, processes typically communicate through shared memory provided at the hardware level. The shared memory can be viewed as an array of shared registers. It is a convenient abstraction to use for programmers. One may also build a register abstraction from a set of processes that communicate by sending messages to each other over a network; this results in an *emulation of shared-memory*. The programmer using this abstraction can develop algorithms using shared memory, without being aware that, behind the scenes, the processes actually communicate by exchanging messages and that there is no physical shared memory. Such an emulation is very appealing because programming with a shared memory is usually considered significantly easier than working with message exchanges, precisely because the programmer can ignore the consistency problems introduced by the distribution of data. Of course, the programmer has to respect the complexity of the emulation.

As we pointed out, studying register specifications and algorithms is also useful when implementing networked storage systems, distributed file systems, and shared working spaces for collaborative work. For example, the abstraction of a distributed storage device that can be accessed through read and write operations is similar to the notion of a register. Not surprisingly, the algorithms that one needs to devise to build a distributed storage system are directly inspired by those used to implement register abstractions.

In this section, we introduce *safe*, *regular*, and *atomic* semantics for registers. To describe them, we consider the behavior of a register when it is accessed concurrently by multiple processes.

4.1.2 Register Overview

Assumptions. Registers store values and can be accessed through two operations, *read* and *write*. A process starts a *read* operation by triggering a ⟨ *Read* ⟩ event and starts a *write* operation by triggering a ⟨ *Write* | v ⟩ event with a value v. We say that a process *invokes* an operation on a register when it triggers the event. The processes in the system use registers for communicating with each other and for storing information.

After a process has invoked an operation like this, the register abstraction may trigger an event that carries the reply from the operation. We say that the process *completes* the operation when this event occurs. Each correct process accesses the registers in a *sequential* manner, which means that after a process has invoked an operation on a register, the process does not invoke any further operation on that register until the previous operation completes. (There were no such restrictions for the broadcast abstractions in Chap. 3.)

A register may store values from an arbitrary domain and is initialized to a special value ⊥. In other words, we assume that some write operation was initially invoked on the register with parameter $\perp$ and completed before any other operation was invoked. (The value $\perp$ cannot be written otherwise.) For presentation simplicity, but without loss of generality, we also assume that the values written to a particular register are unique. This can be implemented by adding unique timestamps provided by the processes to the written values and is similar to the assumption from the previous chapters that messages sent or broadcast are unique.

Some of the presented register abstractions and algorithms restrict the set of processes that may write to and read from a register. The simplest case is a register with one writer and one reader, which is called a $(1, 1)$ register; the writer is a specific process known in advance, and so is the reader. We will also consider registers with one specific writer and N readers, which means that any process can read from the register. It is called a $(1, N)$ register. Finally, a register to which every process may write to and read from is called an (N, N) register. Sometimes a $(1, 1)$ register is also called a *single-writer, single-reader* register, a $(1, N)$ register is called a *single-writer, multi-reader* register, and an (N, N) register is called a *multi-writer, multi-reader* register.

Signature and Semantics. A process interacts with a register abstraction through events. Basically, the register abstraction stores a value, a read operation returns the stored value, and a write operation updates the stored value. More precisely:

1. A process invokes a *read operation* on a register r by triggering a request event ⟨ r, *Read* ⟩ with no input parameters. The register signals that it has terminated a read operation by triggering an indication event ⟨ r, *ReadReturn* | v ⟩, containing a *return value* v as an output parameter. The return value presumably contains the current value of the register.
2. A process invokes a *write operation* on a register r by triggering a request event ⟨ r, *Write* | v ⟩ with one input parameter v, called the *written value*. The register signals that it has terminated a write operation by triggering an indication event ⟨ r, *WriteReturn* ⟩ with no parameters. The write operation serves to update the value in the register.

If a register is accessed by read and write operations of a single process, and we assume there is no failure, we define the specification of a register through the following simple properties:

- *Liveness:* Every operation eventually completes.
- *Safety:* Every read operation returns the value written by the *last* write operation.

In fact, even if a register is accessed by a set of processes one at a time, in a *serial* manner, and if no process crashes, we could still specify a register using those simple properties. By a serial execution we mean that a process does not invoke an operation on a register if some other process has invoked an operation and has not received any reply for the operation. (Note that this notion is stronger than the notion of sequential access introduced earlier.)

Failures. If we assume that processes might fail, say, by crashing, we can no longer require that any process who invokes an operation eventually completes that operation. Indeed, a process might crash right after invoking an operation and may not have the time to complete this operation. We say that the operation has failed. Because crashes are unpredictable, precisely this situation makes distributed computing challenging. We assume that a process who invokes an operation on a register can only fail by crashing (i.e., we exclude other faults for processes that invoke read/write operation, such as arbitrary faults). This restriction is important for implementing registers in the fail-arbitrary model.

Nevertheless, it makes sense to require that if a process p invokes some operation and does not subsequently crash then p eventually gets back a reply to its invocation, i.e., completes the operation. In other words, any process that invokes a read or write operation and does not crash should eventually return from that invocation. In this sense, its operation should not fail. This requirement makes the register *fault-tolerant*. Algorithms with this property are sometimes also called *robust* or *wait-free*.

If we assume that processes access a register in a serial manner, we may at first glance still want to require from a read operation that it returns the value written by the last write operation. However, we need to care about failures when defining the very notion of *last*. To illustrate the underlying issue, consider the following example execution:

> A process p invokes a write operation on a register with a value v and completes this write. Later on, some other process q invokes a write operation on the register with a new value w, and then q crashes before the operation completes. Hence, q does not get any indication that the operation has indeed taken place before it crashes, and the operation has failed. Now, if a process r subsequently invokes a read operation on the register, what is the value that r is supposed to return? Should it be v or w?

In fact, both values may be valid replies depending on what happened. Intuitively, process q may or may not have the time to complete the write operation. In other words, when we require that a read operation returns the last value written, we consider the following two cases as possible:

1. The value returned has indeed been written by the last process that completed its write, even if some other process invoked a write later but crashed. In this case, no future read should return the value written by the failed write; everything happens as if the failed operation was never invoked.
2. The value returned was the input parameter of the last write operation that was invoked, even if the writer process crashed before it completed the operation. Everything happens as if the operation that failed actually completed.

The underlying difficulty is that the failed write operation (by the crashed process q in the example) did not complete and is, therefore, "concurrent" to the last read operation (by process r) that happened after the crash. The same problem occurs even if process q does not fail and is simply delayed. This is a particular problem resulting from the concurrency of two operations, which we discuss now.

Concurrency. When multiple processes access a register in practice, executions are most often not serial (and clearly not sequential). What should we expect a read operation to return when it is concurrent with some write operation? What is the meaning of the "last" write in this context? Similarly, if two write operations were invoked concurrently, what is the "last" value written? Can a subsequent read return one of the values, and then a read that comes even later return the other value?

In this chapter, we specify three register abstractions, called *safe*, *regular*, and *atomic*, which differ mainly in the way we answer these questions. Roughly speaking, a safe register may return an arbitrary value when a write is concurrently ongoing. A regular register, in contrast, ensures a minimal guarantee in the face of concurrent or failed operations, and may only return the previous value or the newly written value. An atomic register is even stronger and provides a strict form of consistency even in the face of concurrency and failures. We also present algorithms that implement these specifications; we will see that algorithms implementing atomic registers are more complex than those implementing regular or safe registers.

To make the specifications more precise, we first introduce some definitions that aim to capture this intuition. For the moment, we assume fail-stop process abstractions, which may only fail by crashing and do not recover after a crash; later in the chapter, we consider algorithms in the fail-recovery model and in the fail-arbitrary model.

4.1.3 Completeness and Precedence

We first define more precise notions for the *completeness* of the execution of an operation and for the *precedence* between different operation executions. When there is no possible ambiguity, we simply take *operations* to mean *operation executions*.

These notions are defined in terms of the events that occur in the interface of a register abstraction, that is, using ⟨ *Read* ⟩, ⟨ *Write* ⟩, ⟨ *ReadReturn* ⟩, and ⟨ *WriteReturn* ⟩ events; the first two represent the *invocation* of an operation, and the latter two indicate the *completion* of an operation. Remember that these events occur at a single indivisible point in time, using a fictional notion of global time that only serves to reason about specifications and algorithms. This global time is not directly accessible to the processes.

We say that an operation is *complete* if its invocation and completion events have *both* occurred. In particular, this means that the process which invokes an operation o does not crash before operation o terminates and the completion event occurs at the invoking algorithm of the process. An operation is said to *fail* when the process that invoked it crashes *before* the corresponding completion event occurs. (We only consider implementations with crash-stop process abstractions here; the corresponding concepts in the fail-recovery and fail-arbitrary models are introduced later.)

The temporal relation between operations is given by the following notions:

- An operation o is said to *precede* an operation o' if the completion event of o occurs before the invocation event of o'. As an immediate consequence of this definition, note that if an operation o invoked by a process p precedes some other operation (possibly invoked by a different process) then o must be complete and its completion event occurred at p.

- If two operations are such that one precedes the other then we say that the operations are *sequential*. If neither one of two operations precedes the other then we say that they are *concurrent*.

Basically, the execution of operations on a register defines a partial order on its read and write operations. If only one process invokes operations then the order is total, according to our assumption that every process operates sequentially on one register. When no two operations are concurrent and all operations are complete, as in a serial execution, the order is also total.

- When a read operation o_r returns a value v, and v was the input parameter of some write operation o_w, we say that operation o_r *reads from* o_w or that value v is *read from* o_w.
- When a write operation (o_w) with input parameter v completes, we say that value v is *written (by o_w)*.

Recall that every value is written only once and, hence, the write operations in the definition are unique.

In the following, we give specifications of various forms of register abstractions and algorithms to implement them. Some algorithms use multiple instances of simpler register abstractions.

4.2 $(1, N)$ **Regular Register**

We start the description of shared-memory abstractions with the specification and two algorithms for a $(1, N)$ *regular* register. This means that one specific process p can invoke a write operation on the register, and any process can invoke a read operation on the register. The notion of regularity, which we explain later, is not considered for multiple writers. (There is no consensus in the distributed computing literature on how to generalize the notion of regularity to multiple writers.)

4.2.1 Specification

The interface and properties of a $(1, N)$ *regular register* abstraction (ONRR) are given in Module 4.1. In short, every read operation that is not concurrent with any write operation returns the last value written. If there is a concurrent write, the read is allowed to return the last value written or the value concurrently being written. Note that if a process invokes a write and crashes (without recovering), the write is considered to be concurrent with any read that did not precede it. Hence, such a read can return the value that was supposed to be written by the failed write or the last value written before the failed write was invoked. In any case, the returned value must be read from some write operation invoked on the register. That is, the value returned by any read operation must be a value that some process has tried to write

Module 4.1: Interface and properties of a $(1, N)$ regular register

Module:

    Name: $(1, N)$-RegularRegister, **instance** *onrr*.

Events:

    Request: ⟨ *onrr, Read* ⟩: Invokes a read operation on the register.

    Request: ⟨ *onrr, Write* | v ⟩: Invokes a write operation with value v on the register.

    Indication: ⟨ *onrr, ReadReturn* | v ⟩: Completes a read operation on the register with return value v.

    Indication: ⟨ *onrr, WriteReturn* ⟩: Completes a write operation on the register.

Properties:

    ONRR1: *Termination:* If a correct process invokes an operation, then the operation eventually completes.

    ONRR2: *Validity:* A read that is not concurrent with a write returns the last value written; a read that is concurrent with a write returns the last value written or the value concurrently written.

(even if the write was not complete), and it cannot be invented out of thin air. The value may be the initial value ⊥ of the register.

To illustrate the specification of a regular register, we depict two executions of operations on one register in Figs. 4.1 and 4.2; the operations are executed by two processes. The notation in the figure uses two dots and a thick line to denote the execution of an operation, where the dots represent the invocation and the completion event. The type of the operation and the parameters are described with text. The execution of Fig. 4.1 is not regular because the first read does not return the last written value. In contrast, the execution in Fig. 4.2 is regular.

As an outlook to the specification of a *safe* register (in Sect. 4.6), which is a weaker abstraction than a regular register, we note that one obtains the *validity* property a safe register by dropping the second part of the *validity* property in Module 4.1, namely, the condition on reads that are not concurrent with any write. When a read is concurrent with a write in a safe register, it may return an arbitrary value.

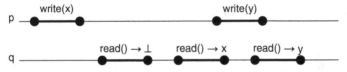

Figure 4.1: A register execution that is not regular because of the first read by process q

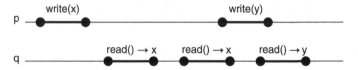

Figure 4.2: A regular register execution

4.2.2 Fail-Stop Algorithm: Read-One Write-All Regular Register

Algorithm 4.1 implements a $(1, N)$ regular register. The algorithm is particularly simple because it uses the fail-stop model and relies on a perfect failure detector. When a process crashes, the failure detector ensures that eventually all correct processes detect the crash (*strong completeness*), and no process is detected to have crashed until it has really crashed (*strong accuracy*).

Algorithm 4.1: Read-One Write-All

Implements:
    $(1, N)$-RegularRegister, **instance** *onrr*.

Uses:
    BestEffortBroadcast, **instance** *beb*;
    PerfectPointToPointLinks, **instance** *pl*;
    PerfectFailureDetector, **instance** $\mathcal{P}$.

upon event $\langle$ *onrr*, *Init* $\rangle$ **do**
    $val := \perp$;
    $correct := \Pi$;
    $writeset := \emptyset$;

upon event $\langle$ $\mathcal{P}$, *Crash* $\mid p$ $\rangle$ **do**
    $correct := correct \setminus \{p\}$;

upon event $\langle$ *onrr*, *Read* $\rangle$ **do**
    trigger $\langle$ *onrr*, *ReadReturn* $\mid val$ $\rangle$;

upon event $\langle$ *onrr*, *Write* $\mid v$ $\rangle$ **do**
    trigger $\langle$ *beb*, *Broadcast* $\mid$ [WRITE, v] $\rangle$;

upon event $\langle$ *beb*, *Deliver* $\mid q$, [WRITE, v] $\rangle$ **do**
    $val := v$;
    trigger $\langle$ *pl*, *Send* $\mid q$, ACK $\rangle$;

upon event $\langle$ *pl*, *Deliver* $\mid p$, ACK $\rangle$ **do**
    $writeset := writeset \cup \{p\}$;

upon $correct \subseteq writeset$ **do**
    $writeset := \emptyset$;
    trigger $\langle$ *onrr*, *WriteReturn* $\rangle$;

The algorithm has each process store a copy of the *current register value* in a local variable *val*. In other words, the value of the register is replicated at all processes. The writer updates the value of all presumably correct processes (i.e., those that it does not detect to have crashed) by broadcasting a WRITE message with the new value. All processes acknowledge the receipt of the new value with an ACK message. The write operation returns when the writer has received an acknowledgment from every process that it considers to be correct. When the write of a new value is complete, all processes that did not crash have stored the new value. The reader simply returns the value that it has stored locally. In other words, the reader *reads one value* and the writer *writes all values*. Hence, Algorithm 4.1 is called "Read-One Write-All."

The algorithm uses a perfect failure-detector abstraction and two underlying communication abstractions: perfect point-to-point links and best-effort broadcast.

We will be using multiple instances of regular registers to build stronger abstractions later in this chapter. As mentioned before, the instances are differentiated by their identifiers, and all messages exchanged using the underlying communication primitives implicitly carry an instance identifier to match the same instance at all processes.

Correctness. The *termination* property is straightforward for any read invocation, because a process simply returns its local value. For a write invocation, *termination* follows from the properties of the underlying communication abstractions (*reliable delivery* of perfect point-to-point links and *validity* of best-effort broadcast) and the *completeness* property of the perfect failure detector (every crashed process is eventually detected by every correct process). Any process that crashes is detected and any process that does not crash sends back an acknowledgment, which is eventually delivered by the writer.

Consider *validity*. Assume that there is no concurrency and all operations are complete. Consider a read invoked by some process p and assume, furthermore, that v is the last value written. Because of the *accuracy* property of the perfect failure detector, at the time when the read is invoked, all processes that did not crash store value v. In particular, also p stores v and returns v, and this is the last value written.

Assume now that the read is concurrent with some write of a value v and the value written prior to v was v' (it may be that v' is the initial value $\perp$). According to the above argument, every process stores v' before the write operation of v was invoked. Because of the properties of the communication abstractions (*no creation* properties), no message is altered and no value is stored by a process unless the writer has invoked a write operation with this value as a parameter. At the time of the read, every process therefore stores either still v' or has *beb*-delivered the WRITE message with v and stores v. The return value of the read is either v or v', as required from a regular register.

Performance. Every write operation requires two communication steps corresponding to the WRITE and ACK exchange between the writer and all processes and $O(N)$ messages. A read operation does not require any communication, it is purely local.

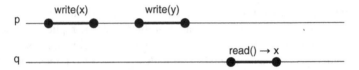

Figure 4.3: A non-regular register execution

4.2.3 Fail-Silent Algorithm: Majority Voting Regular Register

It is easy to see that if the failure detector is not perfect, the "Read-One Write-All" algorithm (Algorithm 4.1) may violate the *validity* property of the register. The execution illustrated in Fig. 4.3 shows how this could happen, even without concurrency and without any failure. When the writer process p falsely suspects process q to have crashed, the write operation may return before receiving the acknowledgment from q and, thus, before q has locally stored the new value y. Hence, the read by q may return x and not the last written value.

In the following, we present Algorithm 4.2 that implements a regular register in the fail-silent model. This algorithm does not rely on any failure detection abstraction. Instead, the algorithm assumes that a majority of the processes is correct. We leave it as an exercise (at the end of the chapter) to show that this majority assumption is actually needed, even when an eventually perfect failure detector can be used.

The general principle of the algorithm requires for the writer and the readers to use a set of *witness* processes that keep track of the most recent value of the register. The witnesses must be chosen in such a way that at least one witness participates in any pair of such operations, and does not crash in the meantime. Every two such sets of witnesses must, therefore, overlap. In other words, they form *quorums*, a collection of sets such that the intersection of every two sets is not empty (Sect. 2.7.3). Majorities are one of the simplest kinds of quorums, which is the reason for calling Algorithm 4.2 "Majority Voting." The algorithm implements a $(1, N)$ regular register, where one specific process is the writer and any process can be a reader.

Similar to the "Read-One Write-All" algorithm presented before, the "Majority Voting" algorithm also has each process store a copy of the *current register value* in a local variable *val*. In addition, the "Majority Voting" algorithm also stores a *timestamp ts* together with the stored value at every process. This timestamp is defined by the writer and represents the number of times the write operation has been invoked.

The algorithm uses a best-effort broadcast instance *beb* and a perfect links instance *pl*. When the unique writer p invokes a write operation with a new value, the process increments its *write-timestamp* and associates it with the value to be written. Then p *beb*-broadcasts a WRITE message to all processes, and has a majority "adopt" this value and the associated timestamp. To *adopt* a value in this context means to store it locally as the current register value. The writer completes the write (and hence returns from the operation) when it has received an acknowledgment from a majority of the processes, indicating that they have indeed adopted the new

---

Algorithm 4.2: Majority Voting Regular Register

Implements:
    $(1, N)$-RegularRegister, **instance** *onrr*.
Uses:
    BestEffortBroadcast, **instance** *beb*;
    PerfectPointToPointLinks, **instance** *pl*.

upon event $\langle$ *onrr, Init* $\rangle$ **do**
    $(ts, val) := (0, \perp)$;
    $wts := 0$;
    $acks := 0$;
    $rid := 0$;
    $readlist := [\perp]^N$;

upon event $\langle$ *onrr, Write* $\mid v$ $\rangle$ **do**
    $wts := wts + 1$;
    $acks := 0$;
    trigger $\langle$ *beb, Broadcast* $\mid$ [WRITE, wts, v] $\rangle$;

upon event $\langle$ *beb, Deliver* $\mid p$, [WRITE, ts', v'] $\rangle$ **do**
    if $ts' > ts$ **then**
        $(ts, val) := (ts', v')$;
    trigger $\langle$ *pl, Send* $\mid p$, [ACK, ts'] $\rangle$;

upon event $\langle$ *pl, Deliver* $\mid q$, [ACK, ts'] $\rangle$ **such that** $ts' = wts$ **do**
    $acks := acks + 1$;
    if $acks > N/2$ **then**
        $acks := 0$;
        trigger $\langle$ *onrr, WriteReturn* $\rangle$;

upon event $\langle$ *onrr, Read* $\rangle$ **do**
    $rid := rid + 1$;
    $readlist := [\perp]^N$;
    trigger $\langle$ *beb, Broadcast* $\mid$ [READ, rid] $\rangle$;

upon event $\langle$ *beb, Deliver* $\mid p$, [READ, r] $\rangle$ **do**
    trigger $\langle$ *pl, Send* $\mid p$, [VALUE, r, ts, val] $\rangle$;

upon event $\langle$ *pl, Deliver* $\mid q$, [VALUE, r, ts', v'] $\rangle$ **such that** $r = rid$ **do**
    $readlist[q] := (ts', v')$;
    if $\#(readlist) > N/2$ **then**
        $v := highestval(readlist)$;
        $readlist := [\perp]^N$;
        trigger $\langle$ *onrr, ReadReturn* $\mid v$ $\rangle$;

---

value and the associated timestamp. It is important to note that a process q will adopt a value v' sent by the writer only if q has not already adopted a value v with a larger timestamp. This might happen if the WRITE message containing v was *beb*-delivered by q *before* the WRITE message containing v'. In this case, process q was also not in the majority that made it possible for p to complete the write of v' before proceeding to writing v.

To read a value, a reader process *beb*-broadcasts a READ message to all processes, every process replies with the stored value and its timestamp, and the reader selects the value with the largest timestamp from a majority of the replies. The processes in this majority act as witnesses of what was written before. This majority does not have to be the same as the one used by the writer. Choosing the largest timestamp ensures that the value written last is returned, provided there is no concurrency. To simplify the presentation of Algorithm 4.2, the reader uses a function *highestval*(S) that takes a list S of timestamp/value pairs as input and returns the value of the pair with the largest timestamp, that is, the value v of a pair $(ts, v) \in S$ such that

$$\text{forall } (ts', v') \in S : ts' < ts \lor (ts', v') = (ts, v).$$

The function is applied to the received pairs as soon as timestamp/value pairs have been received from a majority of the processes.

Note that every WRITE and READ message is tagged with a unique identifier, and the corresponding reply carries this tag. For a write operation, the tag is simply the write-timestamp wts associated with the value written. In the case of a read operation, the tag is a read-request identifier rid, solely used for identifying the messages belonging to different reads. In this way, the reader can figure out whether a given reply message matches a request (and is not a reply in response to an earlier READ message). This mechanism is important to prevent the reader from confusing two replies from different operations and counting them toward the wrong operation. Likewise, the *ack* counter and the list of values in *readlist* must be initialized freshly whenever a new write or read operation starts, respectively. Without these mechanisms, the algorithm may violate the *validity* property of the register.

Correctness. The *termination* property follows from the properties of the underlying communication abstractions and from the assumption that a majority of processes in the system are correct.

For the *validity* property, consider a read operation that is not concurrent with any write. Assume, furthermore, that the read is invoked by process q and the last value written by the writer p is v with associated timestamp wts. This means that, at the time when the read is invoked, a majority of the processes store wts in their timestamp variable ts, and that there is no larger timestamp in the system. This is because the writer uses increasing timestamps. Before returning from the read operation, process q consults a majority of the processes and, hence, receives at least one reply containing timestamp wts. This follows from the use of majority quorums that always intersect. Process q hence returns value v, which is indeed the last value written, because wts is the largest timestamp.

Consider now the case where the read is concurrent with some write of value v with associated timestamp wts, and the previous write was for value v' and timestamp $wts-1$. If any process returns the pair (wts, v) to the reader q then q returns v, which is a valid reply. Otherwise, all replies from more than $N/2$ processes contain v' and associated timestamp $wts - 1$, and q returns v', which is also a valid reply.

Performance. Every write operation requires one communication roundtrip between the writer and a majority of the processes, and every read requires one communication roundtrip between the reader and a majority of the processes. In both operations, $O(N)$ messages are exchanged.

4.3 (1, N) Atomic Register

We give here the specification and two algorithms for a $(1, N)$ *atomic register*. The generalization to multiple writers will be discussed in the next section.

4.3.1 Specification

Consider a $(1, N)$ regular register with initial value $\perp$, and suppose the writer p invokes an operation to write a value v. Because of the regular register specification, nothing prevents a process that reads the register multiple times from returning first v, subsequently $\perp$, then again v, and so on, as long as the reads and the write of p are concurrent. Furthermore, if the writer crashes before completing the write, the operation is not complete, and one subsequent reader might read v, whereas another reader, coming even later, might still return $\perp$. An atomic register is a regular register that prevents such behavior.

The interface and properties of a $(1, N)$ *atomic register* abstraction (ONAR) are given in Module 4.2. A $(1, N)$ atomic register is a regular register that, in addition to the properties of a regular register (Module 4.1) ensures a specific *ordering* property

---

Module 4.2: Interface and properties of a $(1, N)$ atomic register

Module:

    Name: $(1, N)$-AtomicRegister, **instance** *onar*.

Events:

    Request: $\langle$ *onar*, Read $\rangle$: Invokes a read operation on the register.

    Request: $\langle$ *onar*, Write $\mid v$ $\rangle$: Invokes a write operation with value v on the register.

    Indication: $\langle$ *onar*, ReadReturn $\mid v$ $\rangle$: Completes a read operation on the register with return value v.

    Indication: $\langle$ *onar*, WriteReturn $\rangle$: Completes a write operation on the register.

Properties:

    ONAR1–ONAR2: Same as properties ONRR1–ONRR2 of a $(1, N)$ regular register (Module 4.1).

    ONAR3: *Ordering:* If a read returns a value v and a subsequent read returns a value w, then the write of w does not precede the write of v.

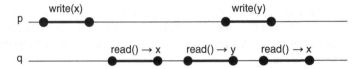

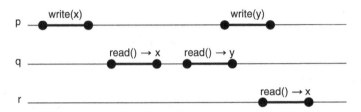

Figure 4.4: A register execution that is not atomic because of the third read by process q

Figure 4.5: Violation of atomicity in the "Read-One Write-All" regular register algorithm

which, roughly speaking, prevents an "old" value from being read by process p, once a "newer" value has been read by process q (even if $p \neq q$). More precisely, this property implies that every operation of an atomic register can be thought to occur at a single indivisible point in time, which lies between the invocation and the completion of the operation.

A $(1, N)$ atomic register prevents that a reader process reads a value w after the completion of a read operation that returned a value v (possibly by another process), when w was written before v. In addition, if the single writer process started to write some value v and crashed before completing this operation, the atomic register ensures that once any reader completes a read operation and returns v, then no subsequent read operation returns a different value.

The execution depicted in Fig. 4.4 is not atomic because the *ordering* property of an atomic register should prevent the last read of process q from returning x after the previous read returned y, given that x was written before y. If the execution is changed so that the last read of q also returns y, the execution becomes atomic. Another atomic execution is the regular execution shown in Fig. 4.2.

It is important to note that none of our previous algorithms implements a $(1, N)$ atomic register, even if no failures occur. We illustrate this through the execution depicted in Fig. 4.5 as a counterexample for Algorithm 4.1 ("Read-One Write-All"), and the execution depicted in Fig. 4.6 as a counterexample for Algorithm 4.2 ("Majority Voting").

The scenario of Fig. 4.5 can occur with Algorithm 4.1 if during the second write operation of process p, the new value y is received and read by process q before it is received by process r. Before receiving the new value, r will continue to read the previous value x, even if its read operation occurs after the read by q.

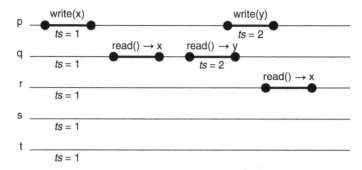

Figure 4.6: Violation of atomicity in the "Majority Voting" regular register algorithm

The scenario of Fig. 4.6 can occur with Algorithm 4.2 if process q has received replies from processes p, q, and s in its second read, and the replies already included timestamp 2 from the second write of p. On the other hand, process r has accessed processes r, s, and t, which have not yet received the WRITE message with timestamp 2 from p.

In the following, we give several algorithms that implement the $(1, N)$ atomic register abstraction. We first describe how to transform an abstract $(1, N)$ regular register into a $(1, N)$ atomic register algorithm; the regular register might be implemented by a fail-stop or fail-silent algorithm, which will determine the system model of the resulting implementation. Such a transformation is modular and helps to understand the fundamental difference between atomic and regular registers. It does not lead to very efficient algorithms, however. We subsequently describe how to directly extend our two regular register algorithms to obtain efficient $(1, N)$ atomic register algorithms.

4.3.2 Transformation: From $(1, N)$ Regular to $(1, N)$ Atomic Registers

This section describes how to transform any $(1, N)$ regular register abstraction into a $(1, N)$ atomic register abstraction. For pedagogical reasons, we divide the transformation in two parts. We first explain how to transform any $(1, N)$ regular register abstraction into a $(1, 1)$ atomic register abstraction and then how to transform any $(1, 1)$ atomic register abstraction into a $(1, N)$ atomic register abstraction. These transformations do not use any other means of communication between processes than the underlying registers.

From $(1, N)$ Regular to $(1, 1)$ Atomic Registers. The first transformation is given in Algorithm 4.3 and realizes the following simple idea. To build a $(1, 1)$ atomic register with process p as writer and process q as reader, we use one $(1, N)$ regular register, also with writer p and reader q. Furthermore, the writer maintains a timestamp that it increments and associates with every new value to be written. The reader also maintains a timestamp, together with the value associated to the highest timestamp that it has read from the regular register so far. Intuitively, the reader

---

Algorithm 4.3: From $(1, N)$ Regular to $(1, 1)$ Atomic Registers

---

Implements:
  $(1, 1)$-AtomicRegister, **instance** *ooar*.

Uses:
  $(1, N)$-RegularRegister, **instance** *onrr*.

upon event ⟨ *ooar*, *Init* ⟩ **do**
    $(ts, val) := (0, \perp)$;
    $wts := 0$;

upon event ⟨ *ooar*, *Write* | v ⟩ **do**
    $wts := wts + 1$;
    trigger ⟨ *onrr*, *Write* | (wts, v) ⟩;

upon event ⟨ *onrr*, *WriteReturn* ⟩ **do**
    trigger ⟨ *ooar*, *WriteReturn* ⟩;

upon event ⟨ *ooar*, *Read* ⟩ **do**
    trigger ⟨ *onrr*, *Read* ⟩;

upon event ⟨ *onrr*, *ReadReturn* | (ts', v') ⟩ **do**
    if $ts' > ts$ **then**
        $(ts, val) := (ts', v')$;
    trigger ⟨ *ooar*, *ReadReturn* | *val* ⟩;

---

stores these items in order to always return the value with the highest timestamp and to avoid returning an old value once it has read a newer value from the regular register.

To implement a $(1, 1)$ atomic register instance *ooar*, Algorithm 4.3 maintains one instance *onrr* of a $(1, N)$ regular register. The writer maintains a writer-timestamp wts, and the reader maintains a timestamp ts, both initialized to 0. In addition, the reader stores the most recently read value in a variable *val*. The algorithm proceeds as follows:

- To *ooar*-write a value v to the atomic register, the writer p increments its timestamp wts and *onrr*-writes the pair (wts, v) into the underlying regular register.
- To *ooar*-read a value from the atomic register, the reader q first *onrr*-reads a timestamp/value pair from the underlying regular register. If the returned timestamp ts' is larger than the local timestamp ts then q stores ts' together with the returned value v in the local variables, and returns v. Otherwise, the reader simply returns the value from val, which it has already stored locally.

Correctness. The *termination* property of the atomic register follows from the same property of the underlying regular register.

Consider *validity* and assume first that a read is not concurrent with any write, and the last value written by p is v and associated with timestamp ts'. The reader-timestamp stored by the reader q is either ts', if q has already read v in some previous read, or a strictly smaller value. In both cases, because of the *validity* property of the regular register, a read by q will return v. Consider now a read that is concurrent with some write of value v and timestamp ts', and the previous write was for value v' and timestamp $ts' - 1$. The reader-timestamp stored by q cannot be larger than ts'. Hence, because of the *validity* property of the underlying regular register, q will return either v or v'; both are valid replies.

Consider now *ordering* and assume that p writes v and subsequently writes w. Suppose that q returns w for some read and consider any subsequent read of q. The reader-timestamp stored by q is either the one associated with w or a larger one. Hence, the last check in the algorithm when returning from a read prevents that the return value was written before w and there is no way for the algorithm to return v.

Performance. The transformation requires only local computation, such as maintaining timestamps and performing some checks, in addition to writing to and reading from the regular register.

From $(1, 1)$ Atomic to $(1, N)$ Atomic Registers. We describe here an algorithm that implements the abstraction of a $(1, N)$ atomic register out of $(1, 1)$ atomic registers. To get an intuition of the transformation, think of a teacher (the writer), who needs to communicate some information to a set of students (the readers), through the abstraction of a traditional blackboard. The board is a good match for the abstraction of a $(1, N)$ register, as long as only the teacher writes on it. Furthermore, it is made of a single physical entity and atomic.

Assume now that the teacher cannot physically gather all students within the same classroom, and hence cannot use one physical board for all. Instead, this global board needs to be emulated with one or several individual boards (i-boards) that can also be written by one person but may only be read by one person. For example, every student can have one or several such electronic i-boards at home, which only he or she can read.

It makes sense to have the teacher write each new piece of information to at least one i-board per student. This is intuitively necessary for the students to eventually read the information provided by the teacher, i.e., to ensure the *validity* property of the register. However, this is not enough to guarantee the *ordering* property of an atomic register. Indeed, assume that the teacher writes two pieces of information consecutively, first x and then y. It might happen that a student reads y and later on, some other student still reads x, say, because the information flow from the teacher to the first student is faster than the flow to the second student. This *ordering* violation is similar to the situation of Fig. 4.5.

One way to cope with this issue is for every student, before terminating the reading of some information, to transmit this information to all other students, through other i-boards. That is, every student would use, besides the i-board devoted to the teacher to provide new information, another one for writing new information to the other students. Whenever a student reads some information from the teacher, the student first writes this information to the i-board that is read by the other students, before returning the information. Of course, the student must in addition also read the i-boards on which the other students might have written newer information. The

Algorithm 4.4: From $(1, 1)$ Atomic to $(1, N)$ Atomic Registers

Implements:
    $(1, N)$-AtomicRegister, **instance** *onar*.

Uses:
    $(1, 1)$-AtomicRegister (multiple instances).

upon event ⟨ *onar, Init* ⟩ **do**
        $ts := 0$;
        $acks := 0$;
        $writing :=$ FALSE;
        $readval := \bot$;
        $readlist := [\bot]^N$;
        forall $q \in \Pi, r \in \Pi$ **do**
                Initialize a new instance *ooar.q.r* of $(1, 1)$-AtomicRegister
                        with writer r and reader q;

upon event ⟨ *onar, Write* | v ⟩ **do**
        $ts := ts + 1$;
        $writing :=$ TRUE;
        forall $q \in \Pi$ **do**
                trigger ⟨ *ooar.q.self, Write* | (ts, v) ⟩;

upon event ⟨ *ooar.q.self, WriteReturn* ⟩ **do**
        $acks := acks + 1$;
        if $acks = N$ **then**
                $acks := 0$;
                if $writing =$ TRUE **then**
                        trigger ⟨ *onar, WriteReturn* ⟩;
                        $writing :=$ FALSE;
                else
                        trigger ⟨ *onar, ReadReturn* | *readval* ⟩;

upon event ⟨ *onar, Read* ⟩ **do**
        forall $r \in \Pi$ **do**
                trigger ⟨ *ooar.self.r, Read* ⟩;

upon event ⟨ *ooar.self.r, ReadReturn* | (ts', v') ⟩ **do**
        $readlist[r] := (ts', v')$;
        if $\#(readlist) = N$ **then**
                $(maxts, readval) := highest(readlist)$;
                $readlist := [\bot]^N$;
                forall $q \in \Pi$ **do**
                        trigger ⟨ *ooar.q.self, Write* | $(maxts, readval)$ ⟩;

teacher adds a timestamp to the written information to distinguish new information
from old one.

The transformation in Algorithm 4.4 implements one $(1, N)$ atomic register
instance *onar* from N^2 underlying $(1, 1)$ atomic register instances. Suppose the
writer of the $(1, N)$ atomic register *onar* is process p (note that the writer is also

a reader here, in contrast to the teacher in the story). The $(1, 1)$ registers are orga-
nized in a $N \times N$ matrix, with register instances called *ooar.q.r* for $q \in \Pi$ and
$r \in \Pi$. They are used to communicate among all processes, from the writer p to all
N readers and among the readers. In particular, register instance *ooar.q.r* is used to
inform process q about the last value read by reader r; that is, process r writes to
this register and process q reads from it. The register instances *ooar.q.p*, which are
written by the writer p, are also used to store the written value in the first place; as
process p may also operate as a reader, these instances have dual roles.

Note that both write and read operations require N registers to be updated; the
acks counter keeps track of the number of updated registers in the write and read
operation, respectively. As this is a local variable of the process that executes the
operation, and as a process executes only one operation at a time, using the same
variable in both operations does not create any interference between reading and
writing. A variable *writing* keeps track of whether the process is writing on behalf
of a write operation, or whether the process is engaged in a read operation and
writing the value to be returned.

Algorithm 4.4 also relies on a timestamp *ts* maintained by the writer, which
indicates the version of the current value of the register. For presentation simplicity,
we use a function *highest*($\cdot$) that returns the timestamp/value pair with the largest
timestamp from a list or a set of such pairs (this is similar to the *highestval* function introduced before, except that the timestamp/value pair is returned whereas
highestval only returns the value). More formally, *highest*(S) with a set or a list of
timestamp/value pairs S is defined as the pair $(ts, v) \in S$ such that

$$\text{forall } (ts', v') \in S \; : \; ts' < ts \lor (ts', v') = (ts, v).$$

The variable *readlist* is a length-N list of timestamp/value pairs; in the algorithm
for reading, we convert it implicitly to the set of its entries. Recall that the function $\#(S)$ denotes the cardinality of a set S or the number of non-$\perp$ entries in a
list S.

Correctness. Because of the *termination* property of the underlying $(1, 1)$ atomic
registers, it is easy to see that every operation in the transformation algorithm
eventually returns.

Similarly, because of the *validity* property of the underlying $(1, 1)$ atomic registers, and due to the choice of the value with the largest timestamp as the return
value, we also derive the *validity* of the $(1, N)$ atomic register.

For the *ordering* property, consider an *onar*-write operation of a value v with associated timestamp ts_v that precedes an *onar*-write of value w with timestamp ts_w;
this means that $ts_v < ts_w$. Assume that a process r *onar*-reads w. According to
the algorithm, process r has written (ts_w, w) to N underlying registers, with identifiers *ooar.q.r* for $q \in \Pi$. Because of the *ordering* property of the $(1, 1)$ atomic
registers, every subsequent read operation from instance *onar* reads at least one of
the underlying registers that contains (ts_w, w), or a pair containing a higher timestamp. Hence, the read operation returns a value associated with a timestamp that is
at least ts_w, and there is no way for the algorithm to return v.

Performance. Every write operation into the $(1, N)$ register requires N writes into $(1, 1)$ registers. Every read from the $(1, N)$ register requires one read from N $(1, 1)$ registers and one write into N $(1, 1)$ registers.

We give, in the following, two direct implementations of $(1, N)$ atomic register abstractions from distributed communication abstractions. The first algorithm is in the fail-stop system model and the second one uses the fail-silent model. These are adaptations of the "Read-One Write-All" and "Majority Voting" $(1, N)$ regular register algorithms, respectively. Both algorithms use the same approach as presented transformation, but require fewer messages than if the transformation would be applied automatically.

4.3.3 Fail-Stop Algorithm: Read-Impose Write-All $(1, N)$ Atomic Register

If the goal is to implement a $(1, N)$ register with one writer and multiple readers, the "Read-One Write-All" regular register algorithm (Algorithm 4.1) clearly does not work: the scenario depicted in Fig. 4.5 illustrates how it fails.

To cope with this case, we define an extension to the "Read-One Write-All" regular register algorithm that circumvents the problem by having the reader also *impose* the value it is about to return on all other processes. In other words, the read operation also *writes back* the value that it is about to return. This modification is described as Algorithm 4.5, called "Read-Impose Write-All." The writer uses a timestamp to distinguish the values it is writing, which ensures the *ordering* property of every execution. A process that is asked by another process to store an older value than the currently stored value does not modify its memory. We discuss the need for this test, as well as the need for the timestamp, through an exercise (at the end of this chapter).

The algorithm uses a request identifier *rid* in the same way as in Algorithm 4.2. Here, the request identifier field distinguishes among WRITE messages that belong to different reads or writes. A flag *reading* used during the writing part distinguishes between the write operations and the write-back part of the read operations.

Correctness. The *termination* and *validity* properties are ensured in the same way as in the "Read-One Write-All" algorithm (Algorithm 4.1). Consider now *ordering* and assume process p writes a value v, which is associated to some timestamp ts_v, and subsequently writes a value w, associated to some timestamp $ts_w > ts_v$. Assume, furthermore, that some process q reads w and, later on, some other process r invokes another read operation. At the time when q completes its read, all processes that did not crash have a timestamp variable ts that is at least ts_w. According to the algorithm, there is no way for r to change its value to v after this time because $ts_v < ts_w$.

Performance. Every write or read operation requires two communication steps, corresponding to the roundtrip communication between the writer or the reader and all processes. At most $O(N)$ messages are needed in both cases.

Algorithm 4.5: Read-Impose Write-All

Implements:
   (1, N)-AtomicRegister, **instance** *onar*.

Uses:
   BestEffortBroadcast, **instance** *beb*;
   PerfectPointToPointLinks, **instance** *pl*;
   PerfectFailureDetector, **instance** $\mathcal{P}$.

upon event ⟨ *onar*, *Init* ⟩ **do**
   $(ts, val) := (0, \perp)$;
   correct := Π;
   writeset := $\emptyset$;
   readval := $\perp$;
   reading := FALSE;

upon event ⟨ $\mathcal{P}$, *Crash* | p ⟩ **do**
   correct := *correct* $\setminus \{p\}$;

upon event ⟨ *onar*, *Read* ⟩ **do**
   reading := TRUE;
   readval := *val*;
   trigger ⟨ *beb*, *Broadcast* | [WRITE, *ts*, *val*] ⟩;

upon event ⟨ *onar*, *Write* | v ⟩ **do**
   trigger ⟨ *beb*, *Broadcast* | [WRITE, *ts* + 1, *v*] ⟩;

upon event ⟨ *beb*, *Deliver* | p, [WRITE, *ts'*, *v'*] ⟩ **do**
   if *ts'* > *ts* **then**
      $(ts, val) := (ts', v')$;
   trigger ⟨ *pl*, *Send* | p, [ACK] ⟩;

upon event ⟨ *pl*, *Deliver* | p, [ACK] ⟩ **then**
   writeset := *writeset* $\cup \{p\}$;

upon *correct* $\subseteq$ *writeset* **do**
   writeset := $\emptyset$;
   if *reading* = TRUE **then**
      reading := FALSE;
      trigger ⟨ *onar*, *ReadReturn* | *readval* ⟩;
   else
      trigger ⟨ *onar*, *WriteReturn* ⟩;

4.3.4 Fail-Silent Algorithm: Read-Impose Write-Majority (1, N) Atomic Register

In this section, we consider a fail-silent model. We describe an extension of our "Majority Voting" (1, N) regular register algorithm (Algorithm 4.2) to implement a (1, N) atomic register.

Algorithm 4.6: Read-Impose Write-Majority (part 1, read)

Implements:
    $(1, N)$-AtomicRegister, **instance** *onar*.

Uses:
    BestEffortBroadcast, **instance** *beb*;
    PerfectPointToPointLinks, **instance** *pl*.

upon event ⟨ *onar*, *Init* ⟩ **do**
    $(ts, val) := (0, \perp)$;
    $wts := 0$;
    $acks := 0$;
    $rid := 0$;
    $readlist := [\perp]^N$;
    $readval := \perp$;
    $reading := \text{FALSE}$;

upon event ⟨ *onar*, *Read* ⟩ **do**
    $rid := rid + 1$;
    $acks := 0$;
    $readlist := [\perp]^N$;
    $reading := \text{TRUE}$;
    trigger ⟨ *beb*, *Broadcast* | [READ, *rid*] ⟩;

upon event ⟨ *beb*, *Deliver* | p, [READ, r] ⟩ **do**
    trigger ⟨ *pl*, *Send* | p, [VALUE, r, ts, val] ⟩;

upon event ⟨ *pl*, *Deliver* | q, [VALUE, r, ts', v'] ⟩ **such that** $r = rid$ **do**
    $readlist[q] := (ts', v')$;
    if $\#(readlist) > N/2$ **then**
        $(maxts, readval) := highest(readlist)$;
        $readlist := [\perp]^N$;
        trigger ⟨ *beb*, *Broadcast* | [WRITE, *rid, maxts, readval*] ⟩;

The algorithm is called "Read-Impose Write-Majority" and shown in Algorithm 4.6–4.7. The implementation of the write operation is similar to that of the "Majority Voting" algorithm: the writer simply makes sure a majority adopts its value. The implementation of the read operation is different, however. A reader selects the value with the largest timestamp from a majority, as in the "Majority Voting" algorithm, but now also imposes this value and makes sure a majority adopts it before completing the read operation: this is the key to ensuring the *ordering* property of an atomic register.

The "Majority Voting" algorithm can be seen as the combination of the "Read-Impose Write-Majority" algorithm with the two ideas that are found in the two-step transformation from $(1, N)$ regular registers to $(1, N)$ atomic registers (Algorithms 4.3 and 4.4): first, the mechanism to store the value with the highest timestamp that was read so far, as in Algorithm 4.3; and, second, the approach of the read implementation to write the value to all other processes before it is returned, as in Algorithm 4.4.

Algorithm 4.7: Read-Impose Write-Majority (part 2, write and write-back)

upon event ⟨ *onar, Write* | *v* ⟩ **do**
 rid := *rid* + 1;
 wts := *wts* + 1;
 acks := 0;
 trigger ⟨ *beb, Broadcast* | [WRITE, *rid*, *wts*, *v*] ⟩;

upon event ⟨ *beb, Deliver* | *p*, [WRITE, *r*, *ts′*, *v′*] ⟩ **do**
 if *ts′* > *ts* **then**
  (*ts*, *val*) := (*ts′*, *v′*);
 trigger ⟨ *pl, Send* | *p*, [ACK, *r*] ⟩;

upon event ⟨ *pl, Deliver* | *q*, [ACK, *r*] ⟩ **such that** *r* = *rid* **do**
 acks := *acks* + 1;
 if *acks* > *N*/2 **then**
  acks := 0;
  if *reading* = TRUE **then**
   reading := FALSE;
   trigger ⟨ *onar, ReadReturn* | *readval* ⟩;
  else
   trigger ⟨ *onar, WriteReturn* ⟩;

Correctness. The *termination* and *validity* properties are ensured in the same way as in Algorithm 4.2 ("Majority Voting"). Consider now the *ordering* property. Suppose that a read operation o_r by process r reads a value v from a write operation o_w of process p (the only writer), that a read operation $o_{r'}$ by process r' reads a different value v' from a write operation $o_{w'}$, also by process p, and that o_r precedes $o_{r'}$. Assume by contradiction that $o_{w'}$ precedes o_w. According to the algorithm, the timestamp ts_v that p associated with v is strictly larger than the timestamp $ts_{v'}$ that p associated with v'. Given that the operation o_r precedes $o_{r'}$, at the time when $o_{r'}$ was invoked, a majority of the processes has stored a timestamp value in ts that is at least ts_v, the timestamp associated to v, according to the write-back part of the algorithm for reading v. Hence, process r' cannot read v', because the timestamp associated to v' is strictly smaller than ts_v. A contradiction.

Performance. Every write operation requires two communication steps corresponding to one roundtrip exchange between p and a majority of the processes, and $O(N)$ messages are exchanged. Every read requires four communication steps corresponding to two roundtrip exchanges between the reader and a majority of the processes, or $O(N)$ messages in total.

4.4 (*N, N*) Atomic Register

4.4.1 Multiple Writers

All registers discussed so far have only a single writer. That is, our specifications of regular and atomic registers introduced in the previous sections do not provide any guarantees when multiple processes write to the same register. It is natural to ask what should happen in the case of multiple writers.

In order to answer this question, we need to formulate an appropriate *validity* property for multiple writers. Indeed, this property requires a read that is not concurrent with any write to return the *last* value written. But, if two processes have written different values v and v' concurrently, before some other process invokes a read operation, then what should this read return? Assuming we make it possible for the reader to return either v or v', do we allow a concurrent reader, or a reader that comes even later, to return the other value? What about a failed write operation? If a process writes a value v and crashes before completing the write, does a reader need to return v or can it return an older value?

In the following, we answer these questions and generalize the specification of atomic registers to multiple writers.

4.4.2 Specification

An (N, N) *atomic register* abstraction (NNAR) links together read and write operations in a stricter way than its single-writer relative. This register abstraction ensures that every failed write appears either as if it was never invoked or as if it completed, i.e., as if the operation was invoked and terminated. Clearly, a failed read operation may always appear as if it was never invoked. In addition, even in the face of concurrency, it must be that the values returned by reads could have been returned by a hypothetical serial execution, where every operation takes place at an indivisible point in time, which lies between the invocation event and the completion event of the operation.

An (N, N) atomic register is a strict generalization of a $(1, N)$ atomic register in the sense that every execution of a $(1, N)$ atomic register is also an execution of an (N, N) atomic register but not vice versa. The interface and properties of an (N, N) atomic register abstraction are given in Module 4.3.

The hypothetical serial execution mentioned before is called a *linearization* of the actual execution. More precisely, a linearization of an execution is defined as a sequence of complete operations that appear atomically, one after the other, which contains at least all complete operations of the actual execution (and possibly some operations that were incomplete) and satisfies the following conditions:

1. every read returns the last value written; and
2. for any two operations o and o', if o precedes o' in the actual execution, then o also appears before o' in the linearization.

We call an execution *linearizable* if there is a way to *linearize* it like this. With this notion, one can reformulate the *atomicity* property of an (N, N) atomic register in Module 4.3 as:

NNAR2': *Atomicity:* Every execution of the register is linearizable.

To implement (N, N) atomic registers, we adopt the same modular approach as for implementing $(1, N)$ atomic registers. We first give a general transformation that

Module 4.3: Interface and properties of an (N, N) atomic register

Module:

    Name: (N, N)-AtomicRegister, **instance** *nnar*.

Events:

    Request: $\langle$ *nnar, Read* $\rangle$: Invokes a read operation on the register.

    Request: $\langle$ *nnar, Write* $\mid v$ $\rangle$: Invokes a write operation with value v on the register.

    Indication: $\langle$ *nnar, ReadReturn* $\mid v$ $\rangle$: Completes a read operation on the register with return value v.

    Indication: $\langle$ *nnar, WriteReturn* $\rangle$: Completes a write operation on the register.

Properties:

    NNAR1: *Termination:* Same as property ONAR1 of a $(1, N)$ atomic register (Module 4.2).

    NNAR2: *Atomicity:* Every read operation returns the value that was written most recently in a hypothetical execution, where every failed operation appears to be complete or does not appear to have been invoked at all, and every complete operation appears to have been executed at some instant between its invocation and its completion.

---

implements an (N, N) atomic register using $(1, N)$ atomic registers. This transformation uses only an array of underlying $(1, N)$ atomic registers and no other way of exchanging information among the processes. We present it to illustrate the fundamental difference between both abstractions. We then give two direct and efficient implementations of (N, N) atomic registers in terms of a fail-stop algorithm and a fail-silent algorithm.

4.4.3 Transformation: From $(1, N)$ Atomic to (N, N) Atomic Registers

We describe how to transform any $(1, N)$ atomic register abstraction into an (N, N) atomic register abstraction, using no other primitives. To get an intuition of this transformation, recall the example of the atomic blackboard on which one teacher writes and from which multiple students read. A multi-writer register corresponds to a blackboard shared by multiple teachers for writing information that is read by a set of students. All teachers should write to a single common board and all students should read from this board. However, only the simpler boards constructed before are available, where every board allows only one teacher to write information. If every teacher uses his or her own board to write information then it will not be clear for a student which information to select and still ensure the atomicity of the common board, i.e., the illusion of one physical common board that all teachers share. The problem is that the student cannot recognize the latest information that was written. Indeed, if some teacher A writes v and then some other teacher B later writes w then a student that looks at the common board afterward should see w. But how can the student know that w is indeed the latest information, given that what is available are simply individual boards, one for each teacher?

The solution is to coordinate the teachers so that they explicitly create a happened-before relation among the information they write. To this end, all teachers associate a global timestamp with every written value. When teacher B writes w, he or she first reads the board and finds v (written by teacher A) and an associated timestamp there. Teacher B now increments the timestamp and associates it with w, representing the very fact that w was written after v and is, therefore, more recent than v. This is the key idea of our transformation.

The transformation in Algorithm 4.8 implements one (N, N) atomic register instance $nnar$ from multiple $(1, N)$ atomic registers. Specifically, it uses an array of N underlying $(1, N)$ atomic register instances, called $onar.p$ for $p \in \Pi$. Every register instance $onar.p$ stores a value and an associated timestamp. Basically, when a process p emulates a write operation with value v to register $nnar$, it first reads all underlying $(1, N)$ registers. Then it selects the largest timestamp, increments it, and associates it with v, the value to be written. Finally, p writes the value and the associated timestamp to the register instance $onar.p$.

To read a value from the multi-writer register, a process p first reads all underlying registers and returns the value with the largest timestamp. It may occur that several registers store the same timestamp with different values. To resolve this ambiguity, process p orders such values according to the rank of the process that writes to the register. (Recall that the rank associates every process with an index between 1 and N.) In other words, process p determines the value with the highest timestamp/rank pair, ordered first by timestamp and second by rank. This defines a total order among the values stored in the underlying registers. We abstract away this order within the function $highest(\cdot)$, which we modify for this algorithm so that it operates on triples of the form (timestamp, rank, value) and returns the timestamp and value from the triple with the largest timestamp/rank pair in our total order.

Correctness. The *termination* property of the (N, N) register follows directly from the corresponding condition of the underlying $(1, N)$ registers.

To show that register instance $nnar$ is *atomic*, we demonstrate that the $nnar$-read and $nnar$-write operations are linearizable, i.e., there exists a hypothetical serial execution with all complete operations of the actual execution, such that (1) every read returns the last value written and (2) for any two operations o_1 and o_2, if o_1 precedes o_2 in the actual execution then o_1 also appears before o_2 in the linearization.

Recall that the algorithm uses a total order on (timestamp, rank, value) tuples, implemented by the function $highest(\cdot)$, and selects the value to return in a read operation accordingly.

It is clear from the algorithm that the timestamps written by two serial operations on $nnar$ are strictly increasing, i.e., if a $nnar$-write operation writes (ts, v) to an underlying register instance $onar.q$ and a subsequent $nnar$-write operation writes (ts', v') to an underlying register instance $onar.q'$ then $ts < ts'$.

Algorithm 4.8: From $(1, N)$ Atomic to (N, N) Atomic Registers

Implements:
    (N, N)-AtomicRegister, **instance** *nnar*.

Uses:
    $(1, N)$-AtomicRegister (multiple instances).

upon event $\langle$ *nnar, Init* $\rangle$ **do**
    $val := \bot$;
    writing := FALSE;
    readlist $:= [\bot]^N$;
    forall $q \in \Pi$ **do**
        Initialize a new instance *onar.q* of $(1, N)$-AtomicRegister
            with writer q;

upon event $\langle$ *nnar, Write* $\mid v$ $\rangle$ **do**
    $val := v$;
    writing := TRUE;
    forall $q \in \Pi$ **do**
        trigger $\langle$ *onar.q, Read* $\rangle$;

upon event $\langle$ *nnar, Read* $\rangle$ **do**
    forall $q \in \Pi$ **do**
        trigger $\langle$ *onar.q, Read* $\rangle$;

upon event $\langle$ *onar.q, ReadReturn* $\mid (ts', v')$ $\rangle$ **do**
    readlist$[q] := (ts', rank(q), v')$;
    if $\#(readlist) = N$ **then**
        $(ts, v) := highest(readlist)$;
        readlist $:= [\bot]^N$;
        if *writing* = TRUE **then**
            writing := FALSE;
            trigger $\langle$ *onar.self, Write* $\mid (ts + 1, val)$ $\rangle$;
        else
            trigger $\langle$ *nnar, ReadReturn* $\mid v$ $\rangle$;

upon event $\langle$ *onar.self, WriteReturn* $\rangle$ **do**
    trigger $\langle$ *nnar, WriteReturn* $\rangle$;

Now, construct the linearization as follows. First, include all *nnar*-write operations according to the total order of their associated timestamp/rank pairs. Second, consider each *nnar*-read operation o_r in the order in which the response occurs in the actual execution, take the value ts and the rank of the writer q associated with the value v returned, and find the *nnar*-write operation o_w, during which process q wrote (ts, v) to instance *onar.q*; place operation o_r after o_w into the linearization, immediately before the subsequent *nnar*-write operation.

It is easy to see that the first condition of linearizability holds from the construction of the linearization, because each read returns the value of the latest preceding write.

To show the second condition of linearizability, consider any two operations o_1 and o_2 in the actual execution such that o_1 precedes o_2. There are four cases to consider:

1. If both are writes, they are in the correct order as argued earlier (their timestamps are strictly increasing).
2. Suppose o_1 is a read and o_2 is a write. The algorithm for the write first reads the underlying registers, selects the highest timestamp/rank pair, and increments this timestamp by one for writing. Then, o_1 occurs before o_2 in the linearization according to its construction.
3. Suppose o_1 is a write and o_2 is a read. As in the previous case, the algorithm for the read first reads the timestamps from all underlying registers and chooses among them a value with a maximal timestamp/rank pair. Thus, o_2 returns a value with associated timestamp generated by o_1 or by a subsequent write. Hence, the construction of the linearization places o_2 after o_1.
4. If o_1 is a read and o_2 is a read, the case is more complex. Suppose that o_1 returns a value v_1 and selected (ts_1, r_1) as highest timestamp/rank pair, and o_2 used a different highest timestamp/rank pair (ts_2, r_2) associated with the return value. As o_2 occurs after o_1 in the actual execution, and as any intervening writes do not decrease the timestamp value, we have $ts_2 \geq ts_1$. If $ts_2 > ts_1$ then the second condition holds by construction of the linearization.

   Otherwise, if $ts_2 = ts_1$, consider process p_1 with rank r_1 and process p_2 with rank r_2. If $r_1 < r_2$ then the write of process p_1 is placed into the linearization before the write of process p_2, and, hence, also o_1 is placed into the linearization before o_2. If $r_1 = r_2$ then the read operations occur also in the correct order in the linearization. The last case, $r_1 > r_2$, however, cannot have occurred in the actual execution: when o_2 is invoked, the underlying register instance $onar.p_1$ still contains the pair (ts_1, v_1) and o_2 would have selected (ts_1, r_1) as the highest timestamp/rank pair. But this contradicts the assumption made above that $(ts_1, r_1) \neq (ts_2, r_2)$.

Performance. Every write operation into the (N, N) atomic register requires N reads from each of the underlying $(1, N)$ registers and one write into a $(1, N)$ register. Every read from the (N, N) register requires N reads from each of the underlying $(1, N)$ registers.

Assume we apply the transformation of Algorithm 4.8 to the "Read-Impose Write-All" fail-stop algorithm (Algorithm 4.5) in order to obtain an (N, N) atomic register algorithm. Every read operation from the (N, N) register would involve N (parallel) communication roundtrips between the reader and all other processes. Furthermore, every write to the (N, N) register would involve N (parallel) communication roundtrips between the writer and all other processes (to determine the largest timestamp), and then another communication roundtrip between the writer and all other processes (to perform the actual writing).

Similarly, assume we apply the transformation of Algorithm 4.8 to "Read-Majority Impose-Majority" algorithm (Algorithm 4.6–4.7) in order to obtain a (N, N) atomic register algorithm. Every read in the (N, N) register would involve

N (parallel) communication roundtrips between the reader and a majority of the processes (to determine the latest value), and then N other communication roundtrips between the reader and a majority of the processes (to impose that value). Furthermore, every write to the (N, N) register would involve N (parallel) communication roundtrips between the writer and a majority (to determine the largest timestamp) and then another communication roundtrip between the writer and a majority (to perform the actual writing).

We present, in the following, two direct implementations of an (N, N) atomic register that are more efficient than the algorithms we obtain through the automatic transformations. Both algorithms use the two main ideas introduced by the transformation, namely, that a writer first consults the memory to obtain the highest timestamp that may have been used by the other writers, and that timestamp/rank pairs are used to extend the order on timestamps. We describe first a fail-stop algorithm and then a fail-silent algorithm.

4.4.4 Fail-Stop Algorithm: Read-Impose Write-Consult-All (N, N) Atomic Register

We describe the "Read-Impose Write-Consult-All" algorithm that implements an (N, N) atomic register in Algorithm 4.9. It uses the fail-stop system model with a perfect failure detector and extends the "Read-Impose Write-All" algorithm for $(1, N)$ atomic registers (Algorithm 4.5) to deal with multiple writers.

In order to get an idea of the issue introduced by multiple writers, it is important to first figure out why the "Read-Impose Write-All" algorithm cannot afford multiple writers. Consider indeed two processes p and q trying to write concurrently to a register, implemented using the "Read-Impose Write-All" algorithm. Due to the use of acknowledgments for read and write operations, if the preceding operation completed and no other operation is invoked, processes p and q both store the same timestamp ts used by that operation. When they proceed to write, different values would become associated with the same timestamp.

To resolve this issue, the algorithm also stores the identity of the process that writes a value together with a timestamp, expressed through the writer's rank, and uses it to determine the highest timestamp. Comparisons employ the same ordering of timestamp/rank pairs as in Algorithm 4.8. Apart from the addition of writer-ranks and the modified comparison, Algorithm 4.9 is the same as Algorithm 4.5.

Correctness. The *termination* property of the atomic register follows from the *completeness* property of the failure detector $\mathcal{P}$ and the underlying channels.

The *atomicity* property follows from the *accuracy* property of $\mathcal{P}$ and from the ordering of timestamp/rank pairs. This order is the same as in Algorithm 4.8 and the argument proceeds analogously.

For demonstrating that the operations of the algorithm are linearizable, we construct the hypothetical sequence of atomic operations as follows. First, include all write operations according to the order on the unique timestamp/rank pair that was included in the WRITE message triggered by the operation. Second, consider each read operation o_r in the order in which the response occurs in the actual execution,

---

Algorithm 4.9: Read-Impose Write-Consult-All

Implements:
    (N, N)-AtomicRegister, **instance** *nnar*.

Uses:
    BestEffortBroadcast, **instance** *beb*;
    PerfectPointToPointLinks, **instance** *pl*;
    PerfectFailureDetector, **instance** $\mathcal{P}$.

upon event $\langle$ *nnar, Init* $\rangle$ **do**
    $(ts, wr, val) := (0, 0, \bot)$;
    correct := Π;
    writeset := $\emptyset$;
    readval := $\bot$;
    reading := FALSE;

upon event $\langle$ $\mathcal{P}$, *Crash* $\mid p$ $\rangle$ **do**
    correct := *correct* $\setminus \{p\}$;

upon event $\langle$ *nnar, Read* $\rangle$ **do**
    reading := TRUE;
    readval := *val*;
    trigger $\langle$ *beb, Broadcast* $\mid$ [WRITE, ts, wr, val] $\rangle$;

upon event $\langle$ *nnar, Write* $\mid v$ $\rangle$ **do**
    trigger $\langle$ *beb, Broadcast* $\mid$ [WRITE, $ts + 1$, $rank(self), v$] $\rangle$;

upon event $\langle$ *beb, Deliver* $\mid p$, [WRITE, ts', wr', v'] $\rangle$ **do**
    if (ts', wr') is larger than (ts, wr) **then**
        $(ts, wr, val) := (ts', wr', v')$;
    trigger $\langle$ *pl, Send* $\mid p$, [ACK] $\rangle$;

upon event $\langle$ *pl, Deliver* $\mid p$, [ACK] $\rangle$ **then**
    writeset := *writeset* $\cup \{p\}$;

upon *correct* $\subseteq$ *writeset* **do**
    writeset := $\emptyset$;
    if *reading* = TRUE **then**
        reading := FALSE;
        trigger $\langle$ *nnar, ReadReturn* $\mid$ *readval* $\rangle$;
    else
        trigger $\langle$ *nnar, WriteReturn* $\rangle$;

---

take the value ts and the rank of the writer q associated with the value v returned, and find the write operation o_w, during which process q wrote (ts, v); place operation o_r after o_w into the sequence, immediately before the subsequent write operation.

The first condition of linearizability is ensured directly by the construction of the linearization, because each read returns the value of the latest preceding write.

To show the second condition of linearizability, consider any two operations o_1 and o_2 in the actual execution such that o_1 precedes o_2. There are four cases to analyze:

1. If both operations are writes then the process p_2 executing o_2 accessed its variable ts and incremented it. As the writer p_1 of o_1 has received an ACK message from p_2 (because p_2 has not been detected by $\mathcal{P}$), the value of ts at process p_2 is at least as large as the timestamp associated to o_1. Thus, the two operations appear in the linearization in the correct order by construction.
2. Suppose o_1 is a read and o_2 is a write. As in the previous case, the algorithm for the writer reads its variable ts and increments it by one for writing. This implies that o_1 occurs before o_2 in the linearization.
3. Suppose o_1 is a write and o_2 is a read. The algorithm for o_2 returns the value in variable val at the reader that is associated to the timestamp in variable ts. According to how processes update their variables and how write operations are ordered, variable ts contains a timestamp that is at least as large as the timestamp written by o_1. This implies that o_2 appears after o_1 in the linearization.
4. If both operations are reads, suppose that o_1 returns a value v_1 associated to a timestamp/rank pair (ts_1, r_1), and o_2 returns a value associated to a different timestamp/rank pair (ts_2, r_2). As o_2 occurs after o_1 in the actual execution, the reader in o_1 received an acknowledgement from all nondetected processes, including the process that executes o_2. The latter process (executing o_2) may only have increased its ts variable in the algorithm; this argument implies that $ts_2 \geq ts_1$.

   We now distinguish two cases. If $ts_2 > ts_1$ then the condition of linearizability holds by construction. Otherwise, if $ts_2 = ts_1$, consider process p_1 with rank r_1 and process p_2 with rank r_2. If $r_1 < r_2$ then the write of process p_1 is placed into the linearization before the write of process p_2, and, hence, also o_1 is placed into the linearization before o_2, as required. Otherwise, it must hold $r_1 > r_2$ because $r_1 \neq r_2$. But, this cannot occur in the actual execution. It would mean that the variable tuple (ts, wr) at the process executing o_2 contains a timestamp/rank pair that is at least as large as (ts_1, r_1) according to the algorithm, because the process received a WRITE message containing (t_1, r_1) during o_1 and updated the variables. But o_2 returns the value associated to (ts_2, r_2), with $ts_2 = ts_1$, and this means that $r_2 \geq r_1$, a contradiction.

Performance. Every read and write in the (N, N) register requires two communication steps, and $O(N)$ messages are exchanged for one operation

4.4.5 Fail-Silent Algorithm: Read-Impose Write-Consult-Majority (N, N) Atomic Register

We describe here how to obtain an algorithm that implements an (N, N) atomic register in a fail-silent model as an extension of our "Read-Impose Write-Majority" algorithm, i.e., Algorithm 4.6–4.7, that implements a $(1, N)$ atomic register.

Let us again consider multiple writers in the single-writer formulation of the algorithm and examine why Algorithm 4.6–4.7 fails to implement an (N, N) atomic

---

Algorithm 4.10: Read-Impose Write-Consult-Majority (part 1, read and consult)

Implements:
(N, N)-AtomicRegister, **instance** *nnar*.

Uses:
BestEffortBroadcast, **instance** *beb*;
PerfectPointToPointLinks, **instance** *pl*.

upon event ⟨ *nnar, Init* ⟩ **do**
$(ts, wr, val) := (0, 0, \bot)$;
$acks := 0$;
$writeval := \bot$;
$rid := 0$;
$readlist := [\bot]^N$;
$readval := \bot$;
$reading := \text{FALSE}$;

upon event ⟨ *nnar, Read* ⟩ **do**
$rid := rid + 1$;
$acks := 0$;
$readlist := [\bot]^N$;
$reading := \text{TRUE}$;
trigger ⟨ *beb, Broadcast* | [READ, *rid*] ⟩;

upon event ⟨ *beb, Deliver* | p, [READ, r] ⟩ **do**
trigger ⟨ *pl, Send* | p, [VALUE, r, ts, wr, val] ⟩;

upon event ⟨ *pl, Deliver* | q, [VALUE, r, ts', wr', v'] ⟩ **such that** $r = rid$ **do**
$readlist[q] := (ts', wr', v')$;
if $\#(readlist) > N/2$ **then**
$(maxts, rr, readval) := highest(readlist)$;
$readlist := [\bot]^N$;
if $reading = \text{TRUE}$ **then**
trigger ⟨ *beb, Broadcast* | [WRITE, *rid, maxts, rr, readval*] ⟩;
else
trigger ⟨ *beb, Broadcast* | [WRITE, *rid, maxts* + 1, rank(*self*), *writeval*] ⟩;

---

register abstraction. Suppose a process p executes a long sequence of write operations. Furthermore, assume that some other correct process q has not received the WRITE messages from p so far, and was, therefore, never included in the majority required to complete those operations. When process q tries to write using its local timestamp, its write operation will fail because its timestamp is smaller than the current value stored by those processes that acknowledged the write operations of p. Compared to the discussion of Algorithm 4.9 before, which uses the fail-stop model, the timestamp of q can fall behind much more here, because q's reply is not needed by p to terminate an operation.

Again, the solution to the problem is to coordinate the timestamps between the processes according to the method introduced by the transformation from $(1, N)$ to (N, N) atomic registers. For extending the "Read-Impose Write-Majority"

Algorithm 4.11: Read-Impose Write-Consult-Majority (part 2, write and write-back)

upon event ⟨ *nnar*, *Write* | *v* ⟩ **do**
    rid := *rid* + 1;
    writeval := *v*;
    acks := 0;
    readlist := [⊥]^N;
    trigger ⟨ *beb*, *Broadcast* | [READ, *rid*] ⟩;

upon event ⟨ *beb*, *Deliver* | *p*, [WRITE, *r*, *ts'*, *wr'*, *v'*] ⟩ **do**
    if (*ts'*, *wr'*) is larger than (*ts*, *wr*) **then**
        (*ts*, *wr*, *val*) := (*ts'*, *wr'*, *v'*);
    trigger ⟨ *pl*, *Send* | *p*, [ACK, *r*] ⟩;

upon event ⟨ *pl*, *Deliver* | *q*, [ACK, *r*] ⟩ **such that** *r* = *rid* **do**
    acks := *acks* + 1;
    if *acks* > *N*/2 **then**
        acks := 0;
        if *reading* = TRUE **then**
            reading := FALSE;
            trigger ⟨ *nnar*, *ReadReturn* | *readval* ⟩;
        else
            trigger ⟨ *nnar*, *WriteReturn* ⟩;

algorithm to multiple writers, we have to determine the "current" timestamp in a distributed fashion. Every writer first consults all processes for timestamps written by other processes, determines the maximal timestamp stored so far, and then selects a higher timestamp to be associated with its write operation. The consultation phase reads the distributed atomic register in the same way as during a read operation.

We give the resulting "Read-Impose Write-Consult-Majority" algorithm in Algorithm 4.10–4.11; it is based on the "Read-Impose Write-Majority" algorithm that implements a single-writer atomic register in the fail-silent system model.

The read operation of the (*N, N*) atomic register algorithm is similar to the single-writer algorithm. The write operation is different in that the writer first invokes the mechanism of the read operation to determine a timestamp to associate with the new value. As in the other multi-writer register algorithms, the algorithm extends timestamps by the rank of the writer process for determining the value to store. The algorithm uses the same order on timestamp/rank pairs as Algorithm 4.8 and the function *highest*(·) from Algorithm 4.8.

Correctness. The *termination* property of the register follows from the correct majority assumption and the properties of the underlying channels. The *atomicity* property follows from the use of a majority quorum during read and write operations and from the ordering of timestamp/rank pairs as in Algorithm 4.8. The linearizability property follows from constructing a linearization order for every execution in the same manner as for Algorithms 4.8 and 4.10–4.11. As the argument contains essentially the same steps as presented twice before, we omit the details.

Performance. Every read or write in the (N, N) register requires four communication steps corresponding to two roundtrip exchanges between the reader or the writer and a majority of the processes. In each case, $O(N)$ messages are exchanged.

4.5 $(1, N)$ Logged Regular Register

So far, we have considered register abstractions for crash-stop process abstractions, which do not recover after a crash. In other words, even if a crashed process recovers, it is excluded from the computation afterward and cannot help other processes reading or writing by storing and witnessing values. In this section, we relax this assumption and enlarge the system model to include recovered processes. This will make the resulting algorithms more robust because they tolerate a wider range of practical failure scenarios. We give the specification of a regular register abstraction and an algorithm that implements this specification in the fail-recovery model.

4.5.1 Precedence in the Fail-Recovery Model

Before defining a register abstraction in the fail-recovery model, we revisit the notion of precedence introduced earlier for the models with crash-stop process abstractions. Recall the assumption that a process accesses every register in a sequential manner, strictly alternating between invocation events and completion events. In the fail-recovery model, a process may crash right after a register abstraction has triggered a completion event of an operation and before the process may react to this event. From the perspective of the register implementation, the operation is complete, but for the calling algorithm, it is not. To reconcile this difference, we extend the notion of precedence among operations to encompass also incomplete operations, for which completion events do not occur.

> An operation o is said to *precede* an operation o' if any of the following two conditions hold:
>
> 1. the completion event of o occurs before the invocation event of o'; or
> 2. the operations are invoked by the same process and the invocation event of o' occurs after the invocation event of o.

Note how this implies that an operation o invoked by some process p may *precede* an operation o' invoked also by process p, even though o may not have completed. For instance, this could occur when p has invoked o, crashed, recovered, and subsequently invoked o'. This was clearly impossible in the system models where processes do not recover from failure.

4.5.2 Specification

The interface and properties of a $(1, N)$ regular register abstraction in the fail-recovery model, called a *logged register*, are given in Module 4.4. Compared to

Module 4.4: Interface and properties of a $(1, N)$ logged regular register

Module:

    Name: $(1, N)$-LoggedRegularRegister, **instance** *lonrr*.

Events:

    Request: $\langle$ *lonrr, Read* $\rangle$: Invokes a read operation on the register.

    Request: $\langle$ *lonrr, Write* $\mid v$ $\rangle$: Invokes a write operation with value v on the register.

    Indication: $\langle$ *lonrr, ReadReturn* $\mid v$ $\rangle$: Completes a read operation on the register with return value v.

    Indication: $\langle$ *lonrr, WriteReturn* $\rangle$: Completes a write operation on the register.

Properties:

    LONRR1: *Termination:* If a process invokes an operation and never crashes, then the operation eventually completes.

    LONRR2: *Validity:* A read that is not concurrent with a write returns the last value written; a read that is concurrent with a write returns the last value written or the value concurrently written.

---

the definition of a $(1, N)$ regular register in the models without recoveries (Module 4.1), only the *termination* property and the notion of precedence that underlies the *validity* property change. Atomic registers in the fail-recovery model with one or multiple writers and with multiple readers can be specified accordingly.

The *termination* property (LONRR1) is similar to the formulation of termination considered before (property ONRR1 of Module 4.1), though expressed here in a different manner. The notion of a "correct process" used in the regular register specification has a different meaning. Because a correct process in the fail-recovery model may crash and recover many times, we do not require that every operation invoked by a correct process eventually completes. It is not possible to require in every case that a process that invokes some operation, crashes, and then recovers, is notified about the completion of the operation. Instead, the *termination* property of a logged regular register requires that only operations invoked by processes that never crash eventually complete.

On the other hand, although the *validity* property (LONRR2) reads exactly as in earlier specifications (e.g., property ONRR2 of Module 4.1), it has a different meaning.

Consider the execution shown in Fig. 4.7. Assume the writer process p invokes an operation to write x and this is the first write operation ever. The process crashes before completing the operation, then recovers, and invokes a second write with value y. At this point in time, some process q concurrently invokes a read operation on the same register. Even though the second write operation of p has already been invoked, it is valid that q reads $\perp$ from the register if the value x is not considered

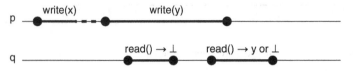

Figure 4.7: An execution of a logged regular register

to have been written. Assume that q subsequently invokes another read operation that is still concurrent with the second write operation of p. This read operation now must no longer return x (but may still return $\perp$ or y) because x was never written to the register. In other words, there is only one last value written before y; it can be either $\perp$ or x, but not both.

In contrast to the logged links and logged broadcast abstractions from the previous chapters, the logged register abstraction delivers its output through ordinary events and not through a special variable that is logged in stable storage. This form was necessary for the communication abstractions because the receiving process could not anticipate, for example, if and how many messages might be delivered by a broadcast abstraction. When accessing shared storage using a register abstraction, however, both indication events, i.e., the ⟨ *ReadReturn* ⟩ and the ⟨ *WriteReturn* ⟩ events, occur only after the process has triggered the corresponding request event beforehand. Furthermore, executing the same register operation multiple times in succession has the same effect as executing it once. This means that even if an indication event is lost because of a crash, when the process recovers later, it can simply restart the operation without losing information or affecting the future behavior of the register.

4.5.3 Fail-Recovery Algorithm: Logged Majority Voting

For implementing a register in the fail-recovery model where all processes can crash, it is easy to see that even implementations of the simplest registers must have access to stable storage and require that a majority of the processes is correct. As before, the fail-recovery algorithm may access local stable storage (through *store* and *retrieve* operations), whose content is not lost after a crash. Furthermore, we assume that a majority of the processes are correct. Remember that a correct process in a fail-recovery model is one that either never crashes or eventually recovers and never crashes again.

Intuitively, we might consider transforming our "Majority Voting" regular register algorithm (i.e., Algorithm 4.2) to deal with process crashes and recoveries simply by logging every new value of any local variable to stable storage upon modification of that variable, and then retrieving all variables upon recovery. This would mean that any delivered message must be stored in stable storage. However, one should be careful with such an automatic transformation, as discussed earlier, because access to stable storage is an expensive operation and should only be used when necessary.

In the following, we describe Algorithm 4.12–4.13, called "Logged Majority Voting," that implements a $(1, N)$ logged regular register. It is a direct extension of Algorithm 4.2. The algorithm stores some variables in persistent storage across invocations, in particular, the current timestamp ts and value val stored in the register, the write-timestamp wts, and the request identifier rid. These values must be logged in one atomic *store* operation; the process accesses them again upon recovery with a *retrieve* operation. We discuss the need of logging with an atomic operation through an exercise (at the end of the chapter).

For communication, the algorithm uses a stubborn point-to-point links abstraction and a stubborn best-effort broadcast abstraction. Remember that stubborn communication primitives ensure that, roughly speaking, if a message is sent or broadcast to a correct process (in the fail-recovery sense), the message is delivered an infinite number of times, unless the sender crashes. This ensures that the process, even if it crashes and recovers a finite number of times, will eventually process every message sent to it. But, the algorithm must take measures to filter out duplicate messages.

Two flags *writing* and *reading* are used to mark the presence of an ongoing write or read operation, respectively. They are necessary to prevent multiply delivered ACK and VALUE messages from triggering duplicate completion events. In contrast to Algorithm 4.2, the "Logged Majority Voting" algorithm employs the request identifier *rid* not only for reads but also for writes. This is necessary because every failed write is restarted during recovery and the collected ACK messages must be attributed to the proper WRITE message.

Note that upon recovery, every process first executes its recovery procedure. The algorithm logs only those variables that must preserve their values across operations, with the exception of the *writing* flag. Logging the *writing* variable is needed for restarting a write operation that may have been left in a partially completed state after a crash.

The communication pattern of Algorithm 4.12–4.13 is similar to the communication induced by Algorithm 4.2 for implementing a regular register in the fail-silent model.

With the same approach as used here to extend Algorithm 4.2 to Algorithm 4.12–4.13 for the fail-recovery model, one can also extend Algorithm 4.6–4.7 ("Read-Impose Write-Majority") and Algorithm 4.10–4.11 ("Read-Impose Write-Consult-Majority") to the fail-recovery model. The resulting algorithms implement a $(1, N)$ atomic register abstraction and an (N, N) atomic register abstraction, respectively, in the fail-recovery model.

Correctness. The *termination* property follows from the properties of the underlying stubborn communication abstractions and the assumption of a majority of the correct processes.

The argument for the *validity* property is similar to the one used for Algorithm 4.2. Consider a read operation that is not concurrent with any write. Assume, furthermore, that the read is invoked by process q and the last value written by the writer p is v with associated timestamp wts. Because the writer logs every timestamp and increments the timestamp for every write, this means that, at the time when the read

---

Algorithm 4.12: Logged Majority Voting (part 1, write)

Implements:
    $(1, N)$-LoggedRegularRegister, **instance** *lonrr*.

Uses:
    StubbornBestEffortBroadcast, **instance** *sbeb*;
    StubbornLinks, **instance** *sl*.

upon event ⟨ *lonrr, Init* ⟩ **do**
    $(ts, val) := (0, \bot)$;
    $wts := 0$;
    $rid := 0$;
    $acklist := [\bot]^N$; $writing :=$ FALSE;
    $readlist := [\bot]^N$; $reading :=$ FALSE;
    $store(wts, ts, val, rid, writing)$;

upon event ⟨ *sbeb, Recovery* ⟩ **do**
    $retrieve(wts, ts, val, rid, writing)$;
    $readlist := [\bot]^N$; $reading :=$ FALSE;
    if $writing =$ TRUE **then**
        $rid := rid + 1$;
        trigger ⟨ *sbeb, Broadcast* | [WRITE, *rid, ts, v*] ⟩;

upon event ⟨ *lonrr, Write* | v ⟩ **do**
    $wts := wts + 1$;
    $(ts, val) := (wts, v)$;
    $rid := rid + 1$;
    $acklist := [\bot]^N$; $writing :=$ TRUE;
    $store(wts, ts, val, rid, writing)$;
    trigger ⟨ *sbeb, Broadcast* | [WRITE, *rid, wts, v*] ⟩;

upon event ⟨ *sbeb, Deliver* | p, [WRITE, r, ts', v'] ⟩ **do**
    if $ts' > ts$ **then**
        $(ts, val) := (ts', v')$;
        $store(ts, val)$;
    trigger ⟨ *sl, Send* | p, [ACK, r] ⟩;

upon event ⟨ *sl, Deliver* | q, [ACK, r] ⟩ **such that** $r = rid$ **do**
    $acklist[q] :=$ ACK;
    if $\#(acklist) > N/2 \wedge writing =$ TRUE **then**
        $acklist := [\bot]^N$; $writing :=$ FALSE;
        $store(writing)$;
        trigger ⟨ *lonrr, WriteReturn* ⟩;

---

is invoked, a majority of the processes have logged v in their variable val and wts in their variable ts, and that there is no larger timestamp in the system. Before returning from the read operation, process q consults a majority of the processes and hence receives at least one reply containing timestamp wts. This follows from the use of majority quorums that always intersect. Process q hence returns value v, which is indeed the last value written, because wts is the largest timestamp.

Algorithm 4.13: Logged Majority Voting (part 2, read)

upon event ⟨ *lonrr*, *Read* ⟩ **do**
    rid := *rid* + 1;
    readlist := [⊥]^N; *reading* := TRUE;
    trigger ⟨ *sbeb*, *Broadcast* | [READ, *rid*] ⟩;

upon event ⟨ *sbeb*, *Deliver* | *p*, [READ, *r*] ⟩ **do**
    trigger ⟨ *sl*, *Send* | *p*, [VALUE, *r*, *ts*, *val*] ⟩;

upon event ⟨ *sl*, *Deliver* | *q*, [VALUE, *r*, *ts'*, *v'*] ⟩ **such that** *r* = *rid* **do**
    readlist[*q*] := (*ts'*, *v'*);
    if #(*readlist*) > *N*/2 ∧ *reading* = TRUE **do**
        v := *highestval*(*readlist*);
        readlist := [⊥]^N; *reading* := FALSE;
        trigger ⟨ *lonrr*, *ReadReturn* | *v* ⟩;

Consider now the case where the read is concurrent with some write of value v with associated timestamp wts, and the previous write was for value v' and timestamp $wts - 1$. If p had crashed during the previous write before it logged v' then no process will ever see v'. Otherwise, if p had logged v' then p has first completed the writing of v' upon recovery. If any process returns wts and v to the reader q then q returns v, which is a valid reply. Otherwise, at least one process replies with v' and associated timestamp $wts - 1$, and q returns v', which is also a valid reply.

Performance. Every write operation requires two communication steps between the writer and a majority of the processes. Similarly, every read operation requires two communication steps between the reader and a majority of the processes. In both cases, $O(N)$ messages are exchanged. Every write operation requires one logging operation by writer and one logging operation by at least a majority of processes (these can be executed in parallel). Thus, every write requires two causally related logging operations.

Note that stubborn links are implemented by retransmitting messages periodically; however, this retransmission can be stopped by a writer and a reader once it has logged the reply from some process or, at the latest, once it receives enough replies and has completed its operation.

4.6 (1, N) Byzantine Safe Register

This section and the following ones consider register abstractions in the fail-arbitrary model, with processes subject to Byzantine faults. The safe register abstraction is introduced first, and regular and atomic registers are discussed subsequently.

Module 4.5: Interface and properties of a $(1, N)$ Byzantine safe register

Module:

    Name: $(1, N)$-ByzantineSafeRegister, **instance** *bonsr*, with writer w.

Events:

    Request: ⟨ *bonsr, Read* ⟩: Invokes a read operation on the register.

    Request: ⟨ *bonsr, Write* | v ⟩: Invokes a write operation with value v on the register. Executed only by process w.

    Indication: ⟨ *bonsr, ReadReturn* | v ⟩: Completes a read operation on the register with return value v.

    Indication: ⟨ *bonsr, WriteReturn* ⟩: Completes a write operation on the register. Occurs only at process w.

Properties:

    BONSR1: *Termination:* If a correct process invokes an operation, then the operation eventually completes.

    BONSR2: *Validity:* A read that is not concurrent with a write returns the last value written.

4.6.1 Specification

Registers with safe semantics have been skipped in the context of crash failures because even simple algorithms were strong enough to provide regular register semantics. With arbitrary-fault process abstractions, it makes sense to consider the $(1, N)$ *Byzantine safe register* abstraction.

A $(1, N)$ Byzantine safe register is basically the same as a $(1, N)$ regular register for crash-stop process failures (Module 4.1), except that its validity property says nothing about the results returned by concurrent operations. More precisely, only reads that are not concurrent with a write must return the last written value; otherwise, a safe register may return any value from its domain. The specification is shown in Module 4.5; it explicitly identifies the one process w that writes to the register.

For the specification and implementation of registers in the fail-arbitrary system model, we assume that writer and reader processes are only subject to crash faults but never exhibit arbitrary (Byzantine) faults. This restriction comes from the inherent difficulty of defining registers operated on by Byzantine processes. As one cannot make statements about the behavior of Byzantine processes, an attempt for such a definition could, therefore, simply ignore their read operations. But arbitrary-faulty writers may influence the values returned by correct processes in complex ways, which is the reason for ruling them out.

In practical systems, this restriction is not significant because the reader and writer processes are usually different from the replicated processes in Π. Readers and writers are often *clients* that access a fault-tolerant service, implemented by the processes in Π, which are called *server processes* in this context. The service has no interest in assuring consistency properties to arbitrary-faulty clients.

4.6.2 Fail-Arbitrary Algorithm: Byzantine Masking Quorum

Distributed implementations of shared storage in the fail-arbitrary model can be separated into two classes: algorithms that use cryptographic digital signatures and algorithms that do not need them. In this section, we introduce a signature-free algorithm that relies on Byzantine masking quorums. An example of a so-called *authenticated-data* algorithm that uses signatures is given in Sect. 4.7.2.

The principal difficulty with extending the "Majority Voting" algorithm (Algorithm 4.2) to tolerate Byzantine faults lies in filtering out wrong timestamps and return values forged by faulty processes. Algorithm 4.14, called "Byzantine Masking Quorum," works only for $N > 4f$. Its write operation proceeds as before: the writer increments a timestamp, sends a timestamp/value pair to all processes, and expects $N - f$ of them to reply with an acknowledgment. But the read operation is different because a Byzantine process may send an arbitrary timestamp and a value that was never written.

In order to eliminate such faulty data, the reader receives timestamp/value pairs from more than $(N + 2f)/2$ processes; such a set of processes is also called a *Byzantine masking quorum* (Sect. 2.7.3). From these values, the reader first eliminates all pairs that occur only f or fewer times and then selects the value from the pair with the highest timestamp. If no pair remains after the elimination, the reader selects a *default value* v_0 from the domain of the register. This filtering and selection operation, starting from a list of timestamp/value pairs, is encapsulated in a function $byzhighestval(\cdot)$. The algorithm implements only safe semantics because v_0 may never have been written to the register.

The other changes from Algorithm 4.2 to 4.14 are to use authenticated links for communication and to explicitly restrict the write operation to the given writer process. Note that all processes know the identity of the writer w and the write operation can only be invoked by process w.

Correctness. Assuming that $N > 4f$, Algorithm 4.14 implements a $(1, N)$ Byzantine safe register. The *termination* property is obvious from the algorithm, because there are $N - f$ correct processes and the algorithm only waits for more than $(N + 2f)/2$ messages of a given type. Because $N - f > (N + 2f)/2$, every correct process eventually stops waiting and returns from an operation.

The *validity* property follows from the use of Byzantine masking quorums. We show that a read operation that is not concurrent with any write returns the last value written. Suppose, process q executes the read and the last written value was v, written by process p with associated timestamp wts. During the write, process p has received ACK messages from more than $(N + 2f)/2$ processes; suppose messages

Algorithm 4.14: Byzantine Masking Quorum

Implements:
    $(1, N)$-ByzantineSafeRegister, **instance** *bonsr*, with writer w.
Uses:
    AuthPerfectPointToPointLinks, **instance** *al*.

upon event ⟨ *bonsr, Init* ⟩ **do**
    $(ts, val) := (0, \bot)$;
    $wts := 0$;
    $acklist := [\bot]^N$;
    $rid := 0$;
    $readlist := [\bot]^N$;

upon event ⟨ *bonsr, Write* | v ⟩ **do**   // only process w
    $wts := wts + 1$;
    $acklist := [\bot]^N$;
    forall $q \in \Pi$ **do**
        trigger ⟨ *al, Send* | q, [WRITE, wts, v] ⟩;

upon event ⟨ *al, Deliver* | p, [WRITE, ts', v'] ⟩ **such that** $p = w$ **do**
    if $ts' > ts$ **then**
        $(ts, val) := (ts', v')$;
    trigger ⟨ *al, Send* | p, [ACK, ts'] ⟩;

upon event ⟨ *al, Deliver* | q, [ACK, ts'] ⟩ **such that** $ts' = wts$ **do**
    $acklist[q] := $ ACK;
    if $\#(acklist) > (N + 2f)/2$ **then**
        $acklist := [\bot]^N$;
        trigger ⟨ *bonsr, WriteReturn* ⟩;

upon event ⟨ *bonsr, Read* ⟩ **do**
    $rid := rid + 1$;
    $readlist := [\bot]^N$;
    forall $q \in \Pi$ **do**
        trigger ⟨ *al, Send* | q, [READ, rid] ⟩;

upon event ⟨ *al, Deliver* | p, [READ, r] ⟩ **do**
    trigger ⟨ *al, Send* | p, [VALUE, r, ts, val] ⟩;

upon event ⟨ *al, Deliver* | q, [VALUE, r, ts', v'] ⟩ **such that** $r = rid$ **do**
    $readlist[q] := (ts', v')$;
    if $\#(readlist) > \frac{N + 2f}{2}$ **then**
        $v := byzhighestval(readlist)$;
        $readlist := [\bot]^N$;
        trigger ⟨ *bonsr, ReadReturn* | v ⟩;

from all f faulty processes are included. Thus, after the completion of the write, more than

$$\frac{N + 2f}{2} - f$$

correct and *informed* processes store the pair (wts, v) in their variables ts and val, and the remaining up to (but less than)

$$N - \frac{N + 2f}{2}$$

correct processes are *uninformed*.

During the read, process q receives more than $(N + 2f)/2$ VALUE messages containing timestamp/value pairs, of which up to f may be from faulty processes and contain arbitrary data, and less than

$$N - \frac{N + 2f}{2}$$

may be from uninformed processes. Subtracting the latter from the former, there are still more than f messages from informed processes and contain the pair (wts, v). Consequently, the function *byzhighestval*$(\cdot)$ does not filter out this pair and wts is the largest timestamp received from any correct process; larger timestamps received from faulty processes occur at most f times and are eliminated. Hence, *byzhighestval*$(\cdot)$ returns v.

Performance. The algorithm uses the same number of messages as Algorithm 4.2 for regular registers in the fail-silent model, from which it is derived. In total, it uses one communication roundtrip and $O(N)$ messages for every operation.

4.7 (1, N) Byzantine Regular Register

When a write operation updates the stored data concurrently to a read operation in Algorithm 4.14, the read may return the default value v_0. Although permitted by safe semantics, this violates *regular* semantics. The problem is that the reader cannot distinguish old timestamp/value pairs and newly written ones from the ones that may have been forged by the faulty processes, and returns v_0 in case of doubt. For extending Algorithm 4.14 to implement a $(1, N)$ *regular* register abstraction, however, the algorithm would need to return either the last written value or the concurrently written one. We define the $(1, N)$ Byzantine regular register abstraction in this section and consider two algorithms to implement it. The first algorithm (Sect. 4.7.2) uses data authentication through digital signatures, where as the second one (Sect. 4.7.3) does not.

4.7.1 Specification

The $(1, N)$ *Byzantine regular register* abstraction is basically the same as a $(1, N)$ regular register, but with an explicit identification of the writer w and the restriction

---

Module 4.6: Interface and properties of a $(1, N)$ Byzantine regular register

Module:

    Name: $(1, N)$-ByzantineRegularRegister, **instance** *bonrr*, with writer w.

Events:

    Request: ⟨ *bonrr, Read* ⟩: Invokes a read operation on the register.

    Request: ⟨ *bonrr, Write* | v ⟩: Invokes a write operation with value v on the register. Executed only by process w.

    Indication: ⟨ *bonrr, ReadReturn* | v ⟩: Completes a read operation on the register with return value v.

    Indication: ⟨ *bonrr, WriteReturn* ⟩: Completes a write operation on the register. Occurs only at process w.

Properties:

    BONRR1–BONRR2: Same as properties ONRR1–ONRR2 in a $(1, N)$ regular register (Module 4.1).

---

of readers and writers to crash faults, as for Byzantine safe registers. The details of the abstraction are given in Module 4.6.

4.7.2 Fail-Arbitrary Algorithm: Authenticated-Data Byzantine Quorum

With the help of digital signatures one can easily circumvent the problem in Algorithm 4.14 mentioned earlier and obtain an implementation of a $(1, N)$ Byzantine regular register. This solution has even better resilience (requiring only $N > 3f$) than Algorithm 4.14 (whose resilience is $N > 4f$).

The idea behind the following "Authenticated-Data Byzantine Quorum" algorithm, shown in Algorithm 4.15, is for the writer to sign the timestamp/value pair and to store it together with the signature at the processes. The writer *authenticates* the data with its signature. The reader verifies the signature on each timestamp/value pair received in a VALUE message and ignores those with invalid signatures. A Byzantine process is thus prevented from returning an arbitrary timestamp and value in the VALUE message, although it may include a signed value with an outdated timestamp. Algorithm 4.15 is now obtained from the "Majority Voting" algorithm in the fail-silent model by adding data authentication and by employing Byzantine (majority) quorums (Sect. 2.7.3) instead of ordinary (majority) quorums.

Note that only the clients, i.e., the reader and the writer, need to perform cryptographic digital signature operations; the server processes simply store the signatures and may ignore their meaning.

Correctness. Under the assumption that $N > 3f$, the *termination* property is straightforward to verify: as there are $N - f$ correct processes, the reader and the

Algorithm 4.15: Authenticated-Data Byzantine Quorum

Implements:
    (1, N)-ByzantineRegularRegister, **instance** *bonrr*, with writer *w*.
Uses:
    AuthPerfectPointToPointLinks, **instance** *al*.

upon event ⟨ *bonrr, Init* ⟩ **do**
    $(ts, val, \sigma) := (0, \bot, \bot)$;
    $wts := 0$;
    $acklist := [\bot]^N$;
    $rid := 0$;
    $readlist := [\bot]^N$;

upon event ⟨ *bonrr, Write* | *v* ⟩ **do**   // only process *w*
    $wts := wts + 1$;
    $acklist := [\bot]^N$;
    $\sigma := sign(self, bonrr\|self\|\text{WRITE}\|wts\|v)$;
    forall $q \in \Pi$ **do**
        trigger ⟨ *al, Send* | *q*, [WRITE, *wts*, *v*, *σ*] ⟩;

upon event ⟨ *al, Deliver* | *p*, [WRITE, *ts′*, *v′*, *σ′*] ⟩ **such that** *p* = *w* **do**
    if $ts' > ts$ **then**
        $(ts, val, \sigma) := (ts', v', \sigma')$;
    trigger ⟨ *al, Send* | *p*, [ACK, *ts′*] ⟩;

upon event ⟨ *al, Deliver* | *q*, [ACK, *ts′*] ⟩ **such that** *ts′* = *wts* **do**
    $acklist[q] := \text{ACK}$;
    if $\#(acklist) > (N + f)/2$ **then**
        $acklist := [\bot]^N$;
        trigger ⟨ *bonrr, WriteReturn* ⟩;

upon event ⟨ *bonrr, Read* ⟩ **do**
    $rid := rid + 1$;
    $readlist := [\bot]^N$;
    forall $q \in \Pi$ **do**
        trigger ⟨ *al, Send* | *q*, [READ, *rid*] ⟩;

upon event ⟨ *al, Deliver* | *p*, [READ, *r*] ⟩ **do**
    trigger ⟨ *al, Send* | *p*, [VALUE, *r*, *ts*, *val*, *σ*] ⟩;

upon event ⟨ *al, Deliver* | *q*, [VALUE, *r*, *ts′*, *v′*, *σ′*] ⟩ **such that** *r* = *rid* **do**
    if $verifysig(q, bonrr\|w\|\text{WRITE}\|ts'\|v'\|, \sigma')$ **then**
        $readlist[q] := (ts', v')$;
        if $\#(readlist) > \frac{N+f}{2}$ **then**
            $v := highestval(readlist)$;
            $readlist := [\bot]^N$;
            trigger ⟨ *bonrr, ReadReturn* | *v* ⟩;

writer receive

$$N - f > \frac{N + f}{2}$$

replies and complete their operations.

To see the *validity* property, consider a read operation by process q that is not concurrent with any write. Assume that some process p executed the last write, and that p has written value v with associated timestamp wts. When the read is invoked, more than $(N + f)/2$ processes have acknowledged to p that they would store wts and v in their local state. The writer has not signed any pair with a larger timestamp than wts. When the reader obtains VALUE messages from more than $(N + f)/2$ processes, at least one of these message originates from a correct process and contains wts, v, and a valid signature from p. This holds because every two sets of more than $(N + f)/2$ processes overlap in at least one correct process, as they form Byzantine quorums. The reader hence returns v, the last written value, because no pair with a timestamp larger than wts passes the signature verification step.

Consider now the case where the read is concurrent with some write of value v with associated timestamp wts, and the previous write was for value v' and timestamp $wts - 1$. If any process returns wts to the reader q then q returns v, which is a valid reply. Otherwise, the reader receives at least one message containing v' and associated timestamp $wts - 1$ from a correct process and returns v', which ensures regular semantics.

Performance. The algorithm uses the same communication pattern as Algorithm 4.2 for regular registers in the fail-silent model and incurs two communication round-trips and $O(N)$ messages for every operation. The algorithm adds the cryptographic operations for creating and verifying digital signatures by the clients.

The same approach can also be used to transform Algorithm 4.6–4.7 for a $(1, N)$ atomic register in the fail-silent model into a $(1, N)$ *Byzantine* atomic register, defined analogously in the fail-arbitrary model.

4.7.3 Fail-Arbitrary Algorithm: Double-Write Byzantine Quorum

In this section, we describe an algorithm with resilience $N > 3f$ that implements a $(1, N)$ Byzantine regular register abstraction and does not use digital signatures. As we have seen with the previous algorithm, digital signatures greatly simplify the design of fail-arbitrary algorithms.

Tolerating less than $N/3$ arbitrary-faulty processes is optimal in this context. For instance, no algorithm for implementing even a safe register on $N = 3$ processes without data authentication tolerates only one Byzantine process. Consider how such an algorithm would operate. Even without concurrency, the read operation should be wait-free, that is, not block after receiving a reply from only $N - f = 2$ processes. Hence, the reader should choose a return value from only two replies. But it may be that the third process is correct and only slow, and one of the replies was forged by the Byzantine process. As the two responses look equally plausible, the reader might return the forged value and violate the *validity* property of the register in this case.

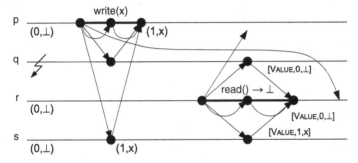

Figure 4.8: A nonregular register execution with one Byzantine process q and a one-phase write algorithm

In order to achieve optimal resilience $N > 3f$ and regular semantics, the writer process p uses two phases to write a new value in Algorithm 4.16–4.17, a *pre-write* phase and a *write* phase. This explains why the algorithm is called "Double-Write Byzantine Quorum."

A two-phase write operation is actually necessary to ensure regular semantics with resilience $N > 3f$, as the execution of a hypothetical algorithm with only one write phase in Fig. 4.8 illustrates. Suppose that the algorithm relies on a timestamp/value pair stored by all processes, like previous algorithms. Initially, every correct process stores $(0, \perp)$. If the algorithm would implement a Byzantine regular register abstraction then a write operation by process p to write the pair $(1, x)$ could have sent this to all processes, receive acknowledgments from processes p, q, and s, and complete. The message from p to process r is delayed. Consider a subsequently invoked read operation by r that obtains VALUE messages with replies from q, r, and s. Process q is Byzantine and replies with $[\text{VALUE}, 0, \perp]$, process r only knows the initial value and sends $[\text{VALUE}, 0, \perp]$, and process s replies with $[\text{VALUE}, 1, x]$. How should the reader select a return value?

- The reader cannot return x, because only one process replied with value x, so the value might have been forged by the faulty process and violate the *validity* property.
- The reader cannot return the initial value $\perp$, because the value x might indeed have been written before the read was invoked, as the execution shows. This would also violate the *validity* property.
- The reader must return *something* as required by the *termination* property. But the reader cannot afford to wait for a reply from process p. It may be that p has crashed and never sends a reply; indeed, if the writer had crashed in the middle of a write and only s had received its (single) message, the replies would represent a valid state.

Hence, the read will not satisfy the properties a regular register.

The two-phase write operation avoids this problem. In the first phase, the writer sends PREWRITE messages with the current timestamp/value pair. Then it waits until it receives PREACK messages from $N - f$ processes, which acknowledge

Algorithm 4.16: Double-Write Byzantine Quorum (part 1, write)

Implements:
   $(1, N)$-ByzantineRegularRegister, **instance** *bonrr*, with writer w.
Uses:
   AuthPerfectPointToPointLinks, **instance** *al*.

upon event $\langle$ *bonrr, Init* $\rangle$ **do**
   $(pts, pval) := (0, \perp)$;
   $(ts, val) := (0, \perp)$;
   $(wts, wval) := (0, \perp)$;
   $preacklist := [\perp]^N$;
   $acklist := [\perp]^N$;
   $rid := 0$;
   $readlist := [\perp]^N$;

upon event $\langle$ *bonrr, Write* $| v$ $\rangle$ **do**   // only process w
   $(wts, wval) := (wts + 1, v)$;
   $preacklist := [\perp]^N$;
   $acklist := [\perp]^N$;
   forall $q \in \Pi$ **do**
      trigger $\langle$ *al, Send* $| q$, [PREWRITE, $wts, wval$] $\rangle$;

upon event $\langle$ *al, Deliver* $| p$, [PREWRITE, $pts', pval'$] $\rangle$
      such that $p = w \wedge pts' = pts + 1$ **do**
   $(pts, pval) := (pts', pval')$;
   trigger $\langle$ *al, Send* $| p$, [PREACK, pts] $\rangle$;

upon event $\langle$ *al, Deliver* $| q$, [PREACK, pts'] $\rangle$ **such that** $pts' = wts$ **do**
   $preacklist[q] := \text{PREACK}$;
   if $\#(preacklist) \geq N - f$ **then**
      $preacklist := [\perp]^N$;
      forall $q \in \Pi$ **do**
         trigger $\langle$ *al, Send* $| q$, [WRITE, $wts, wval$] $\rangle$;

upon event $\langle$ *al, Deliver* $| p$, [WRITE, ts', val'] $\rangle$
      such that $p = w \wedge ts' = pts \wedge ts' > ts$ **do**
   $(ts, val) := (ts', val')$;
   trigger $\langle$ *al, Send* $| p$, [ACK, ts] $\rangle$;

upon event $\langle$ *al, Deliver* $| q$, [ACK, ts'] $\rangle$ **such that** $ts' = wts$ **do**
   $acklist[q] := \text{ACK}$;
   if $\#(acklist) \geq N - f$ **then**
      $acklist := [\perp]^N$;
      trigger $\langle$ *bonrr, WriteReturn* $\rangle$;

that they have stored the data from the PREWRITE message. In the second phase, the writer sends ordinary WRITE messages, again containing the current time-stamp/value pair. It then waits until it receives ACK messages from $N - f$ processes, which acknowledge that they have stored the data from the WRITE message.

Every process stores two timestamp/value pairs, one from the pre-write phase and one from the write phase. Intuitively, the above problem now disappears when

Algorithm 4.17: Double-Write Byzantine Quorum (part 2, read)

upon event ⟨ *bonrr, Read* ⟩ **do**
    $rid := rid + 1$;
    $readlist := [\perp]^N$;
    forall $q \in \Pi$ **do**
        trigger ⟨ *al, Send* | q, [READ, *rid*] ⟩;

upon event ⟨ *al, Deliver* | p, [READ, r] ⟩ **do**
    trigger ⟨ *al, Send* | p, [VALUE, $r, pts, pval, ts, val$] ⟩;

upon event ⟨ *al, Deliver* | q, [VALUE, $r, pts', pval', ts', val'$] ⟩ **such that** $r = rid$ **do**
    if $pts' = ts' + 1 \vee (pts', pval') = (ts', val')$ **then**
        $readlist[q] := (pts', pval', ts', val')$;
    if exists (ts, v) in an entry of *readlist* **such that** *authentic*$(ts, v, readlist) =$ TRUE
    and exists $Q \subseteq readlist$ **such that**
        $\#(Q) > \frac{N+f}{2} \wedge selectedmax(ts, v, Q) =$ TRUE **then**
    $readlist := [\perp]^N$;
    trigger ⟨ *bonrr, ReadReturn* | v ⟩;
    else
        trigger ⟨ *al, Send* | q, [READ, r] ⟩;

the reader is no longer forced to select a value immediately. For example, if q and r reply with the timestamp/value pair $(0, \perp)$ for their pre-written and written pair, and s replies with $(1, x)$ for its pre-written and written pair, then the reader r can infer that one of the three processes must be faulty because the writer received $N - f$ acknowledgments during the pre-write phase for $(1, x)$ (hence, either s sent the wrong written pair or q sent the wrong pre-written pair, as r itself is obviously correct). In this case, process r can safely wait for a reply from the fourth process, which will break the tie.

The algorithm cannot quite satisfy the $(1, N)$ Byzantine regular register abstraction of Module 4.6 in its *termination* property. More precisely, for Algorithm 4.16–4.17, we relax the *termination* property (BONRR1) as follows. Instead of requiring that *every* operation of a correct process eventually terminates, a *read* operation that is concurrent with *infinitely* many write operations may not terminate. In other words, every write eventually completes and either every read eventually completes or the writer invokes infinitely many writes. Hence, algorithms implementing such registers satisfy only this so-called *finite-write termination* property, but are clearly not wait-free. It has been shown that such a relaxation is necessary.

Algorithm 4.16–4.17 relies on Byzantine quorums (Sect. 2.7.3). The reader sends a READ message to all processes as usual and waits for replies containing *two* timestamp/value pairs. According to the algorithm for writing, two cases may occur: either the pre-written timestamp is one higher than the written timestamp or the two pairs are equal; the reader retains such pairs. In any other case, the sender must be faulty and its reply is ignored.

The reader collects such replies in a variable *readlist*, where now every entry consists of two timestamp/value pairs. It stops collecting replies when some entry of *readlist* contains a pair (ts, v) that (1) is found in the entries of more than f processes, and such that (2) there is a Byzantine quorum (Q) of entries in *readlist* whose *highest* timestamp/value pair, selected among the pre-written or written pair of the entries, is (ts, v).

More precisely, a timestamp/value pair (ts, v) is called *authentic* in *readlist*, and the predicate *authentic*$(ts, v, readlist)$ returns TRUE, whenever

$$\#\Big(\{p \mid readlist[p] = (pts', pv', ts', v')$$
$$\wedge \, ((pts', pv') = (ts, v) \vee (ts', v') = (ts, v))\} \Big) \; > \; f.$$

Hence, an authentic timestamp/value pair is found somewhere in the replies of more than f processes and cannot have been forged by a faulty process.

Furthermore, a pair (ts, v) is called a *selected maximum* in a list S with two time-stamp/value pairs in every entry, and the predicate *selectedmax*(ts, v, S) is TRUE, whenever it holds for all $(pts', pv', ts', v') \in S$ that

$$\big(pts' < ts \wedge ts' < ts\big) \vee (pts', pv') = (ts, v) \vee (ts', v') = (ts, v).$$

Thus, a selected maximum pair satisfies, for every entry in S, that it is either equal to one of the timestamp/value pairs in the entry or its timestamp is larger than the timestamps in both pairs in the entry.

Given these notions, the read returns now only if there exists an authentic pair (ts, v) in some entry of *readlist* and a sublist $Q \subseteq readlist$ exists that satisfies $\#(Q) > (N + f)/2$ and *selectedmax*$(ts, v, Q) =$ TRUE.

Note that, the algorithm enforces FIFO-order delivery of all PREWRITE and WRITE messages from the writer to every process, through the timestamp included in these messages. This contrasts with previous algorithms for implementing registers, but here it ensures that a tuple (pts', pv', ts', v') containing the pre-written and written timestamp/value pairs of a correct process always satisfies $pts' = ts'$ or $pts' = ts' + 1$.

When the reader receives a VALUE message with a reply but the condition is not satisfied, the reader sends another READ message to the process and waits for more replies. This is needed to ensure liveness. As a process may not yet have received some messages from a complete write operation, waiting like this ensures that all correct processes eventually reply with timestamps and values that are at least as recent as the last complete write.

Note that, the reader cannot simply wait for the pair with the highest timestamp found anywhere in *readlist* to become authentic, because this might have been sent by a Byzantine process and contain an arbitrarily large timestamp. But, the correct processes send a reply with correct data, and therefore, enough replies are eventually received.

To illustrate the algorithm, consider the execution in Fig. 4.9, where all correct processes initially store $(2, x; 2, x)$ as their two timestamp/value pairs, and process q is Byzantine. Process p now starts to write y, and before it receives enough PREACK messages, process r invokes a read operation. Due to scheduling, the messages

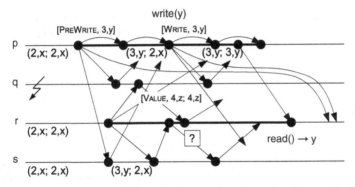

Figure 4.9: Sample execution of the "Double-Write Byzantine Quorum" algorithm implementing a regular register

from p to r are delayed. The reader r obtains the following VALUE messages with responses, each containing a pre-written and a written timestamp/value pair: the forged values $(4, z; 4, z)$ from q, the initial state $(2, x; 2, x)$ from r itself, and the half-way written state $(3, y; 2, x)$ from s. At this point, denoted by $\boxed{?}$ in the figure, the read cannot yet terminate because the only selected maximum in *readlist* is the pair $(4, z)$, but $(4, z)$ is not authentic. Hence, the reader continues by sending an additional READ message. Later on a response from p arrives, containing $(3, y; 3, y)$ from the write phase for value y. The variable *readlist* of the reader now contains four responses, and the sublist of *readlist* containing the responses from processes p, r, and s has $(3, y)$ as its selected maximum. As the pair $(3, y)$ is contained in the responses from p and s, it is also authentic and the read returns y.

Correctness. Assuming that $N > 3f$, the algorithm implements a $(1, N)$ Byzantine regular register abstraction with the relaxed *finite-write termination* property. It is easy to see that every write operation terminates because all $N - f$ correct processes properly acknowledge every PREWRITE and every WRITE message.

   Read operations are only required to terminate when no more write operations are invoked. Assume that the last complete write operation o_w used a timestamp/value pair (ts, v) and a subsequent write operation o'_w failed because the writer crashed; if the writer crashed immediately after starting to execute o'_w, the situation looks for all other processes as if o'_w had never been invoked. Suppose o'_w used timestamp/value pair (ts', v') with $ts' = ts + 1$.

   We distinguish two cases. If the writer crashed before sending any WRITE message during o'_w then since o_w completed, all $N - f$ correct processes eventually store (ts, v) as their written pair and do not change it afterward. Once they all reply with this value to the reader, the pair (ts, v) is authentic and represents a selected maximum of the Byzantine quorum corresponding to the replies of the

$$N - f > \frac{N + f}{2}$$

correct processes. Thus, the read returns v.

Otherwise, if the writer crashed after sending some WRITE message of o'_w then it has previously sent a PREWRITE message containing (ts', v') to all processes. All $N - f$ correct processes eventually store (ts', v') as their pre-written pair and do not change it afterward. Once they all reply with this value to the reader, the pair (ts', v') is authentic and represents a selected maximum of the Byzantine quorum corresponding to the replies of the correct processes. Thus, the read returns v'.

The arguments for these two cases demonstrate that the algorithm satisfies the *finite-write termination* property.

For the *validity* property, consider a read operation o_r and assume the last write operation o_w that completed before the invocation of o_r used a timestamp/value pair (ts, v). The writer may have invoked a subsequent operation to write some value $\bar{v}$. We need to ensure that the value returned by o_r is either v or $\bar{v}$. According to the algorithm, this means that the return value must be associated to timestamp ts or $ts + 1$. From the definition of authentic timestamp/value pairs used by the reader, and because at most f processes might reply with bad values to the reader, only a value written by the writer can be returned. Specifically, because o_w completed, at least $N - 2f > f$ correct processes store a value with timestamp ts or higher in their pre-written and written pair. When their VALUE messages reach the reader during o_r, then (ts, v) or $(ts + 1, \bar{v})$ is authentic. Because the reader uses a Byzantine quorum Q of more than $(N + f)/2$ replies to determine the return value and because Q intersects in at least one correct process with the set of processes storing (ts, v) or $(ts + 1, \bar{v})$, the set Q contains at least one entry in which both timestamps are ts or higher. Thus, the selected maximum cannot contain a smaller timestamp than ts. Hence, o_r returns v or $\bar{v}$, and the *validity* property holds.

Performance. A write operation takes two communication roundtrips between the writer and all processes. A read operation that is not concurrent with a write involves only one communication roundtrip; otherwise, a read operation may continue to send messages as long as writes are concurrently invoked. In the absence of concurrency, both operations require $O(N)$ messages to be exchanged.

4.8 $(1, N)$ Byzantine Atomic Register

Recall the atomic register abstraction introduced in the model with crash-stop processes. Toward its clients, the register appears to execute one common sequence of atomic operations. In the fail-arbitrary model, with our restriction of readers and writers to crash faults, an atomic register obeys the same rules.

Implementing such an atomic register abstraction with Byzantine processes is more difficult than with crash-stop processes. As the presentation of the two $(1, N)$ Byzantine regular register algorithms in the previous section has shown, especially when no data authentication with digital signatures is available, algorithms may involve multiple rounds of communication between client and server processes. In this section, we will present an algorithm where the server processes may send response messages to a reading client spontaneously, without receiving an explicit request before triggering a response. This algorithm achieves the same resilience as our implementations of a Byzantine regular register, namely $N > 3f$, which is optimal.

4.8.1 Specification

A $(1, N)$ *Byzantine atomic register* abstraction is basically the same as the $(1, N)$ atomic register abstraction. The writer w is identified explicitly and the readers and writers are restricted to crash faults, as for the other Byzantine register abstractions. The details of the abstraction are given in Module 4.7.

Module 4.7: Interface and properties of a $(1, N)$ Byzantine atomic register

Module:

    Name: $(1, N)$-ByzantineAtomicRegister, **instance** *bonar*, with writer w.

Events:

    Request: $\langle$ *bonar, Read* $\rangle$: Invokes a read operation on the register.

    Request: $\langle$ *bonar, Write* $\mid v$ $\rangle$: Invokes a write operation with value v on the register. Executed only by process w.

    Indication: $\langle$ *bonar, ReadReturn* $\mid v$ $\rangle$: Completes a read operation on the register with return value v.

    Indication: $\langle$ *bonar, WriteReturn* $\rangle$: Completes a write operation on the register. Occurs only at process w.

Properties:

    BONAR1–BONAR3: Same as properties ONAR1–ONAR3 in a $(1, N)$ atomic register (Module 4.2).

4.8.2 Fail-Arbitrary Algorithm: Byzantine Quorum with Listeners

As noted before, in the context of the "Authenticated-Data Byzantine Quorum" algorithm that implements a Byzantine regular register, adding data authentication with digital signatures can transform a fail-silent atomic register algorithm into a fail-arbitrary one. Thus, adding data authentication to the "Read-Impose Write-Majority" algorithm results in a fail-arbitrary algorithm implementing a $(1, N)$ Byzantine atomic register according to Module 4.7.

Algorithm 4.18–4.19 presented here exploits another idea, more related to the underlying idea of Algorithm 4.14. It requires that a reader obtains the *same* reply value from a Byzantine quorum of processes. But as the writer may concurrently write a new timestamp/value pair to the processes, not all correct processes may send back the same values. To resolve this issue, every server process maintains a

---

Algorithm 4.18: Byzantine Quorum with Listeners (part 1, write)

Implements:
    $(1, N)$-ByzantineAtomicRegister, **instance** *bonar*, with writer w.
Uses:
    AuthPerfectPointToPointLinks, **instance** *al*.

upon event $\langle$ *bonar, Init* $\rangle$ **do**
    $(ts, val) := (0, \perp)$;
    $wts := 0$;
    $acklist := [\perp]^N$;
    $rid := 0$;
    $listening := [\perp]^N$;
    forall $t > 0$ **do** $answers[t] := [\perp]^N$;

upon event $\langle$ *bonar, Write* $\mid v$ $\rangle$ **do**   // only process w
    $wts := wts + 1$;
    $acklist := [\perp]^N$;
    forall $q \in \Pi$ **do**
        trigger $\langle$ *al, Send* $\mid q$, [WRITE, wts, v] $\rangle$;

upon event $\langle$ *al, Deliver* $\mid p$, [WRITE, ts', v'] $\rangle$ **such that** $p = w$ **do**
    if $ts' > ts$ **then**
        $(ts, val) := (ts', v')$;
    forall $q \in \Pi$ such that $listening[q] \neq \perp$ **do**
        trigger $\langle$ *al, Send* $\mid q$, [VALUE, $listening[q], ts, val$] $\rangle$;
    trigger $\langle$ *al, Send* $\mid p$, [ACK, ts] $\rangle$;

upon event $\langle$ *al, Deliver* $\mid q$, [ACK, ts'] $\rangle$ **such that** $ts' = wts$ **do**
    $acklist[q] := \text{ACK}$;
    if $\#(acklist) > (N + f)/2$ **then**
        $acklist := [\perp]^N$;
        trigger $\langle$ *bonar, WriteReturn* $\rangle$;

---

set of *listeners*, which are reader processes of which it knows that they execute a read operation concurrently. Whenever the process receives another WRITE message with a new timestamp/value pair, it forwards the message immediately to all registered listeners. The write operation uses one round and is the same as in several algorithms presented previously.

This algorithm, called "Byzantine Quorum with Listeners," works only if the writer does not crash; under this additional assumption, it implements a $(1, N)$ Byzantine atomic register according to Module 4.7.

The *listening* array represents the listener processes; when $listening[p] = \perp$, then process p is not registered as a listener; when $listening[p] = r$ for some number r, then process p is registered as listener for its read operation with tag r. To stop the forwarding of WRITE messages again, the reader informs all processes when it completes the read operation.

Naturally, if a reader crashes during an operation and the processes think the reader is still listening, another mechanism is needed to prevent excessive

Algorithm 4.19: Byzantine Quorum with Listeners (part 2, read)

upon event ⟨ *bonar, Read* ⟩ **do**
    $rid := rid + 1$;
    forall $t > 0$ **do** $answers[t] := [\bot]^N$;
    forall $q \in \Pi$ **do**
        trigger ⟨ *al, Send* | q, [READ, *rid*] ⟩;

upon event ⟨ *al, Deliver* | p, [READ, r] ⟩ **do**
    $listening[p] := r$;
    trigger ⟨ *al, Send* | p, [VALUE, r, ts, val] ⟩;

upon event ⟨ *al, Deliver* | q, [VALUE, r, ts', v'] ⟩ **such that** $r = rid$ **do**
    if $answers[ts'][q] = \bot$ **then**
        $answers[ts'][q] := v'$;
        if exists (t, v) such that $\#(\{p | answers[t][p] = v\}) > \frac{N+f}{2}$ **then**
            forall $t' > 0$ **do** $answers[t'] := [\bot]^N$;
            forall $q' \in \Pi$ **do**
                trigger ⟨ *al, Send* | q', [READCOMPLETE, *rid*] ⟩;
            trigger ⟨ *bonar, ReadReturn* | v ⟩;

upon event ⟨ *al, Deliver* | p, [READCOMPLETE, r] ⟩ **such that** $r = listening[p]$ **do**
    $listening[p] := \bot$;

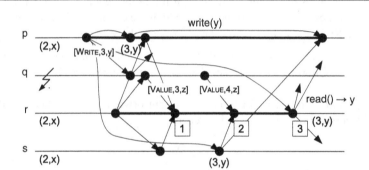

Figure 4.10: Sample execution of the "Byzantine Quorum with Listeners" algorithm implementing an atomic register

communication. The reader collects the returned values in a variable *answers*, which may potentially grow forever. There exist ways, however, to bound the number of occupied, non-$\bot$ entries in *answers* so that there are always $O(fN)$ of them. The algorithm can easily be extended to allow multiple writers.

Figure 4.10 shows an execution of the algorithm. Initially, all correct processes store the timestamp/value pair $(2, x)$, written by process p. Process q is Byzantine. When p starts to write y, it increments the timestamp and sends a WRITE message with $(3, y)$. Concurrently, process r invokes a read operation. At the point denoted by ⬚1, the reader has obtained VALUE messages with $(3, y)$ from p, a forged response $(3, z)$ from q, and the outdated values $(2, x)$ from r itself and from s.

	p	q	r	s
2	-	-	x	x
3	y	z	-	-
4	-	-	-	-

1

	p	q	r	s
2	-	-	x	x
3	y	z	-	y
4	-	z	-	-

2

	p	q	r	s
2	-	-	x	x
3	y	z	y	y
4	-	z	-	-

3

Figure 4.11: Content of the *answers* variable at reader r during the execution shown in Fig. 4.10

Figure 4.11 shows the contents of the *answers* variable of r at this point and two later points during the execution. Before the reader can return a value, it needs to find one row in *answers* (corresponding to a timestamp) for which at least three values are equal.

Note that process s registers r as a listener when it sends the first response with $(2, x)$. Therefore, when process s subsequently delivers the WRITE message from p, it sends another response to r, this time containing $(3, y)$. This response and a forged pair $(4, z)$ are delivered by r before the point denoted by $\boxed{2}$. Process r can still not return a value. Only after r delivers the WRITE message with $(3, y)$ and informs itself as a listener about that (at the point denoted by $\boxed{3}$), it obtains three equal entries in some row of *answers*, which are equal to y. Hence, the reader broadcasts a READCOMPLETE message and returns the value y.

Correctness. Under the assumption that $N > 3f$ and that the writer is correct, the "Byzantine Quorum with Listeners" algorithm implements a $(1, N)$ Byzantine atomic register.

The *termination* property for writes is straightforward to verify: because there are $N - f$ correct processes, the writer receives

$$N - f > \frac{N + f}{2}$$

acknowledgments and completes. A read terminates only when for some time-stamp t and value v, the reader stores $answers[t] = v$ for more than a Byzantine quorum of processes. Suppose that a reader r broadcasts READ messages with tag *rid*. Every correct process eventually receives this message and reacts by sending at least one VALUE message to r with tag *rid*. Consider the first such VALUE message with tag *rid* for every correct process and let (ts, v) be the pair with the largest timestamp among those messages. Those processes that sent a message with a smaller timestamp eventually receive a WRITE message containing (ts, v) as well, because of our additional assumption that the writer is correct. As these processes have registered r as a listener, they forward (ts, v) to r with tag *rid*. The reader eventually receives (ts, v) from more than $(N + f)/2$ processes and returns v.

For the *validity* property, consider a read operation and suppose the most recent complete write operation wrote v with associated timestamp ts. As the writer obtained an acknowledgment from more than $(N + f)/2$ processes, more than

$(N - f)/2$ correct processes store a timestamp/value pair with timestamp at least ts. This means that fewer than $(N - f)/2$ *uninformed* correct processes still store a timestamp smaller than ts. To return a value, the reader must obtain a timestamp/value pair also from more than $(N + f)/2$ processes. But the f Byzantine processes, even with the help of the uninformed processes, cannot create more than $(N + f)/2$ replies containing a timestamp smaller than ts. Hence, the read returns v or a value associated to a higher timestamp.

The same argument also ensures the *ordering* property because once a read returns a value v with associated timestamp ts, every subsequent read can only obtain a Byzantine quorum of replies containing timestamp at least ts. As the writer increments the timestamp in every operation, the replies with higher timestamps contain a value that was written after v.

Performance. The algorithm uses one communication roundtrips and $O(N)$ messages for writes and at least the same number of messages for reads. Because of the messages forwarded to the listeners, it may generate $O(N)$ additional messages for every write that is concurrent to a read.

4.9 Exercises

Exercise 4.1: *Explain why every process needs to maintain a copy of the register value in the "Read-One Write-All" algorithm (Algorithm 4.1).*

Exercise 4.2: *Analogously, explain why every process needs to maintain a copy of the register value in the "Majority Voting" algorithm (Algorithm 4.2).*

Exercise 4.3: *Use the idea of the transformation from $(1, N)$ regular to $(1, 1)$ atomic registers (Algorithm 4.3) to adapt the "Read-One Write-All" algorithm (Algorithm 4.1) to implement a $(1, 1)$ Atomic Register.*

Exercise 4.4: *Use the idea of the transformation from $(1, N)$ regular to $(1, 1)$ atomic registers (Algorithm 4.3) to adapt the "Majority Voting" algorithm (Algorithm 4.2) to implement a $(1, 1)$ Atomic Register.*

Exercise 4.5: *Explain why a timestamp is needed in the "Majority Voting" algorithm (Algorithm 4.2) but not in the "Read-One Write-All" algorithm (Algorithm 4.1).*

Exercise 4.6: *Explain why the request identifier included in WRITE, ACK, READ, and VALUE messages of the "Majority Voting" algorithm (Algorithm 4.2) can be omitted in the "Read-One Write-All" algorithm (Algorithm 4.1).*

Exercise 4.7: *Give an algorithm that implements a $(1, 1)$ atomic register in the fail-silent model and that is more efficient than the "Read-Impose Write-Majority" algorithm (Algorithm 4.6–4.7, which implements a $(1, N)$ atomic register in the fail-silent model).*

Exercise 4.8: *Does any implementation of a regular register require a majority of the correct processes in a fail-silent model with no failure detector? What if an eventually perfect failure detector (Module 2.8) is available?*

Exercise 4.9: *Would the "Majority Voting" algorithm (Algorithm 4.2) still be correct if a process q that receives a WRITE message from the writer p with a timestamp ts' and value v' only acknowledges the message (by sending an ACK message) if ts' is strictly larger that the timestamp ts that q already stores? Note that ts is from a WRITE message that q received previously but contained a more recent value. Explain what happens in the same situation if we consider the "Read-Impose Write-Majority" and then the "Read-Impose Write-Consult-Majority" algorithms.*

Exercise 4.10: *Assume that some algorithm A implements a regular register abstraction with crash-stop processes, in a system where up to $N - 1$ processes can crash. Can we implement a perfect failure detector out of A?*

Exercise 4.11: *Consider the "Logged Majority Voting" algorithm (Algorithm 4.12–4.13) and suppose the store primitive could not log multiple values together atomically. Explain why it is important not to log the timestamp first, before logging the* *value. What could happen if the algorithm separately logs the value after the logging the timestamp?*

Exercise 4.12: *Explain why the writer in the "Logged Majority Voting" algorithm (Algorithm 4.12–4.13) needs to store its timestamp in stable storage.*

4.10 Solutions

Solution 4.1: Algorithm 4.1 ("Read-One Write-All") needs to store a copy of the register value at every process because we assume that any number of processes can crash and any process can read. Assume that the value is not stored at some process q. It is easy to see that after some write operation, all processes might crash except for q. In this case, there is no way for q to return the last value written.

Solution 4.2: Algorithm 4.2 ("Majority Voting") also needs to maintain a copy of the register value at all processes, even if we assume only one reader. Assume that some process q does not maintain a copy. Assume, furthermore, that the writer updates the value of the register: it can do so only by accessing a majority of the processes. If q is in that majority then the writer would have stored the value in a majority of the processes minus one. It might happen that all processes in that majority, except for q, crash. But the set of remaining processes plus q also constitute a majority. A subsequent read in this majority might not return the last value written.

Solution 4.3: The "Read-Impose Write-All" algorithm (Algorithm 4.1) already implements an atomic register if we consider only *one* reader: indeed the scenario of Fig. 4.5, which violates the *ordering* property, involves two readers. Suppose there is an arbitrary process q that is the only reader. The algorithm can even be optimized in such a way that the writer p simply tries to send its value to q and have q store it, and if p detects that q crashes then it gives up. In this case, only the reader would maintain the register value, and the writer would not send any messages to other processes than q.

Solution 4.4: Consider the "Majority Voting" algorithm (Algorithm 4.2) which implements a $(1, N)$ regular register but not a $(1, 1)$ atomic register. It can easily be extended to also satisfy the *ordering* property. According to the idea that underlies Algorithm 4.3, the reader simply stores the timestamp/value pair with the largest timestamp that it has observed so far, and returns this value if the received VALUE messages do not contain a larger timestamp. This can be achieved if the reader always includes its own timestamp/value pair in the variable *readlist*, from which it selects the return value. (The problematic scenario of Fig. 4.6 occurs precisely because the reader has no memory of the previous value read.)

Algorithm 4.20 shows pseudo code for those parts of Algorithm 4.2 that must be modified. It uses the function *highest*($\cdot$) introduced before, which returns the timestamp/value pair with the largest timestamp from its input. With this algorithm,

Algorithm 4.20: Modification of Majority Voting to Implement a $(1, 1)$ Atomic Register

upon event ⟨ *onrr, Read* ⟩ **do**
    $rid := rid + 1$;
    $readlist := [\bot]^N$;
    $readlist[self] := (ts, val)$;
    trigger ⟨ *beb, Broadcast* | [READ, *rid*] ⟩;

upon event ⟨ *beb, Deliver* | *p*, [READ, *r*] ⟩ **do**
    if $p \neq self$ **then**
        trigger ⟨ *pl, Send* | *p*, [VALUE, *r, ts, val*] ⟩;

upon event ⟨ *pl, Deliver* | *q*, [VALUE, *r, ts', v'*] ⟩ **such that** $r = rid$ **do**
    $readlist[q] := (ts', v')$;
    if $\#(readlist) > N/2$ **then**
        $(ts, val) := highest(readlist)$;
        $readlist := \emptyset$;
        trigger ⟨ *onrr, ReadReturn* | *val* ⟩;

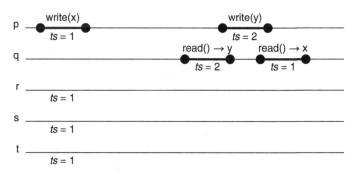

Figure 4.12: Violation of ordering for a $(1, 1)$ atomic register

the scenario of Fig. 4.12 cannot occur, whereas the atomic execution depicted in Fig. 4.2 is possible.

As in the original "Majority Voting" algorithm, every write operation requires one communication roundtrip between the writer and a majority of the processes, and every read operation requires one communication roundtrip between the reader and a majority of the processes. In both cases, $O(N)$ messages are exchanged.

Solution 4.5: The timestamp in Algorithm 4.2 ("Majority Voting") is needed precisely because we do not make use of a perfect failure detector. Without the use of any timestamp, a reader q would not have any means to compare different values from any read majority.

In particular, if process p first writes a value v and subsequently writes a value w, but does not access the same majority in both cases, then q, which is supposed to return w, might have no information about which value is the latest. The timestamp is used to distinguish the values and to help the reader with determining the latest written value.

Such a timestamp is not needed in Algorithm 4.1 ("Read-Impose Write-All") because the writer always accesses all processes that did not crash. The writer can do so because it relies on a perfect failure detector. It is not possible that a reader can obtain different values from the processes, as in the "Majority Voting" algorithm.

Solution 4.6: Every WRITE and READ message in Algorithm 4.2 contains a unique identifier of the request (the timestamp or the value *rid*), which is used to associate the replies (ACK or READ messages) to the request. Because the process does not need a reply from *all* processes to execute an operation (only from a quorum), there may be reply messages from slow processes in transit when the operation completes. If they arrive during an operation invoked subsequently, the process could not associate them to the correct operation and perform an error.

The write operation of the "Read-One Write-All" algorithm, in contrast, always waits for an ACK message from every process that is correct according to the output of the failure detector. For reading, no communication is needed. Because the failure detector satisfies *strong accuracy*, the operation therefore completes only after receiving an ACK message from *every* process that has not crashed. During a subsequent operation, the set *correct* may only have become smaller. Therefore, no message can be and attributed to the wrong operation.

The same argument also demonstrates why the request identifiers are not needed in the "Read-Impose Write-All" and "Read-Impose Write-Consult-All" algorithms (Algorithm 4.5 and 4.9, respectively).

Solution 4.7: The solution is again Algorithm 4.20. It requires one communication roundtrip for every operation. Recall how the reader in the "Read-Impose Write-Majority" algorithm uses another communication roundtrip to impose the timestamp/value pair by writing it back. As there is only one reader here, the next reader is again the same process, and it is sufficient to store the value locally.

It is important that the reader always includes its own value and timestamp when selecting a majority. Otherwise, the reader q might violate the *ordering* property as depicted in the scenario of Fig. 4.12. In the first read, the majority used by q includes the writer p, which has the latest value, but in the second read, q accesses a majority with timestamp 1 and old value x.

Solution 4.8: Assume by contradiction that even with no majority of correct processes, one could implement a regular register in the fail-silent model.

We use a *partitioning* argument, similar to the explanation given earlier in this book why uniform reliable broadcast requires a majority of the correct processes, even if the system is augmented with an eventually perfect failure detector. We partition the system into two disjoint sets of processes, X and Y, such that $|X| = \lceil N/2 \rceil$ and $|Y| = \lfloor N/2 \rfloor$; the writer p is in X and the reader q is in Y. The assumption above means there are correct executions of the algorithm in which all processes of X crash and correct executions where all processes of Y crash.

In particular, process p might return from a write operation with value v, even if none of the processes in Y has witnessed this value. The other processes, including q, were considered to have crashed, even if they did not. Suppose that all processes of X, the only ones that may have witnessed v, crash later; now the reader has no way to learn the value v and might not return the last value written. This shows that a majority of correct processes is necessary.

The same argument implies that an eventually perfect failure detector is not sufficient to circumvent the assumption of a correct majority. The reason is that the failure detector may make incomplete and false suspicions before it is *eventually* complete and accurate. During that initial time, the system may behave as in the fail-silent model. For instance, the write operation may complete even if no process of Y has witnessed the value because all processes of Y might have been falsely suspected.

Solution 4.9: Consider a variant of the "Majority Voting" algorithm, where a process q that receives a WRITE message from the writer p with a timestamp/value pair (ts', v') does not reply with an ACK message if ts' is not strictly larger that the timestamp ts stored by q. The timestamp $ts > ts'$ is associated to a value val, which was written more recently.

Clearly, the only risk here is to violate liveness and to prevent p from completing the write operation with argument v. However, given that q has already stored val, which is associated to a larger timestamp, process p has already completed the write of v. (Remember that the processes are sequential and, in particular, p does not invoke a new operation before completing the current one).

The same argument holds for the "Read-Impose Write-Majority" algorithm because only a single writer is involved and it is sequential.

The situation is different with the "Read-Impose Write-Consult-Majority" algorithm, however, because there are multiple writers. Consider two writers p and q, both sending WRITE messages to some process r, with different values v' and w', respectively, such that w' is associated to a higher timestamp than v'. When r receives w' from q first and v' later from p, it will not send an acknowledgment back to p. If enough other processes crash, it may happen that p does not complete its write operation and violates the *termination* property.

Solution 4.10: The answer is yes. This means that a perfect failure detector is needed to implement a regular register if $N - 1$ processes can crash.

We sketch the idea behind an algorithm $\mathcal{P}^A$ that uses A to implement a perfect failure-detector abstraction (Module 2.6). Recall that a perfect failure detector outputs at every process the identities of other processes that this process detects to have crashed.

Every process p outputs ⟨ *Crash* ⟩ events to detect other processes that should satisfy the *strong completeness* and *strong accuracy* properties of a perfect failure detector.

Algorithm $\mathcal{P}^A$ uses N instances of the $(1, N)$ regular register abstraction, one for every process, such that every process is the writer of exactly one register.

Furthermore, every process p holds a counter k that it periodically increments and writes to its register, using the write operation of algorithm A.

When p invokes the write operation, A triggers an arbitrary exchange of messages among processes, that is, it invokes a primitive that communicates information among different processes through "messages." Suppose that all outputs from the communication primitive inform the "receiving" process about which process has "sent" a particular message by contributing an input value to the primitive. We modify A such that it also adds k to the information that it "sends" in the context of the instance that writes k.

Whenever p "receives" a message like this from a process q, process p remembers q as one of the processes that participated in the instance that wrote k. When the write terminates, then p declares that all processes that did not participate in the instance have crashed and Algorithm $\mathcal{P}^A$ outputs them.

It is easy to see the outputs of $\mathcal{P}^A$ satisfy the *strong completeness* property. Any process that crashes stops participating in the writing and will be permanently detected by every correct process. We argue now that $\mathcal{P}^A$ also ensures the *strong accuracy* property. Assume by contradiction that some process p falsely detects a process q (i.e., before q crashed). In other words, process q does not participate in the instance of the communication abstraction, where p writes k to its register. Given that $N - 1$ processes may crash, suppose that immediately after p completes the write of k, all processes except q crash. Process q might now be required to return k upon reading the register of p using A. But q has no way of distinguishing an execution in which p did write the value k to its register from an execution in which p wrote a different value. Hence, process q might hence violate the *validity* property, contradicting the assumption that A implements a regular register.

Solution 4.11: Suppose that process p writes a value u, then a value v, and finally a value w. While writing u, assume p accesses some process q and not a process r, whereas while writing v, process p accesses r and not q. While writing w, process p again accesses q, which logs first the timestamp, then crashes without logging the associated value, and subsequently recovers. A process s that reads from the register might obtain a reply with a timestamp/value pair from q, but since q only updated its logged timestamp, the value contained is still u. Hence, the read of s may violate the *validity* property of the register.

On the other hand, logging the timestamp after logging the value is not dangerous. In the example scenario, the reader might obtain the new value together with old timestamp and not output the new value. But that is permitted because the write has not completed and, thus, there is no obligation to return the new value. Of course, logging the value and the timestamp separately is not desirable because it incurs two expensive accesses to stable storage.

Solution 4.12: The reason for the writer to log its timestamp in Algorithm 4.12–4.13 is the following. If it crashes and recovers, the writer should not use a smaller timestamp than the one associated with the current value of the register. Otherwise, the reader might return an old value and violate the *validity* property of the register.

4.11 Chapter Notes

- Register specifications were introduced by Lamport in multiple papers (Lamport 1977, 1986a,b), which also defined safe, regular, and atomic semantics. The original definitions were given in the context of a multiprocessor machine, with processes that are concurrent but failure-free, and with only one writer.

- The safe register abstraction provides the weakest guarantees among the three register semantics. When a read is concurrent with a write, a safe register can return an arbitrary value. This may even be a value that no process has ever written or attempted to write (in the sense that the value was an input parameter of an operation), and it may differ from any default value of the register.

  In our system model with processes that send messages to each other, it is easy to prevent that an algorithm invents a value out of thin air. But in a multiprocessor machine as considered by Lamport (1977), the processes might concurrently access some low-level hardware locations that implement a register abstraction, and hence return an arbitrary value. In the fail-arbitrary model, Byzantine processes might deliberately change the stored value, which makes this failure scenario also realistic. Our implementation of a Byzantine safe register abstraction stays on the safe side and returns a default value when it cannot establish if a value has actually been written. For implementations of other Byzantine register abstractions, quorums or digital signatures prevent this problem from occurring.

- Our regular register abstraction corresponds to the notion initially introduced by Lamport. For the case of multiple writers, the regular register abstraction was generalized in three different ways, all stronger than our notion of regular register (Shao, Pierce, and Welch 2003).

- The original notion of an atomic register was close to the one we introduced here. There is a slight difference, however, in the way we gave our definition because we had to take into account the possibility that processes fail, which is typical in a message-passing system. Thus, we had to deal explicitly with the notion of failed operations, in particular with failed write operations.

- The notion of linearizability was introduced by Herlihy and Wing (1990) for arbitrary shared objects, not only register objects with read and write operations. As discussed in the text, our notion of an atomic register is equivalent to a linearizable register when used with crash-stop and with Byzantine process abstractions.

  For defining a "logged" atomic register, however, using the fail-recovery model, one would have to consider a slightly different notion of atomicity, which takes into account the fact that a write operation that was interrupted by a failure has to appear as if it was never invoked or as if it was completed before the next invocation of the same process, which might have recovered, took place (Guerraoui and Levy 2004).

- We considered only registers that store values from an abstract domain, which was not further specified. We did not make any assumption on the possible size of these values. Registers that only store values from a small domain have also been considered (Lamport 1977). Typically, the values of such registers are from some small alphabet, perhaps they store only one bit. Many transformation algorithms have been invented that emulate a register with a given (large) domain from (multiple) registers that store only smaller values (Lamport 1977; Peterson 1983; Vitányi and Awerbuch 1986; Vidyasankar 1988, 1990; Israeli and Li 1993).

- Our implementation of an atomic register from regular registers (the transformation "From $(1, N)$ Regular to $(1, N)$ Atomic Registers" of Sect. 4.3.2) and all our algorithms implementing atomic registers require only a bounded amount of internal memory at every process. Lamport (1986b) has shown that in any such algorithm that is wait-free, a reader process must also write, in the sense that the read operation modifies the state at the processes.

- Fail-silent register implementations with crash-stop processes in a message-passing system and assuming a correct majority were first given for the case of a single writer (Attiya, Bar-Noy, and Dolev 1995). They were later generalized for the case of multiple writers (Lynch and Shvartsman 1997, 2002). Implementations in the fail-recovery model were given more recently (Boichat et al. 2003a; Guerraoui and Levy 2004).

- Failure-detection lower bounds for registers have constituted an active area of research (Delporte-Gallet et al. 2002, 2004, 2010). In particular, and as we discussed through an exercise, in a system where any number of processes can crash and failures cannot be predicted, the weakest failure detector to implement a regular register abstraction is the perfect failure detector.

- Register implementations with Byzantine processes have been considered by Malkhi and Reiter (1998). This work also introduced the concept of Byzantine quorums, the "Byzantine Masking Quorum" algorithm implementing a register with safe semantics, and the "Authenticated-Data Byzantine Quorum" algorithm implementing a register with regular semantics.

- Our Byzantine register abstractions are idealized in the sense that the writer and the reader processes are not Byzantine, that is, they may at most crash but never behave arbitrarily. This simplification models practical scenarios, where a set of fail-arbitrary processes act as "replicas" for the stored data; they are accessed by clients, which are assumed to be under closer control than the replicas. Many distributed storage systems make this assumption.

- The "Double-Write Byzantine Quorum" algorithm was presented by Abraham et al. (2006). It works in a way similar to the implementation of the Byzantine epoch consensus abstraction, which will be considered in Chap. 5.

- Chockler, Guerraoui, and Keidar (2007) show that every distributed implementation of a regular register in the fail-arbitrary model that does *not* use data authentication (with digital signatures) and that should provide wait-free termination for all its operations must store the entire history of the written values. As our "Double-Write Byzantine Quorum" algorithm stores at most two written values, this result explains why the algorithm only satisfies the *finite-write termination* property, but is not wait-free.

- Our "Byzantine Quorums with Listeners" algorithm was introduced by Martin, Alvisi, and Dahlin (2002) and uses the idea of registering the readers as listeners at all processes, in order to ensure that the reads terminate. Because registering a reader modifies the state of a process, it can be seen as another way in which a reader writes to the system.

5. Consensus

Life is what happens to you while you are making other plans.
(John Lennon)

This chapter is devoted to the *consensus* abstraction. The processes use consensus to agree on a common value out of values they initially propose. Reaching consensus is one of the most fundamental problems in distributed computing. Any algorithm that helps multiple processes maintain common state or to decide on a future action, in a model where some processes may fail, involves solving a consensus problem.

We consider multiple variants of consensus in this chapter: *regular*, *uniform*, and *randomized* consensus with crash-stop processes, *logged* consensus with crash-recovery processes, and *Byzantine* and *Byzantine randomized* consensus with arbitrary-fault process abstractions.

There exist a rich set of relations among the nonrandomized consensus algorithms presented in this chapter, which are best highlighted upfront:

- The "Flooding Consensus" algorithm (Algorithm 5.1) and the "Hierarchical Consensus" algorithm (Algorithm 5.2) implement regular consensus in the fail-stop model and rely on a perfect failure detector.
- The "Flooding Uniform Consensus" algorithm (Algorithm 5.3) and the "Hierarchical Uniform Consensus" algorithm (Algorithm 5.2) implement uniform consensus in the fail-stop model and rely also on a perfect failure detector. Each one of them uses the same structure as its nonuniform counterpart.
- The "Leader-Driven Consensus" algorithm in Sect. 5.3 implements uniform consensus in the fail-noisy model with a leader-based approach, assuming that an eventual leader-detector abstraction is available.
- The "Logged Leader-Driven Consensus" algorithm in Sect. 5.4 also uses the leader-based approach to implement uniform consensus in the fail-recovery model.
- In Sect. 5.6, the same leader-based approach is explored for implementing a Byzantine consensus abstraction in the fail-noisy-arbitrary model, with the

C. Cachin et al., *Introduction to Reliable and Secure Distributed Programming*,
DOI: 10.1007/978-3-642-15260-3_5,
© Springer-Verlag Berlin Heidelberg 2011

"Byzantine Leader-Driven Consensus" algorithm. This algorithm works with arbitrary-faulty (Byzantine) processes and relies on a Byzantine eventual leader detector.

- Finally, the "Rotating Coordinator" algorithm in Exercise 5.7 shows a different way to implement uniform consensus in the fail-noisy model than the leader-driven consensus algorithms. It is based on an eventually perfect failure detector.

All three leader-driven consensus algorithms (in the fail-noisy, fail-recovery, and fail-noisy-arbitrary models) have the same structure and execute a sequence of so-called epochs, with a unique leader process for every epoch.

Later, in Chap. 6, we consider extensions and variations of the consensus abstraction. We will show how consensus abstractions can be used to build more sophisticated agreement and coordination abstractions.

5.1 Regular Consensus

5.1.1 Specification

A consensus abstraction is specified in terms of two events, *propose* and *decide*. Each process has an initial value v that it proposes for consensus through a *propose* request, in the form of triggering a $\langle$ *propose* $\mid v \rangle$ event. All correct processes must initially propose a value.

The proposed value is private to the process and the act of proposing is local. This request typically triggers broadcast events through which the processes exchange their proposed values in order to eventually reach agreement. All correct processes have to decide on the same value through a *decide* indication that carries a value v, in the form of processing a $\langle$ *Decide* $\mid v \rangle$ event. The decided value has to be one of the proposed values. A consensus abstraction, in its regular form, satisfies the four properties listed in Module 5.1. The *termination* and *integrity* properties together imply that every correct process decides exactly once. The *validity* property ensures that the consensus primitive may not invent a decision value by itself. The *agreement* property states the main feature of consensus, that every two correct processes that decide indeed decide the same value.

Actually, the consensus abstraction as defined here cannot be implemented in asynchronous systems. The reason is that every deterministic algorithm implementing consensus in the fail-silent model with crash-stop processes has infinite executions, that is, executions where agreement cannot be reached. Therefore, we consider several implementations of consensus in the fail-stop and fail-noisy models, where a failure detector is available.

In the following, we present two different algorithms that implement (regular) consensus in the fail-stop model. Both algorithms rely on a perfect failure-detector abstraction and tolerate $f < N$ process failures. The first algorithm uses a small number of communication steps but a large number of messages. The second algorithm uses fewer messages but more communication steps. We defer the presentation of a fail-noisy consensus algorithm to Sect. 5.3.

Module 5.1: Interface and properties of (regular) consensus

Module:

    Name: Consensus, **instance** c.

Events:

    Request: $\langle\, c,\, Propose \mid v\, \rangle$: Proposes value v for consensus.

    Indication: $\langle\, c,\, Decide \mid v\, \rangle$: Outputs a decided value v of consensus.

Properties:

    C1: *Termination:* Every correct process eventually decides some value.

    C2: *Validity:* If a process decides v, then v was proposed by some process.

    C3: *Integrity:* No process decides twice.

    C4: *Agreement:* No two correct processes decide differently.

5.1.2 Fail-Stop Algorithm: Flooding Consensus

Our first implementation of consensus is the "Flooding Consensus" algorithm (Algorithm 5.1). It uses a perfect failure-detector abstraction and a best-effort broadcast communication abstraction. The basic idea of the algorithm is the following. The processes execute sequential rounds. Each process maintains the set of proposed values that it has seen; this set initially consists of its own proposal. The process typically extends this proposal set when it moves from one round to the next and new proposed values are encountered. In each round, every process disseminates its set in a PROPOSAL message to all processes using the best-effort broadcast abstraction. In other words, the process floods the system with all proposals it has seen in previous rounds. When a process receives a proposal set from another process, it merges this set with its own. In each round, the process computes the union of all proposal sets that it received so far.

A process decides when it has reached a round during which it has gathered all proposals that will ever possibly be seen by any correct process. At the end of this round, the process decides a specific value in its proposal set.

We explain now when a round terminates and a process moves to the next round, as the round structure of the algorithm is not immediately visible in the pseudo code of Algorithm 5.1. Every PROPOSAL message is tagged with the round number in which the message was broadcast. A round terminates at a process p when p has received a message from every process that has not been detected to have crashed by p in that round. That is, a process does not leave a round unless it receives messages, tagged with the number of the round, from all processes that have not been detected to have crashed. To this end, the process collects the set of processes from which it has received a message in round r in variable *receivedfrom*$[r]$.

Algorithm 5.1: Flooding Consensus

Implements:
    Consensus, **instance** c.

Uses:
    BestEffortBroadcast, **instance** beb;
    PerfectFailureDetector, **instance** $\mathcal{P}$.

upon event $\langle$ c, $Init$ $\rangle$ **do**
    $correct := \Pi$;
    $round := 1$;
    $decision := \bot$;
    $receivedfrom := [\emptyset]^N$;
    $proposals := [\emptyset]^N$;
    $receivedfrom[0] := \Pi$;

upon event $\langle$ $\mathcal{P}$, $Crash$ $\mid$ p $\rangle$ **do**
    $correct := correct \setminus \{p\}$;

upon event $\langle$ c, $Propose$ $\mid$ v $\rangle$ **do**
    $proposals[1] := proposals[1] \cup \{v\}$;
    trigger $\langle$ beb, $Broadcast$ $\mid$ [PROPOSAL, 1, $proposals[1]$] $\rangle$;

upon event $\langle$ beb, $Deliver$ $\mid$ p, [PROPOSAL, r, ps] $\rangle$ **do**
    $receivedfrom[r] := receivedfrom[r] \cup \{p\}$;
    $proposals[r] := proposals[r] \cup ps$;

upon $correct \subseteq receivedfrom[round] \wedge decision = \bot$ **do**
    if $receivedfrom[round] = receivedfrom[round-1]$ **then**
        $decision := min(proposals[round])$;
        trigger $\langle$ beb, $Broadcast$ $\mid$ [DECIDED, $decision$] $\rangle$;
        trigger $\langle$ c, $Decide$ $\mid$ $decision$ $\rangle$;
    else
        $round := round + 1$;
        trigger $\langle$ beb, $Broadcast$ $\mid$ [PROPOSAL, $round$, $proposals[round-1]$] $\rangle$;

upon event $\langle$ beb, $Deliver$ $\mid$ p, [DECIDED, v] $\rangle$ **such that** $p \in correct \wedge decision = \bot$ **do**
    $decision := v$;
    trigger $\langle$ beb, $Broadcast$ $\mid$ [DECIDED, $decision$] $\rangle$;
    trigger $\langle$ c, $Decide$ $\mid$ $decision$ $\rangle$;

A process p knows that it is safe to decide when it has seen all proposed values that will ever be seen by the correct processes and be considered for decision. In a round where a new failure is detected, process p is not sure of having exactly the same set of values as the other processes. This might happen when the crashed process(es) have broadcast some value(s) to the other processes but not to p. Every process records in $receivedfrom[r]$ from which processes it has received a proposal in round r; observe that processes in $receivedfrom[r]$ have not crashed up to round r. If a round terminates with the same estimate of correct processes as the

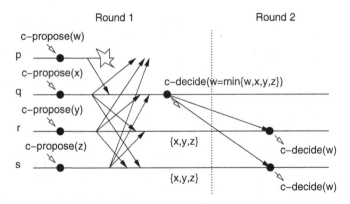

Figure 5.1: Sample execution of flooding consensus

previous round, that is, if PROPOSAL messages from the same set of processes have been received in two consecutive rounds then a decision can be made. This follows because all the messages broadcast by all processes that moved to the current round did reach their destination. Note that a process executes at most N rounds.

To make a decision, the processes can apply any deterministic function to their accumulated proposal set, provided this function is agreed upon in advance and is the same at all processes. In our case, the process decides the minimum value (through function *min* in the algorithm); we implicitly assume here that the set of all possible proposals is totally ordered and the order is known by all processes. A process that decides disseminates the decision to all processes using the best-effort broadcast abstraction.

An execution of the "Flooding Consensus" algorithm is illustrated in Fig. 5.1. Process p crashes during round 1 after broadcasting its proposal. Only process q sees that proposal. No other process crashes. As process q receives proposals in round 1 from all processes and this set is equal to the set of processes at the start of the algorithm in round 0, process q can decide. It selects the minimum value among the proposals and decides value w.

Processes r and s detect the crash of p and cannot decide in round 1. So they advance to round 2. If process r or s would decide based on the proposal set after round 1, they would have decided differently, because the minimum in their proposal sets is, say, x (different from w). But as q has decided, it disseminates its decision through best-effort broadcast. When the decision is delivered, processes r and s also decide w.

Correctness. The *validity* and *integrity* properties follow from the algorithm and from the properties of the broadcast abstraction.

The *termination* property follows from the fact that in round N, at the latest, all processes decide. This is because (1) processes that do not decide keep moving from round to round due to the *strong completeness* property of the failure detector, (2) at least one process needs to fail per round, in order to force the execution of a new round without decision, and (3) there are only N processes in the system.

Consider now *agreement*. Let r be the smallest round in which some correct process p decides and let v be the value it decides. There are two cases to consider. First, assume that process p decides after receiving PROPOSAL messages from the same subset of processes in the two consecutive rounds $r - 1$ and r, i.e., *receivedfrom*$[r]$ = *receivedfrom*$[r - 1]$. Because of the *strong accuracy* property of the failure detector, no process that reaches the end of round r receives a proposal containing a smaller value than v. Let q be any process that moves to round $r + 1$. Either q detects no failure in round r, in which case it also decides v, or q detects some failure and it decides v in round $r + 1$, once it delivers a DECIDED message from p. In the second case, assume that p decides after delivering a DECIDED message from some process q which crashed in round r. Processes that detect the crash of q do not decide in round r but in round $r + 1$, after delivering a DECIDED message from p.

Performance. If there are no failures then the algorithm requires a single communication step since all processes decide at the end of round 1. Each failure may cause at most one additional communication step. Therefore, in the worst case, the algorithm requires N steps if $N - 1$ processes crash in sequence.

In every round, $O(N^2)$ messages are exchanged and $O(N^2)$ DECIDED messages are also exchanged after a process has decided. For each additional round where a process crashes, another $O(N^2)$ message exchanges occur. In the worst case, the algorithm uses $O(N^3)$ messages.

5.1.3 Fail-Stop Algorithm: Hierarchical Consensus

Algorithm 5.2, called "Hierarchical Consensus," shows an alternative way to implement regular consensus in the fail-stop model. This algorithm is interesting because it uses fewer messages than our "Flooding Consensus" algorithm and enables one process to decide before exchanging any messages with the rest of the processes; this process has latency zero. However, to reach a global decision, i.e., for all correct processes to decide, the algorithm requires N communication steps, even in situations where no failure occurs. Algorithm 5.2 is particularly adequate if consensus is used as a service implemented by a set of server processes where the clients are happy to get a response with a decision value as fast as possible, even if not all servers have decided yet.

The "Hierarchical Consensus" algorithm exploits the ranking among the processes given by the *rank*$(\cdot)$ function. The rank is a unique number between 1 and N for every process. Basically, the algorithm ensures that the correct process with the most important rank in the hierarchy imposes its value on all the other processes. For understanding the algorithm, it is important to state that important ranks are low numbers, hence, the highest rank is 1 and the lowest rank is N.

If the process p with rank 1 does not crash in the "Hierarchical Consensus" algorithm, it will impose its value on all other processes by broadcasting a DECIDED message and every correct process will decide the value proposed by p. If p crashes immediately at the start of an execution and the process q with rank 2 is correct then the algorithm ensures that the proposal of q will be decided. The

---

Algorithm 5.2: Hierarchical Consensus

Implements:
    Consensus, **instance** c.

Uses:
    BestEffortBroadcast, **instance** beb;
    PerfectFailureDetector, **instance** $\mathcal{P}$.

upon event $\langle$ c, *Init* $\rangle$ **do**
    detectedranks := $\emptyset$;
    round := 1;
    proposal := $\bot$; *proposer* := 0;
    delivered := $[\text{FALSE}]^N$;
    broadcast := FALSE;

upon event $\langle$ $\mathcal{P}$, *Crash* $\mid p$ $\rangle$ **do**
    detectedranks := *detectedranks* $\cup$ {$rank(p)$};

upon event $\langle$ c, *Propose* $\mid v$ $\rangle$ **such that** *proposal* $= \bot$ **do**
    proposal := v;

upon *round* $= rank(self) \wedge$ *proposal* $\neq \bot \wedge$ *broadcast* $=$ FALSE **do**
    broadcast := TRUE;
    trigger $\langle$ *beb*, *Broadcast* $\mid [\text{DECIDED}, proposal]$ $\rangle$;
    trigger $\langle$ c, *Decide* $\mid proposal$ $\rangle$;

upon *round* $\in$ *detectedranks* $\vee$ *delivered*[*round*] $=$ TRUE **do**
    round := *round* $+ 1$;

upon event $\langle$ *beb*, *Deliver* $\mid p, [\text{DECIDED}, v]$ $\rangle$ **do**
    r := $rank(p)$;
    if $r < rank(self) \wedge r >$ *proposer* **then**
        proposal := v;
        proposer := r;
    delivered[r] := TRUE;

---

heart of the algorithm addresses the case, where p is faulty but crashes only after sending some DECIDED messages and q is correct. A problematic situation would occur when the DECIDED message from p reaches the process s with rank 3 and could cause it to decide, but process q, which has rank 2, might instead detect that p has crashed and go on to impose its value on the other processes. The solution is for process s to wait with deciding until it has heard something from q, either from the failure detector that q has crashed or from q itself in the form of a DECIDED message.

The "Hierarchical Consensus" algorithm works in rounds and relies on a best-effort broadcast abstraction and on a perfect failure detector abstraction $\mathcal{P}$. In round i, the process p with rank i decides its proposal and broadcasts it to all processes in a DECIDED message. All other processes that reach round i wait before taking any actions, until they deliver this message or until $\mathcal{P}$ detects the crash of p.

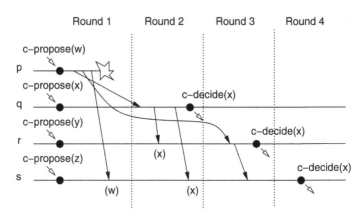

Figure 5.2: Sample execution of hierarchical consensus

No other process than p broadcasts any message in round i. A process collects the *ranks* of the processes detected to have crashed by $\mathcal{P}$ in a variable *detectedranks* (and not the *identities* of the potentially correct ones, as in Algorithm 5.1).

When a process q with rank j receives the proposal of p and q is in round $i < j$ then q adopts this proposal as its own proposal. But, if p crashed, then q may already have progressed past round i because $\mathcal{P}$ detected the crash. In this case, when the DECIDED message from p reaches q only after it has adopted a proposal from a process with a less important rank than i, that is, taken from a DECIDED message in a later round than i, then q must ignore the message from p and not change its proposal.

Consider the example depicted in Fig. 5.2. Process p decides w and broadcasts its proposal to all processes, but crashes. Processes q and r detect the crash before they deliver the proposal of p and advance to the next round. Process s delivers the message from p and changes its own proposal accordingly, i.e., s adopts the value w. In round 2, process q decides its own proposal x and broadcasts this value. This causes s to change its proposal again and now to adopt the value x from q. From this point on, there are no further failures and the processes decide in sequence the same value, namely x, the proposal of q. Even if the message from p reaches process r much later, the process no longer adopts the value from p because it has already adopted a value from process with a less important rank.

Correctness. The *validity* and *integrity* properties follow directly from the algorithm and from the use of the underlying best-effort broadcast abstraction. The *termination* property follows from the *strong completeness* property of the perfect failure detector and from the *validity* property of best-effort broadcast: no process will remain indefinitely blocked in a round and every correct process p will eventually reach round $rank(p)$ and decide in that round.

Consider now the *agreement* property. Let p be the correct process with the most important rank that decides, and suppose it decides some value v. According to the algorithm, every process q with a rank $j > i$ also decides v. As no process suspects

p because p is correct, every other process remains in round i until it receives the DECIDED message from p containing v. This is guaranteed by the *strong accuracy* property of the perfect failure detector. Hence, every process will adopt v in round i. Furthermore, after round i, any other process disregards proposals from processes with more important ranks than process p and any other proposal that it may receive and adopt is also v. This means that all processes decide v.

Performance. The algorithm requires N communication steps to terminate and exchanges $O(N)$ messages in each round. Clearly, the algorithm can be optimized to use fewer messages. For example, a process does not need to send a message to processes with a more important rank because no highly ranked process even looks at a DECIDED message from a process with a less important rank (in this sense, the algorithm is reminiscent of some hierarchies among people).

5.2 Uniform Consensus

5.2.1 Specification

As with reliable broadcast, we can define a uniform variant of consensus. Uniform consensus ensures that no two processes decide different values, whether they are correct or not. The uniform specification is presented in Module 5.2. Its *uniform agreement* property eliminates the restriction to the decisions of the correct processes and requires that every process, whether it later crashes or not, decides the same value. All other properties of uniform consensus are the same as in (regular) consensus.

None of the consensus algorithms we presented so far ensure uniform agreement. Roughly speaking, this is because some of the processes decide too early, without making sure that their decision has been seen by enough processes. Should such an

---

Module 5.2: Interface and properties of uniform consensus

Module:

   Name: UniformConsensus, **instance** *uc*.

Events:

   Request: $\langle\ uc,\ Propose\ |\ v\ \rangle$: Proposes value v for consensus.

   Indication: $\langle\ uc,\ Decide\ |\ v\ \rangle$: Outputs a decided value v of consensus.

Properties:

   UC1–UC3: Same as properties C1–C3 in (regular) consensus (Module 5.1).

   UC4: *Uniform agreement:* No two processes decide differently.

---

early deciding process crash, other processes might have no choice but to decide a different value.

To illustrate the issue in our "Flooding Consensus" algorithm (Algorithm 5.1), consider a scenario where the process p with rank 1 receives messages from all processes at the end of round 1. Assume furthermore that p decides its own proposal value, as this turns out to be the smallest value. However, p crashes shortly after deciding and its message does not reach any other process. The remaining processes move to round 2 without having received the message from p containing its decision. The processes are likely to decide some other value.

To illustrate the same issue in our "Hierarchical Consensus" algorithm (Algorithm 5.2), remember that the process p with rank 1 decides its own proposal in a unilateral way, before sending any messages to other processes and without making sure its proposal is seen by any other process. Hence, if p crashes immediately after deciding, it is likely that the other processes decide a different value.

In the following, we present two uniform consensus algorithms for the fail-stop model that tolerate $f < N$ faulty processes, called "Uniform Flooding Consensus" and "Uniform Hierarchical Consensus," respectively. These two algorithms can be viewed as uniform variants of our "Flooding Consensus" and "Hierarchical Consensus" algorithms, introduced in the previous section. In the next section, we also present a uniform consensus algorithm in the fail-noisy model.

5.2.2 Fail-Stop Algorithm: Flooding Uniform Consensus

Algorithm 5.3, called "Flooding Uniform Consensus," implements uniform consensus using the "flooding" method of Algorithm 5.1 for regular consensus. As in that algorithm, the processes operate in sequential rounds. In each round, they gather a set of proposals from all processes and disseminate their own set to all processes using a best-effort broadcast primitive.

However, there is an important difference to Algorithm 5.1 in that a process can no longer decide after receiving messages from the same set of processes in two consecutive rounds. Recall that a process might have decided and crashed before its proposal set or decision message reached any other process. As this would violate the *uniform agreement* property, the "Flooding Uniform Consensus" algorithm always runs for N rounds and every process decides only in round N. Intuitively, this permits that one process crashes in every round.

The remaining modifications from Algorithm 5.1 to 5.3 result from simplifications: instead of a round-specific proposal set, only one global proposal set is maintained, and the variable *receivedfrom* contains only the set of processes from which the process has received a message in the current round.

Correctness. The *validity* and *integrity* properties follow from the algorithm and from the properties of best-effort broadcast. The *termination* property is ensured here because all correct processes reach round N and decide in that round. More precisely, the *strong completeness* property of the failure detector implies that no correct process waits indefinitely for a message from a process that has crashed, as the crashed process is eventually removed from *correct*. The *uniform agreement*

Algorithm 5.3: Flooding Uniform Consensus

Implements:
    UniformConsensus, **instance** *uc*.

Uses:
    BestEffortBroadcast, **instance** *beb*;
    PerfectFailureDetector, **instance** $\mathcal{P}$.

upon event ⟨ *uc, Init* ⟩ **do**
    correct := Π;
    round := 1;
    decision := ⊥;
    proposalset := ∅;
    receivedfrom := ∅;

upon event ⟨ $\mathcal{P}$, *Crash* | *p* ⟩ **do**
    correct := *correct* \ {*p*};

upon event ⟨ *uc, Propose* | *v* ⟩ **do**
    proposalset := *proposalset* ∪ {*v*};
    trigger ⟨ *beb, Broadcast* | [PROPOSAL, 1, *proposalset*] ⟩;

upon event ⟨ *beb, Deliver* | *p*, [PROPOSAL, *r*, *ps*] ⟩ **such that** *r* = *round* **do**
    receivedfrom := *receivedfrom* ∪ {*p*};
    proposalset := *proposalset* ∪ *ps*;

upon *correct* ⊆ *receivedfrom* ∧ *decision* = ⊥ **do**
    if *round* = *N* **then**
        decision := min(*proposalset*);
        trigger ⟨ *uc, Decide* | *decision* ⟩;
    else
        round := *round* + 1;
        receivedfrom := ∅;
        trigger ⟨ *beb, Broadcast* | [PROPOSAL, *round*, *proposalset*] ⟩;

---

holds because all processes that reach round N have the same set of values in their variable *proposalset*.

Performance. The algorithm requires N communication steps and $O(N^3)$ messages for all correct processes to decide.

5.2.3 Fail-Stop Algorithm: Hierarchical Uniform Consensus

Algorithm 5.4, called "Hierarchical Uniform Consensus," solves uniform consensus in the fail-stop model using a hierarchy among the processes and a series of rounds, similar to our "Hierarchical Consensus" algorithm (Algorithm 5.2). Every process maintains a single proposal value that it broadcasts in the round corresponding to its rank. When it receives a proposal from a more importantly ranked process, it adopts the value.

Algorithm 5.4: Hierarchical Uniform Consensus

Implements:
    UniformConsensus, **instance** *uc*.

Uses:
    PerfectPointToPointLinks, **instance** *pl*;
    BestEffortBroadcast, **instance** *beb*;
    ReliableBroadcast, **instance** *rb*;
    PerfectFailureDetector, **instance** $\mathcal{P}$.

upon event $\langle$ *uc, Init* $\rangle$ **do**
    detectedranks := ∅;
    ackranks := ∅;
    round := 1;
    proposal := ⊥; *decision* := ⊥;
    proposed := $[\bot]^N$;

upon event $\langle$ $\mathcal{P}$, *Crash* | *p* $\rangle$ **do**
    detectedranks := *detectedranks* ∪ {rank(*p*)};

upon event $\langle$ *uc, Propose* | *v* $\rangle$ **such that** *proposal* = ⊥ **do**
    proposal := *v*;

upon *round* = rank(*self*) ∧ *proposal* ≠ ⊥ ∧ *decision* = ⊥ **do**
    trigger $\langle$ *beb, Broadcast* | [PROPOSAL, *proposal*] $\rangle$;

upon event $\langle$ *beb, Deliver* | *p*, [PROPOSAL, *v*] $\rangle$ **do**
    proposed[rank(*p*)] := *v*;
    if rank(*p*) ≥ *round* **then**
        trigger $\langle$ *pl, Send* | *p*, [ACK] $\rangle$;

upon *round* ∈ *detectedranks* **do**
    if *proposed*[*round*] ≠ ⊥ **then**
        proposal := *proposed*[*round*];
    round := *round* + 1;

upon event $\langle$ *pl, Deliver* | *q*, [ACK] $\rangle$ **do**
    ackranks := *ackranks* ∪ {rank(*q*)};

upon *detectedranks* ∪ *ackranks* = {1, . . . , *N*} **do**
    trigger $\langle$ *rb, Broadcast* | [DECIDED, *proposal*] $\rangle$;

upon event $\langle$ *rb, Deliver* | *p*, [DECIDED, *v*] $\rangle$ **such that** *decision* = ⊥ **do**
    decision := *v*;
    trigger $\langle$ *uc, Decide* | *decision* $\rangle$;

The "Hierarchical Uniform Consensus" algorithm uses a perfect failure-detector abstraction $\mathcal{P}$, a best-effort broadcast abstraction to disseminate the proposal, a perfect links abstraction to acknowledge the receipt of a proposal, and a reliable broadcast abstraction to disseminate the decision. We explain the need for the latter after an overview of the algorithm.

In every round of the algorithm, the process whose rank corresponds to the number of the round is the leader, i.e., the most importantly ranked process is the leader of round 1. In contrast to the "Hierarchical Consensus" algorithm, however, a round here consists of two communication steps: within the same round, the leader broadcasts a PROPOSAL message to all processes, trying to impose its value, and then expects to obtain an acknowledgment from all correct processes. Processes that receive a proposal from the leader of the round adopt this proposal as their own and send an acknowledgment back to the leader of the round. If the leader succeeds in collecting an acknowledgment from all processes except those that $\mathcal{P}$ has detected to have crashed, the leader can decide. It disseminates the decided value using a reliable broadcast communication abstraction. As in Algorithm 5.2, a process represents the output from $\mathcal{P}$ and the set of processes who sent an acknowledgment in a set of ranks.

If the leader of a round fails, the correct processes detect this and proceed to the next round. The leader of the next round is the process immediately below the current leader in the hierarchy; the new leader broadcasts its proposal only if it has not already delivered the decision through the reliable broadcast abstraction.

Note that even if the leader fails after disseminating the decision, the reliable broadcast abstraction ensures that if any process decides and stops taking any leadership action then all correct processes will also decide. This property would not be guaranteed by a best-effort broadcast abstraction. (An alternative would have been to use a best-effort broadcast but have processes continue the algorithm even if they receive a decision message.)

Correctness. The *validity* and *integrity* properties follow trivially from the algorithm and from the properties of the underlying communication abstractions.

Consider *termination*. If some correct process decides, it decides because it *rb*-delivered a decision message. Due to the properties of the reliable broadcast abstraction, every correct process eventually *rb*-delivers the decision message and decides. Hence, either all correct processes decide or no correct process decides. Assume by contradiction that there is at least one correct process, and no correct process decides. Let p be the correct process with the most important rank. Due to the *strong completeness* property of the perfect failure detector, every correct process detects the crashes of the processes with more important ranks than p (or *beb*-delivers their PROPOSAL message). Hence, all correct processes reach round $rank(p)$ and, due to the *strong accuracy* property of the failure detector, no process detects the crash of process p or moves to the next round. Therefore, all correct processes wait until a message from p is *beb*-delivered and send an acknowledgment. Process p, the leader of this round, hence succeeds in collecting acknowledgments from all correct processes and decides.

Consider now the *uniform agreement* property, and assume that two processes decide differently. This can only be possible if two processes *rb*-broadcast decision messages with two different proposal values. Consider any two processes p and q such that $rank(q) > rank(p)$ and suppose that p and q *rb*-broadcast two decision values v and v', respectively. Because of the *strong accuracy* property of the failure detector, process q must have adopted v before reaching round $rank(q)$. Hence, it holds $v = v'$, which contradicts the assumption.

Performance. If there are no failures, the algorithm terminates in three communication steps: two steps for the first round and one step for the reliable broadcast. The algorithm exchanges $O(N)$ messages. Each failure of a leader adds two additional communication steps and $O(N)$ additional messages.

5.3 Uniform Consensus in the Fail-Noisy Model

5.3.1 Overview

All consensus and uniform consensus algorithms we have given so far assume a fail-stop model: they rely on a perfect failure detector abstraction $\mathcal{P}$. It is easy to see that in any of those algorithms, a false failure suspicion (i.e., a violation of the *strong accuracy* property of $\mathcal{P}$) might lead to the violation of the *agreement* property of consensus. That is, if a process is detected to have crashed while it is actually correct, then two correct processes might decide differently. On the other hand, in any of those algorithms, not suspecting a crashed process (i.e., violating the *strong completeness* property of $\mathcal{P}$) might lead to the violation of the *termination* property of consensus. This argument shows that the consensus algorithms given so far cannot be used in the fail-noisy model, where the failure detector is only eventually perfect and might make mistakes. (See also the exercises at the end of this chapter.)

In this section, we describe a uniform consensus algorithm in the fail-noisy model, based on an eventual leader detector, which can itself be implemented assuming an eventually perfect failure detector. The algorithm relies on a majority of correct processes and assumes $N > 2f$. This solution is however quite involved, which is the reason for devoting a whole section to this algorithm.

Our fail-noisy uniform consensus algorithm causes the processes to execute a sequence of *epochs*. The epochs are identified with increasing timestamps; every epoch has a designated *leader*, whose task is to reach consensus among the processes. If the leader is correct and no further epoch starts, then the leader succeeds in reaching consensus. But if the next epoch in the sequence is triggered, the processes abort the current epoch and invoke the next one, even if some processes may already have decided in the current epoch.

The core of the algorithm ensures that a subsequent epoch respects the *uniform agreement* property of consensus, such that if a process might already have decided in the current epoch, the decision value becomes fixed. A process that decides in a later epoch must also decide the fixed value.

We introduce two abstractions to build our fail-noisy consensus algorithm. The first one is an *epoch-change* primitive that is responsible for triggering the sequence of epochs at all processes. The second one is an *epoch consensus* abstraction, whose goal is to reach consensus in a given epoch. Since one epoch might be aborted, the consensus algorithm will invoke multiple epoch consensus instances in sequence, governed by the outputs from the epoch-change primitive. Every process must invoke a well-formed sequence of epochs by giving some state information locally to the next instance.

The rest of this section is structured as follows. The next two subsections present the epoch-change and the epoch consensus abstractions and corresponding implementations. The epoch-change primitive can be implemented in a fail-noisy model, relying on an eventual leader detector, but epoch consensus can be implemented in a fail-silent model, provided only that a majority of the processes is correct. We then show a transformation from these two abstractions to uniform consensus. The resulting "Leader-Driven Consensus" algorithm implements uniform consensus in the fail-noisy model.

In fact, there is no difference between regular consensus and its uniform variant in the fail-noisy model. In the exercise section, we will show that any fail-noisy algorithm that solves consensus also solves uniform consensus. Furthermore, we will show that a majority of correct processes is necessary for any fail-noisy algorithm that implements consensus.

Later in this chapter, we will discuss consensus in a fail-arbitrary model, with Byzantine process abstractions. We shall use the same approach based on a sequence of epochs to implement Byzantine consensus. Simply by replacing the implementations of the epoch-change and epoch consensus primitives with fail-arbitrary algorithms, we will use the transformation given here and obtain a Byzantine consensus algorithm.

5.3.2 Epoch-Change

Specification. Our *epoch-change* abstraction signals the start of a new epoch by triggering a $\langle$ *StartEpoch* $\mid ts, \ell \rangle$ event, when a leader is suspected; the event contains two parameters: an *epoch timestamp ts* and a *leader process* ℓ that serve to identify the starting epoch. When this event occurs, we say the process *starts epoch* (ts, ℓ). Apart from the implicit initialization, the epoch-change abstraction receives no requests.

We require that the timestamps in the sequence of epochs that are started at one process are monotonically increasing and that every process receives the same leader for a given epoch timestamp (with the *monotonicity* and *consistency* properties). Eventually, the primitive must cease to start new epochs, and the last epoch started at every correct process must be the same; furthermore, the leader of this last epoch must be correct. This is the *eventual leadership* property. Intuitively, this last leader will then perform all remaining steps of a higher-level module and ensure its termination.

The interface and properties of an epoch-change abstraction are given in Module 5.3. When an epoch-change abstraction is initialized, it is assumed that a default epoch with timestamp 0 and a leader ℓ_0 is active at all correct processes. The value of ℓ_0 is made available to all processes implicitly.

Module 5.3: Interface and properties of epoch-change

Module:

    Name: EpochChange, **instance** *ec.*

Events:

    Indication: $\langle$ *ec, StartEpoch* | ts, ℓ $\rangle$: Starts the epoch identified by timestamp ts with leader ℓ.

Properties:

    EC1: *Monotonicity:* If a correct process starts an epoch (ts, ℓ) and later starts an epoch (ts', ℓ'), then $ts' > ts$.

    EC2: *Consistency:* If a correct process starts an epoch (ts, ℓ) and another correct process starts an epoch (ts', ℓ') with $ts = ts'$, then $\ell = \ell'$.

    EC3: *Eventual leadership:* There is a time after which every correct process has started some epoch and starts no further epoch, such that the last epoch started at every correct process is epoch (ts, ℓ) and process ℓ is correct.

Fail-Noisy Algorithm: Leader-Based Epoch-Change. Our implementation of the epoch-change abstraction is shown in Algorithm 5.5 and called "Leader-Based Epoch-Change." It relies on an eventual leader detector Ω (Module 2.9).

    The epoch-change algorithm is quite simple. Every process p maintains two time-stamps: a timestamp *lastts* of the last epoch that it started (i.e., for which it triggered a $\langle$ *StartEpoch* $\rangle$ event), and the timestamp ts of the last epoch that it attempted to start with itself as leader (i.e., for which it broadcast a NEWEPOCH message, as described next). Initially, the process sets ts to its rank. Whenever the leader detector subsequently makes p trust itself, p adds N to ts and sends a NEWEPOCH message with ts. When process p receives a NEWEPOCH message with a parameter *newts* > *lastts* from some process ℓ *and* p most recently trusted ℓ, then the process triggers a $\langle$ *StartEpoch* $\rangle$ event with parameters *newts* and ℓ. Otherwise, the process informs the aspiring leader ℓ with a NACK message that the new epoch could not be started. When a process receives a NACK message and still trusts itself, it increments ts by N and tries again to start an epoch by sending another NEWEPOCH message.

Correctness. We argue that Algorithm 5.5 implements epoch-change with f crash faults for $N > f$.

    A process p locally maintains the timestamp *lastts* of the most recently started epoch and compares it to the timestamp in every NEWEPOCH message. Hence, the algorithm ensures that p only starts further epochs with higher timestamps. This establishes the *monotonicity* property of epoch-change.

    For the *consistency* property, note that the space of epoch timestamps is partitioned among the N processes because every initializes ts to its rank and increments it by N when it broadcasts a NEWEPOCH message. Hence, no two distinct processes broadcast a NEWEPOCH message with the same timestamp value.

Algorithm 5.5: Leader-Based Epoch-Change

Implements:
    EpochChange, **instance** *ec*.

Uses:
    PerfectPointToPointLinks, **instance** *pl*;
    BestEffortBroadcast, **instance** *beb*;
    EventualLeaderDetector, **instance** Ω.

upon event $\langle$ *ec*, *Init* $\rangle$ **do**
    trusted := ℓ_0;
    lastts := 0;
    ts := *rank*(*self*);

upon event $\langle$ Ω, *Trust* $\mid p$ $\rangle$ **do**
    trusted := *p*;
    if $p = self$ **then**
        ts := *ts* + *N*;
        trigger $\langle$ *beb*, *Broadcast* $\mid$ [NEWEPOCH, *ts*] $\rangle$;

upon event $\langle$ *beb*, *Deliver* $\mid \ell$, [NEWEPOCH, *newts*] $\rangle$ **do**
    if $\ell = trusted \wedge newts > lastts$ **then**
        lastts := *newts*;
        trigger $\langle$ *ec*, *StartEpoch* $\mid$ *newts*, ℓ $\rangle$;
    else
        trigger $\langle$ *pl*, *Send* $\mid \ell$, [NACK] $\rangle$;

upon event $\langle$ *pl*, *Deliver* $\mid p$, [NACK] $\rangle$ **do**
    if *trusted* = *self* **then**
        ts := *ts* + *N*;
        trigger $\langle$ *beb*, *Broadcast* $\mid$ [NEWEPOCH, *ts*] $\rangle$;

The *eventual leadership* property is based on the properties of the leader-detector abstraction. Let q be the correct process that is eventually trusted by all correct processes. At the last time when Ω causes process q to trust itself, q broadcasts a NEWEPOCH message with some timestamp qts that should cause all processes to start an epoch with leader q and timestamp qts. Consider any correct process p that receives this message: p either last trusted q and qts is bigger than its variable *lastts* and, therefore, p starts epoch (qts, t); or the condition does not hold and p sends a NACK message to q. In the latter case, this message causes q to increment its variable ts and to broadcast another NEWEPOCH message. The properties of Ω ensure that eventually all correct processes trust q forever, therefore only q increments its ts variable and all other processes have stopped broadcasting NEWEPOCH messages. Hence, q eventually broadcasts a NEWEPOCH message with a timestamp bigger than the *lastts* variable of p. Because p trusts q when it receives this message, p eventually starts some epoch with timestamp qts^* and leader q. And because q is correct and broadcasts the NEWEPOCH message with timestamp qts^* to all processes, every correct process eventually starts this epoch and stops sending NACK messages.

Suppose that process p above is the last process whose NACK message was delivered to q. Then, because q sends the NEWEPOCH message with timestamp qts^* to all processes, the epoch with timestamp qts^* is also the last epoch that every correct process starts.

Performance. Algorithm 5.5 incurs one communication step and $O(N)$ messages whenever Ω selects a new leader.

5.3.3 Epoch Consensus

Specification. *Epoch consensus* is a primitive similar to consensus, where the processes propose a value and may decide a value. Every epoch is identified by an *epoch timestamp* and has a designated *leader*. As for uniform consensus, the goal of epoch consensus is that all processes, regardless whether correct or faulty, decide the same value (according to the uniform variant of agreement). But epoch consensus is easier to implement than consensus because it only represents an attempt to reach consensus; epoch consensus may not terminate and can be aborted when it does not decide or when the next epoch should already be started by the higher-level algorithm. As another simplification, only the leader proposes a value and epoch consensus is required to decide only when its leader is correct. Because a single epoch consensus may not decide, the higher-level algorithm executes multiple epochs in a logical sequence such that the epoch consensus abstractions in later epochs depend on earlier ones.

More precisely, every instance of *epoch consensus* is associated with a timestamp ts and a leader process ℓ. During initialization, some implementation-specific *state* value is passed to the abstraction at every process. (This feature extends the initialization mechanism as presented so far, but can easily be added in practice.) To start an epoch consensus instance *ep*, the leader ℓ *proposes* a value v with a $\langle$ *Propose* $\mid v$ $\rangle$ request; unlike consensus, the other processes are not required to propose anything. When this occurs, we also say the leader *ep-proposes* v. One way for epoch consensus to terminate is to trigger an indication $\langle$ *Decide* $\mid v$ $\rangle$; when it happens, we say the process *ep-decides* v.

Furthermore, epoch consensus must terminate when the application locally triggers an event $\langle$ *Abort* $\rangle$. After receiving this event, the epoch signals the completion of the abort by returning an event $\langle$ *Aborted* $\mid$ *state* $\rangle$ to the caller, containing some internal state. The caller must use *state* to initialize the next epoch consensus instance in which it participates. Aborts are always triggered externally, an instance does not abort on its own. Different processes may abort epoch consensus independently of each other at different times.

We require that every process runs at most one epoch consensus instance at a time; the process may only initialize a new epoch consensus after the previously active one has aborted or *ep*-decided. Moreover, a process must only initialize an epoch consensus instance with a higher timestamp than that of all instances that it initialized previously, and it must use the state of the most recently aborted epoch consensus instance to initialize the next such instance. A process respecting these rules is said to run a *well-formed* sequence of epochs. Note that the timestamps

Module 5.4: Interface and properties of epoch consensus

Module:

Name: EpochConsensus, **instance** *ep*, with timestamp *ts* and leader process ℓ.

Events:

Request: $\langle$ *ep, Propose* | *v* $\rangle$: Proposes value *v* for epoch consensus. Executed only by the leader ℓ.

Request: $\langle$ *ep, Abort* $\rangle$: Aborts epoch consensus.

Indication: $\langle$ *ep, Decide* | *v* $\rangle$: Outputs a decided value *v* of epoch consensus.

Indication: $\langle$ *ep, Aborted* | *state* $\rangle$: Signals that epoch consensus has completed the abort and outputs internal state *state*.

Properties:

EP1: *Validity:* If a correct process *ep*-decides *v*, then *v* was *ep*-proposed by the leader ℓ' of some epoch consensus with timestamp $ts' \leq ts$ and leader ℓ'.

EP2: *Uniform agreement:* No two processes *ep*-decide differently.

EP3: *Integrity:* Every correct process *ep*-decides at most once.

EP4: *Lock-in:* If a correct process has *ep*-decided *v* in an epoch consensus with timestamp $ts' < ts$, then no correct process *ep*-decides a value different from *v*.

EP5: *Termination:* If the leader ℓ is correct, has *ep*-proposed a value, and no correct process aborts this epoch consensus, then every correct process eventually *ep*-decides some value.

EP6: *Abort behavior:* When a correct process aborts an epoch consensus, it eventually will have completed the abort; moreover, a correct process completes an abort only if the epoch consensus has been aborted by some correct process.

---

from a well-formed sequence of epochs may also skip some values. The "Leader-Driven Consensus" algorithm presented in the next section ensures this property for all processes. Because there is such a correspondence between epochs and epoch consensus instances, we sometimes simply say the "epoch" with timestamp *ets* and mean the instance of epoch consensus with timestamp *ets*.

The properties of epoch consensus are closely related to those of uniform consensus. Its *uniform agreement* and *integrity* properties are the same, and the *termination* condition of epoch consensus is only weakened by assuming the leader is correct. The *validity* property extends the possible decision values to those proposed in epochs with smaller timestamps, assuming a well-formed sequence of epochs. Finally, the *lock-in* property is new and establishes an explicit link on the decision values across epochs: if some process has already *ep*-decided *v* in an earlier epoch of a well-formed sequence then only *v* may be *ep*-decided during this epoch.

The interface and properties of epoch consensus are depicted in Module 5.4. They assume the processes invoke a well-formed sequence of epochs.

Fail-Silent Algorithm: Read/Write Epoch Consensus. Our implementation of epoch consensus is called "Read/Write Epoch Consensus" and shown in Algorithm 5.6. The algorithm uses best-effort broadcast and perfect point-to-point links abstractions.

Multiple instances of epoch consensus may be executed at the same point in time by different processes; but when used in our "Leader-Driven Consensus" algorithm, then every process only runs at most one epoch consensus instance at a time. Different instances never interfere with each other according to our assumption that every instance is identified by a unique epoch timestamp and because point-to-point messages and best-effort broadcast messages are only received from and delivered to other instances with the same timestamp.

Intuitively, the algorithm works as follows. The leader tries to impose a decision value on the processes. The other processes witness the actions of the leader, should the leader fail, and they also witness actions of leaders in earlier epochs. Recall that epoch consensus is initialized with a *state* value, which the previously active epoch consensus returned to the process when it was aborted. The state contains a timestamp and a value. Passing *state* to the next epoch consensus in well-formed sequences serves the *validity* and *lock-in* properties of epoch consensus, as these properties (and no others) link two epochs with different timestamps together.

The algorithm involves two rounds of message exchanges from the leader to all processes. The goal is for the leader to write its proposal value to all processes, who store the epoch timestamp and the value in their state and acknowledge this to the leader. When the leader receives enough acknowledgments, it will *ep*-decide this value. But it may be that the leader of some previous epoch already *ep*-decided some value. To prevent that the epoch violates *lock-in*, the leader must write the previously *ep*-decided value again. Hence, it first reads the state of the processes by sending a READ message. Every process answers with a STATE message containing its locally stored value and the timestamp of the epoch during which the value was last written. The leader receives a quorum of STATE messages and choses the value that comes with the highest timestamp as its proposal value, if one exists. This step uses the function *highest*(·) introduced before. The leader then writes the chosen value to all processes with a WRITE message. The write succeeds when the leader receives an ACCEPT message from a quorum of processes, indicating that they have stored the value locally. The leader now *ep*-decides the chosen value and announces this in a DECIDED message to all processes; the processes that receive this *ep*-decide as well.

As every two quorums overlap in one process, the leader is sure to read any value that may have been *ep*-decided in a previous epoch and to write it again. Quorums play a similar role here as in the replicated implementations of read/write registers from Chap. 4.

When aborted, the epoch consensus implementation simply returns its state, consisting of the timestamp/value pair with the written value, and halts. It is important that the instance performs no further steps.

Algorithm 5.6: Read/Write Epoch Consensus

Implements:
   EpochConsensus, **instance** ep, with timestamp ets and leader ℓ.

Uses:
   PerfectPointToPointLinks, **instance** pl;
   BestEffortBroadcast, **instance** beb.

upon event $\langle\ ep,\ Init\ |\ state\ \rangle$ **do**
   $(valts, val) := state$;
   $tmpval := \perp$;
   $states := [\perp]^N$;
   $accepted := 0$;

upon event $\langle\ ep,\ Propose\ |\ v\ \rangle$ **do**   // only leader ℓ
   $tmpval := v$;
   trigger $\langle\ beb,\ Broadcast\ |\ [\text{READ}]\ \rangle$;

upon event $\langle\ beb,\ Deliver\ |\ \ell,\ [\text{READ}]\ \rangle$ **do**
   trigger $\langle\ pl,\ Send\ |\ \ell,\ [\text{STATE}, valts, val]\ \rangle$;

upon event $\langle\ pl,\ Deliver\ |\ q,\ [\text{STATE}, ts, v]\ \rangle$ **do**   // only leader ℓ
   $states[q] := (ts, v)$;

upon $\#(states) > N/2$ **do**   // only leader ℓ
   $(ts, v) := highest(states)$;
   if $v \neq \perp$ **then**
      $tmpval := v$;
   $states := [\perp]^N$;
   trigger $\langle\ beb,\ Broadcast\ |\ [\text{WRITE}, tmpval]\ \rangle$;

upon event $\langle\ beb,\ Deliver\ |\ \ell,\ [\text{WRITE}, v]\ \rangle$ **do**
   $(valts, val) := (ets, v)$;
   trigger $\langle\ pl,\ Send\ |\ \ell,\ [\text{ACCEPT}]\ \rangle$;

upon event $\langle\ pl,\ Deliver\ |\ q,\ [\text{ACCEPT}]\ \rangle$ **do**   // only leader ℓ
   $accepted := accepted + 1$;

upon $accepted > N/2$ **do**   // only leader ℓ
   $accepted := 0$;
   trigger $\langle\ beb,\ Broadcast\ |\ [\text{DECIDED}, tmpval]\ \rangle$;

upon event $\langle\ beb,\ Deliver\ |\ \ell,\ [\text{DECIDED}, v]\ \rangle$ **do**
   trigger $\langle\ ep,\ Decide\ |\ v\ \rangle$;

upon event $\langle\ ep,\ Abort\ \rangle$ **do**
   trigger $\langle\ ep,\ Aborted\ |\ (valts, val)\ \rangle$;
   halt;   // stop operating when aborted

Correctness. We argue that Algorithm 5.6 implements epoch consensus with timestamp ets and leader ℓ in the fail-noisy model, with f crash faults for $N > 2f$.

We first establish the *lock-in* property of epoch consensus. Suppose some process has *ep*-decided v in an epoch with timestamp $ts' < ts$. The process only *ep*-decided after receiving a DECIDED message with v from the leader ℓ' of epoch ts'. Before sending this message, process ℓ' had broadcast a WRITE message containing v and had collected ACCEPT messages in response from a set $\mathcal{A}$ of more than $N/2$ distinct processes. According to the algorithm, these processes set their variables *val* to v and *valts* to ts'.

Consider the next epoch in which the leader sends a WRITE message, and suppose its timestamp is ts^* and its leader is ℓ^*. Because the state $(valts, val)$ is passed from one epoch consensus instance to the next one in well-formed invocation sequences, this means that no process has changed its *valts* and *val* variables in any epoch between ts' and ts^*. We conclude that every process in $\mathcal{A}$ starts the epoch consensus instance with timestamp ts^* with state $(valts, val) = (ts', v)$. Hence, leader ℓ^* collects STATE messages whose highest timestamp/value tuple is (ts', v) and broadcasts a WRITE message containing v. This implies that a process can only *ep*-decide v and that the set of processes whose variable *val* is equal to v when they abort epoch ts^* is at least $\mathcal{A}$. Continuing this argument until epoch consensus with timestamp ts establishes the *lock-in* property.

To establish the *validity* property, assume that a process *ep*-decides v. It is obvious from the algorithm that a process only *ep*-decides the value v received in a DECIDED message from ℓ; furthermore, every process stores in variable *val* only the value received in a WRITE message from the leader. In both cases, this value comes from the variable *tmpval* of the leader. But in any epoch the leader sets *tmpval* only to the value that it *ep*-proposed or to some value that it received in a STATE message from another process. By backward induction in the sequence of epochs, this shows that v was *ep*-proposed by the leader in some epoch with a timestamp smaller than or equal to ts.

The *uniform agreement* property follows easily from inspecting the algorithm because ℓ sends the same value to all processes in the DECIDED message. Analogously, *integrity* follows from the algorithm.

The *termination* property is also easy to see because when ℓ is correct and no process aborts the epoch, then every correct process eventually receives a DECIDE message and *ep*-decides.

Finally, the *abort behavior* property is satisfied because the algorithm returns $\langle$ *Aborted* $\rangle$ immediately after it has been aborted and only then.

Performance. The "Read/Write Epoch Consensus" algorithm involves five communication steps, assuming that it is not aborted. These steps correspond to the two rounds of messages exchanges between the leader and all processes for reading and for writing, plus the final broadcasting of the decision. One such epoch consensus requires therefore $O(N)$ messages.

Algorithm 5.7: Leader-Driven Consensus

Implements:
    UniformConsensus, **instance** *uc*.

Uses:
    EpochChange, **instance** *ec*;
    EpochConsensus (multiple instances).

upon event ⟨ *uc, Init* ⟩ **do**
    $val := \bot$;
    proposed := FALSE; *decided* := FALSE;
    Obtain the leader ℓ_0 of the initial epoch with timestamp 0 from epoch-change inst. *ec*;
    Initialize a new instance *ep*.0 of epoch consensus with timestamp 0,
        leader ℓ_0, and state $(0, \bot)$;
    $(ets, \ell) := (0, \ell_0)$;
    $(newts, new\ell) := (0, \bot)$;

upon event ⟨ *uc, Propose* | *v* ⟩ **do**
    $val := v$;

upon event ⟨ *ec, StartEpoch* | *newts′, new\ell′* ⟩ **do**
    $(newts, new\ell) := (newts′, new\ell′)$;
    trigger ⟨ *ep.ets, Abort* ⟩;

upon event ⟨ *ep.ts, Aborted* | *state* ⟩ **such that** $ts = ets$ **do**
    $(ets, \ell) := (newts, new\ell)$;
    proposed := FALSE;
    Initialize a new instance *ep.ets* of epoch consensus with timestamp *ets*,
        leader ℓ, and state *state*;

upon $\ell = self \wedge val \neq \bot \wedge proposed =$ FALSE **do**
    proposed := TRUE;
    trigger ⟨ *ep.ets, Propose* | *val* ⟩;

upon event ⟨ *ep.ts, Decide* | *v* ⟩ **such that** $ts = ets$ **do**
    if *decided* = FALSE **then**
        decided := TRUE;
        trigger ⟨ *uc, Decide* | *v* ⟩;

5.3.4 Fail-Noisy Algorithm: Leader-Driven Consensus

This section introduces our "Leader-Driven Consensus" algorithm, implemented from the epoch-change and epoch consensus abstractions. The algorithm provides uniform consensus in a fail-noisy model and runs through a sequence of epochs. The pseudo code in Algorithm 5.7 distinguishes the instances of epoch consensus by their timestamp.

Intuitively, the value that is decided by the consensus algorithm is the value that is *ep*-decided by one of the underlying epoch consensus instances. The algorithm

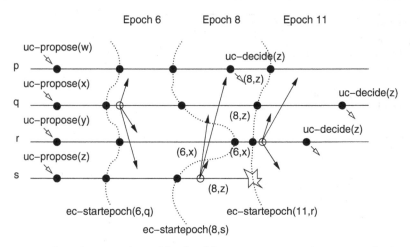

Figure 5.3: Sample execution of leader-driven consensus, using an epoch-change primitive and multiple epoch consensus instances

runs through a sequence of epochs, triggered by ⟨ *StartEpoch* ⟩ events output by the epoch-change primitive. These events also specify timestamp and leader of the next epoch consensus to start. To switch from one epoch to the next, the algorithm aborts the running epoch consensus, obtains its state, and initializes the next epoch consensus with the state. Hence, the algorithm invokes a well-formed sequence of epoch consensus instances.

As soon as a process has obtained the proposal value for consensus from the application and the process is also the leader of the current epoch, it *ep*-proposes this value for epoch consensus. When the current epoch *ep*-decides a value, the process also decides that value in consensus, but continues to participate in the consensus algorithm, to help other processes decide.

When the epoch-change implementation from Algorithm 5.5 and the epoch consensus implementation from Algorithm 5.6 are used underneath the "Leader-Driven Consensus" algorithm, then Algorithm 5.6 can be simplified by omitting the READ message. This does not change the algorithm because the leader of epoch consensus broadcasts READ immediately after it has broadcast a NEWEPOCH message in epoch-change to all processes. Instead, every process may just send the STATE message after initializing the epoch consensus instance, in reply to receiving the NEWEPOCH message.

Figure 5.3 shows a sample execution of the "Leader-Driven Consensus" algorithm with four processes (*p* has rank 1, *q* has rank 2, and so on). Every process proposes a different value and then starts epoch 6 with leader *q*. The open circle depicts that process *q* is the leader and the arrows show that it drives the message exchange in the epoch consensus instance, which is implemented by Algorithm 5.6. Process *q* writes its proposal *x*, but only process *r* receives it and sends an ACCEPT message before the epoch ends; hence, process r updates its state to $(6, x)$. Epoch 8 with leader s starts subsequently and the processes abort the epoch consensus instance with timestamp 6. At process r, epoch 8 starts much later, and r neither receives nor sends any message before the epoch is aborted again. Note that the specification of epoch-change would also permit that process r never starts epoch 8 and moves from epoch 6 to 11 directly.

Process s is the leader of epoch 8. It finds no highest value different from $\perp$ and writes its own proposal z. Subsequently, it sends a DECIDED message and process p ep-decides and uc-decides z in epoch 8. Note that p, q, and s now have state $(8, z)$. Then process s crashes and epoch 11 with leader r starts. The state of r is still $(6, x)$; but it reads value z from p or q, and therefore writes z. As r is correct, all remaining processes ep-decide z in this epoch consensus instance and, consequently, also q and r uc-decide z.

It could also have been that process p crashed immediately after deciding z; in this case, the remaining processes would also have decided z due to the *lock-in* and *agreement* properties of epoch consensus. This illustrates that the algorithm provides uniform consensus.

Correctness. Given an implementation of epoch consensus in the fail-silent model and an implementation of epoch-change in the fail-noisy model, and assuming a majority of correct processes, Algorithm 5.7 implements uniform consensus in the fail-noisy model.

To show the *validity* property, we use an inductive argument on the sequence of epochs that have ever been started at any correct process, ordered by their timestamp. According to the algorithm, a process uc-decides v only when it has ep-decided v in the current epoch consensus; hence, every decision can be attributed to a unique epoch and to a unique instance of epoch consensus. Let ts^* be the smallest timestamp of an epoch consensus in which some process decides v. Then, this process has ep-decided v in epoch consensus with timestamp ts^*. According to the *validity* property of epoch consensus, this means that v was ep-proposed by the leader of some epoch whose timestamp is at most ts^*. Because a process only ep-proposes val when val has been uc-proposed for consensus, the *validity* property follows for processes that uc-decide in epoch ts^*.

Suppose now that the *validity* property of uniform consensus holds for every process that uc-decided in some epoch ts', and consider a correct process that uc-decides in an epoch $ts > ts'$. According to the *lock-in* property of epoch consensus, this process may only ep-decide v and thus only uc-decides v. This shows that the *validity* property holds for decisions in all epochs of well-formed sequences.

In order to establish the *uniform agreement* property, recall from the *validity* property that every decision by the algorithm can be attributed to an ep-decision of some epoch consensus instance. Thus, if two correct processes decide when they are in the same epoch then the *uniform agreement* condition of epoch consensus ensures that the decisions are the same; otherwise, if they decide in different epochs then the *lock-in* property of epoch consensus establishes the *uniform agreement* property.

The *integrity* property is straightforward to verify from the algorithm, because the *decided* flag prevents multiple decisions.

For the *termination* property, observe that the algorithm satisfies the requirements on invoking a well-formed sequence of epoch consensus instances, because of the *monotonicity* and *consistency* properties of the epoch-change primitive and because the algorithm only initializes a new epoch consensus after the previously active one, with a smaller timestamp, has aborted.

According to the *eventual leadership* property of the underlying epoch-change primitive, there exists some epoch with a timestamp ts and leader process ℓ such that no further epoch starts and ℓ is correct. Observe that the algorithm only aborts an instance of epoch consensus when the epoch-change primitive starts another epoch. As this does not occur after starting epoch (ts, ℓ), the *termination* condition for the epoch consensus instance $ep.ts$ now implies that every correct process eventually ep-decides in instance $ep.ts$ and, therefore, also uc-decides immediately after that.

Performance. The complexity of the "Leader-Driven Consensus" algorithm depends entirely on the complexities of the implementations of the underlying epoch-change and epoch consensus primitives, because the algorithm does not directly communicate any messages with a point-to-point link abstraction or a broadcast abstraction.

5.4 Logged Consensus

We consider now the fail-recovery model and address consensus with crash–recovery process abstractions. Recall that such processes may crash and recover arbitrarily often; but when a process eventually ceases to crash and continues to take steps indefinitely, it is still called correct.

We introduce a logged uniform consensus abstraction next. Our approach to implementing it will rely on the "Leader-Driven Consensus" algorithm from the previous section. We introduce also extensions of the epoch-change and epoch consensus abstractions and corresponding implementations for the fail-recovery model. The purpose of the detailed presentation is to demonstrate how multiple abstractions can be composed to survive crashes with subsequent recovery.

5.4.1 Specification

Module 5.5 presents the specification of *logged uniform consensus*. The abstraction results from a small change to the uniform consensus abstraction (Module 5.2), obtained by relaxing the *termination* property and by eliminating the *integrity* property. More precisely, only processes that never crash are required to decide and a process may decide multiple times; both modifications are inevitable in the fail-recovery model.

Recall how our logged links and logged broadcast abstractions store their output messages in a variable in stable storage, from which higher-level modules could

---

Module 5.5: Interface and properties of logged uniform consensus

Module:

    Name: LoggedUniformConsensus, **instance** *luc*.

Events:

    Request: $\langle$ *luc, Propose* $\mid v$ $\rangle$: Proposes value v for consensus.

    Indication: $\langle$ *luc, Decide* $\mid decision$ $\rangle$: Notifies the upper layer that variable *decision* in stable storage contains the decided value of consensus.

Properties:

    LUC1: *Termination:* Every correct process that never crashes eventually log-decides some value.

    LUC2: *Validity:* If a process log-decides v, then v was proposed by some process.

    LUC3: *Uniform agreement:* No two processes log-decide differently.

---

retrieve the output. We adopt the same mechanism for the logged uniform consensus abstraction and for the other primitives in this section. Hence, the event $\langle$ *Decide* $\mid decision$ $\rangle$ in Module 5.5 only gives the name of the logging variable *decision* in stable storage. The module logs the decided value in *decision*, from which the higher layer must retrieve it. We say that the logged primitive *log-decides* the value stored in *decision* when the event $\langle$ *Decide* $\mid decision$ $\rangle$ occurs.

For tolerating crashes with subsequent recovery, a higher-level module may propose the same value multiple times in logged uniform consensus and may also log-decide multiple times. It is assumed that the higher-level module proposes the same value again when it recovers from a crash and the logged uniform consensus abstraction has not log-decided. This ensures that the consensus abstraction eventually terminates and log-decides a value.

In order to adapt Algorithm 5.7 for the fail-recovery model, we need to provide a logged epoch-change abstraction and a logged epoch consensus abstraction that work for crash-recovery process abstractions.

5.4.2 Logged Epoch-Change

Specification. The *logged epoch-change* abstraction is almost the same as its counterpart with crash-stop processes. The only difference concerns the liveness condition, which strengthens some requirements from merely correct processes to processes that never crash. In particular, the *eventual leadership* property of logged epoch-change states that the process ℓ, which is the leader of the last epoch started at every correct process, is not only correct but actually never crashes.

Moreover, the *logged epoch-change* abstraction writes timestamp and leader of the next epoch to start into variables *startts* and *startℓ* in stable storage. This is

---

Module 5.6: Interface and properties of logged epoch-change

Module:

Name: LoggedEpochChange, **instance** *lec*.

Events:

Indication: ⟨ *lec*, *StartEpoch* | *startts*, *startℓ* ⟩: Notifies the upper layer that variables *startts* and *startℓ* in stable storage contain the timestamp and leader of the next epoch to start.

Properties:

LEC1–LEC2: Same as properties EC1–EC2 in epoch-change adapted for log-starting epochs.

LEC3: *Eventual leadership:* There is a time after which every correct process has log-started some epoch and log-starts no further epoch, such that the last epoch log-started at every correct process is epoch (ts, ℓ) and process ℓ never crashes.

---

similar to the delivery mechanism of logged broadcast abstractions. To highlight this difference to epoch-change with crash faults, we say that the abstraction *log-starts* the given epoch when this happens. The specification is shown in Module 5.6.

Fail-Recovery Algorithm: Logged Leader-Based Epoch-Change. An implementation of logged epoch-change is shown in Algorithm 5.8, called "Logged Leader-Based Epoch-Change." It is a direct descendant of Algorithm 5.5 and uses stubborn links and stubborn broadcast instead of perfect links and best-effort broadcast. The timestamp and the leader of the last log-started epoch are logged.

Correctness. The *monotonicity* and *consistency* properties are satisfied in the same way as for the original "Leader-Based Epoch-Change" algorithm. In addition, the value of *startts* is logged whenever it changes.

The *eventual leadership* property is satisfied directly because the eventual leader process ℓ process must be one that *never* crashes. Therefore, the algorithm always terminates at every process after process ℓ receives the last ⟨ *Trust* | ℓ ⟩ from Ω.

Performance. The algorithm incurs one communication step and $O(N)$ messages whenever Ω selects a new leader. It writes to stable storage once for every epoch started.

5.4.3 Logged Epoch Consensus

Specification. The *logged epoch consensus* abstraction plays the same role as the epoch consensus primitive in the consensus algorithm. The only change for the logged variant consists in logging the decision value, which is output after reaching consensus. The ⟨ *Decide* | *epochdecision* ⟩ event specifies the name of a variable *epochdecision* in stable storage, where the decision value is logged. When this event occurs, we say the abstraction *log-decides*. In case that a process crashes before

---

Algorithm 5.8: Logged Leader-Based Epoch-Change

Implements:
    LoggedEpochChange, **instance** *lec*.

Uses:
    StubbornPointToPointLinks, **instance** *sl*;
    StubbornBestEffortBroadcast, **instance** *sbeb*;
    EventualLeaderDetector, **instance** Ω.

upon event $\langle$ *lec, Init* $\rangle$ **do**
    trusted := ℓ_0;
    $(startts, start\ell)$:= $(0, \ell_0)$;
    ts := $rank(self) - N$;

upon event $\langle$ *lec, Recovery* $\rangle$ **do**
    retrieve(*startts*);

upon event $\langle$ Ω, *Trust* $|$ *p* $\rangle$ **do**
    trusted := *p*;
    if *p* = *self* **then**
        ts := $ts + N$;
        trigger $\langle$ *sbeb, Broadcast* $|$ [NEWEPOCH, ts] $\rangle$;

upon event $\langle$ *sbeb, Deliver* $|$ ℓ, [NEWEPOCH, *newts*] $\rangle$ **do**
    if ℓ = *trusted* $\wedge$ *newts* > *startts* **then**
        $(startts, start\ell)$:= $(newts, \ell)$;
        store(*startts, start\ell*);
        trigger $\langle$ *lec, StartEpoch* $|$ *startts, start\ell* $\rangle$;
    else
        trigger $\langle$ *sl, Send* $|$ ℓ, [NACK, *newts*] $\rangle$;

upon event $\langle$ *sl, Deliver* $|$ *p*, [NACK, *nts*] $\rangle$ **such that** *nts* = *ts* **do**
    if *trusted* = *self* **then**
        ts := $ts + N$;
        trigger $\langle$ *sbeb, Broadcast* $|$ [NEWEPOCH, ts] $\rangle$;

---

handling the event, the process may retrieve the epoch's decision value from stable storage upon recovery.

The logged epoch consensus terminates either because it decides or because it is aborted. Although the decided value is returned through a logged variable as described, the local state output by an aborted instance is returned through an ordinary event $\langle$ *Aborted* $|$ *state* $\rangle$. This event may be lost if the process crashes before the higher layer records it, but it does no harm because the layer above can simply abort the logged epoch consensus instance again.

Compared to the epoch consensus abstraction with crash-stop processes, the logged epoch consensus abstraction drops the *integrity* property and reformulates the *termination* property such that every correct process eventually log-decides a value. The detailed specification is shown in Module 5.7.

Module 5.7: Interface and properties of logged epoch consensus

Module:

> **Name:** LoggedEpochConsensus, **instance** *lep*, with timestamp ts and leader process ℓ.

Events:

> **Request:** $\langle$ *lep, Propose* $|$ v $\rangle$: Proposes value v for logged epoch consensus. Executed only by the leader ℓ.

> **Request:** $\langle$ *lep, Abort* $\rangle$: Aborts logged epoch consensus.

> **Indication:** $\langle$ *lep, Decide* $|$ *epochdecision* $\rangle$ Notifies the upper layer that the variable *epochdecision* in stable storage contains the decided value of logged epoch consensus.

> **Indication:** $\langle$ *lep, Aborted* $|$ *state* $\rangle$: Signals that logged epoch consensus has completed the abort and outputs internal state *state*.

Properties:

> **LEP1–LEP4:** Same as the *validity* (EP1), *uniform agreement* (EP2), *lock-in* (EP4), and *abort behavior* (EP6) properties in epoch consensus (Module 5.4), adapted for log-deciding.

> **LEP5:** *Termination:* If the leader ℓ never crashes, has proposed a value, and no correct process aborts this logged epoch consensus instance, then every correct process eventually log-decides some value in this instance.

Fail-Recovery Algorithm: Logged Read/Write Epoch Consensus. We present an implementation of the logged epoch consensus abstraction in Algorithm 5.9, called "Logged Read/Write Epoch Consensus." It results from adapting Algorithm 5.6 from a fail-silent model to a fail-recovery model and also assumes a majority of correct processes. Remember, however, that the notion of correct processes is different in a fail-recovery model: a process is said to be correct in this case if eventually it is permanently up.

Correctness. The main difference between Algorithm 5.9 and Algorithm 5.6 consists in using stubborn point-to-point links and stubborn best-effort broadcast abstractions. The timestamp/value pair maintained by the algorithm is logged and restored after recovery. Local variables used only by the leader are not logged, because the *termination* property of logged epoch consensus assumes that the leader does not crash. All remaining properties are the same as for the underlying algorithm in the fail-silent model.

Performance. The "Logged Read/Write Epoch Consensus" algorithm involves at most five communication steps and $O(N)$ messages until every process terminates and decides. Every process writes twice to stable storage.

Algorithm 5.9: Logged Read/Write Epoch Consensus

Implements:
    EpochConsensus, **instance** *lep*, with timestamp *ets* and leader ℓ.

Uses:
    StubbornPointToPointLinks, **instance** *sl*;
    StubbornBestEffortBroadcast, **instance** *sbeb*;

upon event $\langle$ *lep, Init* | *state* $\rangle$ **do**
    $(valts, val) := state;\ store(valts, val);$
    $tmpval := \perp;$
    $states := [\perp]^N;$
    $accepted := 0;$

upon event $\langle$ *lep, Recovery* $\rangle$ **do**
    $retrieve(valts, val);$

upon event $\langle$ *lep, Propose* | *v* $\rangle$ **do**   // only leader ℓ
    $tmpval := v;$
    trigger $\langle$ *sbeb, Broadcast* | [READ] $\rangle$;

upon event $\langle$ *sbeb, Deliver* | ℓ, [READ] $\rangle$ **do**
    trigger $\langle$ *sl, Send* | ℓ, [STATE, *valts, val*] $\rangle$;

upon event $\langle$ *sl, Deliver* | *q*, [STATE, *ts, v*] $\rangle$ **do**   // only leader ℓ
    $states[q] := (ts, v);$

upon $\#(states) > N/2$ **do**   // only leader ℓ
    $(ts, v) := highest(states);$
    if $v \neq \perp$ **then**
        $tmpval := v;$
    $states := [\perp]^N;$
    trigger $\langle$ *sbeb, Broadcast* | [WRITE, *tmpval*] $\rangle$;

upon event $\langle$ *sbeb, Deliver* | ℓ, [WRITE, *v*] $\rangle$ **do**
    $(valts, val) := (ets, v);\ store(valts, val);$
    trigger $\langle$ *sl, Send* | ℓ, [ACCEPT] $\rangle$;

upon event $\langle$ *sl, Deliver* | *q*, [ACCEPT] $\rangle$ **do**   // only leader ℓ
    $accepted := accepted + 1;$

upon $accepted > N/2$ **do**   // only leader ℓ
    $accepted := 0;$
    trigger $\langle$ *sbeb, Broadcast* | [DECIDED, *tmpval*] $\rangle$;

upon event $\langle$ *sbeb, Deliver* | ℓ, [DECIDED, *v*] $\rangle$ **do**
    $epochdecision := v;\ store(epochdecision);$
    trigger $\langle$ *lep, Decide* | *epochdecision* $\rangle$;

upon event $\langle$ *lep, Abort* $\rangle$ **do**
    trigger $\langle$ *lep, Aborted* | $(valts, val)$ $\rangle$;
    halt;   // stop operating when aborted

Algorithm 5.10: Logged Leader-Driven Consensus (part 1)

Implements:
    LoggedUniformConsensus, **instance** *luc*.

Uses:
    LoggedEpochChange, **instance** *lec*;
    LoggedEpochConsensus (multiple instances).

upon event ⟨ *luc, Init* ⟩ **do**
    val := ⊥; *decision* := ⊥;
    aborted := FALSE; *proposed* := FALSE;
    Obtain the initial leader ℓ_0 from the logged epoch-change instance *lec*;
    Initialize a new instance *lep*.0 of logged epoch consensus with timestamp 0,
        leader ℓ_0, and state $(0, \bot)$;
    $(ets, \ell) := (0, \ell_0)$;
    store(ets, ℓ, decision);

upon event ⟨ *luc, Recovery* ⟩ **do**
    retrieve(ets, ℓ, decision);
    retrieve(startts, startℓ) of instance *lec*;
    $(newts, new\ell) := (startts, start\ell)$;
    retrieve(epochdecision) of instance *lep.ets*;
    if *epochdecision* $\neq \bot \wedge$ *decision* $= \bot$ **then**
        decision := *epochdecision*; *store(decision)*;
        trigger ⟨ *luc, Decide | decision* ⟩;
    aborted := FALSE;

upon event ⟨ *luc, Propose | v* ⟩ **do**
    val := *v*;

5.4.4 Fail-Recovery Algorithm: Logged Leader-Driven Consensus

Algorithm 5.10–5.11, called "Logged Leader-Driven Consensus," shows how the basic "Leader-Driven Consensus" algorithm is adapted for the fail-recovery model. The principal change from "Leader-Driven Consensus" (Algorithm 5.7) lies in logging the current epoch timestamp/leader pair and the decision value.

As the underlying logged epoch-change and logged epoch consensus abstractions may deliver their outputs through variables logged in stable storage, the delivery variables must also be retrieved when the process recovers from a crash. When these values indicate that the underlying module delivered some output before the crash (by log-starting a new epoch or by log-deciding), then the algorithm takes the appropriate steps.

Correctness. The extensions in Algorithm 5.10–5.11 with respect to Algorithm 5.7 make it possible for a process to resume its operation after a crash. All its other properties are the same as for the "Leader-Drive Consensus" algorithm.

The algorithm is prepared to resume in two ways: in case it has missed a ⟨ *StartEpoch* ⟩ event from the epoch-change primitive or when it missed a

---

Algorithm 5.11: Logged Leader-Driven Consensus (part 2)

---

upon event ⟨ *lec, StartEpoch* | *startts, startℓ* ⟩ **do**
　　retrieve(*startts, startℓ*) of instance *lec*;
　　(*newts, newℓ*) := (*startts, startℓ*);

upon (*ets, ℓ*) ≠ (*newts, newℓ*) ∧ *aborted* = FALSE **do**
　　aborted = TRUE;
　　trigger ⟨ *lep.ets, Abort* ⟩;

upon event ⟨ *lep.ts, Aborted* | *state* ⟩ **such that** *ts* = *ets* **do**
　　(*ets, ℓ*) := (*newts, newℓ*); *store*(*ets, ℓ*);
　　aborted = FALSE; *proposed* := FALSE;
　　Initialize a new instance *lep.ets* of logged epoch consensus with timestamp *ets*,
　　　　leader *ℓ*, and state *state*;

upon *ℓ* = *self* ∧ *val* ≠ ⊥ ∧ *proposed* = FALSE **do**
　　proposed := TRUE;
　　trigger ⟨ *lep.ets, Propose* | *val* ⟩;

upon event ⟨ *lep.ts, Decide* | *epochdecision* ⟩ **such that** *ts* = *ets* **do**
　　retrieve(*epochdecision*) of instance *lep.ets*;
　　if *decision* = ⊥ **then**
　　　　decision := *epochdecision*; *store*(*decision*);
　　　　trigger ⟨ *luc, Decide* | *decision* ⟩;

⟨ *Decide* ⟩ event from an epoch consensus instance. Upon recovery, a process retrieves from stable storage the data that it could have missed in these events, which has been logged by the underlying primitives. The algorithm logs also its own state, consisting of the timestamp/leader pair of the current epoch plus the decision value, and retrieves it during recovery. After restoring the internal state, the algorithm examines if some conditions on its state have changed and proceeds to operate as it normally would. This shows that a correct process eventually decides, as required by the *termination* property.

Performance. The "Logged Leader-Driven Consensus" algorithm does not directly involve any communication. It writes to stable storage once for every new epoch that it starts and reads from stable storage when recovering from a crash.

5.5 Randomized Consensus

In this section, we show how to exploit randomization for solving a probabilistic variant of consensus in the fail-silent model, without resorting to a failure detector. Randomization is interesting because any algorithm for consensus must either rely on a failure-detector abstraction (i.e., use a fail-stop or a fail-noisy model) or it must be probabilistic. This follows because one can show that any deterministic consensus algorithm in a fail-silent model has executions that do not terminate, even if only one process may crash; hence, no deterministic algorithm solves consensus in asynchronous systems.

We first state the properties of a *randomized consensus* abstraction and then introduce the abstraction of a *common coin*, which encapsulates various ways of implementing probabilistic choices in consensus algorithms. Finally, we present two consensus algorithms in the randomized fail-silent model. The first algorithm decides on one bit, the second one decides on arbitrary values.

Randomized algorithms extend the basic execution model from Sect. 2.1 so that every process has access to a source of randomness. The local computation part in every step of a process may now additionally depend on the output of a local random source, which picks a random element from a finite set according to a fixed probability distribution. Our algorithms only sample random elements with uniform distribution; we say that the algorithm *flips a coin* in this case and also refer to random sources as *coins*.

5.5.1 Specification

A *randomized consensus* abstraction is in most ways the same as a (regular) consensus abstraction. It uses the same events to *propose* a value and to *decide* a value, and all correct processes must initially propose a value. Randomized consensus also ensures the same *integrity*, *agreement*, and *validity* properties. As before, all correct processes have to decide once, on the same value, and the decided value has to be one of the proposed values.

The liveness property is formulated differently and expressed as *probabilistic termination*; it stipulates that with probability 1, every correct process eventually decides. This probability is induced by the random coin flips in an algorithm and taken over all executions of an algorithm. Randomized consensus ensures the four properties listed in Module 5.8.

Module 5.8: Interface and properties of randomized consensus

Module:

> **Name:** RandomizedConsensus, **instance** *rc*.

Events:

> **Request:** $\langle$ *rc, Propose* $\mid v$ $\rangle$: Proposes value v for consensus.

> **Indication:** $\langle$ *rc, Decide* $\mid v$ $\rangle$: Outputs a decided value v of consensus.

Properties:

> **RC1:** *Probabilistic termination:* With probability 1, every correct process eventually decides some value.

> **RC2–RC4:** Same as properties C2–C4 in (regular) consensus (Module 5.1).

Module 5.9: Interface and properties of a common coin

Module:

    Name: CommonCoin, **instance** *coin*, with domain $\mathcal{B}$.

Events:

    Request: $\langle$ *coin, Release* $\rangle$: Releases the coin.

    Indication: $\langle$ *coin, Output* $\mid b$ $\rangle$: Outputs the coin value $b \in \mathcal{B}$.

Properties:

    COIN1: *Termination:* Every correct process eventually outputs a coin value.

    COIN2: *Unpredictability:* Unless at least one correct process has released the coin, no process has any information about the coin output by a correct process.

    COIN3: *Matching:* With probability at least δ, every correct process outputs the same coin value.

    COIN4: *No bias:* In the event that all correct processes output the same coin value, the distribution of the coin is uniform over $\mathcal{B}$ (i.e., a matching coin outputs any value in $\mathcal{B}$ with probability $\frac{1}{\#(\mathcal{B})}$).

5.5.2 Common Coin

All our randomized consensus algorithms delegate their probabilistic choices to a *common coin* abstraction. A common coin is a primitive that is invoked by triggering an event $\langle$ *Release* $\rangle$ at every process; we say that a process *releases* the coin because the coin's value is unpredictable before the first process invokes the coin. The value c of the coin is output to every process through an event $\langle$ *Output* $\mid c$ $\rangle$. The common coin abstraction is summarized in Module 5.9.

We assume that every correct process releases its coin initially. A common coin has an output domain $\mathcal{B}$ and is characterized by four properties. The first property ensures *termination*. The second property keeps the coin value secret until the first process releases the coin.

The third and fourth properties specify the probability distribution of the coin output. In particular, we require that with probability at least $\delta > 0$, the outputs of all correct processes *match* because they are equal; we call such a coin δ-matching. If the coin outputs match always, i.e., when $\delta = 1$, we say the coin *matches perfectly*. Furthermore, given that all coin outputs actually match, the distribution of the coin must be *unbiased*, that is, uniform over $\mathcal{B}$. We assume the coin to be unbiased for simplicity. However, a common coin with any constant bias is good enough for achieving termination in most randomized consensus algorithms. (But note that *some* bias is necessary because a coin cloud match with probability 1 but always output the same value).

One can implement a common coin abstraction purely with local computation, for instance, when all processes flip coins independently. Such coins are typically less useful than common coins realized by a distributed algorithm.

Consider the following local common-coin implementation, called the "Independent Choice" coin: upon releasing the coin, every process simply selects a value at random from $\mathcal{B}$ according to the uniform distribution and outputs it. If the domain is one bit then this realizes a 2^{-N+1}-matching common coin, because the probability that every process selects some b is 2^{-N}, for $b \in \{0, 1\}$.

Another possible common coin algorithm is the "Beacon" coin. An external trusted process, called the *beacon*, periodically chooses an unpredictable random value and broadcasts it at predefined times. When an algorithm accesses a sequence of common coin abstractions, then for the k-th coin, every process receives the k-th random value from the beacon and outputs it. This coin matches always. Unfortunately, it is very difficult to integrate the beacon into a distributed algorithm in an asynchronous system.

Of course, more realistic implementations of the common-coin abstraction are needed for realizing the concept in practical distributed systems. As mentioned in the notes at the end of the chapter, several such methods exist.

5.5.3 Randomized Fail-Silent Algorithm: Randomized Binary Consensus

Algorithm 5.12–5.13 is simply called "Randomized Binary Consensus;" it relies on a majority of correct processes to make progress and on a common coin abstraction for terminating and reaching agreement. The agreement domain is one bit; we show in the next section how to extend the algorithm for consensus on arbitrary values. The algorithm operates in sequential rounds, where the processes try to ensure that the same value is proposed by a majority of the processes in each round. If there is no such value, the processes resort to the coin abstraction and let it select a value to propose in the next round. Unless the processes agree in the first round, the probability that the processes agree in a subsequent round depends directly on the matching probability of the common coin. This probability is strictly greater than zero. Therefore, if the algorithm continues to execute rounds, it terminates eventually with probability 1.

Each round of the "Randomized Binary Consensus" algorithm consists of two phases. In the first phase, every correct process proposes a value by sending it to all processes with a best-effort broadcast primitive. Then it receives proposals from a quorum of processes. If a process observes that all responses contain the same phase-one proposal value then it proposes that value for the second phase. If a process does not obtain a unanimous set of proposals in the first phase, the process simply proposes $\perp$ for the second phase. Note that as a result of this procedure, if two processes propose a value different from $\perp$ for the second phase, they propose exactly the same value. Let this value be called v^*.

The purpose of the second phase is to verify if v^* was also observed by enough other processes. After a process receives $N - f$ phase-two messages, it checks if more than f phase-two proposals are equal to v^*, and may decide this value if there

---

Algorithm 5.12: Randomized Binary Consensus (phase 1)

Implements:
    RandomizedConsensus, **instance** rc, with domain $\{0, 1\}$.

Uses:
    BestEffortBroadcast, **instance** beb;
    ReliableBroadcast, **instance** rb;
    CommonCoin (multiple instances).

upon event $\langle\ rc,\ Init\ \rangle$ **do**
    $round := 0;\ phase := 0;$
    $proposal := \bot;$
    $decision := \bot;$
    $val := [\bot]^N;$

upon event $\langle\ rc,\ Propose\ |\ v\ \rangle$ **do**
    $proposal := v;$
    $round := 1;\ phase := 1;$
    trigger $\langle\ beb,\ Broadcast\ |\ [\textsc{Phase-1}, round, proposal]\ \rangle;$

upon event $\langle\ beb,\ Deliver\ |\ p,\ [\textsc{Phase-1}, r, v]\ \rangle$ **such that** $phase = 1 \wedge r = round$ **do**
    $val[p] := v;$

upon $\#(val) > N/2 \wedge phase = 1 \wedge decision = \bot$ **do**
    if exists $v \neq \bot$ **such that** $\#(\{p \in \Pi \mid val[p] = v\}) > N/2$ **then**
        $proposal := v;$
    else
        $proposal := \bot;$
    $val := [\bot]^N;$
    $phase := 2;$
    trigger $\langle\ beb,\ Broadcast\ |\ [\textsc{Phase-2}, round, proposal]\ \rangle;$

---

are enough of them. A process that receives v^* in the second phase, but is unable to collect enough v^* values to decide, starts a new round with v^* as its proposal.

Finally, it is possible that a process does not receive v^* in the second phase (either because no such value was found in phase one or simply because it has received only $\bot$ in phase two). In this case, the process starts a new round, with a new proposal that it sets to the value output by the common coin abstraction. To ensure that the coin abstraction makes progress, *every* process invokes the coin (and not only those that need the coin output). Every process initializes a new coin instance after collecting the phase-two proposals and immediately releases the coin. During the invocation of the common coin abstraction, a process pretends to be in an imaginary phase 0; this prevents it from receiving phase-one or phase-two proposals out of context.

When a process is ready to decide after outputting the coin, it abandons the round structure of the algorithm. Instead, it distributes a DECIDED message with the decision value using a reliable broadcast abstraction for simplicity. Every process decides upon receiving this message. The step of broadcasting a DECIDED

Algorithm 5.13: Randomized Binary Consensus (phase 2)

---

upon event ⟨ *beb, Deliver* | *p*, [PHASE-2, *r*, *v*] ⟩ **such that** *phase* = 2 ∧ *r* = *round* **do**
    val[*p*] := *v*;

upon #(*val*) ≥ *N* − *f* ∧ *phase* = 2 ∧ *decision* = ⊥ **do**
    phase := 0;
    Initialize a new instance *coin.round* of CommonCoin with domain {0, 1};
    trigger ⟨ *coin.round, Release* ⟩;

upon event ⟨ *coin.round, Output* | *c* ⟩ **do**
    if exists *v* ≠ ⊥ such that #({*p* ∈ *Π* | *val*[*p*] = *v*}) > *f* **then**
        decision := *v*;
        trigger ⟨ *rb, Broadcast* | [DECIDED, *decision*] ⟩;
    else
        if exists *p* ∈ *Π*, *w* ≠ ⊥ such that *val*[*p*] = *w* **then**
            proposal := *w*;
        else
            proposal := *c*;
        val := [⊥]^N;
        round := *round* + 1; *phase* := 1;
        trigger ⟨ *beb, Broadcast* | [PHASE-1, *round*, *proposal*] ⟩;

upon event ⟨ *rb, Deliver* | *p*, [DECIDED, *v*] ⟩ **do**
    decision := *v*;
    trigger ⟨ *rc, Decide* | *decision* ⟩;

---

message is actually not needed, as demonstrated in an exercise (at the end of the chapter).

Figure 5.4 demonstrates why randomization is necessary and shows an execution of a deterministic variant of Algorithm 5.12–5.13. At first glance, it may seem that a deterministic solution could allow a majority in the first phase to be reached faster. For instance, suppose that when a process receives a majority of ⊥ in the second phase of a round, it selects deterministically the first non-⊥ value received so far instead of selecting a value at random. Unfortunately, a deterministic choice allows executions where the algorithm never terminates, as we explain now.

Consider three processes *p*, *q*, and *r*, with initial values 1, 0, and 0, respectively. Each process proposes its own value for the first phase of the round. Consider the following execution for the first phase:

- Process *p* receives values from itself and from *q*. As both values differ, *p* proposes ⊥ for the second phase.
- Process *q* receives values from itself and from *p*. As both values differ, *q* proposes ⊥ for the second phase.
- Process *r* receives values from itself and from *q*. As both values are the same, *r* proposes 0 for the second phase.

Now consider the following execution for the second phase:

- Process *p* receives values from itself and from *q*. As both values are ⊥ and the process cannot propose ⊥ in the next round, it needs to choose a value. According

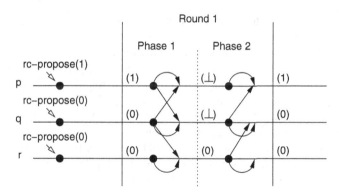

Figure 5.4: Role of randomization

to our variant, p deterministically selects value 1 for the first phase of the next round.

- Process q receives values from itself and from r. As one of the values is 0, q proposes 0 for the first phase of the next round.
- Process r receives values from itself and from q. As one of the values is 0, r proposes 0 for the first phase of the next round.

This execution is clearly possible. Note that in this example, no process crashes, no message is lost, and only some messages are delayed. The processes move to the next round as soon as they receive a majority of messages. Unfortunately, the result of this execution is that the input values for the next round are exactly the same as for this round. The same execution sequence could be repeated indefinitely. Randomization prevents such infinite executions from occurring as there will be a round where p also selects 0 as the value for the next round.

Correctness. We argue why the algorithm implements randomized consensus under the assumption that $N > 2f$. The following observation helps with the analysis. If two processes send a PHASE-2 message in the same round and both messages contain a proposal different from $\perp$ then the two proposals are equal to some value u. This holds because every process has received phase-one proposals from a quorum of more than $N/2$ processes and set its phase-two value to $\perp$ *unless all* received phase-one proposals were equal. But in this case, because every two quorums overlap, every other process that sends a PHASE-2 message must also have received at least one PHASE-1 message containing u.

For the *validity* property, observe that if all processes start a particular round with the same proposal value v then every correct process receives only PHASE-2 messages containing v, consequently broadcasts a DECIDED message with v in the same round, and eventually decides v. No process decides a different value.

Note that there is a positive probability that the common coin outputs the same value to all processes and this value is a uniformly chosen random bit. If all coin outputs are the same and are equal to the unique value v that may be contained in a PHASE-2 message then every process sets its proposal to this value before moving to the next round. Using the same argument as for *validity*, this observation implies the *termination* property.

The *integrity* property is obvious from the algorithm.

The observation made earlier proves the *agreement* property for two processes that broadcast the DECIDED messages during the same round. Note that when some process broadcasts a DECIDED message with v, then it has received $N - f$ phase-two messages and more than f of them contained v. Hence, every process obtains also at least one phase-two message with v among the $N - f$ phase-two messages that it collects, and no process sets its proposal to the value from the common coin. Because now all processes move to the next round with proposal v, they eventually also decide v, according to the argument to show *validity*.

Performance. Every round of the algorithm involves two communication steps and $O(N^2)$ messages. Since the unique value u that may be contained in a PHASE-2 message is determined before the coin is released by any process and because the coin value is unpredictable until that time, with probability at least $\delta/2$, every process obtains a coin that is equal to u. If this happens, the algorithm terminates. Hence, the expected number of rounds executed by a correct process is proportional to $1/\delta$.

5.5.4 Randomized Fail-Silent Algorithm: Randomized Consensus with Large Domain

The "Randomized Binary Consensus" algorithm can only decide on one-bit values. This restriction has been introduced because the processes sometimes set their proposal values to an output of the common coin and the coin outputs one bit. We now extend this algorithm so that it decides on arbitrary values.

A common coin abstraction can also be initialized with an arbitrary domain, but there are two issues with this choice. First, if we retain the structure of Algorithm 5.12–5.13, the coin abstraction must only output values that have been proposed in order to ensure the *validity* property; otherwise, the processes might decide on a random value output by the common coin. The second issue is that all processes should initialize a particular instance of the common coin with the *same* domain; but we cannot use the set of all proposed values for the domain, because the processes do not know this a priori (otherwise, they would already have reached consensus).

A solution is implemented in the "Randomized Consensus with Large Domain" algorithm and shown in Algorithm 5.14. It needs a somewhat relaxed common coin abstraction compared to Module 5.9, which does not require that all processes invoke the common coin with the same domain. Instead, every process simply uses the set of proposed values that it is aware of. This set grows and should eventually become stable, in the sense that every correct process invokes the common coin with the same set. This coin abstraction satisfies all properties of Module 5.9 once that every process initializes the coin with the same domain. Otherwise, the coin abstraction only ensures the *termination* property. Note that also this coin

Algorithm 5.14: Randomized Consensus with Large Domain (extends Algorithm 5.12–5.13)

Implements:
    RandomizedConsensus, **instance** *rc*.

Uses:
    BestEffortBroadcast, **instance** *beb*;
    ReliableBroadcast, **instance** *rb*;
    CommonCoin (multiple instances).

// Except for the event handlers below with the extensions mentioned here, it is
// the same as Algorithm 5.12–5.13.

upon event ⟨ *rc, Init* ⟩ **do**
    ...
    values := ∅;

upon event ⟨ *rc, Propose* | *v* ⟩ **do**
    ...
    values := *values* ∪ {*v*};
    trigger ⟨ *rb, Broadcast* | [PROPOSAL, *v*] ⟩;

upon event ⟨ *rb, Deliver* | *p*, [PROPOSAL, *v*] ⟩**do**
    values := *values* ∪ {*v*};

upon #(*val*) > *N*/2 ∧ *phase* = 2 ∧ *decision* = ⊥ **do**
    Initialize a new instance *coin.round* of CommonCoin with domain *values*;
    ...

---

abstraction is realized by the "Independent Choice" method, for example, where every process simply selects a value at random from the domain that it knows.

In Algorithm 5.14, every process additionally disseminates its initial proposal with reliable broadcast, and every process collects the received proposals in a variable *values*. A process then initializes the common coin with domain *values*. This ensures that the coin always outputs a value that has been proposed. (Note that *values* is different from the array *val*, which contains the received proposal values.)

Correctness. Because Algorithm 5.14 for large domains directly extends the "Binary Randomized Consensus" algorithm, most of its properties carry over to the extended algorithm. In particular, the *validity*, *integrity*, and *agreement* properties hold directly.

For the *termination* property, observe that eventually, all correct processes have *rb*-delivered the same PROPOSAL messages, and therefore, their *values* variables are equal. After this time, the common coin satisfies the properties of Module 5.9 and outputs a matching value with probability at least δ, as in the binary algorithm. Note that disseminating the proposals by reliable broadcast and not simply by best-effort broadcast is crucial for termination.

Performance. With an implementation of the reliable broadcast abstraction as shown in Chap. 3, the cost of the "Randomized Consensus with Large Domain" algorithm increases to $O(N^3)$ messages from the binary case. The number of required communication steps remains the same. Moreover, the probability of terminating in a given round now depends on the number of different proposals; with k different proposals, this probability is at least δ/k. When all N processes propose different values, then the expected number of rounds taken by the algorithm is proportional to N/δ.

5.6 Byzantine Consensus

This section and the next consider consensus with arbitrary-fault process abstractions. We first discuss the specification of Byzantine consensus and its implementation in the fail-noisy-arbitrary model. Our implementation uses the same approach as the "Leader-Driven Consensus" algorithm from Sect. 5.3, which is structured into epochs. The next section will present a randomized Byzantine consensus abstraction and its implementation. This algorithm is an extension of the "Randomized Binary Consensus" algorithm from Sect. 5.5.

5.6.1 Specifications

A consensus primitive for arbitrary-fault or Byzantine process abstractions offers very similar guarantees to a consensus primitive for crash-stop processes. It should allow all processes to reach a common decision despite the presence of faulty ones, in order for the correct processes to coordinate their actions. There are two differences, however.

A first difference lies in the behavior of Byzantine processes: the abstraction cannot require anything from them. Therefore, we restrict all its properties to correct processes. The second difference is more profound. The *validity* property of consensus requires that every value decided by a (correct) process has been proposed by some process. Intuitively, the consensus primitive must not decide a value that comes out of the blue and that was not proposed by any process. We would like to maintain this guarantee for Byzantine consensus. But because a faulty and potentially malicious process can pretend to have proposed arbitrary values, we must formulate *validity* in another way. We discuss *weak* and *strong* notions of validity for Byzantine consensus in the following.

The *weak* variant of the *validity* property maintains this guarantee only for executions in which all processes are correct and none of them is Byzantine. It considers the case that all processes propose the same value and requires that an algorithm only decides the proposed value in this case. Moreover, the algorithm must decide a value that was actually proposed and not invented out of thin air. If some processes are actually faulty, an arbitrary value may be decided. The *weak Byzantine consensus* abstraction implements this validity notion, as specified in Module 5.10. Its other properties (*termination*, *integrity*, and *agreement*) correspond directly to the consensus abstraction (Module 5.1).

Module 5.10: Interface and properties of weak Byzantine consensus

Module:

    Name: WeakByzantineConsensus, **instance** *wbc*.

Events:

    Request: ⟨ *wbc, Propose* | *v* ⟩: Proposes value *v* for consensus.

    Indication: ⟨ *wbc, Decide* | *v* ⟩: Outputs a decided value *v* of consensus.

Properties:

    WBC1: *Termination:* Every correct process eventually decides some value.

    WBC2: *Weak validity:* If all processes are correct and propose the same value v, then no correct process decides a value different from v; furthermore, if all processes are correct and some process decides v, then v was proposed by some process.

    WBC3: *Integrity:* No correct process decides twice.

    WBC4: *Agreement:* No two correct processes decide differently.

Naturally, an application designer may not be satisfied with the *weak validity* notion because situations with one or more Byzantine processes might be common. The *strong* variant of *validity* for Byzantine consensus tolerates arbitrary-fault processes and instead requires the decision value to be the value proposed by the correct processes. If not all of them propose the same value, the decision value must still be a value proposed by a correct process or may be some special symbol □. The latter denotes a default value that indicates no valid decision was found (however, it is permitted that a correct process proposes □). In other words, if all correct processes propose the same value then Byzantine consensus decides this value, and otherwise, it may decide some value proposed by a correct process or □. Importantly, the decision value cannot originate only from the Byzantine processes.

The *(strong) Byzantine consensus* abstraction shown in Module 5.11 implements this *strong validity* property. The only change from weak Byzantine consensus is *strong validity*. Note that the *strong validity* property does *not* imply the weak one, because strong validity allows the primitive to decide □, whereas *weak validity* requires (only if all processes are correct) that the decided value was proposed by some (correct) process. Hence, the two Byzantine consensus notions are not comparable.

One can transform an implementation of weak Byzantine consensus into a Byzantine consensus primitive with strong validity. Exercise 5.11 at the end of the chapter explores this question.

Recall how the uniform variant of consensus, with crash-fault process abstractions, prevented a process from deciding an inconsistent value if the process later crashed. Note that in our model, a fail-arbitrary process is either correct throughout its execution or faulty from the start. A faulty process might behave in arbitrary ways

---

Module 5.11: Interface and properties of (strong) Byzantine consensus

Module:

    Name: ByzantineConsensus, **instance** bc.

Events:

    Request: $\langle\ bc,\ Propose \mid v\ \rangle$: Proposes value v for consensus.

    Indication: $\langle\ bc,\ Decide \mid v\ \rangle$: Outputs a decided value v of consensus.

Properties:

    BC1 and **BC3–BC4:** Same as properties WBC1 and WBC3–WBC4 in weak Byzantine consensus (Module 5.10).

    BC2: *Strong validity:* If all correct processes propose the same value v, then no correct process decides a value different from v; otherwise, a correct process may only decide a value that was proposed by some correct process or the special value $\square$.

---

and also influence the environment, which should be prepared for this eventuality. Therefore, one cannot define a useful Byzantine consensus primitive that represents the guarantee given by uniform consensus.

The next two sections introduce epoch-change and epoch consensus primitives in the Byzantine model. The abstractions are basically the same as their counterparts in the model with crash-stop processes, but their implementations differ for tolerating fail-arbitrary processes. Once these primitives are implemented in the fail-arbitrary model, they are used in Sect. 5.6.4 underneath the "Leader-Driven Consensus" algorithm (presented in Sect. 5.3) to implement a weak Byzantine consensus abstraction.

In order to satisfy the *agreement* property in the fail-arbitrary model, our implementations of (weak and strong) Byzantine consensus use $N > 3f$ processes. This is optimal.

5.6.2 Byzantine Epoch-Change

Specification. The epoch-change primitive in the Byzantine model has the same interface and satisfies the same properties as the epoch-change primitive with crash-stop processes. Its specification is shown in Module 5.12.

Fail-Noisy-Arbitrary Algorithm: Byzantine Leader-Based Epoch-Change. The "Byzantine Leader-Based Epoch-Change" implementation of Byzantine epoch-change is shown in Algorithm 5.15. Like Algorithm 5.5, which implements epoch-change tolerating crash faults, it relies on an eventual leader detector (in the Byzantine variant). But, it is conceptually simpler than the epoch-change implementation with crash faults. Algorithm 5.15 outputs at all correct processes a sequence of timestamps that always increases by 1. The leader of an epoch with timestamp ts is computed deterministically from ts, using the function $leader(\cdot)$ introduced in

---

Module 5.12: Interface and properties of Byzantine epoch-change

---

Module:

    Name: ByzantineEpochChange, **instance** *bec*.

Events:

    Indication: $\langle$ *bec*, *StartEpoch* $\mid ts, \ell$ $\rangle$: Starts the epoch identified by timestamp ts with leader ℓ.

Properties:

    BEC1–BEC3: Same as properties EC1–EC3 of epoch-change (Module 5.3).

Sect. 2.6.5. (The value of *leader(ts)* is process whose rank is ts, if $ts \bmod N \neq 0$, or the process with rank N, if $ts \bmod N = 0$.) Hence, the leader rotates in a round-robin fashion.

The algorithm maintains a timestamp *lastts* of the most recently started epoch and a timestamp *nextts*, which is equal to *lastts* $+ 1$ during the period when the process has broadcast a NEWEPOCH message but not yet started the epoch with timestamp *nextts*. Whenever the process observes that the leader of the current epoch is different from the process that it most recently trusted, the process begins to switch to the next epoch by broadcasting a NEWEPOCH message to all processes. Alternatively, the process also begins to switch to the next epoch after receiving NEWEPOCH messages from more than f distinct processes. Once the process receives more than $2f$ NEWEPOCH messages (from distinct processes) it starts the epoch.

A process waits for NEWEPOCH messages from more than f processes before switching to a new epoch because the Byzantine processes alone must not be able to trigger an epoch-change without cause. At least one correct process that no longer trusts the leader of the current epoch is also needed for switching.

Correctness. We show that Algorithm 5.15 implements epoch-change for $N > 3f$, with f Byzantine processes. We begin with the *monotonicity* and *consistency* properties. It is obvious from the algorithm that the timestamps of two successive epochs started by a correct process increase by 1. Furthermore, the leader of an epoch is derived deterministically from its timestamp.

To show the *eventual leadership* property, more precisely, its first condition, notice that every correct process sends a NEWEPOCH message for starting a new epoch whenever the leader of the current epoch is not the process that it trusts. Furthermore, there exists a time when the leader detector has caused every correct process to trust the same process ℓ^* forever. Hence, eventually no correct process sends any further NEWEPOCH messages. When all NEWEPOCH messages among correct processes have been delivered and the highest epoch started by a correct process has timestamp ts^*, then this process has received more than $2f$ NEWEPOCH messages with timestamp ts^*. As more than f of those messages were sent by correct processes, every correct process has also sent a NEWEPOCH message with

---

Algorithm 5.15: Byzantine Leader-Based Epoch-Change

Implements:
    ByzantineEpochChange, **instance** *bec.*

Uses:
    AuthPerfectPointToPointLinks, **instance** *al*;
    ByzantineLeaderDetector, **instance** *bld.*

upon event ⟨ *bec, Init* ⟩ **do**
    lastts := 0; *nextts* := 0;
    trusted := 0;
    newepoch := $[\perp]^n$;

upon event ⟨ *bld, Trust* | *p* ⟩ **do**
    trusted := *p*;

upon *nextts* = *lastts* ∧ *trusted* ≠ leader(*lastts*) **do**
    nextts := *lastts* + 1;
    forall *q* ∈ *Π* **do**
        trigger ⟨ *al, Send* | *q*, [NEWEPOCH, *nextts*] ⟩;

upon event ⟨ *al, Deliver* | *p*, [NEWEPOCH, *ts*] ⟩ **such that** *ts* = *lastts* + 1 **do**
    newepoch[*p*] := NEWEPOCH;

upon #(*newepoch*) > *f* ∧ *nextts* = *lastts* **do**
    nextts := *lastts* + 1;
    forall *q* ∈ *Π* **do**
        trigger ⟨ *al, Send* | *q*, [NEWEPOCH, *nextts*] ⟩;

upon #(*newepoch*) > 2*f* ∧ *nextts* > *lastts* **do**
    lastts := *nextts*;
    newepoch := $[\perp]^n$;
    trigger ⟨ *bec, StartEpoch* | *lastts*, leader(*lastts*) ⟩;

---

timestamp ts^* according to the algorithm. Thus, every correct process eventually receives at least $N - f > 2f$ NEWEPOCH messages with timestamp ts^* and starts the epoch with timestamp ts^* and no further epoch. The second condition of *eventual leadership* is evident because the leader is computed by the *leader*(·) function from the timestamp.

Performance. Algorithm 5.15 incurs one communication step and $O(N^2)$ messages whenever the leader detector selects a new leader at enough correct processes.

5.6.3 Byzantine Epoch Consensus

Specification. An epoch consensus abstraction in the Byzantine model has the same interface and satisfies almost the same properties as the (uniform) epoch consensus abstraction for crash-stop processes. Only its *agreement* property differs in a minor way as it only refers to decisions of correct processes.

Module 5.13: Interface and properties of Byzantine epoch consensus

Module:

Name: ByzantineEpochConsensus, **instance** *bep*, with timestamp ts and leader process ℓ.

Events:

Request: $\langle$ *bep, Propose* $|\ v\ \rangle$: Proposes value v for epoch consensus. Executed only by the leader ℓ.

Request: $\langle$ *bep, Abort* $\rangle$: Aborts epoch consensus.

Indication: $\langle$ *bep, Decide* $|\ v\ \rangle$: Outputs a decided value v of epoch consensus.

Indication: $\langle$ *bep, Aborted* $|$ *state* $\rangle$: Signals that epoch consensus has completed the abort and outputs internal state *state*.

Properties:

BEP1, BEP3–BEP6: Same as properties EP1 and EP3–EP6 of epoch consensus (Module 5.4).

BEP2: *Agreement:* No two correct processes *ep*-decide differently.

As before, the properties require a *well-formed* sequence of epochs, where a process initializes a Byzantine epoch consensus instance only with a higher timestamp than that of all instances that it initialized previously, and the process must use the state returned by the most recently aborted instance to initialize the next such instance. The specification is given in Module 5.13.

For describing a Byzantine epoch-change algorithm later, we use an abstraction called conditional collect, which is defined and implemented next.

Conditional Collect. The purpose of a primitive for *conditional collect (CC)*, specified in Module 5.14, is to collect information in the system, in the form of messages from all processes, in a consistent way. The abstraction is invoked at every process by an event $\langle$ *Input* $|\ m\ \rangle$ with an input message m; it outputs a vector M with n entries indexed by processes, through an event $\langle$ *Collected* $|\ M\ \rangle$ at every process, such that $M[p]$ is either equal to UNDEFINED or corresponds to the input message of process p.

A conditional collect primitive is parameterized by an output predicate $C(\cdot)$, defined on an N-vector of messages, and it should only output a collected vector that satisfies the predicate. The output predicate must be specified at the time when the primitive is initialized, in terms of an efficiently computable Boolean function on a vector of messages. The output predicate is fixed and cannot be changed afterward (for instance, the function must not access variables that may concurrently be updated). Furthermore, every correct process must specify the same output predicate.

A conditional collect primitive should collect the same vector of messages at every correct process such that this vector satisfies the output predicate. Naturally,

---

Module 5.14: Interface and properties of conditional collect

Module:

    Name: ConditionalCollect, **instance** cc, with leader ℓ and output predicate C.

Events:

    Request: $\langle\ cc,\ Input\ |\ m\ \rangle$: Inputs a message m.

    Indication: $\langle\ cc,\ Collected\ |\ M\ \rangle$: Outputs a vector M of collected messages.

Properties:

    CC1: *Consistency:* If the leader is correct, then every correct process collects the same M, and this M contains at least $N - f$ messages different from UNDEFINED.

    CC2: *Integrity:* If some correct process collects M with $M[p] \neq$ UNDEFINED for some process p and p is correct, then p has input message $M[p]$.

    CC3: *Termination:* If all correct processes input compliant messages and the leader is correct, then every correct process eventually collects some M such that $C(M) =$ TRUE.

---

the correct processes must all input messages that will satisfy the predicate; otherwise, this goal cannot be achieved. More precisely, we say that the correct processes input *compliant* messages when each correct process p inputs a message m_p and any N-vector M with $M[p] = m_p$ satisfies $C(M)$.

Since this goal may be difficult to reach in general, the primitive additionally identifies one special process ℓ, called the leader, and is required to output the same vector M that satisfies $C(M)$ at all correct processes only when the leader is correct (this is expressed by the *consistency* and *termination* properties). Regardless of whether the leader is correct, the *integrity* property demands that the primitive must not modify the input messages of the correct processes in transit. Note that with a faulty leader, some inputs may be omitted in the output vector of a correct process, and the outputs of two correct processes may differ.

The following fail-arbitrary algorithm, called "Signed Conditional Collect," implements conditional collect with Byzantine processes. It uses two communication rounds and assumes a digital signature scheme. In the first round, every process signs its input message and sends it together with the signature to the leader over a point-to-point link. The leader collects enough messages (at least $N - f$) such that they satisfy the output predicate. In the second round, the leader sends the collected and signed messages to all processes, using authenticated point-to-point links. After receiving such a vector M accompanied by a vector Σ of signatures and before outputting M, a process verifies that for every entry $M[p] \neq$ UNDEFINED, the value $\Sigma[p]$ represents a valid signature from process p.

The details are shown in Algorithm 5.16, where the function $\#(M)$ introduced before also denotes the number of entries in a vector M different from UNDEFINED.

Algorithm 5.16: Signed Conditional Collect

Implements:
    ConditionalCollect, **instance** cc, with leader ℓ and output predicate C.

Uses:
    AuthPerfectPointToPointLinks, **instance** al.

upon event $\langle\, cc, Init \,\rangle$ **do**
    $messages := [\textsc{Undefined}]^N;\ \Sigma := [\perp]^N;$
    $collected := \textsc{False};$

upon event $\langle\, cc, Input \mid m \,\rangle$ **do**
    $\sigma := sign(self, cc\|self\|\textsc{Input}\|m);$
    trigger $\langle\, al, Send \mid \ell, [\textsc{Send}, m, \sigma] \,\rangle;$

upon event $\langle\, al, Deliver \mid p, [\textsc{Send}, m, \sigma] \,\rangle$ **do**   // only leader ℓ
    if $verifysig(p, cc\|p\|\textsc{Input}\|m, \sigma)$ **then**
        $messages[p] := m;\ \Sigma[p] := \sigma;$

upon $\#(messages) \geq N - f \wedge C(messages)$ **do**   // only leader ℓ
    forall $q \in \Pi$ **do**
        trigger $\langle\, al, Send \mid q, [\textsc{Collected}, messages, \Sigma] \,\rangle;$
    $messages := [\textsc{Undefined}]^N;\ \Sigma := [\perp]^N;$

upon event $\langle\, al, Deliver \mid \ell, [\textsc{Collected}, M, \Sigma] \,\rangle$ **do**
    if $collected = \textsc{False} \wedge \#(M) \geq N - f \wedge C(M) \wedge$
        $(\text{forall } p \in \Pi \text{ such that } M[p] \neq \textsc{Undefined}, \text{ it holds}$
        $verifysig(p, cc\|p\|\textsc{Input}\|M[p], \Sigma[p]))$ **then**
        $collected := \textsc{True};$
        trigger $\langle\, cc, Collected \mid M \,\rangle;$

An alternative algorithm for conditional collect without digital signatures is the subject of an exercise (at the end of the chapter).

Correctness. Assuming that $N > 3f$, the "Signed Conditional Collect" algorithm implements the conditional collect abstraction. Based on our assumption that the correct processes input compliant messages, the *consistency* and *termination* properties follow easily because they assume that the leader is correct. The *integrity* property holds because every process signs its input and the algorithm never outputs a vector that contains a message with an invalid signature.

Performance. The algorithm incurs two communication steps. In every step, the leader either receives a message from every process or sends a message to every process. In total, there are $O(N)$ messages.

Fail-Arbitrary Algorithm: Byzantine Read/Write Epoch Consensus. We now present algorithm "Byzantine Read/Write Epoch Consensus," which implements an instance *bep* of Byzantine epoch consensus with timestamp *ets* and leader process ℓ. As with the "Read/Write Epoch Consensus" algorithm in the fail-noisy model, there may exist multiple instances with different timestamps in the system. But when used

---

Algorithm 5.17: Byzantine Read/Write Epoch Consensus (part 1, read phase)

Implements:
    ByzantineEpochConsensus, **instance** *bep*, with timestamp *ets* and leader process ℓ.

Uses:
    AuthPerfectPointToPointLinks, **instance** *al*;
    ConditionalCollect, **instance** *cc*, with leader ℓ and predicate *sound*($\cdot$).

upon event $\langle$ *bep, Init* | *epochstate* $\rangle$ **do**
    $(valts, val, writeset) := epochstate$;
    $written := [\bot]^N$; $accepted := [\bot]^N$;

upon event $\langle$ *bep, Propose* | v $\rangle$ **do**   // only leader ℓ
    if $val = \bot$ **then** $val := v$;
    forall $q \in \Pi$ **do**
        trigger $\langle$ *al, Send* | q, [READ] $\rangle$;

upon event $\langle$ *al, Deliver* | p, [READ] $\rangle$ **such that** $p = \ell$ **do**
    trigger $\langle$ *cc, Input* | [STATE, *valts, val, writeset*] $\rangle$;

upon event $\langle$ *cc, Collected* | *states* $\rangle$ **do**
    // $states[p] = $ [STATE, ts, v, ws] or $states[p] = $ UNDEFINED
    $tmpval := \bot$;
    if exists $ts \geq 0, v \neq \bot$ from S such that $binds(ts, v, states)$ **then**
        $tmpval := v$;
    else if exists $v \neq \bot$ such that $unbound(states) \wedge states[\ell] = $ [STATE, $\cdot, v, \cdot$] **then**
        $tmpval := v$;
    if $tmpval \neq \bot$ **then**
        if exists ts such that $(ts, tmpval) \in writeset$ **then**
            $writeset := writeset \setminus \{(ts, tmpval)\}$;
        $writeset := writeset \cup \{(ets, tmpval)\}$;
        forall $q \in \Pi$ **do**
            trigger $\langle$ *al, Send* | q, [WRITE, *tmpval*] $\rangle$;

---

to build our (Byzantine) consensus algorithm, every process executes a well-formed sequence of Byzantine epoch consensus instances and invokes at most one instance at a time. We also assume that ets is contained implicitly in every message sent by the algorithm over the point-to-point link communication primitives. As every correct process invokes a sequence of Byzantine epoch consensus instances with unique timestamps, we sometimes refer to the "epoch" with a timestamp ets instead of the instance with timestamp ets.

At a high level, Algorithm 5.17–5.18 consists of a *read phase* followed by a *write phase*, like the basic algorithm that works for crash-stop processes. We say that a process *writes a value* v when it sends a WRITE message to all processes containing v during the write phase.

According to the specification of Byzantine epoch consensus, the algorithm is initialized with a value *state*, output by the Byzantine epoch consensus instance that the process ran previously. This value determines its local state and contains

Algorithm 5.18: Byzantine Read/Write Epoch Consensus (part 2, write phase)

upon event $\langle$ *al, Deliver* $|$ p, [WRITE, v] $\rangle$ **do**
    written[p] := v;

upon exists v such that $\#(\{p \mid written[p] = v\}) > \frac{N+f}{2}$ **do**
    $(valts, val) := (ets, v)$;
    written := $[\bot]^N$;
    forall $q \in \Pi$ **do**
        trigger $\langle$ *al, Send* $|$ q, [ACCEPT, *val*] $\rangle$

upon event $\langle$ *al, Deliver* $|$ p, [ACCEPT, v] $\rangle$ **do**
    accepted[p] := v;

upon exists v such that $\#(\{p \mid accepted[p] = v\}) > \frac{N+f}{2}$ **do**
    accepted := $[\bot]^N$;
    trigger $\langle$ *bep, Decide* $|$ v $\rangle$;

upon event $\langle$ *bep, Abort* $\rangle$ **do**
    trigger $\langle$ *bep, Aborted* $|$ $(valts, val, writeset)$ $\rangle$;
    halt;   // stop operating when aborted

(1) a timestamp/value pair (*valts, val*) with the value that the process received most recently in a Byzantine quorum of WRITE messages, during the epoch with time-stamp *valts*, and (2) a set *writeset* of timestamp/value pairs with one entry for every value that this process has ever written (where the timestamp denotes the most recent epoch in which the value was written).

The read phase obtains the states from all processes to determine whether there exists a value that may already have been *bep*-decided. In the case of crash faults, it was sufficient that the leader alone computed this value and wrote it; with Byzantine processes the leader might write a wrong value. Thus, every process must repeat the computation of the leader and write a value, in order to validate the choice of the leader.

The algorithm starts by the leader sending a READ message to all processes, which triggers every process to invoke a conditional collect primitive. Every process inputs a message [STATE, *valts, val, writeset*] containing its state. The leader in conditional collect is the leader ℓ of the epoch.

The conditional collect primitive determines whether there exists a value (from an earlier epoch) that must be written during the write phase; if such a value exists, the read phase must identify it or conclude that no such value exists. To this end, we introduce a predicate *sound*(S) on an N-vector S of STATE messages, to be used in the conditional collect primitive. An entry of S may be *defined* and contain a STATE message or may be *undefined* and contain UNDEFINED. In every defined entry, there is a timestamp ts, a value v, and a set of timestamp/value pairs, representing the writeset of the originating process. When process ℓ is correct, at least $N - f$ entries in the collected S are defined; otherwise, more than f entries may be undefined.

The predicate *sound*(·) is formulated in terms of two conditions. Together they determine whether the STATE messages in S indicate that a certain timestamp/value pair (ts, v) occurs often enough among the defined entries of S so that a process may already have *bep*-decided v in an earlier epoch. If yes, value v must be written.

The first condition collects evidence for such a value, which consists of a Byzantine quorum of defined entries in S. A suitable timestamp/value pair is one with the *highest* timestamp among some Byzantine quorum of defined entries in S. If such a pair exists then its value is a candidate for being written again in this epoch consensus instance. (However, it could also be a value from a forged entry of a Byzantine process; the second condition will filter out such values.)

Formally, we use the function $\#(S)$ to denote the number of *defined* entries in S and introduce a predicate *quorumhighest*(ts, v, S), which returns TRUE whenever the timestamp/value pair (ts, v) appears in an entry of S and contains the largest timestamp among some Byzantine quorum of entries in S. In other words, *quorumhighest*(ts, v, S) is TRUE whenever $S[p] = [\text{STATE}, ts, v, ws]$ for some p and some ws and

$$\#\Big(\{p \mid S[p] = [\text{STATE}, ts', v', ws'] \\ \wedge (ts' < ts \vee (ts', v') = (ts, v))\}\Big) > \frac{N + f}{2},$$

and FALSE otherwise.

The second condition determines whether a value v occurs in some writeset of an entry in S that originates from a correct process; because up to f entries in S may be from faulty processes, these must be filtered out. When the writeset of more than f processes contains (ts, v) with timestamp ts or a higher timestamp than ts, then v is *certified* and some correct process has written v in epoch ts or later. To capture this, we define a predicate *certifiedvalue*(ts, v, S) to be TRUE whenever

$$\#\Big(\{p \mid S[p] = [\text{STATE}, \cdot, \cdot, ws'] \\ \wedge \text{ there exists } (ts', v') \in ws' \text{ such that } ts' \geq ts \wedge v' = v\}\Big) > f,$$

and FALSE otherwise. As will become clear, a process never writes $\bot$; therefore, the value $\bot$ is never certified for any timestamp.

For a timestamp/value pair (ts, s) occuring in S, we say that S *binds ts to v* whenever $\#(S) \geq N - f$ and

$$\text{quorumhighest}(ts, v, S) = \text{TRUE} \wedge \text{certifiedvalue}(ts, v, S) = \text{TRUE}.$$

We abbreviate this by writing *binds*(ts, v, S).

When $\#(S) \geq N - f$ and the timestamps from a Byzantine quorum of entries in S are equal to 0 (the initial timestamp value), then we say that S *is unbound* and abbreviate this by writing *unbound*(S).

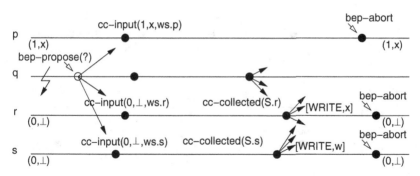

Figure 5.5: Sample execution of a Byzantine epoch consensus instance, with timestamp 6 and Byzantine leader q

Finally, the predicate *sound(S)* is TRUE if and only if there exists a time-stamp/value pair (ts, v) in S such that S binds ts to v or S is unbound, that is,

$$sound(S) \equiv \big(\text{there exists } (ts, v) \text{ such that } binds(ts, v, S)\big) \vee unbound(S).$$

Every correct process initializes the conditional collect primitive with this predicate $sound(\cdot)$.

As we will see, the inputs of the correct processes are compliant when they all input a STATE message to the conditional collect primitive. When the leader is correct, conditional collect outputs a vector S that satisfies $sound(S) = $ TRUE. If S binds ts to some $v \neq \perp$ then the process must write v; otherwise, S is unbound and the process writes the value from the leader ℓ, which it finds in $S[\ell]$. The process sends a WRITE message to all processes with the value. In case $sound(S) = $ FALSE, the leader must be faulty and the process halts.

When a process has received more than $(N + f)/2$ WRITE messages from distinct processes containing the same value v, it sets its state to (ets, v) and broadcasts an ACCEPT message with v over the authenticated point-to-point links. When a process has received more than $(N + f)/2$ ACCEPT messages from distinct processes containing the same value v, it *bep*-decides v.

A sample execution of the algorithm for some epoch 6 with a Byzantine leader process q is shown in Fig. 5.5. One instance of Byzantine epoch consensus is invoked with timestamp 6 and leader process q. The initial states of the correct processes are the timestamp/value pair $(1, x)$ and writeset $ws_p = \{(1, x)\}$ at p, the pair $(0, \perp)$ and $ws_r = \{(1, x)\}$ at r, and the pair $(0, \perp)$ and $ws_s = \emptyset$ at s. (This state may result from an instance of Byzantine epoch consensus, which executed previously in a well-formed sequence of epochs and has been aborted.)

The leader q initially broadcasts a READ message, to which all processes respond by invoking the conditional collect abstraction with their state. Note that, we cannot tell if the Byzantine leader has *bep*-proposed any value or not. However, we do

Epoch 7

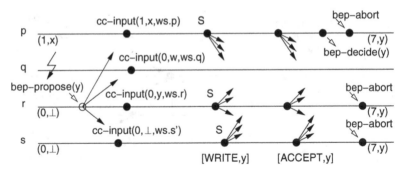

Figure 5.6: Sample execution of a Byzantine epoch consensus instance, with timestamp 7 and leader r

observe that leader q influences the execution of conditional collect such that process p never collects any output and processes r and q collect the respective output states

$$S_r = [[1, x, ws_p], [0, x, \{(1, x), (2, w)\}], [0, \perp, ws_r], \text{UNDEFINED}]$$
$$S_s = [\text{UNDEFINED}, [0, w, \emptyset], [0, \perp, ws_r], [0, \perp, ws_s]].$$

Note that $S_r \neq S_s$ is permitted because the leader is Byzantine, and furthermore, the discrepancy $S_r[q] \neq S_s[q]$ is also allowed because it concerns the output of the Byzantine process q. Process r finds that $(1, x)$ is the highest timestamp in a Byzantine quorum of entries in S_r and that x is certified, therefore $binds(1, x, S_r) = \text{TRUE}$. However, process s determines that $unbound(S_s) = \text{TRUE}$ and writes value w, taken from $S_s[q]$. No process receives enough WRITE messages to proceed with the algorithm. Subsequently, all correct processes bep-abort the Byzantine epoch consensus instance. Their states remain almost the same as at the start of the execution: the timestamp/value pairs are unchanged, and only the writeset of s changes to $ws'_s = \{(6, w)\}$.

Figure 5.6 depicts a second execution of Byzantine epoch consensus, now with timestamp 7 and correct leader r. All correct processes start with the state they had after the execution of epoch 6 from Fig. 5.5. Note that, the leader r now bep-proposes y, broadcasts a READ message, and acts as the leader in the conditional collect primitive. Because of this, all correct processes collect the *same* output vector S (as guaranteed by the *consistency* and *termination* properties of Module 5.14).

Assuming that the Byzantine process q inputs a timestamp/value pair of $(0, w)$ and an empty writeset to the conditional collect, its output vector may be

$$S = [\text{UNDEFINED}, [0, w, \emptyset], [0, y, ws_r], [0, \perp, ws'_s]].$$

This vector is unbound, because it only contains timestamp 0 in the defined entries. Therefore, the correct processes write the value y from leader r in epoch 7. Processes p, r, and s receive enough WRITE messages to change their states to $(7, y)$ and to broadcast an ACCEPT message. These messages cause process p to bep-decide x. Before any other message arrives, all correct processes bep-abort the Byzantine epoch consensus instance. Note that, the state of all correct processes is now $(7, y)$ and all their writesets include $(7, y)$.

Correctness. Algorithm 5.17–5.18 implements Byzantine epoch consensus with timestamp ets and leader ℓ with f Byzantine faults for $N > 3f$.

We first demonstrate the *lock-in* property of Byzantine epoch consensus. Suppose some correct process has bep-decided v in an epoch consensus instance with timestamp $ts' < ts$. The process only bep-decided after collecting ACCEPT messages containing v from more than $(N + f)/2$ processes; among the processes that sent those messages, there exists a set $\mathcal{A}$ of more than

$$\frac{N + f}{2} - f > f$$

correct processes. According to the algorithm, they all set their variables val to v and $valts$ to ts'.

The members of $\mathcal{A}$ only sent an ACCEPT message after collecting WRITE messages containing v from more than $(N + f)/2$ processes; among these processes, there exists a set $\mathcal{W}$ of more than

$$\frac{N + f}{2} - f > f$$

correct processes. According to the algorithm, they all added (ts', v) to their variable *writeset*.

Consider the next instance of Byzantine epoch consensus with timestamp $ts^* > ets$, in which any correct process p collects *states* from conditional collect such that $binds(ts^*, v^*, states)$ for some $v^* \neq \bot$. We claim that $v^* = v$.

To see this, observe that no correct process has sent a WRITE message in any epoch between ts' and ts^*. This means that no correct process has changed its $valts$, val, and *writeset* variables (even if faulty processed did send WRITE messages, there would not have been enough of them). By the assumption about how a correct process passes the state from one epoch to the next, every process in $\mathcal{A}$ starts epoch ts^* with its state containing $(valts, val) = (ts', v)$. Furthermore, every process in $\mathcal{W}$ starts epoch ts^* with a variable *writeset* that contains (ts', v). The *integrity* property of conditional collect ensures that these state values are not modified in transit by the primitive. Hence, the vector *states* output to p satisfies that $quorumhighest(ts', v, states) = $ TRUE because the state from at least one member of $\mathcal{A}$ is contained in every Byzantine quorum. Furthermore, $certifiedvalue(ts', v, states) = $ TRUE because the writesets of all processes in $\mathcal{W}$ include (ts', v).

Consequently, process p writes v, and any other correct process that writes also writes v. This proves the claim and implies that a correct process can only *bep*-decide v in epoch ts^*. Furthermore, the set of correct processes that set their variable *val* to v and variable *valts* to a value at least as large as ts' when they abort epoch ts^* is now at least $\mathcal{A}$. Using the same reasoning, the set of correct processes whose *writeset* variable contains (ts', v) is also at least $\mathcal{A}$. Continuing this argument until epoch ts establishes the *lock-in* property.

To show the *validity* property, assume that a correct process *bep*-decides v. It is obvious from the algorithm that a correct process only *bep*-decides for the value v received in an ACCEPT message from a Byzantine quorum of processes and that any correct process only sends an ACCEPT message with v after receiving v in a WRITE message from a Byzantine quorum of processes. Moreover, any correct process only sends a WRITE message with v in two cases: either (1) after collecting a vector *states* that binds ts to v or (2) after collecting *states* that is unbound and taking v from *states*$[\ell]$, which was input by the leader ℓ. In case (2), the *validity* property is satisfied. In case (1), we continue by applying the same argument inductively, backward in the well-formed sequence of epochs, until we reach an epoch where *states* is unbound; in that epoch, the reasoning for case (2) applies. This shows that v was *bep*-proposed by the leader in some epoch with timestamp $ts' \leq ts$.

For the *agreement* property, observe how any correct process that *bep*-decides v must have received more than $(N + f)/2$ ACCEPT messages with v. As a correct process only sends one ACCEPT message in an epoch and as $N > 3f$, it is not possible that another correct process receives more than $(N + f)/2$ ACCEPT messages with a value different from v. The *agreement* property follows. The *integrity* property is easy to see from this and directly from the algorithm.

To show the *termination* property, we demonstrate that all correct processes input compliant STATE messages to the conditional collect abstraction, and therefore $sound(S) =$ TRUE when at least $N - f$ entries of S are those STATE messages. To see this, suppose the state of a correct process contains a pair (ts, v); the pair is either $(0, \bot)$ or was assigned after receiving a Byzantine quorum of WRITE messages in epoch ts. In the latter case, no output vector S containing this pair could be unbound. As

$$\frac{N + f}{2} > 2f,$$

it follows from the algorithm that v is also in the writeset of more than f correct processes. Consider now the pair (ts', v') with the largest timestamp $ts' \geq ts$ held by a correct process. This pair has the maximum timestamp in the state of a Byzantine quorum of correct processes. In addition, the writesets of more than f correct processes contain (ts', v'). Hence, conditional collect with a correct leader may obtain a vector S such that $binds(ts', v'S)$. Alternatively, if a Byzantine quorum of correct processes input a state with timestamp 0, the algorithm can find an unbound S. Hence, conditional collect eventually outputs S such that $sound(S)$ holds.

If process ℓ is correct then every correct process collects the same vector with at least $N - f$ entries different from UNDEFINED, according to the *consistency* property of conditional collect. Hence, every correct process eventually assigns *tmpval* $\neq \perp$ and sends a WRITE message containing some value *tmpval*. More precisely, all

$$N - f > \frac{N + f}{2}$$

correct processes write the same *tmpval*. Hence, every correct process eventually sends an ACCEPT message to all processes with *tmpval* and every correct process eventually *bep*-decides, because no aborts occur.

Finally, the *abort behavior* property is satisfied because the algorithm returns an event ⟨ *Aborted* | *state* ⟩ immediately and only if it has been aborted.

Performance. Algorithm 5.17–5.18 takes three communication steps plus the steps of the underlying conditional collect implementation. With the "Signed Conditional Collect" algorithm, the algorithm for Byzantine epoch consensus requires five communication steps. As all processes send messages to each other, there are $O(N^2)$ messages in total.

5.6.4 Fail-Noisy-Arbitrary Algorithm: Byzantine Leader-Driven Consensus

Given implementations of the Byzantine epoch-change and Byzantine epoch consensus abstractions, the "Leader-Driven Consensus" algorithm presented in the fail-noisy model provides weak Byzantine consensus. In particular, the "Byzantine Leader-Driven Consensus" algorithm in the fail-noisy-arbitrary model, shown in Algorithm 5.19, differs from its counterpart with crash-stop processes only by using underlying abstractions with Byzantine processes.

Recall that the Byzantine epoch-change primitive uses a Byzantine eventual leader-detection abstraction. According to its properties, Algorithm 5.19 for Byzantine consensus must periodically give feedback when the elected leader does not perform well. A correct process does that whenever the leader of an epoch takes too long before deciding. Specifically, whenever a new epoch begins and a new

---

Algorithm 5.19: Byzantine Leader-Driven Consensus

Implements:
    WeakByzantineConsensus, **instance** *wbc*.

Uses:
    ByzantineEpochChange, **instance** *bec*;
    ByzantineEpochConsensus (multiple instances);
    ByzantineLeaderDetector, **instance** *bld*.

// The algorithm is the same as the "Leader-Driven Consensus" in Algorithm 5.7, with
// the handler below added and these differences:
// – it uses the Byzantine epoch-change and Byzantine epoch consensus primitives;
// – whenever a new epoch instance is initialized, it increases T and executes *starttimer*(T).

upon event ⟨ *Timeout* ⟩ **do**
    trigger ⟨ *bld, Complain* | ℓ ⟩;

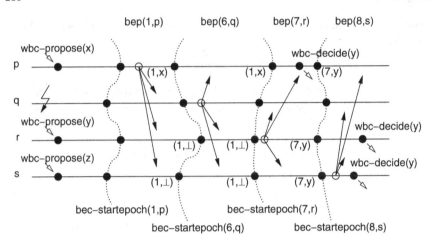

Figure 5.7: Sample execution of Byzantine leader-driven consensus

instance *bep.ets* of epoch consensus with timestamp *ets* is initialized, every process also starts a timeout service with delay T, set to an estimate of how long the epoch should take before deciding. The delay is increased every time before the timeout is restarted. If the timeout expires before the epoch instance *bep*-decides then the process complains about the current leader ℓ and triggers an event $\langle$ *bld,* *Complain* $| \ell \rangle$.

When the "Byzantine Leader-Based Epoch-Change" algorithm and the "Byzantine Read/Write Epoch Consensus" algorithm (Algorithms 5.15 and 5.17–5.18) are called from Algorithm 5.19, we can simplify them in two ways.

First, the READ message may be omitted. As the leader of the epoch sends a READ message immediately after obtaining enough NEWEPOCH messages and starting the epoch consensus algorithm in the new epoch, every process simply invokes conditional collect with its STATE message, upon initializing the epoch consensus instance.

Second, in the first epoch consensus instance invoked by Algorithm 5.19, the conditional collect primitive for reading the state of all processes may be skipped because all processes, apart from the leader, store the default state initially. Only the initial leader needs to disseminate its state using the authenticated perfect links.

An execution of Algorithm 5.19 with Algorithm 5.17–5.18 implementing Byzantine epoch consensus is shown in Fig. 5.7. The Byzantine epoch-change primitive (*bec*) starts four epochs, denoted by $bep(1, p)$ for the epoch with timestamp 1 and leader p, by $bep(6, q)$ for epoch 6 with leader q, and so on. Process q is Byzantine. In epoch 1, the leader process p manages to write its proposal value x, sends an ACCEPT message, and changes its state to $(1, x)$, but the epoch aborts before any other process sends an ACCEPT message. Epoch 6 with the Byzantine leader q subsequently proceeds exactly as shown in Fig. 5.5; then, epoch 7 with leader r executes as illustrated in Fig. 5.6. During this epoch, process p *bep*-decides y and consequently *wbc*-decides y. In epoch 8, the leader process s writes value y again; the remaining correct processes *bep*-decide and *wbc*-decide y as well.

Correctness. As the primitives underlying the "Byzantine Leader-Driven Consensus" algorithm are the same as in the fail-noisy model and as the algorithm is the same as "Leader-Driven Consensus," its correctness follows from the same reasoning as applied in the fail-noisy model.

Performance. The "Byzantine Leader-Driven Consensus" algorithm does not use a communication primitive directly. Its performance is, therefore, given by the implementations of the underlying Byzantine epoch-change and Byzantine epoch consensus primitives.

5.7 Byzantine Randomized Consensus

The preceding section introduced consensus with processes subject to Byzantine faults and presented an implementation that needs an eventual leader detector primitive to guarantee termination. Analogous to consensus with crash-stop processes, one can also resort to randomization and consider randomization in the fail-arbitrary model. A primitive for Byzantine randomized consensus and its implementation are the subject of this section.

5.7.1 Specification

The *Byzantine randomized consensus* abstraction differs from the (strong) Byzantine consensus primitive (Module 5.11) only in the *termination* property. In all other respects, the two notions are the same. The primitive inherits its *probabilistic termination* property directly from randomized consensus (Module 5.8) and must decide with probability 1. The abstraction is shown in Module 5.15.

5.7.2 Randomized Fail-Arbitrary Algorithm: Byzantine Randomized Binary Consensus

We present Algorithm 5.20–5.21, which implements Byzantine randomized consensus on one-bit values and works under the assumption $N > 5f$. The algorithm is called "Byzantine Randomized Binary Consensus" and is very similar to Algorithm 5.12–5.13 in the randomized fail-silent model. In particular, it also proceeds in global rounds and every round consists of two phases. In phase one, the processes exchange their proposals. In phase two, they determine if enough processes proposed the same value. If one process observes a large number (more than $2f$) of phase-two messages with the same proposal then this process may decide. If a process observes enough phase-two messages with the same value v to be sure that v is the proposal of a correct process (the value occurs more than than f times) then the process adopts v as its own proposal. All processes then access a common

---

Module 5.15: Interface and properties of Byzantine randomized consensus

Module:

    Name: ByzantineRandomizedConsensus, **instance** *rc*.

Events:

    Request: ⟨ *brc, Propose* | v ⟩: Proposes value v for consensus.

    Indication: ⟨ *brc, Decide* | v ⟩: Outputs a decided value v of consensus.

Properties:

    BRC1: Same as property RC1 in randomized consensus (Module 5.8).

    BRC2–BRC4: Same as properties BC2–BC4 in (strong) Byzantine consensus
    (Module 5.11).

---

coin and if they have not yet decided or adopted a value in this round, they use the output from the coin as their proposal for the next round.

To simplify the description, the processes continue to participate in the algorithm after deciding, with their proposal set to the decided value. This helps the other processes decide. One could alternatively make every correct process abandon the rounds, by adopting the method implemented in the fail-silent variant of the algorithm (Algorithm 5.12–5.13).

In the fail-arbitrary model, Byzantine quorums of more than $(N + f)/2$ processes replace the majority quorums, and the phase-two votes are disseminated with a Byzantine consistent broadcast primitive instead of simple best-effort broadcast.

Note that the common coin abstraction of Module 5.14 also exists in the fail-arbitrary model, considering that it only states conditions on the output of the correct processes. The "Independent Choice" method to implement a common coin, whereby every process simply selects a random value on its own and independently from the others, also works in the Byzantine model. It implements a coin that matches with probability at least 2^{-N+f}.

The algorithm achieves the *strong validity* property of Byzantine consensus, as is easy to see because the domain is binary. Adapting this fail-arbitrary algorithm to larger domains (while retaining strong validity) requires more work than for the large-domain extension in the fail-silent model from Algorithm 5.14.

Correctness. We argue why the algorithm implements Byzantine randomized consensus under the assumption that $N > 5f$. The following two observations help with the analysis.

First, if two correct processes broadcast a PHASE-2 message in the same round and both messages contain a proposal different from $\bot$ then the two proposals are equal to some value u, which we call the *majority value* of the round. This holds because every correct process p has received phase-one proposals from $N - f$ processes, which also form a Byzantine quorum of more than $(N + f)/2$ processes. Then p sets its phase-two value to $\bot$, *unless* a Byzantine quorum among the received

---

Algorithm 5.20: Byzantine Randomized Binary Consensus (phase 1)

Implements:
    ByzantineRandomizedConsensus, **instance** *brc*, with domain $\{0, 1\}$.

Uses:
    AuthPerfectPointToPointLinks, **instance** *al*;
    ByzantineConsistentBroadcast (multiple instances);
    CommonCoin (multiple instances).

upon event $\langle$ *brc, Init* $\rangle$ **do**
    round := 0; *phase* := 0;
    proposal := $\bot$;
    decision := $\bot$;
    val := $[\bot]^N$;

upon event $\langle$ *brc, Propose* $\mid v$ $\rangle$ **do**
    proposal := *v*;
    round := 1; *phase* := 1;
    forall $q \in \Pi$ **do**
        trigger $\langle$ *al, Send* $\mid q$, [PHASE-1, *round, proposal*] $\rangle$;

upon event $\langle$ *al, Deliver* $\mid p$, [PHASE-1, *r, v*] $\rangle$ **such that** *phase* $= 1 \wedge r = round$ **do**
    val[*p*] := *v*;

upon $\#(val) \geq N - f \wedge phase = 1$ **do**
    if exists $v \neq \bot$ such that $\#(\{p \in \Pi \mid val[p] = v\}) > \frac{N+f}{2}$ **then**
        proposal := *v*;
    else
        proposal := $\bot$;
    val := $[\bot]^N$;
    phase := 2;
    forall $p \in \Pi$ **do**
        Initialize a new instance *bcb.round.p* of ByzantineConsistentBroadcast;
    trigger $\langle$ *bcb.round.self, Broadcast* $\mid$ [PHASE-2, *round, proposal*] $\rangle$;

---

phase-one proposals were equal to the same value. Recall that if *p* obtains a Byzantine quorum of messages from distinct processes then every other Byzantine quorum of such messages includes at least one of those messages that was sent by a correct process in the system. Hence, every Byzantine quorum of phase-one messages contains the majority value *u* at least once.

Second, if some correct process *bcb*-delivers more than $2f$ PHASE-2 broadcasts in some round *r* that contain a value *v* then every correct process *bcb*-delivers more than *f* PHASE-2 broadcasts in round *r* that contain *v*. This follows from the *consistency* property of the underlying Byzantine consistent broadcast abstraction and because there are only *N* such broadcast instances in every round. Note that *v* must be the majority value of the round. Consequently, if some correct process decides *v* in round *r* then every correct process sets its proposal value to *v* at the end of round *r*.

Algorithm 5.21: Byzantine Randomized Binary Consensus (phase 2)

---

upon event ⟨ *bcb.round.p*, *Deliver* | *p*, [PHASE-2, *r*, *v*] ⟩ **such that**
    phase = 2 ∧ *r* = *round* **do**
  val[*p*] := *v*;

upon #(*val*) ≥ *N* − *f* ∧ *phase* = 2 **do**
  phase := 0;
  Initialize a new instance *coin.round* of CommonCoin with domain {0, 1};
  trigger ⟨ *coin.round*, *Release* ⟩;

upon event ⟨ *coin.round*, *Output* | *c* ⟩ **do**
  if exists *v* ≠ ⊥ such that #({*p* ∈ *Π* | *val*[*p*] = *v*}) > 2*f* **then**
    if *decision* = ⊥ **then**
      decision := *v*;
      trigger ⟨ *brc*, *Decide* | *decision* ⟩;
    proposal := *v*;
  else if exists *w* ≠ ⊥ such that #({*p* ∈ *Π* | *val*[*p*] = *w*}) > *f* **then**
    proposal := *w*;
  else
    proposal := *c*;
  val := [⊥]^N;
  round := *round* + 1; *phase* := 1;
  forall *q* ∈ *Π* **do**
    trigger ⟨ *al*, *Send* | *q*, [PHASE-1, *round*, *proposal*] ⟩;

To show the *validity* property, note that when all correct processes start a round
with the same proposal v, then all correct processes obtain at least $N - 2f$ entries
in *val* equal to v in phase one (the Byzantine processes might broadcast a different
proposal). As

$$N - 2f > \frac{N + f}{2}$$

under the assumption that $N > 5f$, all correct processes also broadcast a PHASE-
2 message containing v. Every correct process, therefore, obtains at least $N - 2f$
entries in *val* equal to v in phase two (again subtracting the values from Byzantine
processes). As also $N - 2f > 2f$ under the assumption of the algorithm, every
correct process decides v in this case and also ends the round with its proposal equal
to v. For the case when not all correct processes propose the same value initially,
then the algorithm may obviously decide any value, since the domain is binary.

The *integrity* property holds because a process maintains the variable *decision* as
a guard to check if it has already decided previously.

For the *agreement* property, recall the two observations given earlier. Hence, if
some correct process decides the majority value v in round r then correct processes
may only decide v in round r. If not all processes decide then v remains the only possible decision value because all correct processes enter round $r + 1$ with a proposal
value of v, as shown under the *validity* property.

Every correct process advances through the rounds of the algorithm because it waits for more than $(N + f)/2$ PHASE-1 messages and for $N - f$ PHASE-2 broadcasts, but all $N - f$ correct processes eventually broadcast such messages.

A correct process decides as soon as it receives the majority value of the round from more than $2f$ processes. At the end of every round, the correct processes either set their proposal to the majority value or to the common coin output. At the latest when the coin values at all correct processes match, the algorithm is guaranteed to decide in the next round and therefore satisfies *termination*.

Performance. Every round of the algorithm involves one communication step with $O(N^2)$ messages plus N parallel instances of Byzantine consistent broadcast, which takes at least two communication steps. Depending on the implementation of the broadcast primitive according to Sect. 3.10, this adds two communication steps and $O(N^3)$ messages or three communication steps with only $O(N^2)$ messages. On top of this comes the cost of implementing the common coin abstraction. As in Algorithm 5.12–5.13, the expected number of rounds that a correct process executes before terminating is proportional to $1/\delta$.

5.8 Exercises

Exercise 5.1: *What would happen in our "Flooding Consensus" algorithm if it accepted a beb-delivered* DECIDED *message from process p even if $p \notin$ correct?*

Exercise 5.2: *Our "Hierarchical Consensus" algorithm requires N communication steps for all correct processes to decide. Suggest a slight modification that enables it to run in $N - 1$ steps.*

Exercise 5.3: *Can we also optimize our "Flooding Uniform Consensus" algorithm to save one communication step, such that all correct processes always decide after $N - 1$ communication steps? Consider simply the case of a system of two processes.*

Exercise 5.4: *Consider all our fail-stop consensus algorithms ("Hierarchical (Uniform) Consensus" and "Flooding (Uniform) Consensus," Algorithms 5.1–5.4). Explain why none of those algorithms would be correct if the failure detector turns out not to be perfect.*

Exercise 5.5: *Explain why any fail-noisy consensus algorithm actually solves uniform consensus.*

Exercise 5.6: *Explain why any fail-noisy algorithm that implements consensus (or epoch consensus) requires a majority of the correct processes.*

Exercise 5.7: *Give a fail-noisy consensus algorithm that assumes a correct majority of the processes and uses an eventually perfect failure-detector abstraction. It should use a round-based approach in such a way that (1) in any execution where the process p with rank 1 is never suspected, p imposes its proposal value as the consensus decision, (2) in any execution where p crashes initially and the process q with rank 2 is never suspected, q imposes its proposal value, and so on, such that if all processes with a more important rank than k initially crash then the process with rank k imposes its proposal unless it is suspected.*

Exercise 5.8: *Consider Algorithm 5.6, "Leader-Driven Consensus," in the fail-noisy model, with the epoch-change and epoch consensus primitives implemented by Algorithm 5.5 and Algorithm 5.6, respectively. Suppose that the process ℓ_0, which is the leader of the initial epoch, is correct, and furthermore, that all processes initially trust process ℓ_0. How can you simplify the algorithm so that it uses fewer communication steps than Algorithm 5.6 to decide under these assumptions?*

Exercise 5.9: *The "Randomized Binary Consensus" algorithm (Algorithm 5.12–5.13) uses a reliable broadcast primitive to disseminate a* DECIDED *message. Modify the algorithm and remove the* DECIDED *message. Recall that the* DECIDED *message ensures that all correct processes terminate and describe an alternative way for ensuring termination.*

Exercise 5.10: *Discuss the notion of validity for Byzantine consensus abstractions with binary domain, i.e., such that processes can only propose 0 or 1.*

Exercise 5.11: *How can one transform any algorithm for weak Byzantine consensus into one for (strong) Byzantine consensus? This exercise answers this question in two steps.*

Consider a validated Byzantine consensus *primitive, with a third variation of validity condition called* anchored validity. *It reflects the intuition that a correct process can somehow recognize an acceptable decision value for consensus. Every process (even a Byzantine one) may propose a value that is acceptable in this way, and it would be enough for the consensus abstraction to decide on any value with this property, no matter from where it originates. The strong validity notion, in contrast, requires that all correct processes propose the* same *(acceptable) value, which is difficult to ensure in practice, or the decision might be the special symbol* □.

To formalize anchored validity, *we introduce a predicate* $P(\cdot)$ *on proposal values and every process invokes a Byzantine consensus abstraction with* P, *determined by the application that is interested in the decision of consensus. The predicate is either true or false, can be evaluated locally and efficiently by every process, and yields the same verdict on a given value when evaluated by any correct process. In this sense, the predicate anchors the validity of a decision in the application. A* validated Byzantine consensus *abstraction is now the same as our two Byzantine consensus abstractions (Modules 5.10 and 5.11) with the following notion of* anchored validity:

> Every correct process only decides a value v such that $P(v) =$ TRUE.
> Moreover, if all processes are correct and propose v, then no correct process decides a value different from v.

It is assumed that every correct process proposes a value that satisfies P.

Take now any algorithm that implements weak Byzantine consensus and transform it as follows: whenever a process proposes a value v or delivers a message from another process containing a value v, which the other process (if correct) may have proposed, then verify that $P(v)$ holds; proceed only if $P(v) =$ TRUE and halt otherwise. This gives a Byzantine consensus algorithm with anchored validity and completes the first step of this transformation.

For the second step, describe a transformation of validated Byzantine consensus to (strong) Byzantine consensus, that is, describe an algorithm that implements the Byzantine consensus abstraction from a validated Byzantine consensus abstraction. The solution is easier when digital signatures are available.

Exercise 5.12: *Implement a conditional collect abstraction with an algorithm that does not use digital signatures. As a hint, recall the differences between the two implementations of Byzantine consistent broadcast in Sect. 3.10.*

Exercise 5.13: *Consider the execution of the "Byzantine Read/Write Epoch Consensus" algorithm illustrated in Fig. 5.6. Start with the same initial states of* *all correct processes. Describe an execution that results in some correct process bep-deciding x, where additionally one correct process never sends any* ACCEPT *message.*

5.9 Solutions

Solution 5.1: Consider a variant of the "Flooding Consensus" algorithm that accepts a DECIDED message from any process p (as long as *decision* $= \bot$), even if $p \notin correct$. This algorithm may violate the *agreement* property. In the following, we describe an execution with at least three processes that demonstrates this.

It may occur that p decides in round 1 and then crashes. No other process delivers the PROPOSAL message from p of round 1, but the DECIDED message from p, sent using best-effort broadcast, may still reach others at some later time. All other processes detect that p has crashed and progress to round 2 without receiving a PROPOSAL message from p, hence $p \in crashed$ and $p \notin receivedfrom[1]$ for them. Note that p might have decided its own value v, which is smaller than any other proposed value, and no other process is yet aware of v. As p was detected by the failure detector to have crashed, the other processes may proceed without waiting for any further messages from p. Suppose some correct process q decides a value $v' \neq v$ (the fact that p decided v does not violate the *agreement* property because p is not correct). If the DECIDED message from p now reaches a third process r that has not yet decided then r decides v. This violates *agreement* because q and r are correct.

Solution 5.2: The lowest-ranked process t, which has rank N and broadcasts last, does not need to broadcast its message. Indeed, the only process that uses t's broadcast value is t itself. Hence, process t decides its proposal just *before* it would have broadcast it (not when it has delivered it).

Solution 5.3: The answer is no. We argue here that in the case of two processes, the "Flooding Uniform Consensus" algorithm needs two communication steps because a decision cannot be reached by all correct processes after one step. (The interested reader can extend this argument to a system of $N > 2$ processes.)

Consider a system with two processes p and q and assume that every process must decide after executing only one round in the algorithm. We describe an execution where the processes do not reach uniform agreement; thus, the algorithm need at least two rounds. Suppose that p and q propose two different values v and w, respectively. Without loss of generality, assume that $v < w$. In the following execution, process p is faulty.

During the first round, p and q send their values to each other. Process p receives its own value and q's value and decides at the end of the round by our assumption. It decides v, the smaller value, and then crashes. Now, assume that the message from p to q in round one is delayed arbitrarily. There is a time after which q detects p to have crashed because of the *strong completeness* property of the perfect failure detector. As q cannot know that p actually did send a message, q reaches the end of the first round and must decide. Process q decides its own value w, which violates *uniform agreement*.

Note that in the original algorithm, where the processes decide only after two rounds, the above scenario cannot occur. This is because p crashes *before* it can decide (in fact, it never decides); later on, q decides w.

Solution 5.4: A violation of *strong completeness* property of the perfect failure detector could lead to the violation of the *termination* property of consensus as follows. In all our fail-stop algorithms, there is at least one critical point where a process p waits to deliver a message from a process q or to detect the crash of process q. Should q crash and p never detect the crash of q, p would remain blocked forever and never decide.

Consider now *strong accuracy*. If it does not hold, our "Flooding Consensus" algorithm, for instance, could violate the *agreement* property in the scenario of Fig. 5.1: if process q crashes after deciding 3, and p is falsely suspected to have crashed by processes r and q, then r and q will decide 5. A similar scenario can occur for "Hierarchical Consensus."

Solution 5.5: Consider any fail-noisy consensus algorithm that implements consensus but not uniform consensus. This means that there is an execution where two processes p and q decide differently and one of them crashes, so that the algorithm violates *uniform agreement*. Assume that process p crashes. With an eventually perfect failure detector, it might be the case that p has not crashed but is falsely suspected to have crashed by all other processes. Process q would decide the same as in the previous execution, and the algorithm would even violate the regular *agreement* property.

Solution 5.6: We explain this for the case of a system of four processes p, q, r, and s. Assume by contradiction that there is a fail-noisy consensus algorithm that tolerates the crash of two processes. Assume that p and q propose a value v, whereas r and s propose a different value v'. Consider an execution E_1 where p and q crash initially: in this execution, r and s decide v' to respect the *validity* property of consensus. Consider also an execution E_2 where r and s crash initially: in this scenario, p and q decide v. With an eventually perfect failure detector, a third execution E_3 is possible: the one where no process crashes, p and q falsely suspect r and s, and r and s falsely suspect p and q. In this execution E_3, processes p and q decide v, just as in execution E_1 (they execute the same steps as in E_1, and cannot distinguish E_3 from E_1 up to the decision point), whereas r and s decide v', just as in execution E_2 (they execute the same steps as in E_2, and cannot distinguish E_3 from E_2 up to the decision point). *Agreement* would hence be violated.

A similar argument applies to epoch consensus.

Solution 5.7: We give here an algorithm based on the "rotating coordinator" approach, which causes the process p with rank k to impose its proposal in round k, when all processes with more important ranks initially crash and p is never suspected. Although Algorithm 5.7 also implements consensus in the fail-noisy model, it uses a different structure because the process that imposes its proposal is chosen by the eventual leader detector abstraction.

Algorithm 5.22: Rotating Coordinator (part 1)

Implements:
    UniformConsensus, **instance** *uc*.

Uses:
    EventuallyPerfectFailureDetector, **instance** $\Diamond \mathcal{P}$;
    BestEffortBroadcast, **instance** *beb*;
    UniformReliableBroadcast, **instance** *urb*.

upon event $\langle$ *uc, Init* $\rangle$ **do**
    round := 1;
    suspected := $\emptyset$;
    proposal := $\bot$;
    sentpropose := FALSE; *sentvote* := FALSE;
    estimate := $\bot$; *votes* := $[\bot]^N$;

upon event $\langle$ $\Diamond \mathcal{P}$, *Suspect* $\mid p$ $\rangle$ **do**
    suspected := *suspected* $\cup$ $\{p\}$;

upon event $\langle$ $\Diamond \mathcal{P}$, *Restore* $\mid p$ $\rangle$ **do**
    suspected := *suspected* $\setminus$ $\{p\}$;

upon event $\langle$ *uc, Propose* $\mid v$ $\rangle$ **such that** *proposal* = $\bot$ **do**
    proposal := *v*;

upon *leader(round)* = *self* $\wedge$ *proposal* $\neq$ $\bot$ $\wedge$ *sentpropose* = FALSE **do**
    sentpropose := TRUE;
    trigger $\langle$ *beb, Broadcast* $\mid$ [PROPOSE, *round, proposal*] $\rangle$;

upon event $\langle$ *beb, Deliver* $\mid p$, [PROPOSE, *r, v*] $\rangle$ **such that** *r* = *round* **do**
    estimate := *v*;   // proposal received from *p* = *leader(round)*

upon (*estimate* $\neq$ $\bot$ $\vee$ *leader(round)* $\in$ *suspected*) $\wedge$ *sentvote* = FALSE **do**
    sentvote := TRUE;
    trigger $\langle$ *beb, Broadcast* $\mid$ [VOTE, *round, estimate*] $\rangle$;

Algorithm 5.22–5.23, called "Rotating Coordinator," proceeds in rounds such that the process with rank k acts as a leader for round k. All other processes act as witnesses. Every process goes sequentially from round k to round $k + 1$, and no process ever jumps to a higher round. The leader of round k is determined from the round number by the function *leader*($\cdot$) introduced before.

Every process maintains a current *proposal* that it tries to impose as the decision value. In the first phase of every round, the leader sends its proposal to all processes using a best-effort broadcast primitive. Every process waits until it receives the proposal v from the leader or until it suspects the leader to have crashed. A process then broadcasts a VOTE message containing either v or the special value $\bot$. After receiving a quorum of such votes, a process may decide when it received only votes equal

---

Algorithm 5.23: Rotating Coordinator (part 2)

---

upon event ⟨ *beb*, *Deliver* | *p*, [VOTE, *r*, *v*] ⟩ **such that** *r* = *round* **do**
    votes[*p*] := *v*;

upon #(*votes*) > *N*/2 ∧ *sentvote* = TRUE **do**
    V := {*v* | there exists *p* ∈ *Π* such that *votes*[*p*] = *v*};
    if exists *v* ≠ ⊥ such that *V* = {*v*} **then**
        trigger ⟨ *urb*, *Broadcast* | [DECIDED, *v*] ⟩;
        proposal := *v*;
    else if exists *v* ≠ ⊥ such that *V* = {*v*, ⊥} **then**
        proposal := *v*;
    round := *round* + 1;
    sentpropose := FALSE; *sentvote* := FALSE;
    estimate := ⊥; *votes* := [⊥]^N;

upon event ⟨ *urb*, *Deliver* | *p*, [DECIDED, *v*] ⟩ **do**
    trigger ⟨ *uc*, *Decide* | *v* ⟩;

---

to v; otherwise, if it received at least one vote of v, it updates its proposal and sets it to v. The decision is disseminated with a uniform reliable broadcast abstraction.

Concurrently to executing the rounds, every process records the output of the eventually perfect failure detector and maintains a set of suspected processes. The majority quorum ensures that once a process decides v, every correct process updates its proposal to v.

Correctness. The *validity* property follows directly from the algorithm and from the properties of the underlying communication abstractions. Consider now *termination*. If some correct process decides, it reacts to a DECIDED message that is *urb*-delivered through the underlying uniform reliable broadcast instance *urb*. Because of its *agreement* property, every correct process eventually *urb*-delivers the DECIDED message and decides. It remains to show that some correct process eventually decides. Toward a contradiction, assume that there is at least one correct process but no correct process decides. Consider the point in time after which all faulty processes have crashed, all faulty processes are suspected forever by every correct process, and no correct process is ever suspected. Suppose that after this time, some process starts a new round in which the leader is a correct process. Unless some process has already decided, all correct processes reach this round. Consequently, the leader manages to impose its proposal on all correct processes, none of them votes ⊥, and all of them broadcast a DECIDED message in this round.

To show the *uniform agreement* property, assume that some process has *urb*-broadcast a decision with value v in some round r. This means that the value v has been proposed by the leader of round r; as the deciding process *beb*-delivered a quorum of VOTE messages that contained v, every correct process has received at least one VOTE message with v as well, by the quorum intersection property. Hence, value v is locked in the sense that any server may only proceed to round $r + 1$ with its *proposal* variable equal to v. In particular, the leader of round $r + 1$, and the leaders of all subsequent rounds, may only propose v. This ensures no process *urb*-broadcasts a DECIDED message with a value different from v. Furthermore, a process only *uc*-decides when it *urb*-delivers a DECIDED message. Together with the *no duplication* property of the underlying uniform reliable broadcast, this argument also demonstrates that the algorithm satisfies *integrity*.

Performance. If no process fails or is suspected to have failed then three communication steps and $O(N^2)$ messages are required for all correct processes to decide.

Solution 5.8: By opening up the underlying epoch-change and epoch consensus abstractions, we obtain an algorithm that uses only three communication steps. When process ℓ_0, as the leader of the initial epoch, has proposed a value v_ℓ, it directly tries to impose v_ℓ by writing it in epoch 0, without first consulting the other processes and reading their local states. It may skip the first round of message exchanges for reading because in the initial epoch, process ℓ_0 knows that no decision could have been made in a previous epoch (as there is no previous epoch). This first round in every epoch consensus instance is actually only needed to make sure that the leader will propose a value that might have been decided (more precisely, to ensure the *lock-in* property of epoch consensus). The algorithm, therefore, saves one communication phase by directly having ℓ_0 write v_ℓ and all correct processes decide after three communication steps.

Solution 5.9: Observe that the DECIDED message is only necessary because a process stops participating in the next round after sending this message. If every process instead continues with the algorithm and participates for at least one more round, all correct processes eventually decide. To make this work and to let the processes progress through both phases of the next round, one has to remove the two clauses *decision* $= \bot$ from the conditions that guard the exits from phase one and two, respectively. Furthermore, a process must now only decide if *decision* $= \bot$.

The modified algorithm works because during the round in which the first process decides some value v, all processes obtain at least one phase-two proposal with $v \neq \bot$. This means that they set their proposal to v for moving to the next round. According to the *validity* property, every correct process now decides in the next round.

Solution 5.10: Consider a binary Byzantine consensus abstraction with weak validity. If it is somehow known that all correct processes have proposed the same value and the primitive decides differently then there must be one faulty process that proposed this other value.

For Byzantine consensus with strong validity, every decided value was actually proposed by a correct process. This is an intuitive and useful property of Byzantine consensus with a binary domain. Unfortunately, if the domain has more than two values then strong validity does not guarantee this property in all situations. (It is possible, however, to maintain this intuitive property at the cost of reducing the resilience of algorithms that implement the abstraction, that is, when the number of Byzantine processes that can be tolerated decreases with as the domain size grows.)

Solution 5.11: For completeness, Module 5.16 summarizes the validated Byzantine consensus primitive.

Module 5.16: Interface and properties of validated Byzantine consensus

Module:

    Name: ValidatedByzantineConsensus, **instance** *vbc*, with predicate $P(\cdot)$.

Events:

    Request: $\langle$ *vbc, Propose* $\mid v$ $\rangle$: Proposes value v for consensus.

    Indication: $\langle$ *vbc, Decide* $\mid v$ $\rangle$: Outputs a decided value v of consensus.

Properties:

    VBC1 and **VBC3–VBC4:** Same as properties WBC1 and WBC3–WBC4 in weak Byzantine consensus (Module 5.10).

    VBC2: *Anchored validity:* Every correct process only decides a value v such that $P(v) = \text{TRUE}$. Moreover, if all processes are correct and propose v, then no correct process decides a value different from v.

A solution for the requested transformation, called "From Anchored Validity to Strong Validity," is shown in Algorithm 5.24 and provides Byzantine consensus based on a validated Byzantine consensus abstraction.

The transformation adds one round of point-to-point message exchange among the processes, in which they sign and send their proposal values to each other, before invoking validated Byzantine consensus. Any value that has been proposed by more than f processes, as certified by their signatures, is considered valid, as is the default value $\square$.

If a process observes a value proposed by more than f processes, it proposes this value for validated consensus. As it may be that all correct processes propose different values, the algorithm may also propose the default value $\square$ once it has received $N - f$ point-to-point messages with valid signatures.

As shown in Exercise 5.10, if the domain is binary, this method actually guarantees that the Byzantine consensus primitive never decides $\square$.

Correctness. The transformation requires that $N > 3f$. Every correct process eventually receives PROPOSAL messages with valid signatures from all $N - f$ correct processes. If all correct processes propose the same value v then every correct process proposes v for validated consensus, because $N - 2f > f$ and there are only f Byzantine processes. In any case, a proposal for validated consensus must be justified with signatures from more than f processes or must contain the value $\square$; the *validproposed* predicate ensures this. Hence, the *strong validity* property follows.

The other properties of Byzantine consensus follow directly from the algorithm and from the underlying validated Byzantine consensus primitive.

Algorithm 5.24: From Anchored Validity to Strong Validity

Implements:
    ByzantineConsensus, **instance** bc.

Uses:
    AuthPerfectPointToPointLinks, **instance** al;
    ValidatedByzantineConsensus, **instance** vbc, with predicate $validproposed(\cdot)$.

function $validproposed((v, \Sigma))$ **returns** Boolean **is**
    if $\#(\{p \in \Pi \mid verifysig(p, bc\|\text{PROPOSAL}\|v, \Sigma[p]) = \text{TRUE}\}) > f$ **then**
        return TRUE;
    else if $v = \square$ **then**
        return TRUE;
    else
        return FALSE;

upon event $\langle\, bc, Init \,\rangle$ **do**
    $proposals := [\bot]^N$; $\Sigma := [\bot]^N$;

upon event $\langle\, bc, Propose \mid v \,\rangle$ **do**
    $\sigma := sign(self, bc\|\text{PROPOSAL}\|v)$;
    forall $q \in \Pi$ **do**
        trigger $\langle\, al, Send \mid q, [\text{PROPOSE}, v, \sigma] \,\rangle$;

upon event $\langle\, al, Deliver \mid p, [\text{PROPOSE}, v, \sigma] \,\rangle$ **do**
    if $proposals[p] = \bot \land verifysig(p, bc\|\text{PROPOSAL}\|v, \sigma)$ **then**
        $proposals[p] := v$; $\Sigma[p] := \sigma$;

upon exists $v \neq \bot$ such that $\#(\{p \in \Pi \mid proposals[p] = v\}) > f$ **do**
    $proposals := [\bot]^N$;
    trigger $\langle\, vbc, Propose \mid (v, \Sigma) \,\rangle$;

upon $\#(proposals) \geq N - f$ **do**
    $proposals := [\bot]^N$;
    trigger $\langle\, vbc, Propose \mid (\square, \Sigma) \,\rangle$;

upon event $\langle\, vbc, Decide \mid (v', \Sigma') \,\rangle$ **do**
    trigger $\langle\, bc, Decide \mid v' \,\rangle$;

Performance. The algorithm adds one communication step to the underlying validated Byzantine consensus abstraction with $O(N^2)$ additional messages.

Solution 5.12: Algorithm 5.25, called "Echo Conditional Collect," implements a conditional collect abstraction and uses no digital signatures. Its relation to Algorithm 5.16, which also implemented conditional collect but used signatures, is similar to the relation between Algorithm 3.16 ("Authenticated Echo Broadcast") and Algorithm 3.17 ("Signed Echo Broadcast") for Byzantine consistent broadcast.

To start the algorithm, every correct process broadcasts a SEND message containing m to all processes using an authenticated perfect point-to-point links instance al.

Algorithm 5.25: Echo Conditional Collect

Implements:
    ConditionalCollect, **instance** cc, with leader ℓ and output predicate C.

Uses:
    AuthPerfectPointToPointLinks, **instance** al.

upon event $\langle\ cc,\ Init\ \rangle$ **do**
    $received := [\text{FALSE}]^N$;
    $echos := [\bot]^N \times [\bot]^N$;
    $messages := [\text{UNDEFINED}]^N$;   // only leader ℓ
    $choice := \bot$; $collected := \text{FALSE}$;

upon event $\langle\ cc,\ Input\ |\ m\ \rangle$ **do**
    forall $q \in \Pi$ **do**
        trigger $\langle\ al,\ Send\ |\ q, [\text{SEND}, m]\ \rangle$;

upon event $\langle\ al,\ Deliver\ |\ p, [\text{SEND}, m]\ \rangle$ **do**
    if $received[p] = \text{FALSE}$ **then**
        $received[p] := \text{TRUE}$;
        forall $q \in \Pi$ **do**
            trigger $\langle\ al,\ Send\ |\ q, [\text{ECHO}, p, m]\ \rangle$;

upon event $\langle\ al,\ Deliver\ |\ p, [\text{ECHO}, s, m]\ \rangle$ **do**
    $echos[s, p] := m$;
    if $self = \ell\ \wedge\ \#(\{q\ |\ echos[s, q] = m\}) > 2f\ \wedge\ messages[s] = \bot$ **then**
        $messages[s] := m$;   // only leader ℓ

upon $self = \ell\ \wedge\ \#(messages) \geq N - f\ \wedge\ C(messages)$ **do**   // only leader ℓ
    forall $q \in \Pi$ **do**
        trigger $\langle\ al,\ Send\ |\ q, [\text{CHOICE}, messages]\ \rangle$;
    $messages := [\text{UNDEFINED}]^N$;

upon event $\langle\ al,\ Deliver\ |\ \ell, [\text{CHOICE}, M]\ \rangle$ **do**
    if $choice = \bot\ \wedge\ \#(M) \geq N - f\ \wedge\ C(M)$ **then**
        $choice := M$;

upon $choice \neq \bot\ \wedge\ collected = \text{FALSE}\ \wedge$ (**forall** $s \in \Pi$ such that
        $choice[s] = m$, it holds $\#(\{q\ |\ echos[s, q] = m\}) > f$) **do**
    $collected := \text{TRUE}$;
    trigger $\langle\ cc,\ Collected\ |\ choice\ \rangle$;

Whenever a process al-delivers a SEND message containing some m from sender p (for the first time), it broadcasts a message [ECHO, p, m] to all processes over the authenticated links. Until the end of the algorithm, every process continuously counts how many ECHO messages that it delivers (counting only those from distinct senders) with respect to every other process.

The leader process ℓ initializes an N-vector *messages* to $[\text{UNDEFINED}]^N$ and whenever it al-delivers more than $2f$ messages [ECHO, s, m] with the same m for some process s from distinct senders, it sets $messages[s] := m$. The leader continues to collect messages like this until *messages* contains at least $N - f$ entries different from UNDEFINED and $C(messages)$ holds. Once this is the case, the leader *al*-sends a message [CHOICE, *messages*] to all processes.

Finally, when a process p *al*-delivers a message [CHOICE, M] from ℓ and for every s such that $M[s] = m \neq$ UNDEFINED, process p receives also more than f messages [ECHO, s, m], then p outputs the collected vector M. Note that, this involves waiting for ECHO and CHOICE messages simultaneously.

Correctness. It is not difficult to verify that this algorithm implements conditional collect for $N > 3f$. Briefly, the *integrity* property follows because for every collected M with $M[s] \neq$ UNDEFINED where process s is correct, at least one correct process has sent an ECHO message containing $M[s]$ and thus, process s must also have input $M[s]$.

Furthermore, if the leader ℓ is correct, even when no faulty process sends any ECHO message then there are $N - f > 2f$ correct processes that do send ECHO messages for every input they receive from a correct process. As the correct processes input compliant messages, ℓ eventually broadcasts a CHOICE message with M that satisfies $C(M)$ and with at least $N - f$ entries different from UNDEFINED. Every correct process that receives this message is also guaranteed to receive f or more ECHO messages for every entry, as required to make progress; hence, it collects the vector M from ℓ that satisfies $C(M)$, as required by the *consistency* and *termination* properties.

Performance. The algorithm incurs three communication steps, as all processes wait for the CHOICE message from the leader and the leader may send it only after receiving enough ECHO messages. The number of messages is $O(N^2)$.

Compared to Algorithm 5.16, the algorithm uses only authenticated links but no digital signatures; verifying the authenticity of $O(N^2)$ point-to-point messages is usually much more efficient than verifying $O(N)$ digital signatures. On the other hand, Algorithm 5.16 uses only $O(N)$ messages. Thus, the "Echo Conditional Collect" algorithm trades lower computational efficiency for an increased number of messages compared to the "Signed Conditional Collect" algorithm.

Solution 5.13: The execution shown in Fig. 5.8 may result as follows. Suppose the Byzantine process q does not input any value. Then

$$S = [[1, x, ws_p], \text{UNDEFINED}, [0, y, ws_r], [0, \bot, ws_s]].$$

As the leader r is correct, all correct processes collect the same output vector S. This vector binds timestamp 1 to x, because timestamp 1 is the maximum timestamp in the three defined entries, and because $(1, x) \in ws_p$ and $(1, x) \in ws_r$. Therefore, the correct processes write value x in epoch 7. When processes p and r receive enough WRITE messages, they change their state to $(7, x)$ and each broadcast an ACCEPT message. These messages, together with a forged ACCEPT message with value x from the Byzantine process q, cause process p to *bep*-decide x. Process s *bep*-aborts before it sends an ACCEPT message.

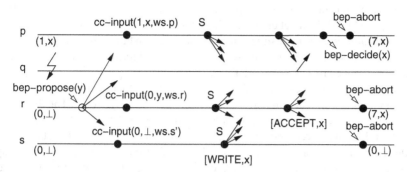

Figure 5.8: Sample execution of a Byzantine epoch consensus instance, with timestamp 7 and leader r, in which process p *bep*-decides x

5.10 Chapter Notes

- The consensus problem is the single most important problem in distributed computing and has become a recurrent theme during the development of the field. The consensus problem has originally been introduced in its Byzantine variant by Lamport, Shostak, and Pease (1982) for synchronous systems, under the name of "Byzantine agreement." When considered in asynchronous systems, it has commonly been called "consensus."

- After Fischer, Lynch, and Paterson (1985) had proved that no deterministic algorithm implements consensus in a fail-silent model, even if only one process fails, alternative models were explored. On the one hand, Dwork, Lynch, and Stockmeyer (1988) introduced models of partially synchronous systems, where reaching consensus becomes possible. On the other hand, Ben-Or (1983) and Rabin (1983) proposed to use randomized algorithms for consensus. Many consensus algorithms have used the fail-stop system model or the fail-noisy system model, which represent partially synchronous systems. The timing information in these models is available via the failure-detector abstraction. It is an elegant way to encapsulate the timing assumptions of partially synchronous systems (Chandra and Toueg 1996).

- Our fail-stop consensus algorithms (the "Flooding Consensus" and "Hierarchical Consensus" algorithms, together with their uniform variants, from Algorithms 5.1–5.4) go back to the earliest published consensus algorithms by Lamport, Shostak, and Pease (1982). These algorithms are also reminiscent of the "phase-king" approach used for implementing consensus in synchronous systems (Berman and Garay 1989).

- The "Leader-Driven Consensus" algorithm from Sect. 5.3 is a modular formulation of the "Paxos" consensus algorithm, which can be extracted from the total-order broadcast algorithm with the same name (Lamport 1998). A total-order broadcast algorithm with a similar structure has previously been used in viewstamped replication (Oki and Liskov 1988). The Paxos algorithm has been analyzed in a number of papers (De Prisco, Lampson, and Lynch 2000; Lampson 2001). Boichat et al. (2003a,b) present the Paxos algorithm in terms of an abortable consensus abstraction. The variant given here is from Cachin (2009).

- The "Rotating Coordinator" fail-noisy consensus algorithm (from Exercise 5.7) was introduced by Chandra and Toueg (1996).

- The "Leader-Driven Consensus" algorithm and the "Rotating Coordinator" algorithm both implement uniform consensus in the fail-noisy model. The difference is that the former algorithm uses the eventual leader detector (Ω) whereas the latter relies on an eventually perfect failure detector ($\Diamond\mathcal{P}$). In practice, the leader-detector-based algorithm often works faster. If Ω outputs an accurate estimate of a correct leader process ℓ, the messages between ℓ and all other processes are not delayed, and process ℓ becomes the first leader, then the "Leader-Driven Consensus" algorithm will terminate very fast. On the other hand, the "Rotating Coordinator" algorithm proceeds according to a fixed order among the processes and may waste several rounds with faulty coordinators until it hits a correct coordinator process, even if $\Diamond\mathcal{P}$ outputs accurate failure information.

- Lower bounds for consensus using failure detectors were first given by Chandra, Hadzilacos, and Toueg (1996) and refined later (Delporte-Gallet et al. 2002, 2004, 2010).

- Guerraoui (2000) shows that any fail-noisy algorithm that solves regular consensus also solves uniform consensus (Exercise 5.5). Furthermore, Chandra and Toueg (1996) and Guerraoui (2000) show that any fail-noisy consensus algorithm (using an unreliable failure detector) requires a majority of correct processes (Exercise 5.6).

- The randomized consensus algorithms in the fail-silent model presented in this chapter are from Ezhilchelvan, Mostefaoui, and Raynal (2001). They generalize older randomized algorithms for binary consensus (Ben-Or 1983; Rabin 1983). The "Randomized Binary Consensus" algorithm and the "Rotating Coordinator" algorithm are members of the same family of indulgent consensus algorithms (Guerraoui and Raynal 2004).

- The "Independent Choice" implementation of the common coin corresponds to the first randomized consensus algorithm of Ben-Or (1983). It has exponentially small (in N) matching probability, which lets our consensus implementations based on it terminate in an exponential number of steps (in N) only. Rabin (1983) proposed two coin implementations with perfect matching probability: the "Beacon" coin and an implementation from predistributed information, based on cryptographic secret sharing (Shamir 1979). Canetti and Rabin (1993) subsequently introduced the first common coin without predistributed secrets that leads to efficient consensus algorithms (that is, they terminate in a polynomial number of steps instead of exponentially many). A practical common coin implementation from distributed cryptography has been developed by Cachin, Kursawe, and Shoup (2005). All these algorithms use the randomized fail-arbitrary model, and can typically be simplified for the fail-silent model.

- After the Byzantine agreement problem formulated by Lamport, Shostak, and Pease (1982) had triggered interest in the consensus abstraction, the work on consensus in asynchronous systems focused on crash-stop processes for a long time. Only more recently, Byzantine consensus and algorithms in the fail-noisy-arbitrary model have again received considerable attention. The revived interest started with the "practical Byzantine fault-tolerance" (PBFT) algorithm from the work of Castro and Liskov (2002). Several variants and optimizations of it have been explored since (Doudou et al. 2005; Abd-El-Malek et al. 2005; Abraham et al. 2006; Martin and Alvisi 2006; Kotla et al. 2009). Most of them are formulated as Byzantine total-order broadcast algorithms (see Sect. 6.2) with a very practical focus.
- Our "Byzantine Leader-Driven Consensus" algorithm is the Byzantine consensus algorithm inherent in PBFT (Castro and Liskov 2002); PBFT itself implements a Byzantine total-order broadcast abstraction (see Chap. 6.2). More precisely, with the two optimizations mentioned in Sect. 5.6.4 applied, the algorithm involves an initial message from the leader to all processes and two rounds of echoing the message among all processes. This is the same communication pattern as first used in the reliable broadcast algorithm of Bracha (1987) (our "Authenticated Double-Echo Broadcast" algorithm from Chap. 3), and it is also used during the normal-case operation of a view in the PBFT algorithm.
- As becomes clear from our formulation, the "Leader-Driven Consensus" algorithm in the fail-noisy model and the "Byzantine Leader-Driven Consensus" algorithm in the fail-arbitrary model use the same basic structure. This resemblance between the original algorithms, Paxos and viewstamped replication on the one hand (Lamport 1998; Oki and Liskov 1988), and PBFT on the other hand (Castro and Liskov 2002), is not immediately evident. It has only become clear over time, through a series of works addressing their similarity (Lampson 2001; Li et al. 2007; Liskov 2010; Milosevic et al. 2009; Cachin 2009).
- The conditional collect primitive is used by the "Byzantine Read/Write Epoch Consensus" algorithm, which implements the Byzantine epoch consensus abstraction. The primitive is inspired by the weak interactive consistency (WIC) abstraction defined by Milosevic, Hutle, and Schiper (2009), who used it to simplify Byzantine consensus algorithms. Compared to WIC, conditional collect introduces a leader into the specification for ensuring termination. The "Echo Conditional Collect" algorithm for conditional collect without signatures (from Exercise 5.12) is contained in PBFT (Castro and Liskov 2002).
- The validated Byzantine consensus primitive and the anchored validity notion (from Exercise 5.11) were introduced by Cachin et al. (2001). A similar notion of validity in the fail-arbitrary model has been used by Ben-Or and El-Yaniv (2003).

6. Consensus Variants

God does not often clap his hands. When he does, everybody should dance.
(African Proverb)

This chapter describes variants of the consensus abstraction introduced in the previous chapter. These variants are motivated by applications of consensus to areas like fault-tolerant, replicated services, and distributed databases.

In the variants we consider here, just like in consensus, the processes need to make consistent decisions, such as agreeing on one common value. However, most of the abstractions extend or change the interface of consensus, in order to satisfy the specific coordination requirements of an application.

The abstractions we will study here include *total-order broadcast, terminating reliable broadcast, fast consensus, (nonblocking) atomic commitment, group membership,* and *view synchrony.* We will mainly focus on fail-stop algorithms for implementing these abstractions. But we also consider *Byzantine total-order broadcast* and *Byzantine fast consensus* and give implementations for them in the fail-arbitrary model. Some further variants of the total-order broadcast abstraction are discussed in the exercise section. But other variants of consensus represent unexplored territory, in the sense that determining adequate means to specify and implement these abstractions in other system models is an area of current research.

6.1 Total-Order Broadcast

6.1.1 Overview

Earlier in the book (in Sect. 3.9), we discussed FIFO-order and causal-order (reliable) broadcast abstractions and their implementation. FIFO-order broadcast requires that messages from the same process are delivered in the order that the sender has broadcast them. For messages from different senders, FIFO-order broadcast does not guarantee any particular order of delivery. Causal-order broadcast

C. Cachin et al., *Introduction to Reliable and Secure Distributed Programming,*
DOI: 10.1007/978-3-642-15260-3_6,
© Springer-Verlag Berlin Heidelberg 2011

enforces a global ordering for all messages that causally depend on each other: such messages need to be delivered in the same order and this order must respect causality. But causal-order broadcast does not enforce any ordering among messages that are causally unrelated, or "concurrent" in this sense. In particular, if a process p broadcasts a message m_1 and a process q concurrently broadcasts a message m_2 then the messages might be delivered in different orders by the processes. For instance, p might deliver first m_1 and then m_2, whereas q might deliver first m_2 and then m_1.

A *total-order (reliable) broadcast* abstraction orders all messages, even those from different senders and those that are not causally related. More precisely, total-order broadcast is a reliable broadcast communication abstraction which ensures that all processes deliver the same messages in a common global order. Whereas reliable broadcast ensures that processes agree on the same *set* of messages they deliver, total-order broadcast ensures that they agree on the same *sequence* of messages; the set of delivered messages is now ordered.

The total-order broadcast abstraction is sometimes also called *atomic broadcast* because the message delivery occurs as if the broadcast were an indivisible "atomic" action: the message is delivered to all or to none of the processes and, if the message is delivered, every other message is ordered either before or after this message. This section considers total-order broadcast among crash-stop process abstractions. Total-order broadcast with Byzantine processes is the subject of Sect. 6.2.

Total-order broadcast is the key abstraction for maintaining consistency among multiple replicas that implement one logical service, whose behavior can be captured by a deterministic state machine. A state machine consists of variables representing its state together with commands that update these variables and may produce some output. Commands consist of *deterministic* programs, such that the outputs of the state machine are solely determined by the initial state and the sequence of commands previously executed. Most practical services can be modeled like this. Any service implemented by the state machine can be made fault-tolerant by replicating it on different processes. Total-order broadcast ensures that all replicas deliver the commands from different clients in the same order, and hence maintain the same state.

For instance, this paradigm can be applied to implement highly available shared objects of arbitrary types in a distributed system, that is, objects with much more powerful semantics than the read-write (register) objects studied earlier in the book (Chap. 4). According to the state-machine replication paradigm, each process hosts a replica of the object. A client broadcasts every method invocation on the object to all replicas using the total-order broadcast primitive. This will ensure that all replicas keep the same state and that all responses are equal. In short, the use of total-order broadcast ensures that the object is highly available, yet it appears as if it were a single logical entity accessed in a sequential and failure-free manner, which provides operations that act atomically on its state. We will return to this topic in the exercise section.

Module 6.1: Interface and properties of regular total-order broadcast

Module:

  Name: TotalOrderBroadcast, **instance** *tob*.

Events:

  Request: ⟨ *tob, Broadcast* | m ⟩: Broadcasts a message m to all processes.

  Indication: ⟨ *tob, Deliver* | p, m ⟩: Delivers a message m broadcast by process p.

Properties:

  TOB1: *Validity:* If a correct process p broadcasts a message m, then p eventually delivers m.

  TOB2: *No duplication:* No message is delivered more than once.

  TOB3: *No creation:* If a process delivers a message m with sender s, then m was previously broadcast by process s.

  TOB4: *Agreement:* If a message m is delivered by some correct process, then m is eventually delivered by every correct process.

  TOB5: *Total order:* Let m_1 and m_2 be any two messages and suppose p and q are any two correct processes that deliver m_1 and m_2. If p delivers m_1 before m_2, then q delivers m_1 before m_2.

6.1.2 Specifications

Many specifications of the total-order broadcast abstraction can be considered. We focus here on two variants that both extend a corresponding reliable broadcast abstraction. The first is a regular variant that ensures total ordering only among the correct processes. The second is a uniform variant that ensures total ordering with respect to all processes, including the faulty processes as well.

The specification of a *regular total-order broadcast* abstraction is depicted in Module 6.1. The interface is the same as in the (regular) reliable broadcast abstraction (Module 3.2 from Sect. 3.3), and also its first four properties (TOB1–TOB4) are the same as before (properties RB1–RB4). The only difference consists in the added *total order* property.

The second specification defines *uniform total-order broadcast* and is depicted in Module 6.2. The interface is the same as in the uniform reliable broadcast abstraction (Module 3.3); its first four properties (UTOB1–UTOB4) map directly to those of uniform reliable broadcast (URB1–URB4) in Sect. 3.4 and extend it with the *uniform total order* property.

Other combinations of the *total order* or *uniform total order* properties with reliable and uniform reliable broadcast properties are possible and lead to slightly different specifications. For conciseness, we omit describing all the corresponding modules and refer to an exercise (at the end of the chapter) for a logged total-order broadcast abstraction.

Module 6.2: Interface and properties of uniform total-order broadcast

Module:

    Name: UniformTotalOrderBroadcast, **instance** *utob*.

Events:

    Request: $\langle$ *utob*, *Broadcast* $\mid m$ $\rangle$: Broadcasts a message m to all processes.

    Indication: $\langle$ *utob*, *Deliver* $\mid p, m$ $\rangle$: Delivers a message m broadcast by process p.

Properties:

    UTOB1–UTOB3: Same as properties TOB1–TOB3 in regular total-order broadcast (Module 6.1).

    UTOB4: *Uniform agreement:* If a message m is delivered by some process (whether correct or faulty), then m is eventually delivered by every correct process.

    UTOB5: *Uniform total order:* Let m_1 and m_2 be any two messages and suppose p and q are any two processes that deliver m_1 and m_2 (whether correct or faulty). If p delivers m_1 before m_2, then q delivers m_1 before m_2.

It is important to note that the *total order* property is orthogonal to the FIFO-order and causal-order properties discussed in Sect. 3.9. It is possible that a total-order broadcast abstraction does not respect causal order. On the other hand, as we pointed out, FIFO-order broadcast and causal-order broadcast abstractions do not enforce total order: the processes may deliver some messages in different order to different processes.

6.1.3 Fail-Silent Algorithm: Consensus-Based Total-Order Broadcast

In the following, we give a total-order broadcast algorithm that implements the abstraction of Module 6.1 and is called "Consensus-Based Total Order" because it relies on consensus. The pseudo code is shown in Algorithm 6.1. It uses a reliable broadcast abstraction and multiple instances of a (regular) consensus abstraction as underlying building blocks.

The intuition behind Algorithm 6.1 is the following. Messages are first disseminated using a reliable broadcast instance with identifier *rb*. Recall that reliable broadcast imposes no particular order on delivering the messages, so every process simply stores the delivered messages in a set of unordered messages. At any point in time, it may be that no two processes have the same sets of unordered messages in their sets. The processes then use the consensus abstraction to decide on one set, order the messages in this set, and finally deliver them.

More precisely, the algorithm implementing a total-order broadcast instance *tob* works in consecutive rounds. As long as new messages are broadcast, the processes keep on moving sequentially from one round to the other. There is one consensus

---

Algorithm 6.1: Consensus-Based Total-Order Broadcast

Implements:
    TotalOrderBroadcast, **instance** *tob*.

Uses:
    ReliableBroadcast, **instance** *rb*;
    Consensus (multiple instances).

upon event ⟨ *tob*, *Init* ⟩ **do**
    unordered := ∅;
    delivered := ∅;
    round := 1;
    wait := FALSE;

upon event ⟨ *tob*, *Broadcast* | *m* ⟩ **do**
    trigger ⟨ *rb*, *Broadcast* | *m* ⟩;

upon event ⟨ *rb*, *Deliver* | *p*, *m* ⟩ **do**
    if *m* ∉ *delivered* **then**
        unordered := *unordered* ∪ {(*p*, *m*)};

upon *unordered* ≠ ∅ ∧ *wait* = FALSE **do**
    wait := TRUE;
    Initialize a new instance *c.round* of consensus;
    trigger ⟨ *c.round*, *Propose* | *unordered* ⟩;

upon event ⟨ *c.r*, *Decide* | *decided* ⟩ **such that** *r* = *round* **do**
    forall (*s*, *m*) ∈ *sort*(*decided*) **do**   // by the order in the resulting sorted list
        trigger ⟨ *tob*, *Deliver* | *s*, *m* ⟩;
    delivered := *delivered* ∪ *decided*;
    unordered := *unordered* \ *decided*;
    round := *round* + 1;
    wait := FALSE;

---

instance for every round, such that the instance of round r has identifier $c.r$, for $r = 1, 2, \ldots$. The processes use the consensus instance of round r to decide on a set of messages to assign to that round number. Every process then *tob*-delivers all messages in the decided set according to some deterministic order, which is the same at every process. This will ensure the *total order* property.

The r-th consensus instance, invoked in round r, decides on the messages to deliver in round r. Suppose that every correct process has *tob*-delivered the same messages up to round $r - 1$. The messages of round r are delivered according to a deterministic and locally computable order, agreed upon by all processes in advance, such as the lexicographic order on the binary representation of the message content or based on low-level message identifiers. Once that the processes have decided on a set of messages for round r, they simply apply a deterministic function $sort(\cdot)$ to the decided set messages, the function returns an ordered list of messages, and the processes deliver the messages in the given order. Hence, the algorithm ensures

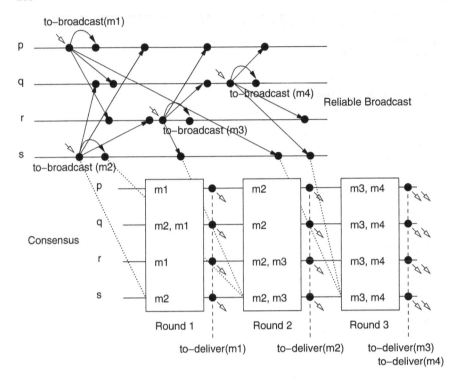

Figure 6.1: Sample execution of consensus-based total-order broadcast

that there is one global sequence of messages that are *tob*-delivered by the correct processes.

In each instance of consensus, every process starts with a (possibly different) set of messages to be ordered. Each process simply proposes the set of messages it has already *rb*-delivered (from the reliable broadcast primitive) and not yet *tob*-delivered (according to the total-order semantics). The properties of consensus ensure that all processes decide the same set of messages for the instance. In addition, Algorithm 6.1 uses a flag *wait* to ensure that a new round is not started before the previous round has terminated.

An execution of the algorithm is illustrated in Fig. 6.1. The figure is unfolded into two parallel flows: that of the reliable broadcasts, used to disseminate the messages, and that of the consensus instances, used to order the messages. Messages received from the reliable broadcast module are proposed to the next instance of consensus. For instance, process s proposes message m_2 to the first instance of consensus. As the first instance of consensus decides message m_1, process s resubmits m_2 (along with m_3 that it has received meanwhile) to the second instance of consensus.

Correctness. The *no creation* property follows from the *no creation* property of the reliable broadcast abstraction and from the *validity* property of the consensus abstraction. The *no duplication* property follows from the *no duplication* property of the reliable broadcast abstraction and from the *integrity* property of the consensus abstraction, combined with the check that no message contained in the variable *delivered* is added to the set *unordered*.

Consider the *agreement* property. Assume that some correct process p *to*-delivers some message m. According to the algorithm, p must have decided a set of messages that contains m in some round. Every correct process eventually decides the same set of messages in that round because of the algorithm and the *termination* property of consensus. Hence, every correct process eventually *to*-delivers m.

Consider the *validity* property of total-order broadcast, and let p be some correct process that *to*-broadcasts a message m. Assume by contradiction that p never *to*-delivers m. This means that m is never included in a set of decided messages at any correct process. Due the *validity* property of reliable broadcast, every correct process eventually *rb*-delivers m. Therefore, there is some round in which every correct process proposes a set of unordered messages to consensus that contains m. The *validity* property of consensus now ensures that p decides a batch of messages that includes m and *to*-delivers m in the same round.

Consider now the *total order* property. Let p and q be any two correct processes that *to*-deliver some message m_2. Assume that p *to*-delivers some distinct message m_1 before m_2. If p *to*-delivers m_1 and m_2 in the same round then due to the *agreement* property of consensus, q must have decided the same set of messages in that round. Thus, q also *to*-delivers m_1 before m_2, as we assume that the messages decided in one round are *to*-delivered in the same order by every process, determined in a fixed way from the set of decided messages. Assume that m_1 is contained in the set of messages decided by p in an earlier round than m_2. Because of the *agreement* property of consensus, q must have decided the same set of messages in the earlier round, which contains m_1. Given that processes proceed sequentially from one round to the other, q must also have *to*-delivered m_1 before m_2.

Performance. To *to*-deliver a message when no failures occur, and by merging a fail-stop reliable broadcast algorithm with a fail-stop consensus algorithm as presented in previous chapters, three communication steps and $O(N)$ messages are required.

Variant. By replacing the regular consensus abstraction with a uniform one, Algorithm 6.1 implements a uniform total-order broadcast abstraction.

6.2 Byzantine Total-Order Broadcast

6.2.1 Overview

Total-order broadcast is an important primitive also in the fail-arbitrary model. Intuitively, it gives the same guarantees as total-order broadcast in a system with crash-stop processes, namely that every correct process delivers the same sequence of messages over time.

Recall the Byzantine broadcast primitives from Chap. 3, in which every instance only delivered one message. Because total-order broadcast concerns multiple messages, its specification does not directly extend these basic one-message primitives, but uses the same overall approach as the total-order broadcast abstraction with crash-stop processes. In particular, every process may repeatedly broadcast a message and every process may deliver many messages.

For implementing total-order broadcast in the fail-arbitrary model, however, one cannot simply take the algorithm from the fail-silent model in the previous section and replace the underlying consensus primitive with Byzantine consensus. We present an algorithm with the same underlying structure, but suitably extended for the fail-arbitrary model. But first we introduce the details of the specification.

6.2.2 Specification

A *Byzantine total-order broadcast* abstraction lets every process repeatedly broadcast messages by triggering a request event $\langle$ *Broadcast* $\mid m \rangle$. An indication event $\langle$ *Deliver* $\mid p, m \rangle$ delivers a message m with sender p to a process. For an instance *btob* of Byzantine total-order broadcast, we also say a process *btob*-broadcasts a message and *btob*-delivers a message.

The sender identification in the output holds only when process p is correct, because a Byzantine process may behave arbitrarily. The abstraction ensures the same *integrity* property as the Byzantine broadcast primitives of Chap. 3, in the sense that every message delivered with sender p was actually broadcast by p, if p is correct, and could not have been forged by Byzantine processes. The other properties of Byzantine total-order broadcast are either exactly the same as those of total-order broadcast among crash-stop processes (*validity*, *agreement*, and *total order*) or correspond directly to the previous abstraction (*no duplication*). The specification is given in Module 6.3.

6.2.3 Fail-Noisy-Arbitrary Algorithm:
Rotating Sender Byzantine Broadcast

Implementations of Byzantine broadcast abstractions are more complex than their counterparts with crash-stop processes because there are no useful failure-detector abstractions in the fail-arbitrary model. But an algorithm may rely on the eventual leader detector primitive (Module 2.9) that is usually accessed through an underlying consensus abstraction.

Here we introduce Algorithm 6.2, called "Rotating Sender Byzantine Broadcast," which relies on a Byzantine consensus primitive, similar to the "Consensus-Based Total-Order Broadcast" algorithm from the previous section. As before, the processes proceed in rounds and invoke one instance of Byzantine consensus in every round. Furthermore, every process disseminates the *btob*-broadcast messages using a low-level communication primitive.

However, the processes cannot simply reliably broadcast the *btob*-broadcast messages and propose a set of *btob*-undelivered messages received from reliable

---

Module 6.3: Interface and properties of Byzantine total-order broadcast

Module:

Name: ByzantineTotalOrderBroadcast, **instance** *btob*.

Events:

Request: $\langle$ *btob, Broadcast* | *m* $\rangle$: Broadcasts a message *m* to all processes.

Indication: $\langle$ *btob, Deliver* | *p, m* $\rangle$: Delivers a message *m* broadcast by process *p*.

Properties:

BTOB1: *Validity:* If a correct process *p* broadcasts a message *m*, then *p* eventually delivers *m*.

BTOB2: *No duplication:* No correct process delivers the same message more than once.

BTOB3: *Integrity:* If some correct process delivers a message *m* with sender *p* and process *p* is correct, then *m* was previously broadcast by *p*.

BTOB4: *Agreement:* If a message *m* is delivered by some correct process, then *m* is eventually delivered by every correct process.

BTOB5: *Total order:* Let m_1 and m_2 be any two messages and suppose *p* and *q* are any two correct processes that deliver m_1 and m_2. If *p* delivers m_1 before m_2, then *q* delivers m_1 before m_2.

---

broadcast to consensus. The reason lies in the more demanding validity properties of Byzantine consensus compared to consensus with processes that may only crash. In the (strong) Byzantine consensus primitive, a "useful" decision value that carries some undelivered messages results only if *all* correct processes propose exactly the same input. But without any further structure on the message dissemination pattern, the correct processes may never propose the same value, especially because further *btob*-broadcast messages may arrive continuously. Weak Byzantine consensus offers no feasible alternative either, because it ensures validity only if all processes are correct. In the presence of a single Byzantine process, it may never output any useful decision.

The solution realized by Algorithm 6.2 circumvents this problem by imposing more structure on what may be proposed in a consensus instance. The algorithm proceeds in global rounds; in round *r*, a process only proposes a single message for consensus and one that is *btob*-broadcast by the *designated sender* for the round, determined from the round number by the function *leader*($\cdot$) introduced before.

More precisely, a process first relays every *btob*-broadcast message to all others in a DATA message over an authenticated link primitive *al*. Every DATA message contains a sequence number, assigned by the sender, to provide FIFO order among its DATA messages. Every correct process, therefore, *al*-delivers the same ordered sequence of DATA messages from every correct sender. The receiver stores the

Algorithm 6.2: Rotating Sender Byzantine Broadcast

Implements:
    ByzantineTotalOrderBroadcast, **instance** *btob*.

Uses:
    AuthPerfectPointToPointLinks, **instance** *al*;
    ByzantineConsensus (multiple instances).

upon event ⟨ *btob, Init* ⟩ **do**
    $unordered := ([])^N$;
    $delivered := \emptyset$;
    $round := 1$;
    $wait :=$ FALSE;
    $lsn := 0$;
    $next := [1]^N$;

upon event ⟨ *btob, Broadcast* | *m* ⟩ **do**
    $lsn := lsn + 1$;
    forall $q \in \Pi$ **do**
        trigger ⟨ *al, Send* | *q*, [DATA, *lsn, m*] ⟩;

upon event ⟨ *al, Deliver* | *p*, [DATA, *sn, m*] ⟩ **such that** $sn = next[p]$ **do**
    $next[p] := next[p] + 1$;
    if $m \notin delivered$ **then**
        append($unordered[p], m$);

upon exists p such that $unordered[p] \neq [] \wedge wait =$ FALSE **do**
    $wait :=$ TRUE;
    Initialize a new instance *bc.round* of Byzantine consensus;
    if $unordered[leader(round)] \neq []$ **then**
        $m :=$ head($unordered[leader(round)]$);
    else
        $m := \square$;
    trigger ⟨ *bc.round, Propose* | *m* ⟩;

upon event ⟨ *bc.r, Decide* | *m* ⟩ **such that** $r = round$ **do**
    $s :=$ leader($round$);
    if $m \neq \square \wedge m \notin delivered$ **then**
        $delivered := delivered \cup \{m\}$;
        trigger ⟨ *btob, Deliver* | *s, m* ⟩;
    remove($unordered[s], m$);
    $round := round + 1$;
    $wait :=$ FALSE;

undelivered *btob*-broadcast messages from every sender in a queue according to the order of their arrival.

Concurrently, every process runs through rounds Byzantine consensus instances. In every round, it proposes the first message in the queue corresponding to the designated sender s of the round for consensus. When a process finds no message in the queue of process s, it proposes the symbol $\square$ for consensus. When consensus decides on a message, the process *btob*-delivers it; if consensus decides □then no message is *btob*-delivered in this round. (Recall that Byzantine consensus may decide □ unless all correct processes have proposed the same value.)

The variable *unordered* is an array of lists, one for every process in the system. It is initialized to an array of empty lists, denoted by $([])^N$. Lists can be manipulated with the operations introduced before, in Chap. 3: an element x can be appended to a list L by the function *append*(L, x), and an element x can be removed from L by the function *remove*(L, x). We also use a new function *head*(L) here, which returns the first element in L.

Correctness. Note that the algorithm preserves FIFO order by design, and *btob*-delivers messages from the same sender in the order they were *btob*-broadcast. Intuitively, the algorithm maintains N ordered message queues, one for every process, and propagates the messages from every sender through the corresponding queue. These queues are synchronized at all correct processes. Every round of consensus may cut off the first message in each queue and deliver it, or may decide not to deliver a message.

It may happen that the consensus instance of a round decides a message sent by sender s, but some process p does not find the message in the queue *unordered*$[s]$. It is safe for the process to deliver the message nevertheless, because the queue must be empty; this follows because a correct s sends its messages in the same order to all processes. Hence, whenever any correct process enters a new round, the queue *unordered*$[s]$ contains a unique message at its head or is empty.

The *validity* property now follows easily because a *btob*-broadcast message m from a correct sender is eventually contained in the sender's queue at every correct process. Eventually, there is a round corresponding to the sender of m, in which every correct process proposes m for consensus. According to the *strong validity* property of Byzantine consensus, message m is *btob*-delivered at the end of this round.

The *no duplication* property is evident from the algorithm and the checks involving the *delivered* variable. The *agreement* and *total order* properties follow from the round structure and from the *termination* and *agreement* properties of the underlying Byzantine consensus primitive.

Finally, the *integrity* property holds because a correct process, in round r, only proposes for consensus a message received over an authenticated link from the sender $s = leader(r)$ or the value □. According to the *strong validity* property of Byzantine consensus, the decided value must have been proposed by a correct process (unless it is □); therefore, the algorithm may only *btob*-deliver a message from sender s in round r.

Performance. The algorithm adds one communication step with $O(N)$ messages for every broadcast message to the cost of the underlying Byzantine consensus instances. Every delivered message requires at least one instance of Byzantine consensus, which is the most expensive part of the algorithm.

The algorithm is conceptually simple, but suffers from the problem that it may not be efficient. In particular, depending on the network scheduling, it may invoke an arbitrary number of Byzantine consensus instances until it delivers a particular message m from a correct sender in the totally ordered sequence. This happens when the algorithm *btob*-delivers messages from Byzantine senders before m or when the consensus primitive decides □.

We discuss a more efficient algorithm, which never wastes a Byzantine consensus instance without atomically delivering some message, in the exercises (at the end of the chapter).

Variant. Algorithm 6.2, our Byzantine total-order broadcast algorithm, uses Byzantine consensus in a modular way. If we would break up the modular structure and integrate the rounds of Algorithm 6.2 with the round-based and leader-based approach of the "Byzantine Leader-Driven Consensus" algorithm for Byzantine consensus, we would save several steps and obtain a much more efficient algorithm. Even more savings would be possible from integrating the resulting algorithm with the implementation of the Byzantine eventual leader-detection abstraction, which is used underneath the "Byzantine Leader-Driven Consensus" algorithm.

6.3 Terminating Reliable Broadcast

6.3.1 Overview

The goal of the reliable broadcast abstraction introduced earlier in the book (Sect. 3.3) is to ensure that if a message is delivered to a process then it is delivered to all correct processes (in the uniform variant).

As its name indicates, *terminating reliable broadcast (TRB)* is a form of reliable broadcast with a specific termination property. It is used in situations where a given process s is known to have the obligation of broadcasting some message to all processes in the system. In other words, s is an expected source of information in the system and all processes must perform some specific processing according to some message m to be delivered from the source s. All the remaining processes are thus waiting for a message from s. If s broadcasts m with best-effort guarantees and does not crash, then its message will indeed be delivered by all correct processes.

Consider now the case where process s crashes and some other process p detects that s has crashed without having seen m. Does this mean that m was not broadcast? Not really. It is possible that s crashed while broadcasting m. In fact, some processes might have delivered m whereas others might never do so. This can be problematic for an application. In our example, process p might need to know whether it should keep on waiting for m, or if it can know at some point that m will never be delivered by any process. The same issue may arise when the processes are waiting for a set of messages broadcast by multiple senders, of which some are known to broadcast a message but others might never broadcast a message.

At this point, one may think that the problem of the faulty sender could have been avoided if s had used a uniform reliable broadcast primitive to broadcast m. Unfortunately, this is not the case. Consider process p in the example just given. The use of a uniform reliable broadcast primitive would ensure that, if some other process q delivered m then p would eventually also deliver m. However, p cannot decide if it should wait for m or not. Process p has no means to distinguish the case where some process q has delivered m (and p can indeed wait for m), from the case where no process will ever deliver m (and p should definitely not keep waiting for m).

The TRB abstraction adds precisely this missing piece of information to reliable broadcast. TRB ensures that every process p either delivers the message m from the sender or some failure indication $\triangle$, denoting that m will never be delivered (by any process). This indication is given in the form of a specific message $\triangle$ delivered to the processes, such that $\triangle$ is a symbol that does not belong to the set of possible messages that processes broadcast. TRB is a variant of consensus because all processes deliver the same message, i.e., either message m from the sender or the indication $\triangle$.

TRB is similar to the Byzantine consistent broadcast and Byzantine reliable broadcast abstractions (of Sects. 3.10 and 3.11) in two ways: first, there is only one process s that sends a message and this process is known, and second, the broadcast abstraction delivers at most one message. With respect to termination, TRB differs from the Byzantine broadcast abstractions, however: When the sender s is faulty, a Byzantine broadcast abstraction may not deliver a message, but TRB always delivers an output, regardless of whether process s is correct.

6.3.2 Specification

The properties of TRB are depicted in Module 6.4. Note that the abstraction is defined for a specific sender process s, which is known to all processes in advance. Only the sender process broadcasts a message; all other processes invoke the algorithm and participate in the TRB upon initialization of the instance. According to Module 6.4, the processes may not only deliver a message m but also "deliver" the special symbol $\triangle$, which indicates that the sender has crashed.

We consider here the *uniform* variant of the problem, where agreement is uniformly required among any pair of processes, be they correct or not.

6.3.3 Fail-Stop Algorithm: Consensus-Based Uniform Terminating Reliable Broadcast

Algorithm 6.3, called "Consensus-Based Uniform Terminating Reliable Broadcast," implements uniform TRB using three underlying abstractions: a perfect failure detector instance $\mathcal{P}$, a uniform consensus instance uc, and a best-effort broadcast instance beb.

Algorithm 6.3 works by having the sender process s disseminate a message m to all processes using best-effort broadcast. Every process waits until it either receives the message broadcast by the sender process or detects the crash of the sender. The properties of a perfect failure detector and the *validity* property of the broadcast ensure that no process waits forever. If the sender crashes, some processes may *beb*-deliver m and others may not *beb*-deliver any message.

Module 6.4: Interface and properties of uniform terminating reliable broadcast

Module:

    Name: UniformTerminatingReliableBroadcast, **instance** *utrb*, with sender *s*.

Events:

    Request: ⟨ *utrb*, *Broadcast* | *m* ⟩: Broadcasts a message *m* to all processes. Executed only by process *s*.

    Indication: ⟨ *utrb*, *Deliver* | *p*, *m* ⟩: Delivers a message *m* broadcast by process *p* or the symbol △.

Properties:

    UTRB1: *Validity:* If a correct process *p* broadcasts a message *m*, then *p* eventually delivers *m*.

    UTRB2: *Termination:* No process delivers more than one message.

    UTRB3: *Integrity:* If a correct process delivers some message *m*, then *m* was either previously broadcast by process *s* or it holds $m = \triangle$.

    UTRB4: *Uniform Agreement:* If any process delivers a message *m*, then every correct process eventually delivers *m*.

Then all processes invoke the uniform consensus abstraction to agree on whether to deliver *m* or the failure notification △. Every process proposes either *m* or △ in the consensus instance, depending on whether the process has delivered *m* (from the best-effort broadcast primitive) or has detected the crash of the sender (in the failure detector). The decision of the consensus abstraction is then delivered by the algorithm. Note that, if a process has not *beb*-delivered any message from *s* then it learns *m* from the output of the consensus primitive.

An execution of the algorithm is illustrated in Fig. 6.2. The sender process *s* crashes while broadcasting *m* with the best-effort broadcast primitive. Therefore, processes *p* and *q* receive *m*, but process *r* does not; instead, *r* detects the crash of *s*. All remaining processes use the consensus primitive to decide on the value to be delivered. In the example of the figure, the processes decide to deliver *m*, but it would also be possible that they decide to deliver △ (since *s* has crashed).

Correctness. Consider first the *validity* property of uniform TRB. Assume that *s* does not crash and *utrb*-broadcasts a message *m*. Due to the *strong accuracy* property of the perfect failure detector, no process detects a crash of *s*. Due to the *validity* property of best-effort broadcast, every correct process *beb*-delivers *m* and proposes *m* for uniform consensus. By the *termination* and *validity* properties of uniform consensus, all correct processes including *s* eventually decide *m*. Thus, process *s* eventually *utrb*-delivers *m*.

To see the *termination* property, observe how the *no duplication* property of best-effort broadcast and the *integrity* property of consensus ensure that no process

---

Algorithm 6.3: Consensus-Based Uniform Terminating Reliable Broadcast

---

Implements:
    UniformTerminatingReliableBroadcast, **instance** *utrb*, with sender *s*.

Uses:
    BestEffortBroadcast, **instance** *beb*;
    UniformConsensus, **instance** *uc*;
    PerfectFailureDetector, **instance** $\mathcal{P}$.

upon event ⟨ *utrb, Init* ⟩ **do**
    proposal := ⊥;

upon event ⟨ *utrb, Broadcast* | *m* ⟩ **do**   // only process *s*
    trigger ⟨ *beb, Broadcast* | *m* ⟩;

upon event ⟨ *beb, Deliver* | *s, m* ⟩ **do**
    if *proposal* = ⊥ **then**
        proposal := *m*;
        trigger ⟨ *uc, Propose* | *proposal* ⟩;

upon event ⟨ $\mathcal{P}$, *Crash* | *p* ⟩ **do**
    if *p* = *s* ∧ *proposal* = ⊥ **then**
        proposal := △;
        trigger ⟨ *uc, Propose* | *proposal* ⟩;

upon event ⟨ *uc, Decide* | *decided* ⟩ **do**
    trigger ⟨ *utrb, Deliver* | *s, decided* ⟩;

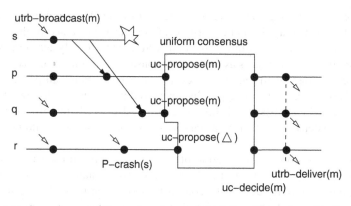

Figure 6.2: Sample execution of consensus-based uniform terminating reliable broadcast

uc-decides more than once. Therefore, every process also *utrb*-delivers at most one message. The *strong completeness* property of the failure detector, the *validity* property of best-effort broadcast, and the *termination* property of consensus ensure furthermore that every correct process eventually *utrb*-delivers a message.

The *integrity* property of uniform TRB follows directly from the *no creation* property of best-effort broadcast and from the *validity* property of consensus: if a process *utrb*-delivers a message m then either $m = \triangle$ or m was *utrb*-broadcast by process s.

Finally, the *uniform agreement* property of uniform consensus implies also the *uniform agreement* property of TRB.

Performance. The algorithm requires the execution of one underlying uniform consensus instance, invokes a best-effort broadcast primitive to broadcast one message, and accesses a perfect failure detector. The algorithm does not add anything to the cost of these primitives. If no process fails and ignoring the messages sent by the failure detector, the algorithm exchanges $O(N)$ messages and requires one additional communication step for the initial best-effort broadcast, on top of the uniform consensus primitive.

Variant. Our TRB specification has a *uniform agreement* property. As for reliable broadcast, we could specify a regular variant of TRB with a regular *agreement* property that refers only to messages delivered by correct processes. In that case, Algorithm 6.3 can still be used to implement regular TRB when the underlying uniform consensus abstraction is replaced by a regular one.

6.4 Fast Consensus

6.4.1 Overview

The consensus primitive plays a central role in distributed programming, as illustrated by the many variants and extensions of consensus presented in this chapter. Therefore, a consensus algorithm with good performance directly accelerates many implementations of other tasks as well. Many consensus algorithms invoke multiple communication steps with rounds of message exchanges among all processes. But some of these communication steps may appear redundant, especially for situations in which all processes start with the same proposal value. If the processes had a simple way to detect that their proposals are the same, consensus could be reached faster.

This section introduces a variation of the consensus primitive with a requirement to terminate particularly fast under favorable circumstances. A *fast consensus* abstraction is a specialization of the consensus abstraction from Chap. 5 that must terminate in *one round* when all processes propose the same value. In other words, the abstraction imposes a performance condition on consensus algorithms for the case of equal input values and requires that every process decides after one communication step. This improvement is not for free, and comes at the price of lower resilience.

With the fast consensus primitive, we introduce a performance criterion into a module specification for the first time in this book. This is a common practice for more elaborate abstractions. One has to look inside algorithms that implement the

---

Module 6.5: Interface and properties of uniform fast consensus

Module:

    Name: UniformFastConsensus, **instance** *ufc*.

Events:

    Request: ⟨ *ufc, Propose* | *v* ⟩: Proposes value *v* for consensus.

    Indication: ⟨ *ufc, Decide* | *v* ⟩: Outputs a decided value *v* of consensus.

Properties:

    UFC1: *Fast termination:* If all processes propose the same value then every correct process decides some value after one communication step. Otherwise, every correct process eventually decides some value.

    UFC2: *Validity:* If a process decides *v*, then *v* was proposed by some process.

    UFC3: *Integrity:* No process decides twice.

    UFC4: *Uniform agreement:* No two processes decide differently.

---

abstraction for judging whether it satisfies the property, in contrast to the usual safety properties, for which the correctness of an algorithm can be verified from its behavior at the module interface alone.

6.4.2 Specification

We consider the fast consensus primitive in its uniform variant. The specification of a *uniform fast consensus* primitive is shown in Module 6.5. Compared to the uniform consensus abstraction (specified in Module 5.2), the interface and three of the four properties (*validity*, *integrity*, and *uniform agreement*) remain the same, only the termination condition changes. The strengthened *fast termination* property requires that every correct process decides after one communication step, in all those executions where the proposal values of all processes are the same.

    The number of communication steps used by a primitive is directly determined by the algorithm that implements it. Recall that a communication step of a process occurs when a process sends a message to another process and the latter receives this message. Basic communication steps are typically encapsulated by some underlying modules, such as perfect point-to-point links and best-effort broadcast. Therefore, one also has to consider the implementations of the underlying modules to determine the performance of an algorithm.

6.4.3 Fail-Silent Algorithm: From Uniform Consensus to Uniform Fast Consensus

One can add fast termination to any consensus implementation in a modular way. We present such a transformation "From Uniform Consensus to Uniform Fast

---

Algorithm 6.4: From Uniform Consensus to Uniform Fast Consensus

---

Implements:
    UniformFastConsensus, **instance** *ufc*.

Uses:
    BestEffortBroadcast, **instance** *beb*;
    UniformReliableBroadcast, **instance** *urb*;
    UniformConsensus, **instance** *uc*.

upon event ⟨ *uc, Init* ⟩ **do**
    proposal := ⊥;
    decision := ⊥;
    val := [⊥]^N;

upon event ⟨ *ufc, Propose* | *v* ⟩ **do**
    proposal := *v*;
    trigger ⟨ *beb, Broadcast* | [PROPOSAL, *proposal*] ⟩;

upon event ⟨ *beb, Deliver* | *p*, [PROPOSAL, *v*] ⟩ **do**
    val[*p*] := *v*;
    if #(*val*) = *N* − *f* ∧ *decision* = ⊥ **then**
        if exists *v* ≠ ⊥ such that #({*p* ∈ *Π* | *val*[*p*] = *v*}) = *N* − *f* **then**
            decision := *v*;
            trigger ⟨ *ufc, Decide* | *v* ⟩;
            trigger ⟨ *urb, Broadcast* | [DECIDED, *decision*] ⟩;
        else
            if exists *v* ≠ ⊥ such that #({*p* ∈ *Π* | *val*[*p*] = *v*}) ≥ *N* − 2*f* **then**
                proposal := *v*;
            val := [⊥]^N;
            trigger ⟨ *uc, Propose* | *proposal* ⟩;

upon event ⟨ *urb, Deliver* | *p*, [DECIDED, *v*] ⟩ **do**
    if *decision* = ⊥ **then**
        decision := *v*;
        trigger ⟨ *ufc, Decide* | *v* ⟩;

upon event ⟨ *uc, Decide* | *v* ⟩ **do**
    if *decision* = ⊥ **then**
        decision := *v*;
        trigger ⟨ *ufc, Decide* | *v* ⟩;

Consensus" in Algorithm 6.4. It is a fail-silent algorithm and comes at the cost of reduced resilience. Specifically, implementing fast consensus requires that $N > 3f$ instead of only $N > 2f$. The algorithm additionally uses a uniform reliable broadcast primitive.

The transformation first performs one round of all-to-all message exchanges, in which every process broadcasts its proposal value with best-effort guarantees. When a process receives only messages with the same proposal value v in this round, from $N - f$ distinct processes, it decides v. This step ensures the *fast termination* property; such a process *decides fast*. Otherwise, if the messages received in the first round contain multiple distinct values, but still more than $N - 2f$ messages contain the same proposal value w, the process adopts w as its own proposal value. Unless the process has already decided, it then invokes an underlying uniform consensus primitive with its proposal and lets it agree on a decision.

In order to ensure that the algorithm terminates under all circumstances, even if some process, say p, has decided fast and does not invoke the underlying consensus module, the algorithm additionally asks p to reliably broadcast its decision value with a *uniform agreement* guarantee. Hence, if p is correct, every correct process may, eventually, decide after receiving the decision value from the fast-deciding process.

The heart of the transformation is the condition under which a process adopts another proposal value after the first round. Namely, it may occur that some processes decide fast, say, some value v, but others resort to the uniform consensus primitive. In this case, the algorithm must ensure that v remains the only possible decision value. The condition achieves that because a process that decides fast has received v from $N - f$ processes. As at most f of these processes may fail and because $N > 3f$, every other correct process still receives v from at least $N - 2f$ processes. Hence, all processes propose v in the underlying consensus primitive.

Correctness. For the *fast termination* property, observe first that if all processes propose the same value v then every process may indeed decide after one communication step, that is, after receiving $N - f$ PROPOSAL messages containing v. Otherwise, the algorithm terminates under the combination of the $N > 3f$ condition with the assumptions made about the underlying consensus implementation, because every correct process either decides fast and *urb*-broadcasts its decision or invokes the uniform consensus instance *uc*. If no correct process reliably broadcasts a decision then all of them invoke uniform consensus and its *termination* property ensures termination.

The *validity* property is straightforward to verify from the algorithm. The role of the variable *decision* ensures that no process decides twice and establishes the *integrity* property.

Given this discussion, we now consider the *uniform agreement* property. There are three cases to consider: First, suppose two processes decide some value v after the first round. As each of them has *beb*-delivered $N - f$ PROPOSAL messages containing v, but there are a total of N processes only and $N > 3f$, a message from some sender must have been *beb*-delivered by both processes. Hence, they decide the same value.

For the second case, assume no process *urb*-broadcasts a DECIDED message. Then every process *ufc*-decides after *uc*-deciding, and *agreement* follows from the *agreement* property of uniform consensus.

In the third case, some process has decided fast and received $N - f$ messages with the same proposal v in the first round. Therefore, every other process that receives $N - f$ messages in the first round finds at least $N - 2f$ among them containing v. Hence, every process may only *uc*-propose v in the underlying uniform consensus primitive. According to its *validity* property, it *uc*-decides v.

Performance. If the initial proposal values are not the same for all processes then the transformation adds at most communication step to the underlying uniform consensus primitive.

6.5 Fast Byzantine Consensus

6.5.1 Overview

One can also require that a Byzantine consensus primitive decides fast and takes only one round in executions where all proposed values are the same. This section introduces a *fast Byzantine consensus* abstraction with this feature.

Compared to fast consensus with crash-stop process abstractions, however, one cannot require that an algorithm always decides in one round whenever all correct processes propose the same value. The reason is that Byzantine processes might propose arbitrary values, and a correct process cannot distinguish such a value from a value proposed by a correct process. As illustrated by the different *validity* properties for Byzantine consensus introduced in the previous chapter, ensuring a particular consensus decision value in the fail-arbitrary model may be problematic. Our fast Byzantine consensus abstraction, therefore, adopts the approach that was already taken for weak Byzantine consensus; it requires a fast decision only in executions where all processes are correct.

Compared to the previous abstractions of Byzantine consensus, deciding fast in executions with unanimous proposals requires to lower the resilience. Specifically, the algorithm presented here assumes that $N > 5f$; one can show that this is optimal.

6.5.2 Specification

Our notion of *fast Byzantine consensus* is specified by Module 6.6. It has the same request and indication events as all consensus abstractions. The primitive corresponds to a (strong) Byzantine consensus primitive with the strengthened *fast termination* property (that is, properties FBC2–FBC4 are the same as properties BC2–BC4 of Module 5.11).

The *fast termination* property requires that any fast Byzantine consensus algorithm terminates after one communication step if all correct processes propose the same value, but only in failure-free executions, that is, in executions without Byzantine processes.

A variant of fast Byzantine consensus with a stronger *fast termination* property is explored in an exercise (at the end of the chapter). It does not restrict fast decisions to executions with only correct processes.

6.5.3 Fail-Arbitrary Algorithm: From Byzantine Consensus to Fast Byzantine Consensus

As was the case for fast consensus in the fail-stop model, fast Byzantine consensus can be realized in a modular way from a Byzantine consensus abstraction.

Module 6.6: Interface and properties of fast Byzantine consensus

Module:

    Name: FastByzantineConsensus, **instance** *fbc*.

Events:

    Request: $\langle$ *fbc, Propose* $\mid v$ $\rangle$: Proposes value v for consensus.

    Indication: $\langle$ *fbc, Decide* $\mid v$ $\rangle$: Outputs a decided value v of consensus.

Properties:

    FBC1: *Fast termination:* If all processes are correct and propose the same value, then every correct process decides some value after one communication step. Otherwise, every correct process eventually decides some value.

    FBC2: *Strong validity:* If all correct processes propose the same value v, then no correct process decides a value different from v; otherwise, a correct process may only decide a value that was proposed by some correct process or the special value $\square$.

    FBC3: *Integrity:* No correct process decides twice.

    FBC4: *Agreement:* No two correct processes decide differently.

We describe a transformation "From Byzantine Consensus to Fast Byzantine Consensus" in Algorithm 6.5. The transformation is similar to Algorithm 6.4, but requires some changes. These concern the lowered resilience of the algorithm, it requires $N > 5f$, and the higher numbers of equal values that are needed to decide fast. One can show that this condition is necessary.

As a minor difference to the previous algorithm, every process always invokes the underlying (strong) Byzantine consensus primitive here, even after deciding fast. Recall that in Algorithm 6.4, only processes that did not decide fast proposed a value to the uniform consensus primitive. This change simplifies the algorithm and avoids complications arising when broadcasting a decision value with Byzantine processes.

Correctness. We argue why Algorithm 6.5 provides fast Byzantine consensus if $N > 5f$. The *fast termination* property follows directly from the algorithm because of the assumption that all processes must be correct and propose the same value, in order to decide in one round. Hence, no Byzantine process could interfere by sending a different value. Furthermore, a process may either decide fast, i.e., after receiving only equal PROPOSAL messages or after deciding in the underlying Byzantine consensus instance *bc*. Because every correct process *bc*-proposes a value, it also *bc*-decides a value by the properties of Byzantine consensus.

The *strong validity* property holds because the underlying (strong) Byzantine consensus primitive satisfies the same *strong validity* property, and the algorithm directly maps proposal values to the primitive and decision values from the primitive to fast consensus.

Algorithm 6.5: From Byzantine Consensus to Fast Byzantine Consensus

---

Implements:
  FastByzantineConsensus, **instance** *fbc*.

Uses:
  AuthPerfectPointToPointLinks, **instance** *al*;
  ByzantineConsensus, **instance** *bc*.

upon event ⟨ *fbc, Init* ⟩ **do**
    proposal := □;
    decision := ⊥;
    val := $[⊥]^N$;

upon event ⟨ *fbc, Propose* | *v* ⟩ **do**
    proposal := *v*;
    forall *q* ∈ *Π* **do**
        trigger ⟨ *al, Send* | *q*, [PROPOSAL, *proposal*] ⟩;

upon event ⟨ *al, Deliver* | *p*, [PROPOSAL, *v*] ⟩ **do**
    val[*p*] := *v*;
    if #(*val*) = *N* − *f* **then**
        if exists *v* ≠ ⊥ such that #({*p* ∈ *Π* | *val*[*p*] = *v*}) = *N* − *f* **then**
            decision := *v*;
            trigger ⟨ *fbc, Decide* | *v* ⟩;
        if exists *v* ≠ ⊥ such that #({*p* ∈ *Π* | *val*[*p*] = *v*}) > $\frac{N-f}{2}$ **then**
            proposal := *v*;
        val := $[⊥]^N$;
        trigger ⟨ *bc, Propose* | *proposal* ⟩;

upon event ⟨ *bc, Decide* | *v* ⟩ **do**
    if *decision* = ⊥ **then**
        decision := *v*;
        trigger ⟨ *fbc, Decide* | *v* ⟩;

The variable *decision* protects a process from deciding more than once, and this establishes the *integrity* property.

For the *agreement* property, consider first the case where two correct processes *p* and *q* decide fast. Note that among the PROPOSAL messages received by a correct process, at least *N* − 2*f* were sent by correct processes. Because *N* > 5*f*, the two sets of *N* − 2*f* PROPOSAL messages from correct processes collected by *p* and *q* overlap (actually, in more than *f* messages). Therefore, the same value *v* is contained in the sets of *p* and *q*, and both processes also decide *v* fast.

Next, suppose that some correct process *p* decides a value *v* fast and another correct process *q* *fbc*-decides after *bc*-deciding. The fact that *p* decided fast implies that it received at least *N* − *f* PROPOSAL messages containing *v*. As there are only *N* processes in the system overall, at most *f* further correct processes may have proposed a value different from *v*. Hence, every other correct process receives *v* in at least *N* − 3*f* PROPOSAL messages, accounting for the potentially different proposals from the up to f further correct processes and for the PROPOSAL messages from the f Byzantine processes. As

$$N - 3f > \frac{N - f}{2}$$

under the assumption for the algorithm, it follows that every correct process bc-proposes v in the underlying consensus primitive. Hence, every correct process bc-decides v and therefore, also process q fbc-decides v.

Finally, if no process decides fast then the *agreement* property directly follows from the underlying Byzantine consensus primitive.

Performance. The transformation adds one round of message exchanges among all processes and one communication step to the underlying Byzantine consensus primitive.

6.6 Nonblocking Atomic Commit

6.6.1 Overview

The unit of data processing in a distributed information system is a *transaction*. Among other applications, transactions are a central concept for the design of database management systems. A transaction corresponds to a portion of a program that is delimited by a *begin* statement and an *end* statement. A transaction typically satisfies *atomic* semantics in two senses:

Concurrency atomicity: All transactions appear to execute one after the other, i.e., they are *serializable*; serializability is usually guaranteed through some *distributed locking* scheme or with some *optimistic concurrency control* mechanism.

Failure atomicity: Every transaction appears to execute either completely and thereby *commits* or not at all, in which case it is said to *abort*.

Ensuring these two forms of atomicity in a distributed environment is not trivial because the transaction might be accessing information on different processes, called *data managers*, which maintain the relevant data items. The data managers may have different local state and different opinions on whether the transaction should commit or not. For example, some data managers might observe conflicting concurrent data accesses, whereas others might not. Similarly, some data managers might detect logical or physical problems that prevent a transaction from committing. For instance, there may not be enough money to make a bank transfer, there may be concurrency-control problems, such as the risk of violating serializability in a database system, or there could be a storage issue, such as when the disk is full and a data manager has no way to guarantee the durability of the transaction's updates.

Despite differences between their opinions, all data managers need to make sure that they either all discard the new updates, in case the transaction aborts, or make them visible, in case the transaction commits. In other words, all data managers need to agree on the same outcome for the transaction.

The *nonblocking atomic commit* (NBAC) abstraction is used precisely to solve this problem in a reliable way. The processes, each representing a data manager, agree on the outcome of a transaction, which is either to *commit* or to *abort* the transaction. Every process initially proposes a value for this decision, which is either a COMMIT value or an ABORT value, depending on its local state and opinion about the transaction.

By proposing COMMIT for a transaction, a process expresses that it is willing and able to commit the transaction. Typically, a process witnesses the absence of any problem during the execution of the transaction. Furthermore, the process promises to make the update of the transaction permanent. This, in particular, means that the process has stored the temporary update of the transaction in stable storage: should it crash and recover, it can install a consistent state including all updates of the committed transaction.

By proposing ABORT, a data manager process vetoes the commitment of the transaction and states that it cannot commit the transaction. This may occur for many reasons, as we pointed out earlier.

6.6.2 Specification

The *nonblocking atomic commit* abstraction is defined by $\langle\ Propose\ |\ v\ \rangle$ and $\langle\ Decide\ |\ v\ \rangle$ events, which are similar to those in the interface of the consensus abstraction, but require that v is either COMMIT or ABORT. The abstraction satisfies the properties listed in Module 6.7. At first glance, the problem looks like binary consensus: the processes propose one of two values and need to decide on a common final value. There is, however, a fundamental difference: in consensus, any proposed value can be decided. In the atomic commit abstraction, a value of COMMIT cannot be decided if any of the processes has proposed ABORT (this would mean that some data managers can indeed commit the transaction and ensure its durability whereas others cannot). When a process expresses its veto to a transaction by proposing ABORT, the NBAC abstraction must honor this. As another difference to consensus, nonblocking atomic commit may decide ABORT also if some process crashes, even though all processes have proposed COMMIT.

6.6.3 Fail-Stop Algorithm: Consensus-Based Nonblocking Atomic Commit

Algorithm 6.6 implements nonblocking atomic commit using three underlying abstractions: a perfect failure detector $\mathcal{P}$, a uniform consensus instance uc, and a best-effort broadcast abstraction *beb*. In order to distinguish the value proposed to the NBAC abstraction from the value proposed to the underlying consensus abstraction, we call the first a *vote* and the second a *proposal*.

The algorithm works as follows. Every process p broadcasts its initial vote (ABORT or COMMIT) to all other processes using best-effort broadcast. Then it waits to hear something from every process q in the system: either to *beb*-deliver the vote of q or to detect the crash of q. If p detects the crash of any process or receives a vote ABORT from any process then p directly (without waiting for more messages)

Module 6.7: Interface and properties of nonblocking atomic commit

Module:

    Name: NonBlockingAtomicCommit, **instance** *nbac*.

Events:

    Request: $\langle$ *nbac, Propose* $\mid v$ $\rangle$: Proposes value $v =$ COMMIT or $v =$ ABORT for the commit.

    Indication: $\langle$ *nbac, Decide* $\mid v$ $\rangle$: Outputs the decided value for the commit.

Properties:

    NBAC1: *Termination:* Every correct process eventually decides some value.

    NBAC2: *Abort-Validity:* A process can only decide ABORT if some process proposes ABORT or a process crashes.

    NBAC3: *Commit-Validity:* A process can only decide COMMIT if no process proposes ABORT.

    NBAC4: *Integrity:* No process decides twice.

    NBAC5: *Uniform Agreement:* No two processes decide differently.

---

invokes the consensus abstraction with ABORT as its proposal. If p receives the vote COMMIT from all processes then p invokes consensus with COMMIT as its proposal. Once the consensus abstraction *uc*-decides, every process *nbac*-decides according to the outcome of consensus.

Correctness. The *termination* property of nonblocking atomic commit follows from the *validity* property of best-effort broadcast, from the *termination* property of consensus, and from the *strong completeness* property of the perfect failure detector. The *uniform agreement* property of NBAC directly follows from that of the uniform consensus abstraction. Furthermore, the *integrity* property of NBAC holds because the *no duplication* property of best-effort broadcast and the *integrity* property of uniform consensus ensure that no process *nbac*-decides twice.

Consider now the two *validity* properties of NBAC. The *commit-validity* property requires that COMMIT is *nbac*-decided only if all processes *nbac*-propose COMMIT. Assume by contradiction that some process p *nbac*-proposes ABORT, whereas some process q *nbac*-decides COMMIT. According to the algorithm, for q to *nbac*-decide COMMIT, it must also have *uc*-decided COMMIT in the consensus primitive. Because of the *validity* property of consensus, some process r must have proposed COMMIT to the consensus abstraction. Given the *validity* property of the best-effort broadcast primitive, one can distinguish two cases: either process p (that votes ABORT) crashes and process r does not *beb*-deliver the vote from p or r *beb*-delivers the vote ABORT from p. In both cases, according to the algorithm, process r proposes ABORT to uniform consensus: a contradiction. Consider now the *abort-validity* property of NBAC. It requires that ABORT is *nbac*-decided only

Algorithm 6,6: Consensus-Based Nonblocking Atomic Commit

Implements:
    NonBlockingAtomicCommit, **instance** *nbac*.

Uses:
    BestEffortBroadcast, **instance** *beb*;
    UniformConsensus, **instance** *uc*;
    PerfectFailureDetector, **instance** $\mathcal{P}$.

upon event $\langle$ *nbac, Init* $\rangle$ **do**
    voted := $\emptyset$;
    proposed := FALSE;

upon event $\langle$ $\mathcal{P}$, *Crash* $\mid p$ $\rangle$ **do**
    if *proposed* = FALSE **then**
        trigger $\langle$ *uc, Propose* $\mid$ ABORT $\rangle$;
        proposed := TRUE;

upon event $\langle$ *nbac, Propose* $\mid v$ $\rangle$ **do**
    trigger $\langle$ *beb, Broadcast* $\mid v$ $\rangle$;

upon event $\langle$ *beb, Deliver* $\mid p, v$ $\rangle$ **do**
    if v = ABORT $\wedge$ *proposed* = FALSE **then**
        trigger $\langle$ *uc, Propose* $\mid$ ABORT $\rangle$;
        proposed := TRUE;
    else
        voted := *voted* $\cup$ $\{p\}$;
        if *voted* = Π $\wedge$ *proposed* = FALSE **do**
            trigger $\langle$ *uc, Propose* $\mid$ COMMIT $\rangle$;
            proposed := TRUE;

upon event $\langle$ *uc, Decide* $\mid$ *decided* $\rangle$ **do**
    trigger $\langle$ *nbac, Decide* $\mid$ *decided* $\rangle$;

---

if some process *nbac*-proposes ABORT or some process crashes. Assume by contradiction that all processes *nbac*-propose a vote of COMMIT and no process crashes, whereas some process *p* *nbac*-decides ABORT. For *p* to *nbac*-decide *Abort*, due the *validity* property of uniform consensus, some process *q* must *uc*-propose ABORT. According to the algorithm and the *strong accuracy* property of the failure detector though, *q* only *uc*-proposes ABORT if some process *nbac*-proposes *Abort* or $\mathcal{P}$ detects a process crash: a contradiction.

Performance. The algorithm requires one execution of the consensus abstraction. In addition to the cost of consensus and the messages communicated by the perfect failure detector, the algorithm exchanges $O(N^2)$ messages and requires one communication step for the initial best-effort broadcast.

Variant. One could define a nonuniform (regular) variant of nonblocking atomic commit, by requiring only *agreement* (for any two *correct* processes) and not *uniform agreement* (for any two processes). However, this abstraction would not be useful in a practical setting to coordinate the termination of a transaction in a distributed database system. Indeed, the very fact that some process has decided to commit a transaction might trigger an external action: say, the process has delivered some cash through a bank machine. Even if that process has crashed, its decision is important and other processes should reach the same outcome.

6.7 Group Membership

6.7.1 Overview

Some of our algorithms from the previous sections were required to make decisions based on information about which processes were operational, crashed, or otherwise faulty. At any point during the computation, every process maintains information about some other processes in the system, whether they are up and running, whether one specific process can be a trusted leader, and so on. In the algorithms we considered, this information is provided by a failure detector module available at each process. According to the properties of a failure detector, this information reflects the actual status of failures in the system more or less accurately. In any case, the outputs of the failure detector modules at different processes are not always the same. In particular, different processes may get notifications about process failures in different orders and, in this way, obtain a different perspective of the system's evolution. If there was a way to provide better coordinated failure notifications, faster and simpler algorithms might become possible.

A *group membership* (GM) abstraction provides consistent and accurate information about which processes have crashed and which processes are correct. The output of a group membership primitive is better coordinated and at a higher abstraction level than the outputs of failure detectors and leader election modules.

In a second role, a membership abstraction enables dynamic changes in the group of processes that constitute the system. Throughout this book, we have assumed a static set Π of N processes in our system model. No new process could join the set of processes, be included in the system, and participate in the computation. Likewise, a process in Π could not voluntarily leave the system or become excluded by an administrator. And after a process had crashed, our algorithms would eventually ignore it, but the process was still part of the system.

A group membership primitive also coordinates such join and leave operations and provides a dynamic set of processes in the system. As with failure notifications, it is desirable that group-membership information is provided to the processes in a consistent way.

To simplify the presentation of the group membership concept, however, we will only describe how it implements its first role above, i.e., to give consistent information about process crashes in a system with otherwise static membership. We assume that the initial membership of the group is the complete set of processes, and subsequent membership changes are solely caused by crashes. We do not consider explicit join and leave operations, although they are important for practical systems. Group membership introduces a new notion that defines the current set of active processes in the system, which is also the basis for modeling join and leave operations. One can easily extend our basic abstraction with such operations. Reference pointers to the literature and to practical systems that support such operations are given in the notes at the end of this chapter.

6.7.2 Specification

A group is the set of processes that participate in the computation. At any point in time, the current membership of the group is called the *group view*, or simply the *view*. More precisely, a view $V = (id, M)$ is a tuple that contains a unique numeric *view identifier* id and a set M of *view member* processes. Over time, the system may evolve through multiple views. The initial group view is the entire system, denoted by $V_0 = (0, \Pi)$, which contains view identifier 0 and includes the complete set of processes Π in the system. The group membership abstraction provides information about a new view V through an indication event $\langle View \mid V \rangle$. When a process outputs a view V, it is said to *install* a new view V, after going through a *view change*. Group membership offers no request events to the layer above.

We consider a *monotone group membership* abstraction, where all correct processes install multiple new views in a sequence with monotonically increasing view identifiers. Furthermore, when two different processes install a view with the same identifier, the view memberships must be the same. Compared to the outputs of our failure-detector abstractions, views therefore offer much better coordination among the processes.

The group membership abstraction is characterized by the properties listed in Module 6.8. Its *uniform agreement* and *monotonicity* properties require that every

---

Module 6.8: Interface and properties of group membership

Module:

> **Name:** GroupMembership, **instance** *gm*.

Events:

> **Indication:** $\langle$ *gm*, *View* $\mid$ V $\rangle$: Installs a new view $V = (id, M)$ with view identifier id and membership M.

Properties:

> **GM1:** *Monotonicity:* If a process p installs a view $V = (id, M)$ and subsequently installs a view $V' = (id', M')$, then $id < id'$ and $M \supseteq M'$.

> **GM2:** *Uniform Agreement:* If some process installs a view $V = (id, M)$ and another process installs some view $V' = (id, M')$, then $M = M'$.

> **GM3:** *Completeness:* If a process p crashes, then eventually every correct process installs a view (id, M) such that $p \notin M$.

> **GM4:** *Accuracy:* If some process installs a view (id, M) with $q \notin M$ for some process $q \in \Pi$, then q has crashed.

process installs a sequence of views with increasing identifiers and shrinking membership, as mentioned earlier. The *completeness* and *accuracy* properties are similar to those of the perfect failure detector abstraction and dictate the conditions under which a process can be excluded from a group.

6.7.3 Fail-Stop Algorithm: Consensus-Based Group Membership

Algorithm 6.7, which is called "Consensus-Based Group Membership," implements the group membership abstraction assuming a uniform consensus abstraction and a perfect failure-detector abstraction. At initialization, each process installs a view including all the processes in the system. From that point on, the algorithm remains idle until some process detects that another process has crashed. As different processes may detect crashes in different orders, a new view cannot be output immediately after detecting a failure and in a unilateral way; the processes first need to coordinate about the composition of the new view. The algorithm executes an instance of uniform consensus to decide which processes are to be included in the next view. A process invokes consensus only after it has detected that at least one member of the current view have crashed. The *wait* flag is used to prevent a process from triggering a new consensus instance before the previous consensus

---

Algorithm 6.7: Consensus-Based Group Membership

Implements:
    GroupMembership, **instance** *gm*.

Uses:
    UniformConsensus (multiple instance);
    PerfectFailureDetector, **instance** $\mathcal{P}$.

upon event $\langle$ *gm, Init* $\rangle$ **do**
    $(id, M) := (0, \Pi)$;
    correct := Π;
    wait := FALSE;
    trigger $\langle$ *gm, View* $\mid (id, M)$ $\rangle$;

upon event $\langle$ $\mathcal{P}$, *Crash* $\mid p$ $\rangle$ **do**
    correct := *correct* $\setminus \{p\}$;

upon *correct* $\subsetneq M \wedge$ *wait* = FALSE **do**
    $id := id + 1$;
    wait := TRUE;
    Initialize a new instance *uc.id* of uniform consensus;
    trigger $\langle$ *uc.id, Propose* $\mid$ *correct* $\rangle$;

upon event $\langle$ *uc.i, Decide* $\mid M'$ $\rangle$ **such that** $i = id$ **do**
    $M := M'$;
    wait := FALSE;
    trigger $\langle$ *gm, View* $\mid (id, M)$ $\rangle$;

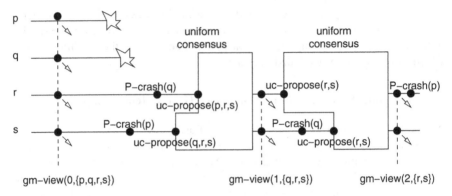

Figure 6.3: Sample execution of consensus-based group membership

instance has terminated. When the consensus decides, a new view is delivered. In order to preserve the *uniform agreement* property, a process p may sometimes install a view containing a process that p already knows to have crashed, because the perfect failure-detector module at p has already output that process. In this case, after installing that view, p will initiate a new consensus instance to trigger the installation of another view that would exclude the crashed process.

An execution of the "Consensus-Based Group Membership" algorithm is illustrated in Fig. 6.3. In the execution with four processes p, q, r, and s, the first two processes, p and q, crash initially. Process s subsequently detects the crash of p and initiates a consensus instance to define a new view without p. Process r then detects the crash of q and proposes a different view to consensus. The first consensus instance decides the proposal from s, and, as a result, process p is excluded from the view with identifier 1. As process r has already detected the crash of q, it triggers another consensus instance to exclude q. Eventually, process s also detects the crash of q and also participates in the second consensus instance to install the view with identifier 2. This view includes only the correct processes.

As a possible optimization of the algorithm, consider the moment when a process has decided on a set M' in an instance of uniform consensus and is about to start a new view (id, M'). Then the process might also set *correct* to *correct* $\cap$ M', for accelerating the detection of crashed processes.

Algorithm 6.7 actually provides stronger guarantees than required by the group membership abstraction. In particular, it satisfies a *linear* group membership property in the sense that every process installs the *same* sequence of views and never skips a view in the sequence. In contrast, the *monotonicity* property would actually allow that a process installs a view with a much higher identifier than its current view, or that all process skip a view with a particular identifier. Furthermore, the algorithm also ensures a *strict* form of the *monotonicity* property, in that the membership of a view installed after the current one is always strictly smaller than the membership of the current view. Monotonicity allows a subsequent view to have the same membership. There are practical group communication systems that exploit this flexibility of our group membership abstraction.

Correctness. The *monotonicity* property follows directly from the algorithm, because a process only initiates the formation of a new view when its set *correct* becomes properly contained in the current view membership. The *uniform agreement* property follows directly from the *uniform agreement* property of the underlying consensus abstraction.

The *completeness* property follows from the *strong completeness* property of the perfect failure-detector abstraction, which says that if a process p crashes then eventually every correct process detects the crash. According to the algorithm, there will be a consensus instance in which every proposal value no longer includes p. By the *validity* property of consensus, this means that they eventually install a view that does not include p.

The *accuracy* property of the group membership algorithm follows analogously from the use of the perfect failure detector $\mathcal{P}$. As some process p proposed a set of processes to consensus that did not include a process q, process q must have been detected to have crashed by process p. In this case, the *strong accuracy* property of $\mathcal{P}$ implies that q must have crashed.

Performance. The algorithm requires at most one consensus execution for each process that crashes.

Variant. We focus here only on the uniform variant of the group membership abstraction: a regular group membership abstraction is specified by replacing the *uniform agreement* property with a regular *agreement* property. An algorithm implementing a regular group membership abstraction might use regular consensus instead of uniform consensus.

6.8 View-Synchronous Communication

6.8.1 Overview

The *view-synchronous communication* abstraction is also called *view-synchronous broadcast* and integrates two abstractions introduced earlier: reliable broadcast and group membership. In the following, we discuss a subtle issue that arises when these two primitives are combined. This difficulty motivates the introduction of view-synchronous communication as a new first-class primitive.

Consider the following scenario of a group of processes exchanging messages, where one of them, say, process q, crashes. Assume that this failure is detected and that the membership abstraction installs a new view $V = (id, M)$ at the processes such that $q \notin M$. Suppose that after V has been installed, some process p delivers a message m that was originally broadcast by q. Note that such a scenario is possible, as nothing in the specification of reliable broadcast prevents a message that was broadcast by a process that has failed from being delivered later. In fact, in order to ensure the *agreement* property of reliable broadcast, messages originally broadcast by q are typically relayed by other processes, especially for the case where q has failed. However, it feels strange and counterintuitive for the application programmer to handle a message from a process q in view V, from which q has been expelled. It would, thus, be desirable for p to simply discard m. Unfortunately, it may also happen that some other process r has already delivered m *before* installing view V. So, in this scenario, the communication primitive is faced with two conflicting goals: to ensure the reliability of the broadcast, which means that m must be delivered by p, but, at the same time, to guarantee the consistency of the view information, which means that m cannot be delivered in the new view and p must discard it.

The solution to this dilemma, which is offered by view-synchronous communication, integrates the installation of views with the delivery of messages and orders every new view with respect to the message flow. If a message m is delivered by a (correct) process before it installs a view V then m should be delivered by all processes that install V, *before* they install the view. This abstraction is also called *view-synchronous broadcast* because it gives the illusion that failures are synchronized and appear to happen atomically with respect to the delivered messages.

6.8.2 Specification

View-synchronous communication extends both the reliable broadcast abstraction and the group membership abstraction: as a consequence, its interface contains the events of both primitives. Specifically, the interface of a view-synchronous communication primitive contains a request event ⟨ *Broadcast* | m ⟩ to broadcast a message m, an indication event ⟨ *Deliver* | p, m ⟩ that outputs a message m from sender p (from Module 3.2), and another indication event ⟨ *View* | V ⟩, which installs view V (from Module 6.8). The abstraction adds two more events used for synchronization with the communication layer above; these are introduced after the formal definition.

Module 6.9 states the properties of *view-synchronous communication*; it defines the view synchrony concept as the combination of group membership, in a uniform variant as considered in the previous section, with the regular variant of reliable broadcast. Other combinations are possible, in particular combinations of regular and uniform variants and, optionally, adding the properties of FIFO delivery order and causal delivery order for reliable broadcast. Given such a wide choice, there are many different possible flavors of view-synchronous communication.

In Module 6.10, we introduce a *uniform view-synchronous communication* abstraction, obtained by combining the group membership abstraction with the uniform reliable broadcast abstraction.

The new element in the specification of view-synchronous communication, which integrates the way that messages should be delivered with respect to view changes, lies in the *view inclusion* property that first appears in Module 6.9. We say that a process *delivers* or *broadcasts* a message m *in a view* V if the process delivers or broadcasts m, respectively, after installing view V and before installing any subsequent view. The *view inclusion* property requires that every message must be

---

Module 6.9: Interface and properties of view-synchronous communication

Module:

    Name: ViewSynchronousCommunication, **instance** *vs.*

Events:

    Request: $\langle$ *vs, Broadcast* $\mid m$ $\rangle$: Broadcasts a message m to all processes.

    Indication: $\langle$ *vs, Deliver* $\mid p, m$ $\rangle$: Delivers a message m broadcast by process p.

    Indication: $\langle$ *vs, View* $\mid V$ $\rangle$: Installs a new view $V = (id, M)$ with view identifier id and membership M.

    Indication: $\langle$ *vs, Block* $\rangle$: Requests that no new messages are broadcast temporarily until the next view is installed.

    Request: $\langle$ *vs, BlockOk* $\rangle$: Confirms that no new messages will be broadcast until the next view is installed.

Properties:

    VS1: *View Inclusion:* If some process delivers a message m from process p in view V, then m was broadcast by p in view V.

    VS2–VS5: Same as properties RB1–RB4 in (regular) reliable broadcast (Module 3.2).

    VS6–VS9: Same as properties GM1–GM4 in group membership (Module 6.8).

---

delivered only in the same view in that it was broadcast. This solves the problem mentioned before, as the condition implies that messages coming from processes that have already been excluded from a view can no longer be delivered.

In order to make the *view inclusion* property feasible, the interface and properties of view-synchronous communication contain an additional feature. As messages must be delivered in the same view in which they are broadcast, the view change poses a problem: if new messages are continuously broadcast then the installation of a new view may be postponed indefinitely. In other words, it is not possible to implement the view-synchronous communication abstraction without any control on the broadcast pattern. Therefore, the interface of this abstraction includes two specific events that handle the interaction between the view-synchronous communication primitive and the layer above (i.e., the application layer). They provide flow control through a $\langle$ *Block* $\rangle$ indication event and a $\langle$ *BlockOk* $\rangle$ request event. By triggering the $\langle$ *Block* $\rangle$ event, the view-synchronous communication layer requests that the higher layer stops broadcasting messages in the current view. When the higher-level module agrees to that, it acknowledges the block request with the $\langle$ *BlockOk* $\rangle$ event.

We assume that the layer above is well behaved and that whenever it is asked to stop broadcasting messages (through a request to block), then it indeed does not trigger any further broadcasts after acknowledging the request to block. It may again

---

Module 6.10: Interface and properties of uniform view-synchronous communication

Module:

    Name: UniformViewSynchronousCommunication, **instance** *uvs*.

Events:

    Request: ⟨ *uvs, Broadcast* | *m* ⟩: Broadcasts a message *m* to all processes.

    Indication: ⟨ *uvs, Deliver* | *p, m* ⟩: Delivers a message *m* broadcast by process *p*.

    Indication: ⟨ *uvs, View* | *V* ⟩: Installs a new view $V = (id, M)$ with view identifier *id* and membership *M*.

    Indication: ⟨ *uvs, Block* ⟩: Requests that no new messages are broadcast temporarily until the next view is installed.

    Request: ⟨ *uvs, BlockOk* ⟩: Confirms that no new messages will be broadcast until the next view is installed.

Properties:

    UVS1–UVS4 and **UVS6–UVS9:** Same as properties VS1–VS4 and VS6–VS9 in view-synchronous communication (Module 6.9).

    UVS5: Same as property URB4 (*uniform agreement*) in uniform reliable broadcast (Module 3.3).

---

broadcast new messages after the next view is installed. On the other hand, we require from the view-synchronous communication abstraction that it only requests the higher layer to block if a view change is imminent, i.e., only if a process that is a member of the current view has failed and a new view must be installed. (We do not explicitly state these properties in Modules 6.9 and 6.10 as we consider them to be of a different nature than the *view inclusion* property.)

6.8.3 Fail-Stop Algorithm: TRB-Based View-Synchronous Communication

Algorithm 6.8–6.9, called "TRB-Based View-Synchronous Communication," implements the view-synchronous communication abstraction according to Module 6.9. The keys element of the algorithm is a collective *flush* procedure, executed by the processes after they receive a view change from the underlying group membership primitive and before they install this new view at the view-synchronous communication level. During this step, every process uses an instance of the uniform TRB primitive to rebroadcast all messages that it has view-synchronously delivered in the current view.

    The algorithm for an instance *vs* of view-synchronous communication works as follows. During its normal operation within a view $V = (vid, M)$, a process simply adds *vid* to every message that it receives for *vs*-broadcast and broadcasts it in a DATA message using an underlying best-effort broadcast primitive *beb*. When

---

Algorithm 6.8: TRB-Based View-Synchronous Communication (part 1, data transmission)

Implements:
    ViewSynchronousCommunication, **instance** *vs*.

Uses:
    UniformTerminatingReliableBroadcast (multiple instances);
    GroupMembership, **instance** *gm*;
    BestEffortBroadcast, **instance** *beb*.

upon event ⟨ *vs*, *Init* ⟩ **do**
    $(vid, M) := (0, \emptyset)$;   // current view $V = (vid, M)$
    flushing := FALSE; *blocked* := TRUE;
    inview := $\emptyset$;
    delivered := $\emptyset$;
    pendingviews := [];
    trbdone := $\emptyset$;

upon event ⟨ *vs*, *Broadcast* | *m* ⟩ **such that** *blocked* = FALSE **do**
    inview := *inview* ∪ $\{(self, m)\}$;
    delivered := *delivered* ∪ $\{m\}$;
    trigger ⟨ *vs*, *Deliver* | *self*, *m* ⟩;
    trigger ⟨ *beb*, *Broadcast* | [DATA, *vid*, *m*] ⟩;

upon event ⟨ *beb*, *Deliver* | *p*, [DATA, *id*, *m*] ⟩ **do**
    if $id = vid \wedge blocked = $ FALSE $\wedge m \notin delivered$ **then**
        inview := *inview* ∪ $\{(p, m)\}$;
        delivered := *delivered* ∪ $\{m\}$;
        trigger ⟨ *vs*, *Deliver* | *p*, *m* ⟩;

---

a process *beb*-delivers a DATA message with a view identifier that matches *vid*, the identifier of the current view, it immediately *vs*-delivers the message contained inside. Every process also maintains a set *inview*, with all sender/message pairs for the messages that it *vs*-delivered during the normal operation of the current view.

The collective flush procedure is initiated when the group membership primitive installs a new view. Each process first requests from its caller that it stops *vs*-broadcasting messages in the current view. The higher layer agrees to this with a ⟨ *BlockOk* ⟩ event at each process. When the view-synchronous communication algorithm receives this event, it stops *vs*-delivering new messages and discards any DATA message that still arrives via the underlying best-effort broadcast primitive. The process then proceeds to resending all messages that it *vs*-delivered in the old view using a TRB primitive.

Every process initializes one instance of uniform TRB for each process in M, the membership of the old view, and rebroadcasts its set *inview* with the TRB instance for which it is the sender. Eventually, when the TRB instances have delivered such sets (or the failure indication) from all processes in M, each process computes the union of these sets. The result is a global set of messages that have been *vs*-delivered by those processes in view V that have not crashed so far. Each process then

Algorithm 6.9: TRB-Based View-Synchronous Communication (part 2, view change)

---

upon event ⟨ *gm, View* | V' ⟩ **do**
    if $V' = (0, M')$ for some M' **then**   // start the initial view
        $(vid, M) := (0, M')$;
        blocked := FALSE;
    else
        append(*pendingviews, V'*);

upon *pendingviews* $\neq$ [] $\wedge$ *flushing* = FALSE **do**   // start collective flush procedure
    flushing := TRUE;
    trigger ⟨ *vs, Block* ⟩;

upon event ⟨ *vs, BlockOk* ⟩ **do**
    blocked := TRUE;
    forall $p \in M$ **do**
        Initialize a new instance *utrb.vid.p* of uniform terminating reliable
            broadcast with sender p;
        if $p = self$ **then**
            trigger ⟨ *utrb.vid.p, Broadcast* | *inview* ⟩;

upon event ⟨ *utrb.id.p, Deliver* | p, iv ⟩ **such that** $id = vid$ **do**
    trbdone := *trbdone* $\cup$ $\{p\}$;
    if $iv \neq \triangle$ **then**
        forall $(s, m) \in iv$ such that $m \notin delivered$ **do**
            delivered := *delivered* $\cup$ $\{m\}$;
            trigger ⟨ *vs, Deliver* | s, m ⟩;

upon *trbdone* = $M \wedge$ *blocked* = TRUE **do**   // ready to install new view
    V := *head*(*pendingviews*); *remove*(*pendingviews, V*);
    $(vid, M) := V$;
    correct := *correct* $\cap$ M;
    flushing := FALSE; *blocked* := FALSE;
    inview := $\emptyset$;
    trbdone := $\emptyset$;
    trigger ⟨ *vs, View* | (vid, M) ⟩;

---

vs-delivers any message contained in this set that it has not yet *vs*-delivered, before it installs the new view.

Note that discarding DATA messages from the old view during the flush procedure and later causes no problem, because if a message is *vs*-delivered by any correct process in the old view then it will be rebroadcast through the TRB abstraction and *vs*-delivered as well.

Whenever a process *vs*-delivers a message during the algorithm, it verifies that the message has not been *vs*-delivered before. The algorithm maintains a variable *delivered* for this purpose that stores all *vs*-delivered messages so far (in the current view and in earlier views).

The new views output by the underlying group membership abstraction are appended to a queue *pendingviews*. This ensures that they do not get lost and are still

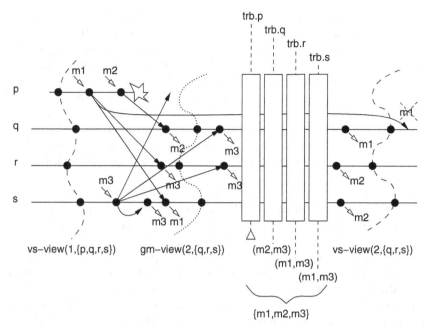

Figure 6.4: Sample execution of the TRB-based view synchronous algorithm

processed in the same sequence as installed by group membership. When a process has started to handle messages in a new view, it keeps checking this queue; as soon as it finds another view at the head of the queue, it invokes the flush procedure and this leads to the next view change. Variable *pendingviews* is a list of views; recall that our operations on lists are *append*(L, x) to append an element x to a list L, *remove*(L, x) to remove x from L, and *head*(L), which returns the first element in L.

An example execution of the algorithm is shown in Fig. 6.4. Process p *vs*-broadcasts two messages m_1 and m_2 and then crashes. Message m_1 arrives at r and s via best-effort broadcast and is immediately *vs*-delivered, but the best-effort broadcast to q is delayed. On the other hand, message m_2 is *vs*-delivered by q but not by r and s, because the sender p crashed. Additionally, process s also *vs*-broadcasts a message m_3, which is soon *vs*-delivered by all correct processes, before a view change is initiated. When the underlying membership module installs a new view and excludes p from the group, the flush procedure starts. The processes initialize an instance of TRB for each process in the old view, and each process broadcasts the set of messages that it has *vs*-delivered in the old view. For instance, the TRB with sender q outputs m_2 and m_3, since q has not yet *vs*-delivered m_1. The union of all sets output by the TRB instances, $\{m_1, m_2, m_3\}$, must be *vs*-delivered by every correct process before it installs the new view. Note that the best-effort broadcast DATA message with m_1 is eventually delivered to q, but is discarded because it is not from the current view at q.

Correctness. Consider first the *view inclusion* property. Let m be any message that is *vs*-delivered by some process q with sender p in a given view V. If q is the sender of the message then q directly *vs*-delivers the message upon *vs*-broadcasting it, in the same view. Consider now the case where the sender p is a different process. There are two possibilities. Either process q *vs*-delivers m in response to *beb*-delivering a DATA message containing m or in response to *utrb*-delivering the rebroadcast set of delivered messages from some process r. In the first case, the algorithm checks if the view in which the message was *vs*-broadcast is the current one, and if not, the message is discarded. In the second case, process r has *utrb*-broadcast its set *delivered*, which contains only messages that have been *vs*-broadcast and *vs*-delivered in the current view.

The *no creation* broadcast property directly follows from the properties of the underlying best-effort broadcast and TRB abstraction. The *no duplication* broadcast property follows from the use of the variable *delivered* and the check, applied after *beb*-delivering a DATA message, that only messages *vs*-broadcast in the current view are *vs*-delivered. Consider the *agreement* broadcast property (VS5). Assume that some correct process p has *vs*-delivered a message m. Every correct process eventually *vs*-delivers m after *beb*-delivering it, or if a new view needs to be installed, upon *utrb*-delivering a set of delivered messages from the same view that contains m. To show the *validity* property of broadcast, let p be some correct process that *vs*-broadcasts a message m. Process p directly *vs*-delivers m and, because of the *agreement* broadcast property, every correct process eventually *vs*-delivers m.

Consider now the properties inherited from group membership. The *monotonicity*, *uniform agreement* (VS7), and *accuracy* properties directly follow from the corresponding properties of the underlying group membership abstraction and from the algorithm, which preserves the order of views. The *completeness* property is ensured by the *completeness* property of the underlying group membership primitive, the *termination* property of TRB, and the assumption that the higher-level module is well behaved (i.e., it stops *vs*-broadcasting messages when it is asked to do so).

Performance. During periods where the view does not need to change, the cost of view-synchronously delivering a message is the same as the cost of a best-effort broadcast, that is, one single message transmission. For a view change from a view (vid, M), however, the algorithm requires the execution of a group membership instance, plus the (parallel) execution of one TRB for each process in M, in order to install the new view. Considering the consensus-based algorithms used to implement group membership and TRB primitives, installing a new view requires $1 + |M|$ consensus instances. In an exercise (at the end of the chapter), we discuss how to optimize Algorithm 6.8–6.9 by running a single instance of consensus to agree both on the new view and on the set of messages to be *vs*-delivered before the new view is installed.

6.8.4 Fail-Stop Algorithm: Consensus-Based Uniform View-Synchronous Communication

The view-synchronous broadcast algorithm of the previous section (Algorithm 6.8–6.9) implements view-synchronous communication (Module 6.9). It is uniform in the sense that no two processes, be they correct or not, install different views. The algorithm is *not* uniform in the message-delivery sense, as required by uniform view-synchronous communication (Module 6.10). That is, one process might view-synchronously deliver a message and crash, but no other process delivers that message. For instance, the sender p of a message m could *vs*-deliver m and its best-effort broadcast might reach only one other process q, which also *vs*-delivers m. But, if p and q crash without any further actions then no other process ever learns anything about m.

One might think that Algorithm 6.8–6.9 could be made to satisfy the *uniform agreement* broadcast property of Module 6.10 simply by replacing the underlying best-effort broadcast abstraction with a uniform reliable broadcast primitive (say, instance *urb*). However, the following scenario illustrates that this does not work. Suppose process p *vs*-broadcasts m, *urb*-broadcasts m, and then *vs*-delivers m after *urb*-delivering it. The only guarantee here is that all correct processes will eventually *urb*-deliver m; they might do so after installing a new view, however, which means that m would not be *vs*-delivered correctly.

We present Algorithm 6.10–6.11, called "Consensus-Based Uniform View-Synchronous Communication," which ensures uniform agreement in two ways: first, in the sense of group membership and, second, in the sense of reliable broadcast. In other words, Algorithm 6.10–6.11 implements uniform view-synchronous communication (Module 6.10).

The algorithm invokes a uniform consensus primitive directly and relies on a perfect failure-detector abstraction, but does not use group membership or TRB. It works as follows. When a process *vs*-broadcasts a message m, it *beb*-broadcasts a DATA message with m and the current view identifier, and adds m to the set of messages it has *beb*-broadcast. When a process p extracts such an m from a *beb*-delivered DATA message originating from the same view, it adds q to the set of processes $ack[m]$ that have acknowledged m. Then p *beb*-broadcasts m and thereby acknowledges m, if it did not do so already, and adds m to its set of messages it has *beb*-broadcast. The latter set is stored in a variable *pending*, which contains all messages that a process has received in the current view.

The process maintains also a variable *delivered* with all messages that it has ever *vs*-delivered. When all processes in the current view are contained in $ack[m]$ at a given process p, then p *vs*-delivers the message m and adds m to *delivered*. As the reader might recall from Chap. 3, the same approach has already been used in Algorithm 3.4.

If any process detects the crash of at least one member of the current view, the process initiates a collective flush procedure as in Algorithm 6.8–6.9 from the previous section. The process first broadcasts (using best-effort guarantees) its set *pending*, containing all messages received in the current view; note that some

Algorithm 6.10: Consensus-Based Uniform View-Synchronous Communication (part 1)

Implements:
    UniformViewSynchronousCommunication, **instance** *uvs*.

Uses:
    UniformConsensus (multiple instances);
    BestEffortBroadcast, **instance** *beb*;
    PerfectFailureDetector, **instance** $\mathcal{P}$.

upon event ⟨ *uvs, Init* ⟩ **do**
    $(vid, M) := (0, \Pi)$;   // current view $V = (vid, M)$
    $correct := \Pi$;
    flushing := FALSE; *blocked* := FALSE; *wait* := FALSE;
    pending := ∅;
    delivered := ∅;
    forall m **do** $ack[m] := ∅$;
    $seen := [\bot]^N$;
    trigger ⟨ *uvs, View* | (vid, M) ⟩;

upon event ⟨ *uvs, Broadcast* | m ⟩ **such that** *blocked* = FALSE **do**
    $pending := pending \cup \{(self, m)\}$;
    trigger ⟨ *beb, Broadcast* | [DATA, $vid, self, m$] ⟩;

upon event ⟨ *beb, Deliver* | p, [DATA, id, s, m] ⟩ **do**
    if $id = vid \wedge blocked = $ FALSE **then**
        $ack[m] := ack[m] \cup \{p\}$;
        if $(s, m) \notin pending$ **then**
            $pending := pending \cup \{(s, m)\}$;
            trigger ⟨ *beb, Broadcast* | [DATA, vid, s, m] ⟩;

upon exists $(s, m) \in pending$ such that $M \subseteq ack[m] \wedge m \notin delivered$ **do**
    $delivered := delivered \cup \{m\}$;
    trigger ⟨ *uvs, Deliver* | s, m ⟩;

---

messages in *pending* might not have been *vs*-delivered. As soon as a process p has collected the set *pending* from every other process that p did not detect to have crashed, it proposes a new view through an instance of uniform consensus. The view consists of all processes that are correct according to the failure detector output at p.

Apart from a new candidate view, process p also proposes the collection of *pending* sets received from *all* processes in the candidate view. The union of these sets contains all messages that the processes have "seen" and potentially *vs*-delivered in the ending view. The consensus primitive then decides on a new view and on such a collection of sets. Before installing the new view, each process parses all sets of pending messages in the consensus decision and *vs*-delivers those messages that it has not *vs*-delivered yet. Finally, the process installs the new view decided by consensus and resumes the normal operation in the next view.

Algorithm 6.11: Consensus-Based Uniform View-Synchronous Communication (part 2)

---

upon event ⟨ $\mathcal{P}$, *Crash* | p ⟩ **do**
    correct := *correct* \ {p};

upon *correct* $\subsetneq M \wedge$ *flushing* = FALSE **do**
    flushing := TRUE;
    trigger ⟨ *uvs*, *Block* ⟩;

upon event ⟨ *uvs*, *BlockOk* ⟩ **do**
    blocked := TRUE;
    trigger ⟨ *beb*, *Broadcast* | [PENDING, *vid*, *pending*] ⟩;

upon event ⟨ *beb*, *Deliver* | p, [PENDING, *id*, *pd*] ⟩ **such that** *id* = *vid* **do**
    seen[p] := *pd*;

upon (forall $p \in$ *correct* : *seen*[p] $\neq \perp$) $\wedge$ *wait* = FALSE **do**
    wait := TRUE;
    vid := *vid* + 1;
    Initialize a new instance *uc.vid* of uniform consensus;
    trigger ⟨ *uc.vid*, *Propose* | (*correct*, *seen*) ⟩;

upon event ⟨ *uc.id*, *Decide* | (M', S) ⟩ **such that** *id* = *vid* **do**   // install new view
    forall $p \in M'$ such that $S[p] \neq \perp$ **do**
        forall (s, m) $\in S[p]$ such that $m \notin$ *delivered* **do**
            delivered := *delivered* $\cup$ {m};
            trigger ⟨ *uvs*, *Deliver* | s, m ⟩;
    flushing := FALSE; *blocked* := FALSE; *wait* := FALSE;
    pending := $\emptyset$;
    forall m **do** *ack*[m] := $\emptyset$;
    seen := $[\perp]^N$;
    M := M';
    trigger ⟨ *uvs*, *View* | (*vid*, M) ⟩;

Correctness. The arguments for correctness are similar to those of Algorithm 6.8–6.9. The *view inclusion* property directly follows from the algorithm because no process buffers a message from the previous view when it installs the next view.

We first consider the broadcast-related properties. The *delivered* variable ensures that no message is *vs*-delivered twice, which demonstrates the *no duplication* property. It is also easy to see that a message can only be *vs*-delivered if some process has indeed *vs*-broadcast it, as stated by the *no creation* property.

The *validity* property follows because a correct process p includes every message in its set *pending*. As p is correct and, therefore, never detected by the failure detector, this set is always contained in the decision of the uniform consensus instance that switches to the next view. Process p *vs*-delivers every one of its messages at the latest before installing the next view.

For the *uniform agreement* property, consider any process that *vs*-delivers some message m. If the process does this during the flush procedure that installs a new view then all correct processes install the same new view as well and *vs*-deliver m.

Otherwise, the process *vs*-delivers m because every process in the current view has acknowledged m, and it follows that all correct processes must have stored the message in their *pending* variable. Hence, during the next view change, m is contained in the set of all "seen" messages and is eventually *vs*-delivered by every correct process.

The properties related to group membership follow directly from the algorithm, because it contains almost the same steps as the "Consensus-Based Group Membership" algorithm from Sect. 6.7, which also uses uniform consensus and perfect failure-detector primitives.

Performance. During periods where the view does not change, the cost of *vs*-delivering a message is the same as the cost of a reliable broadcast, namely $O(N^2)$ messages and only two communication steps. To install a new view, the algorithm requires the parallel execution of best-effort broadcasts for all processes in the view, followed by an execution of uniform consensus to agree on the next view. The algorithm uses only one instance of uniform consensus and is therefore more efficient than Algorithm 6.8–6.9, which may invoke up to $N + 1$ instances of uniform consensus for a view change.

6.9 Exercises

Exercise 6.1: *Would it make sense to add the* total-order *property of total-order broadcast to a best-effort broadcast abstraction?*

Exercise 6.2: *What happens in our "Consensus-Based Total-Order Broadcast" algorithm (Algorithm 6.1) if the set of messages delivered in a round is not sorted deterministically after deciding in the consensus abstraction, but before it is proposed to consensus? What happens in that algorithm if the set of messages decided on by consensus is not sorted deterministically at all?*

Exercise 6.3: *The "Consensus-Based Total-Order Broadcast" algorithm (Algorithm 6.1) transforms a consensus abstraction (together with a reliable broadcast abstraction) into a total-order broadcast abstraction. Describe a transformation between these two primitives in the other direction, that is, implement a (uniform) consensus abstraction from a (uniform) total-order broadcast abstraction.*

Exercise 6.4: *Discuss algorithms for total-order broadcast in the fail-silent model.*

Exercise 6.5: *Discuss the specification of total-order broadcast and its implementation in the fail-recovery model.*

Exercise 6.6: *Discuss the relation between Byzantine consensus and Byzantine total-order broadcast.*

Exercise 6.7: *Design a more efficient Byzantine total-order broadcast algorithm than Algorithm 6.2, in which every underlying consensus instance decides at least one message that can be btob-delivered. Use digital signatures and a Byzantine consensus primitive with the* anchored validity *property, as introduced in Exercise 5.11.*

Exercise 6.8: *Give a specification of a state-machine replication abstraction and design an algorithm to implement it using a total-order broadcast primitive.*

Exercise 6.9: *Consider a fault-tolerant service, implemented by a replicated state machine, from the perspective of a group of clients. Clients invoke operations on the service and expect to receive a response. How do the clients access the replicated state-machine abstraction from Exercise 6.8? What changes if the replicated state-machine abstraction is implemented in the fail-arbitrary model, with Byzantine processes?*

Exercise 6.10: *Can we implement a TRB abstraction with an eventually perfect failure-detector abstraction ($\Diamond\mathcal{P}$) if we assume that at least one process can crash?*

Exercise 6.11: *Can we implement a perfect failure-detector abstraction $\mathcal{P}$ from multiple TRB instances, such that every process can repeatedly broadcast messages, in a model where any number of processes can crash?*

Exercise 6.12: *Consider the fast Byzantine consensus abstraction with the following stronger form of the* fast *termination property. It guarantees a one-round decision in any execution as long as all* correct *processes propose the same value:*

> **FBC1':** *Strong fast termination:* If all correct processes propose the same value, then every correct process decides some value after one communication step. Otherwise, every correct process eventually decides some value.

Describe how to modify Algorithm 6.5 such that it transforms a Byzantine consensus abstraction into fast Byzantine consensus with strong fast termination. As a hint, we add that the strong fast termination *property can only be achieved under the assumption that $N > 7f$.*

Exercise 6.13: *Recall that our implementation of a nonblocking atomic commit (NBAC) abstraction (Algorithm 6.6) relies on consensus. Devise two algorithms that do not use consensus and implement relaxations of the NBAC abstraction, where the* termination *property has been replaced with:*

1. Weak termination: *Let p be some process that is known to the algorithm; if p does not crash then all correct processes eventually decide.*
2. Very weak termination: *If no process crashes then all processes eventually decide.*

Exercise 6.14: *Can we implement a NBAC primitive with an eventually perfect failure detector $\Diamond \mathcal{P}$, if we assume that at least one process can crash? What if we consider a weaker specification of NBAC, in which the (regular or uniform)* agreement *property is not required?*

Exercise 6.15: *Do we need the perfect failure-detector primitive $\mathcal{P}$ to implement NBAC if we consider a system where at least two processes can crash, but a majority is correct? What if we assume that at most one process can crash?*

Exercise 6.16: *Give an algorithm that implements a view-synchronous communication abstraction such that a single consensus instance is used for every view change (unlike Algorithm 6.8–6.9), and every process directly vs-delivers every message after vs-broadcasting it or after first learning about the existence of the message (unlike Algorithm 6.10–6.11).*

6.10 Solutions

Solution 6.1: The resulting abstraction would not make much sense in a failure-prone environment, as it would not preclude the following scenario. Assume that a process p broadcasts several messages with best-effort properties and then crashes. Some correct processes might end up delivering all those messages (in the same order) whereas other correct processes might end up not delivering any message.

Solution 6.2: If the deterministic sorting is done prior to proposing the set for consensus, instead of a posteriori upon deciding, the processes would not agree on a set but on a sequence of messages. But if they *to*-deliver the messages in decided order, the algorithm still ensures the *total order* property.

If the messages, on which the algorithm agrees in consensus, are never sorted deterministically within every batch (neither a priori nor a posteriori), then the *total order* property does not hold. Even if the processes decide on the same batch of messages, they might *to*-deliver the messages within this batch in a different order. In fact, the *total order* property would be ensured only with respect to *batches* of messages, but not with respect to individual messages. We thus get a coarser granularity in the total order.

We could avoid using the deterministic sort function at the cost of proposing a single message at a time in the consensus abstraction. This means that we would need exactly as many consensus instances as there are messages exchanged between the processes. If messages are generated very slowly by processes, the algorithm ends up using one consensus instance per message anyway. If the messages are generated rapidly then it is beneficial to use several messages per instance: within one instance of consensus, several messages would be gathered, i.e., every message of the consensus algorithm would concern several messages to *to*-deliver. Agreeing on large batches with many messages at once is important for performance in practice, because it considerably reduces the number of times that the consensus algorithm is invoked.

Solution 6.3: Given a total-order broadcast primitive *to*, a consensus abstraction is obtained as follows: When a process proposes a value v in consensus, it *to*-broadcasts v. When the first message is *to*-delivered containing some value x, a process decides x. Since the total-order broadcast delivers the same sequence of messages at every correct process, and every *to*-delivered message has been *to*-broadcast, this reduction implements a consensus abstraction.

Solution 6.4: Our algorithm for total-order broadcast in the fail-stop model works also in the fail-silent model, as it does not use a failure-detector abstraction directly, but uses primitives for reliable broadcast and consensus. Algorithms for reliable broadcast can be realized in the fail-silent model, assuming a majority of correct processes. The consensus abstraction cannot be implemented in the fail-silent model, as explained in Chap. 5, only in the fail-noisy or in the randomized fail-silent models.

Solution 6.5: We introduce a specification of total-order broadcast in the fail-recovery model and an algorithm that implements it.

We apply the same approach as used to derive "logged" abstractions in the previous chapters. We depart from an abstraction designed for the fail-stop model and adapt its interface with adjacent modules to use logged delivery, add logging operations for relevant states, and define a recovery procedure. Any underlying primitives are implemented in the fail-recovery model as well.

We illustrate here only the uniform variant of logged total-order broadcast, presented in Module 6.11. Its interface is similar to the interface of the logged

Module 6.11: Interface and properties of logged uniform total-order broadcast

Module:

    Name: LoggedUniformTotalOrderBroadcast, **instance** *lutob*.

Events:

    Request: ⟨ *lutob, Broadcast* | *m* ⟩: Broadcasts a message *m* to all processes.

    Indication: ⟨ *lutob, Deliver* | *delivered* ⟩: Notifies the upper layer of potential updates to variable *delivered* in stable storage, where *delivered* is a sequence of sender/message pairs.

Properties:

    LUTOB1–LUTOB4: Same as properties LURB1–LURB4 of logged uniform reliable broadcast (Module 3.6).

    LUTOB5: *Logged uniform total order:* For any two processes p and q, suppose p log-delivers a sequence of messages dp and q log-delivers a sequence of messages dq. Then dp is either a prefix of dq or dq is a prefix of dp.

---

broadcasts from Chap. 3 (see Module 3.5, for instance), with the only change that variable *delivered*, used to *log-deliver* messages from the primitive, is now an ordered list and no longer a set. Newly log-delivered messages are always appended to *delivered*. Recall that the abstraction log-delivers a message m from sender s whenever an event ⟨ *Deliver* | *delivered* ⟩ occurs such that *delivered* contains a pair (s, m) for the first time.

To implement the abstraction, we present algorithm "Logged Uniform Total-Order Broadcast" in Algorithm 6.12; it closely follows the algorithm for the fail-stop model presented in Sect. 6.1 and works as follows. Every message in a total-order broadcast request is disseminated using the underlying uniform reliable broadcast primitive for the fail-recovery model. The total-order broadcast algorithm maintains two variables with messages: a set *unordered* of messages that have been delivered by the underlying reliable broadcast module, and a list *delivered*, containing the totally ordered sequence of log-delivered messages. The algorithm operates in a sequence of rounds and invokes one logged uniform consensus primitive per round. At the end of every round, it sorts the newly decided batch of messages and appends them to *delivered*.

The algorithm starts a new instance of logged uniform consensus whenever it notices that there are unordered messages that have not yet been ordered by the consensus instances of previous rounds. When proposing a batch of messages for consensus in some round, the algorithm logs the proposal in stable storage. The *wait* flag is also used to ensure that consensus instances are invoked in serial order.

During the recovery operation after a crash, the total-order algorithm runs again through all rounds executed before the crash and executes the same consensus instances once more. (We assume that the runtime environment re-instantiates all instances of consensus that had been dynamically initialized before the crash.) This

---

Algorithm 6.12: Logged Uniform Total-Order Broadcast

Implements:
   LoggedUniformTotalOrderBroadcast, **instance** *lutob*.

Uses:
   LoggedUniformReliableBroadcast, **instance** *lurb*;
   LoggedUniformConsensus (multiple instances).

upon event ⟨ *lutob, Init* ⟩ **do**
   unordered := ∅; *delivered* := [];
   round := 1;
   recovering := FALSE; *wait* := FALSE;
   forall $r > 0$ **do** *proposals*[r] := ⊥;

upon event ⟨ *Recovery* ⟩ **do**
   unordered := ∅; *delivered* := [];
   round := 1;
   recovering := TRUE; *wait* := FALSE;
   retrieve(*proposals*);
   if *proposals*[1] ≠ ⊥ **then**
      trigger ⟨ *luc.*1, *Propose* | *proposals*[1] ⟩;

upon event ⟨ *lutob, Broadcast* | m ⟩ **do**
   trigger ⟨ *lurb, Broadcast* | m ⟩;

upon event ⟨ *lurb, Deliver* | *lurbdelivered* ⟩ **do**
   unordered := *unordered* ∪ *lurbdelivered*;

upon *unordered* \ *delivered* ≠ ∅ ∧ *wait* = FALSE ∧ *recovering* = FALSE **do**
   wait := TRUE;
   Initialize a new instance *luc.round* of logged uniform consensus;
   proposals[*round*] := *unordered* \ *delivered*;
   store(*proposals*);
   trigger ⟨ *luc.round, Propose* | *proposals*[*round*] ⟩;

upon event ⟨ *luc.r, Decide* | *decided* ⟩ **such that** r = *round* **do**
   forall (s, m) ∈ *sort*(*decided*) **do**   // by the order in the resulting sorted list
      append(*delivered*, (s, m));
   store(*delivered*);
   round := *round* + 1;
   if *recovering* = TRUE **then**
      if *proposals*[*round*] ≠ ⊥ **then**
         trigger ⟨ *luc.round, Propose* | *proposals*[*round*] ⟩;
      else
         recovering := FALSE;
   else
      wait := FALSE;
   trigger ⟨ *lutob, Deliver* | *delivered* ⟩;

---

ensures that every instance of consensus actually decides. Because the algorithm proposes the logged message batches again for consensus, every consensus instance is always invoked with exactly the same parameters. Although it may not be strictly needed (depending on the implementation of consensus), this is consistent with the invariant that each process proposes the message batch stored in stable storage.

The algorithm has the interesting feature of never storing the set of unordered messages and not logging the delivered sequence for its own use (however, the algorithm must write *delivered* to stable storage for log-delivering its output). These two data structures are simply reconstructed from scratch upon recovery, based on the stable storage kept internally by the reliable broadcast primitive and by the consensus primitive. Because the initial values proposed for each consensus instance are logged, the process may invoke all past instances of consensus again to obtain the same sequence of messages ordered and delivered in previous rounds.

The algorithm requires at least one communication step to execute the reliable broadcast primitive and at least two communication steps to execute every consensus instance. Therefore, even if no failures occur, at least three communication steps are required.

Solution 6.6: The Byzantine total-order broadcast and the Byzantine consensus primitives stand in a similar relation to each other as their counterparts with crash-stop processes, which was discussed in Exercise 6.3. As demonstrated through Algorithm 6.2, Byzantine consensus can be used to implement Byzantine total-order broadcast.

An emulation in the other direction works as well, assuming that $N > 3f$. The processes run a Byzantine total-order broadcast primitive and broadcast the proposal from consensus. Once that the first $N - f$ messages from distinct senders have been delivered by total-order broadcast, the processes apply a deterministic decision function. It decides a value v in Byzantine consensus if more than f messages were equal to v; otherwise, it decides $\Box$. This emulation shows that Byzantine total-order broadcast can be used to implement Byzantine consensus.

Solution 6.7: A simple solution, which solves the problem almost but not completely, works like this. Every process maintains a variable *undelivered* with the set of input messages that it has itself *btob*-broadcast, but that have not yet been *btob*-delivered. In parallel, the processes execute rounds of Byzantine consensus with the *anchored validity* property. For every consensus instance, a process p computes a digital signature σ on the round number and its current set of undelivered messages, and proposes the tuple $(p, undelivered, \sigma)$ for consensus. The predicate implementing anchored validity verifies that a proposal contains only messages that have not yet been delivered up to the current round, that there is at least one undelivered message, and that the signature in the proposal is valid.

In order to prevent that a correct process stalls the sequence of consensus executions because its set *undelivered* is empty, the processes also periodically exchange their proposals for consensus, using point-to-point links. When a process with an empty set of input messages receives a proposal, it adopts the proposal of the other process and proposes it in consensus. When consensus decides a set of messages from some sender process s, every process *btob*-delivers all messages in a deterministic order. Because the signature on the proposal is valid, the messages must have been *btob*-broadcast by sender s (if s is correct).

According to the *anchored validity* notion and the predicate imposed by the correct processes, this algorithm decides and *btob*-delivers at least one message in every round of consensus. It may violate the *validity* property of Byzantine total-order broadcast, though, because consensus may forever avoid to decide on the set of messages sent by a particular correct process.

An extension of this algorithm avoids the above problem. To ensure that every *btob*-broadcast message m from a correct sender s is eventually *btob*-delivered, the sender first constructs a triple (m, s, σ), containing a signature σ on the message, and sends this triple to all processes using authenticated point-to-point links. Every process now maintains the received triples containing undelivered messages in its *undelivered* variable.

An initial dissemination phase is added to every round; in the second phase of the round, the processes again execute an instance of Byzantine consensus with anchored validity. In the dissemination phase, every process signs its variable *undelivered* and sends it with the signature in an UNDELIVERED message to all processes. Every process waits to receive such UNDELIVERED messages containing only valid signatures from more than f processes.

A process then enters the second phase of the round and proposes the received list of $f + 1$ UNDELIVERED messages to Byzantine consensus. The predicate implementing anchored validity verifies that a proposal contains UNDELIVERED messages signed by more than f distinct processes, that no (*btob*-level) message contained in it has yet been delivered up to the current round, that there is at least one undelivered message, and that the signatures in all triples are valid. When consensus decides a proposal, the algorithm proceeds like before and *btob*-delivers all messages extracted from the triples in a deterministic order.

The extended algorithm ensures the *validity* property because a triple (m, s, σ) with a *btob*-broadcast message m, sent by a correct process s, and with signature σ is eventually contained in the *undelivered* set of every correct process. In the next round after that time, every UNDELIVERED message therefore contains m. Since the Byzantine consensus instance decides a set of more than f UNDELIVERED messages, at least one of them is from a correct process and contains also m.

Solution 6.8: A state machine consists of variables and commands that transform its state and may produce some output. Commands consist of deterministic programs such that the outputs of the state machine are solely determined by the initial state and by the sequence of commands that it has executed. A state machine can be made fault-tolerant by replicating it on different processes.

A replicated state-machine abstraction can be characterized by the properties listed in Module 6.12. Basically, its interface presents two events: first, a request event ⟨ *Execute* | *command* ⟩ that a client uses to invoke the execution of a program *command* of the state machine; and, second, an indication event ⟨ *Output* | *response* ⟩,

---

Module 6.12: Interface and properties of a replicated state machine

Module:

    Name: ReplicatedStateMachine, **instance** *rsm*.

Events:

    Request: ⟨ *rsm, Execute* | *command* ⟩: Requests that the state machine executes the command given in *command*.

    Indication: ⟨ *rsm, Output* | *response* ⟩: Indicates that the state machine has executed a command with output *response*.

Properties:

    RSM1: *Agreement:* All correct processes obtain the same sequence of outputs.

    RSM2: *Termination:* If a correct process executes a command, then the command eventually produces an output.

---

which is produced by the state machine and carries the output from executing the last command in parameter *response*. For the sake of brevity, we assume that the *command* parameter of the execution operation includes both the name of the command to be executed and any relevant parameters.

As an example, an atomic register could be implemented as a state machine. In this case, the state of the machine would hold the current value of the register and the relevant commands would be (1) a *write(v)* command that writes a value v to the register and outputs a parameter-less response, which only indicates that the write concluded, and (2) a *read* command that causes the state machine to output the value of the register as the response. Of course, more sophisticated objects can be replicated the same way.

Algorithm 6.13 implements a replicated state-machine primitive simply by disseminating all commands to execute using a uniform total-order broadcast primitive. When a command is delivered by the broadcast module, the process executes it on the state machine, and outputs the response.

As the state machine is deterministic, is started from the same initial state at every process, and every process executes the same sequence of commands, all responses are equal.

Solution 6.9: Every client assigns unique identifiers to its own commands. A client sends an identifier/command pair to one replica first using a point-to-point message (a replica is a process that executes the replicate state machine). When it receives this, the replica executes the command on the state machine and includes the originating client and the command identifier together with the command description. When the client does not receive a response to a command after some time, it resends the same identifier/command pair to another replica.

Algorithm 6.13: Replicated State Machine using Total-Order Broadcast

---

Implements:
    ReplicatedStateMachine, **instance** *rsm*.

Uses:
    UniformTotalOrderBroadcast, **instance** *utob*;

upon event ⟨ *rsm*, *Init* ⟩ **do**
    state := initial state;

upon event ⟨ *rsm*, *Execute* | *command* ⟩ **do**
    trigger ⟨ *utob*, *Broadcast* | *command* ⟩;

upon event ⟨ *utob*, *Deliver* | *p*, *command* ⟩ **do**
    (*response*, *newstate*) := execute(*command*, *state*);
    state := *newstate*;
    trigger ⟨ *rsm*, *Output* | *response* ⟩;

All replicas process the outputs of the state machine; we assume that every response also carries the command from which it is produced, including the originating client and the identifier. When the state machine at a replica outputs a response, the replica obtains the client from which the command originated and sends the response with the command identifier back to the client, using a point-to-point message. A client must wait to receive the first response for every command identifier and may discard duplicate responses.

Almost the same scheme works with Byzantine processes. Even though a client might send the command to some Byzantine replicas, the client eventually hits a correct replica by repeatedly sending the command to different replicas. Once it sends the command to a correct replica, the state machine eventually executes the command and outputs a response. But as the Byzantine replicas may send a wrong response to the client, the client needs to receive $f + 1$ matching responses with a given command identifier: this ensures that at least one of the responses is from a correct replica.

Solution 6.10: The answer is no. Consider an instance *trb* of TRB with sender process s. We show that it is impossible to implement TRB from an eventually perfect failure-detector primitive $\Diamond\mathcal{P}$ if even one process can crash.

Consider an execution E_1, in which process s crashes initially and observe the possible actions for some correct process p: due to the *termination* property of TRB, there must be a time T at which p *trb*-delivers $\triangle$.

Consider a second execution E_2 that is similar to E_1 up to time T, except that the sender s is correct and *trb*-broadcasts some message m, but all communication messages to and from s are delayed until after time T. The failure detector behaves in E_2 as in E_1 until after time T. This is possible because the failure detector is only eventually perfect. Up to time T, process p cannot distinguish E_1 from E_2 and *trb*-delivers $\triangle$. According to the *agreement* property of TRB, process s must *trb*-deliver △ as well, and *s* delivers exactly one message due to the *termination* property. But this contradicts the *validity* property of TRB, since *s* is correct, has *trb*-broadcast some message $m \neq \triangle$, and must *trb*-deliver *m*.

Solution 6.11: The answer is yes and shows that the perfect failure detector is not only sufficient to implement TRB but also necessary. In other words, the TRB abstraction is equivalent to a perfect failure detector primitive.

Consider a model where any number of processes can crash and suppose that for every process *p*, multiple instances of TRB with *p* as sender are available. We explain how to construct a perfect failure detector from these primitives. The idea behind the transformation is to have every process repeatedly invoke instances of TRB with all processes in the system as senders. If one such instance with sender *s* ever *trb*-delivers △ at process *p*, the module $\mathcal{P}$ at *p* detects *s* to have crashed from then on.

The transformation satisfies the *strong completeness* property of $\mathcal{P}$ because the TRB abstraction delivers △ if the sender *s* has crashed by its *termination* property. On the other hand, the *strong accuracy* property of $\mathcal{P}$ (which states that if a process is detected, then it has crashed) holds because the properties of TRB imply that process *P* only delivers △ when the sender *s* has crashed.

Solution 6.12: The only change to Algorithm 6.5 concerns the number of equal proposal values necessary to decide fast. The algorithm as stated before decides fast if all $N - f$ received PROPOSAL messages contain the same value. Clearly, even one Byzantine process could prevent fast termination according to the strong notion by sending a different proposal value and causing it to be received by all correct processes. More generally, the algorithm must tolerate that at most *f* of the received proposal messages are different from the rest and still decide fast. Reducing the bound for deciding fast to finding $N - 2f$ equal values among the $N - f$ received proposal messages achieves this.

The modified algorithm still ensures *agreement* under the assumption that $N > 7f$. Again, there are three cases to consider: two correct processes *p* and *q* decide fast both, or *p* decides fast and *q* decides after *bc*-deciding, or both decide after *bc*-deciding. Only the second case changes substantially compared to Algorithm 6.5. If *p* decides fast, it has received $N - f$ PROPOSAL messages and found a common value *v* in at least $N - 2f$ of them. As the system contains *N* processes, also every other correct process must have received PROPOSAL messages from at least $N - 2f$ of those processes whose proposal was received by *p*. No more than *f* of these processes might be Byzantine; thus, every correct process must have at least $N - 3f$ proposals containing *v*. But the assumption that $N > 7f$ implies that

$$N - 3f > \frac{N - f}{2}$$

and, therefore, every correct process adopts *v* as its proposal and *bc*-proposes *v*. Applying the same argument as before, it follows that also process *q* decides *v* in fast Byzantine consensus.

All other properties of fast Byzantine consensus follow from the same arguments as used to show the correctness of Algorithm 6.5.

Solution 6.13: Both algorithms are reminiscent of atomic commit methods used by some practical distributed transaction processing systems.

1. The first algorithm may rely on the globally known process p to enforce termi-nation. The algorithm uses a perfect failure detector P and works as follows. All processes send their proposal over a point-to-point link to p. This process collects the proposals from all processes that P does not detect to have crashed. Once process p knows something from every process in the system, it may decide unilaterally. In particular, it decides COMMIT if all processes propose COMMIT and no process is detected by P, and it decides ABORT otherwise, i.e., if some process proposes ABORT or is detected by P to have crashed. Process p then uses best-effort broadcast to send its decision to all processes. Any process that delivers the message with the decision from p decides accordingly. If p crashes, then all processes are blocked.
   Of course, the algorithm could be improved in some cases, because the pro-cesses might figure out the decision by themselves, such as when p crashes after some correct process has decided, or when some correct process decides ABORT. However, the improvement does always work: if all correct processes pro-pose COMMIT but p crashes before any other process then no correct process can decide. This algorithm is also known as the "Two-Phase Commit" (2PC) algorithm. It implements a variant of atomic commitment that is *blocking*.
2. The second algorithm is simpler because it only needs to satisfy termination if all processes are correct. All processes use best-effort broadcast to send their proposals to all processes. Every process waits to deliver proposals from all other processes. If a process obtains the proposal COMMIT from all processes, then it decides COMMIT; otherwise, it decides ABORT. Note that this algorithm does not make use of any failure detector.

Solution 6.14: The answer is no. To explain why, we consider an execution E_1, where all processes are correct and propose COMMIT, except for some process p that proposes ABORT and crashes initially, without sending any message. All correct processes must therefore decide ABORT in E_1, as deciding COMMIT would violate the *commit-validity* property. Let T be the time at which the first (correct) process q decides ABORT. It does so presumably after receiving some output of $\diamond P$, which indicated that p crashed.

   Consider now an execution E_2 that is similar to E_1 except that p is correct and proposes COMMIT, but all its messages are delayed until after time T. The failure detector behaves in E_2 as in E_1 until time T and suspects p to have crashed; this is possible because $\diamond P$ is only eventually perfect. Hence, no process apart from p can distinguish between E_1 and E_2 and q also decides ABORT in E_2. But this violates the *abort-validity* property, as all processes are correct and propose COMMIT, yet they decide ABORT.

In this argument, the (uniform or regular) *agreement* property of NBAC was not explicitly needed. This shows that even a specification of NBAC where *agreement* was not needed could not be implemented with an eventually perfect failure detector if some process crashes.

Solution 6.15: Consider first a system where at least two processes can crash but a majority is correct. We will argue that in this case the perfect failure detector is not needed. Specifically, we exhibit a failure detector that is strictly weaker than the perfect failure detector ($\mathcal{P}$) in a precise sense, but that is strong enough to implement NBAC.

The failure-detector abstraction in question is called the *anonymously perfect* perfect failure detector, and denoted by $?\mathcal{P}$. This failure detector ensures the *strong completeness* and *eventual strong accuracy* properties of an eventually perfect failure detector (Module 2.8), plus the following property:

> *Anonymous detection:* Every correct process eventually outputs a failure indication value F if and only if some process has crashed.

Recall that an eventually perfect failure-detector primitive is not sufficient to implement NBAC, as shown in Exercise 6.14.

Given that we assume a majority of correct processes and given that the failure detector $?\mathcal{P}$ satisfies at least the properties of an eventually perfect failure detector, one can use $?\mathcal{P}$ to implement a uniform consensus primitive (for instance, using the fail-noisy Algorithm 5.7 from Chap. 5).

We now describe how to implement NBAC with the help of a $?\mathcal{P}$ abstraction and a uniform consensus primitive. The NBAC algorithm works as follows. All processes initially use a best-effort broadcast primitive *beb* to send their proposal to all processes. Every process p waits (1) to *beb*-deliver COMMIT from all processes, or (2) to *beb*-deliver ABORT from some process, or (3) for $?\mathcal{P}$ to output F. In case (1), process p invokes consensus and proposes COMMIT. In cases (2) and (3), p invokes consensus with proposal ABORT. When the consensus primitive outputs a decision, p also decides this value for NBAC. It is easy to see that the algorithm implements NBAC, since the *anonymous detection* property gives the processes enough information to decide correctly.

Now we discuss in which sense $?\mathcal{P}$ is strictly weaker than $\mathcal{P}$. Assume a system where at least two processes can crash. Consider an execution E_1 where two processes p and q crash initially, and an execution E_2 where only p initially crashes. Let r be any correct process. Using $?\mathcal{P}$, at any particular time T, process r cannot distinguish between executions E_1 and E_2 if the messages of q are delayed until after T. When process r obtains an output F from $?\mathcal{P}$, it knows that some process has indeed crashed but not which one. With $\mathcal{P}$, process r would know precisely which process crashed.

Hence, in a system where two processes can crash but a majority is correct, a perfect failure-detector primitive $\mathcal{P}$ is not needed to implement NBAC. There is a failure-detector abstraction $?\mathcal{P}$, called the anonymously perfect failure detector, which is strictly weaker than $\mathcal{P}$ and strong enough to implement NBAC.

Consider now the second part of the exercise. Assume that at most one process can crash. We argue that in such a system, we can emulate a perfect failure-detector abstraction given a primitive for NBAC. The algorithm causes all processes to go through sequential rounds. In each round, the processes use best-effort broadcast to send an "I-am-alive" message to all processes, and then invoke an instance of NBAC. In a given round, every process p waits for NBAC to decide on an outcome: if the outcome is COMMIT then p moves to the next round; if the outcome is ABORT then p waits to *beb*-deliver $N - 1$ messages and declares the process that should have sent the missing message to have crashed. Clearly, this algorithm emulates the behavior of a perfect failure detector $\mathcal{P}$ in a system where at most one process crashes.

Solution 6.16: Algorithm 6.14–6.15 for view-synchronous communication presented here uses a reliable broadcast primitive, a uniform consensus module, and a perfect failure-detector abstraction.

The algorithm combines the simple communication approach of Algorithm 6.8–6.9 with methods from Algorithm 6.10–6.11; it works as follows. When a process detects the crash of at least one member of the current view, the process

---

Algorithm 6.14: Direct Consensus-Based View-Synchronous Communication (part 1)

Implements:
    ViewSynchronousCommunication, **instance** *vs.*

Uses:
    UniformConsensus, (multiple instances);
    BestEffortBroadcast, **instance** *beb*;
    PerfectFailureDetector, **instance** $\mathcal{P}$.

upon event $\langle$ *vs, Init* $\rangle$ **do**
    $(vid, M) := (0, \Pi)$;   // current view $V = (vid, M)$
    $correct := \Pi$;
    flushing := FALSE; *blocked* := FALSE; *wait* := FALSE;
    inview := $\emptyset$;
    delivered := $\emptyset$;
    seen := $[\bot]^N$;
    trigger $\langle$ *vs, View* $|$ (vid, M) $\rangle$;

upon event $\langle$ *vs, Broadcast* $|$ m $\rangle$ **such that** *blocked* = FALSE **do**
    inview := *inview* $\cup$ $\{(self, m)\}$;
    delivered := *delivered* $\cup$ $\{m\}$;
    trigger $\langle$ *vs, Deliver* $|$ *self, m* $\rangle$;
    trigger $\langle$ *beb, Broadcast* $|$ $[\text{DATA}, vid, m]$ $\rangle$;

upon event $\langle$ *beb, Deliver* $|$ p, $[\text{DATA}, id, m]$ $\rangle$ **do**
    if $id = vid \wedge blocked = \text{FALSE} \wedge m \notin delivered$ **then**
        inview := *inview* $\cup$ $\{(p, m)\}$;
        delivered := *delivered* $\cup$ $\{m\}$;
        trigger $\langle$ *vs, Deliver* $|$ p, m $\rangle$;

Algorithm 6.15: Direct Consensus-Based View-Synchronous Communication (part 2)

upon event ⟨ $\mathcal{P}$, *Crash* | p ⟩ **do**
    correct := *correct* \ {p};

upon *correct* $\subsetneq M \land$ *flushing* = FALSE **do**
    flushing := TRUE;
    trigger ⟨ *vs*, *Block* ⟩;

upon event ⟨ *vs*, *BlockOk* ⟩ **do**
    blocked := TRUE;
    trigger ⟨ *beb*, *Broadcast* | [INVIEW, *vid*, *inview*] ⟩;

upon event ⟨ *beb*, *Deliver* | p, [INVIEW, *id*, *iv*] ⟩ **such that** $id = vid$ **do**
    seen[p] := *iv*;

upon (forall $p \in$ *correct* : *seen*[p] $\neq \bot$) $\land$ *wait* = FALSE **do**
    wait := TRUE;
    vid := *vid* + 1;
    Initialize a new instance *uc.vid* of uniform consensus;
    trigger ⟨ *uc.vid*, *Propose* | (*correct*, *seen*) ⟩;

upon event ⟨ *uc.id*, *Decide* | (M', S) ⟩ **such that** $id = vid$ **do**   // install new view
    forall $p \in M'$ such that $S[p] \neq \bot$ **do**
        forall (s, m) $\in S[p]$ such that $m \notin$ *delivered* **do**
            delivered := *delivered* $\cup$ {m};
            trigger ⟨ *vs*, *Deliver* | s, m ⟩;
    flushing := FALSE; *blocked* := FALSE; *wait* := FALSE;
    inview := $\emptyset$;
    seen := $[\bot]^N$;
    M := M';
    trigger ⟨ *vs*, *View* | (*vid*, M) ⟩;

initiates a collective flush procedure as in the algorithms of Sect. 6.8. The purpose of the flush procedure is again to collect all messages that have been view-synchronously delivered by at least one process (that has not been detected to have crashed). These messages must be *vs*-delivered by all processes that are about to install the new view. To execute the flush procedure, each process first blocks the normal message flow as before (by triggering a ⟨ *Block* ⟩ output event for the layer above and waiting for the corresponding ⟨ *BlockOk* ⟩ input event). Once the message flow is blocked, the process stops broadcasting and delivering view-synchronous application messages. The process then broadcasts its set of *vs*-delivered messages in the current view (stored in variable *inview*) to every other process.

As soon as a process p has collected the *vs*-delivered message set from every other process that p did not detect to have crashed, p proposes a new view through a consensus instance. More precisely, process p proposes to consensus the new set of view members as well as their corresponding sets of *vs*-delivered messages (in variable *seen*). Because the flush procedure might be initiated by processes which have detected different failures (or detected the failures in a different order), and, furthermore, some processes might fail during the flush procedure, different processes might propose different values to consensus. But it is important to note that each of these proposals contains a valid set of processes for the next view and a valid set of *vs*-delivered messages. (The only risk here is to end up *vs*-delivering fewer or more messages of processes which have crashed, but this does no harm.) Consensus guarantees that the same new view is selected by all correct processes. Before installing the new view, process p parses the *vs*-delivered message sets of all other processes that proceed to the new view and *vs*-delivers those messages that it has not *vs*-delivered yet. Finally, p installs the new view and resumes the normal operation within the view.

Any message is *vs*-delivered by its sender immediately after the message is *vs*-broadcast. The message is also added to the set *inview* of messages *vs*-delivered by the sender. If the sender remains correct, the message will be *vs*-delivered before the next view change by the algorithm described earlier (remember that the algorithm uses a perfect failure detector). Furthermore, the set of *vs*-delivered messages (from the variable *seen* of some process) will be made available to all noncrashed processes as an output of the consensus instance that decides on the next view. Since all correct processes parse this set for missing messages before they install the next view, all contained messages are *vs*-delivered in the same view at all correct processes.

During periods where the view does not need to change, the cost of *vs*-delivering a message is the same as the cost of a best-effort broadcast, that is, only $O(N)$ messages and one communication step. To install a new view, the algorithm requires every process to broadcast one message using best-effort broadcast and to execute one instance of uniform consensus to agree on the next view.

6.11 Chapter Notes

- Total-order broadcast is probably the most important abstraction for practical applications of distributed programming. It has, therefore, received a lot of interest, starting with the pioneering work of Lamport (1978). Schneider (1990) gives a concise introduction to total-order broadcast and state-machine replication.
- Our total-order broadcast specifications and the algorithm implementing total-order broadcast in the fail-stop model are inspired by the work of Chandra and Toueg (1996) and of Hadzilacos and Toueg (1993). These implementations are instructive because they are modular and use consensus as an abstract primitive. In practice, system implementors have preferred optimized monolithic implementations of total-order broadcast, such as the "Paxos" algorithm (Lamport 1998) or viewstamped replication (Oki and Liskov 1988), whose consensus mechanisms we discussed in Chap. 5. Many systems deployed today provide total-order broadcast; one representative implementation is described by Chandra, Griesemer, and Redstone (2007).

- Our total-order broadcast specification and the algorithm in the fail-recovery model (in Exercise 6.5) were defined only more recently (Boichat et al. 2003a; Boichat and Guerraoui 2005; Rodrigues and Raynal 2003).

- We considered that messages that need to be totally ordered were broadcast to all processes in the system, and hence it was reasonable to have all processes participate in the ordering activity. As for reliable broadcast, it is also possible to formulate a total-order multicast abstraction where the sender can select the subset of processes to which the message needs to be sent, and require that no other process besides the sender and the multicast set participates in the ordering (Rodrigues, Guerraoui, and Schiper 1998; Guerraoui and Schiper 2001).

- It is possible to design total-order algorithms with crash-stop processes that exploit particular features of concrete networks. Such algorithms can be seen as sophisticated variants of the basic approach taken by the algorithms presented here (Chang and Maxemchuck 1984; Veríssimo et al. 1989; Kaashoek and Tanenbaum 1991; Moser et al. 1995; Rodrigues et al. 1996; Rufino et al. 1998; Amir et al. 2000).

- Byzantine total-order broadcast has a shorter history than its counterpart with crash-stop processes. Our Byzantine atomic broadcast algorithms in Sect. 6.2 and Exercise 6.7 follow the modular presentation by Cachin et al. (2001). In contrast to this, the PBFT algorithm of Castro and Liskov (2002) and many subsequent algorithms (Doudou et al. 2005; Abd-El-Malek et al. 2005; Abraham et al. 2006; Martin and Alvisi 2006; Kotla et al. 2009; Guerraoui et al. 2010) implement Byzantine total-order broadcast directly.

- The TRB problem was studied by Hadzilacos and Toueg (1993) in the context of crash failures. This abstraction is a variant of the "Byzantine Generals" problem (Lamport, Shostak, and Pease 1982). While the original Byzantine Generals problem uses a fail-arbitrary model with processes that might behave arbitrarily and maliciously, the TRB abstraction assumes that processes may only fail by crashing.

- The fast consensus abstraction and the algorithm that implements it were discussed by Brasileiro et al. (2001). Our description in Sect. 6.4 follows their presentation.

- The fast Byzantine consensus abstraction in Sect. 6.5 and its variant from Exercise 6.12 have been introduced by Song and van Renesse (2008).

- The atomic commit problem, sometimes also called "atomic commitment," was introduced by Gray (1978), together with the "Two-Phase Commit" algorithm, which we studied in Exercise 6.13. The atomic commit problem corresponds to our nonblocking atomic commit (NBAC) abstraction without the *termination* property.

- The nonblocking atomic commit problem has been introduced by Skeen (1981) and was refined later (Guerraoui 2002; Delporte-Gallet et al. 2004). Our "Consensus-Based Non-Blocking Atomic Commit" algorithm presented in this chapter is a modular variant of Skeen's decentralized three-phase algorithm. It is more modular in the sense that we encapsulate many subtle issues of NBAC within consensus.

• The group membership problem was initially discussed by Birman and Joseph
  (1987). They also introduced the view-synchronous communication abstraction.
  Both primitives have been implemented in the influential ISIS System. The specification of view-synchronous communication presented here was introduced
  by Friedman and van Renesse (1996). This is a strong specification as it ensures
  that messages are always delivered in the same view, in which they were broadcast. Weaker specifications were also considered (Babaoglu et al. 1997; Fekete
  et al. 2001; Lesley and Fekete 2003; Pereira et al. 2003). A comprehensive
  survey of group communication specifications and systems providing view-
  synchronous communication is presented by Chockler, Keidar, and Vitenberg
  (2001).

7. Concluding Remarks

The world must be coming to an end. Children no longer obey their parents and
every man wants to write a book.
(Writing on a tablet, unearthed not far from Babylon and dated back to 2800 B.C.)

In many areas of computing, theory and practice were able to sediment a number of basic abstractions that are now taught to students and provided to programmers, in the forms of libraries or programming-language constructs.

The basic abstractions of sequential computing include data structures like *set*, *record*, and *array*, as well as control structures like *if-then-else*, and *loops*. In concurrent computing, fundamental abstractions include *thread*, *mutex*, *transaction*, and *semaphore*, whereas the underlying abstractions of operating systems include *address space* and *file*.

This book studies abstractions for distributed programming: *broadcast*, *shared memory*, *consensus*, and its variants. It describes their realization in distributed systems that are prone to failures and subject to attacks. Some of these abstractions may become – if they are not already – the basic building blocks for building reliable and secure distributed applications.

We mention in the following some systems that support (a subset of) these abstractions. We also mention alternative books that describe the underlying algorithms and implementations from a different perspective.

7.1 Implementation in *Appia*

Many abstractions introduced in the book have been implemented in the *Appia* library. This library is written in Java and was developed with the goal of supporting flexible protocol compositions. *Appia* was originally built for pedagogical purposes (Miranda, Pinto, and Rodrigues 2001). It has subsequently been used in many different research projects and is available freely (Miranda et al. 2009).

C. Cachin et al., *Introduction to Reliable and Secure Distributed Programming*,   341
DOI: 10.1007/978-3-642-15260-3_7,
© Springer-Verlag Berlin Heidelberg 2011

The first edition of this book contained implementations in *Appia* of many of its algorithms for crash-stop process abstractions. They are available online from the book's website at http://distributedprogramming.net.

Studying actual implementations of the algorithms greatly enhances the understanding of those details that have not been covered in the high-level descriptions. Knowledge about the practical issues makes a big difference when moving to a real environment.

7.2 Further Implementations

In the following, we enumerate other systems and programming libraries that implement some of the abstractions we considered in this book. For some libraries, the list also contains pointers to detailed technical descriptions or to more theoretical studies of their algorithmic aspects.

V: The V distributed system was developed at Stanford University as part of a research project to explore communication issues in distributed systems. The process group abstraction was introduced there to encapsulate distribution (Cheriton and Zwaenepoel 1985).

Amoeba: The Amoeba microkernel-based distributed operating system was developed at the Vrije University of Amsterdam to devise applications on a collection of workstations or single board computers (Kaashoek et al. 1989).

Delta-4: The Delta-4 project was a European research project under the ESPRIT Programme that defined an architecture to build dependable system based on reliable (group) communication abstractions. Many of the ideas underlying Delta-4 were later incorporated in the FT-CORBA standard (Powell 1991, 1994).

Replicated RPC: Circus was one of the first systems to use the group communication abstraction to access replicated servers. It included a replicated remote-procedure call facility implemented in Berkeley Unix (Cooper 1984a,b).

ISIS, Horus, Ensemble, and Spinglass: The ISIS system was developed at Cornell University to realize and experiment with the abstractions of group membership and the view-synchronous communication (Birman and Joseph 1987). ISIS, the first in a suite of four related systems, was a commercial product that was deployed in air-traffic control and stock-market applications. For many years, it represented the reference system in the area (Birman and van Renesse 1993; Birman 1999). Horus was a modular implementation of ISIS (van Renesse et al. 1996), and Ensemble was an implementation of Horus written in the ML programming language with several optimizations of the communication stack (Hayden 1998). Spinglass, the youngest in the family, was based on gossip-based algorithms and designed for highly scalable systems (Birman et al. 2001).

Transis: Transis is a group communication system developed at the Hebrew University of Jerusalem. It defines algorithms for both local-area and wide-are networks. The work on this system highlighted the importance of uniform primitives (Amir et al. 1992).

Psync, Consul, Cactus, and Coyote: Psync was the first one in a suite of group communication systems inspired by the x-kernel protocol composition framework (Peterson et al. 1989). Consul was one of the first systems to relax total order based on application semantics for improved performance (Mishra et al. 1993). Cactus was a follow-up on Consul based on a microprotocol decomposition of group services. Many useful lessons on protocol composition were extracted from this work (Bhatti et al. 1998).

GARF, OGS, and BAST: These constitute a suite of distributed programming libraries developed at EPFL. The consensus abstraction was promoted as a first class citizen of the libraries. A fine-grained composition methodology was proposed to guide the programmer (Garbinato et al. 1995; Felber and Guerraoui 2000; Guerraoui et al. 2000).

Arjuna: Arjuna is an object-oriented distributed system developed at the University of Newcastle upon Tyne, which integrates group communication and transaction abstractions (Parrington et al. 1995).

Totem: Developed at the University of California at Santa Barbara, Totem is a group communication protocol suite well-known for a very efficient implementation of total order broadcast on a LAN. It was used to build FT-CORBA compliant systems (Moser et al. 1995; Amir et al. 1995).

Spread: Spread is a group communication system with support for wide-area communication and provides also message encryption and authentication (Amir et al. 2000; Spread Concepts LLC 2010).

JGroups: Written in Java, JGroups is a group communication protocol suite targeted at application servers and data centers; it is widely used at the time of writing this book (Ban 2010).

PBFT: This implementation of Byzantine total-order broadcast using the PBFT algorithm has been developed at the Massachusetts Institute of Technology (Castro and Liskov 2002). Because it is freely available, it has been taken up and extended by several other research projects that build systems for secure distributed programming in the fail-arbitrary model.

SINTRA: The Secure Intrusion-Tolerant Replication Architecture (SINTRA) prototype was developed at IBM Research in order to demonstrate Byzantine total-order broadcast and randomized Byzantine consensus primitives using cryptography (Cachin and Poritz 2002).

UpRight: UpRight is an open-source library for crash-tolerant and Byzantine-tolerant state machine replication (Clement et al. 2009). It incorporates ideas from some of the most efficient Byzantine total-order broadcast protocols developed after the appearance of PBFT.

BFT-SMaRt: SMaRt is a high-performance Byzantine-fault-tolerant state machine replication library developed in Java with simplicity and robustness as primary requirements (Bessani and Sousa 2010). Its main objective is to provide a code base for building dependable services and for implementing new algorithms.

7.3 Further Reading

This book has introduced the most important concepts of distributed programming, according to our understanding. We aimed at formulating the abstractions in a concise manner and at reducing the algorithms to their essential structure. Having mastered the abstractions in this book, the reader is now well positioned to explore the world of distributed programming further. One may choose between two principle directions:

- The *theory of distributed computing* offers a rich conceptual framework that gives deep insights in the phenomena arising from distributed and concurrent programming. The theory develops not only positive results by establishing abstractions and implementing them, but gives also equally important negative results, which characterize impossibilities by formulating models in which certain tasks are provably unsolvable (Lynch 1989).
- The *practice of distributed computing* develops implementations and deploys distributed systems in the real world. For succeeding in practice, a deep understanding of communication networks and operating systems, their capabilities and limitations, is necessary. Many aspects that have been neglected in this book become very important, such as the typical behavior of a system and not only its worst-case behavior (on which this book focused). But building an actual system and deploying it on a global scale, in production systems with tens of thousands of nodes, is for many the ultimate reward.

We close this book with some pointers to related books on distributed programming. Some books choose different abstractions than those we studied in this book, whereas other books choose the same abstractions but present them in a different manner.

Lynch (1996), Attiya and Welch (2004): These books introduce the theory of distributed computing and address aspects like complexity, which we did not cover here. They contain important impossibility results and prove them in detail. Both are written at an advanced level. Lynch (1996) presents algorithms in a very abstract way, making it easier to prove their correctness in a modular and precise manner. Attiya and Welch (2004) consider different computing models, including the message-passing model and the shared-memory model, with special emphasis on their similarities and the discrepancies between them. These two books are ideally suited for the reader who wants to further explore the theory of distributed computing.

Tel (2000), Kshemkalyani and Singhal (2008): The book of Tel (2000) is formulated at an introductory level and contains a comprehensive overview of distributed algorithms and the related theory. It emphasizes more detailed (and perhaps more realistic) network abstractions than the ones considered here. Kshemkalyani and Singhal (2008) give a broad introduction to the principles of distributed systems. The book presents many facets of the theory of distributed systems, but also covers some topics from related domains, such as cryptographic authentication, self-stabilization, and peer-to-peer systems.

Veríssimo and Rodrigues (2001), Birman (2005): These books take the perspective of the designer of a distributed system and discuss crucial architectural decisions for achieving dependability.

Tanenbaum and v. Steen (2002), Coulouris, Dollimore, and Kindberg (2005): These books present the operating system perspective of a distributed system, including aspects like transactions, security, and naming.

Charron-Bost, Pedone, and Schiper (2010): This book contains a collection of works on replication, which were originally presented at a seminar entitled "A 30-Year Perspective on Replication" held in 2007. Their common theme is to use replication as a way to tolerate faults. Replication is also the main method that has been used in this book to realize reliable and secure distributed programming abstractions. This collection contains survey chapters written by most of the people who have contributed to developing state-of-the-art replication techniques.

References

Abadi, M. and P. Rogaway (2002). Reconciling two views of cryptography (the computational soundness of formal encryption). *Journal of Cryptology 15*(2), 103–127.

Abd-El-Malek, M., G. R. Ganger, G. R. Goodson, M. K. Reiter, and J. J. Wylie (2005). Fault-scalable byzantine fault-tolerant services. In *Symposium on Operating Systems Principles (SOSP 2005)*, pp. 59–74.

Abraham, I., G. Chockler, I. Keidar, and D. Malkhi (2006). Byzantine disk Paxos: Optimal resilience with Byzantine shared memory. *Distributed Computing 18*(5), 387–408.

Aguilera, M., W. Chen, and S. Toueg (2000). Failure detection and consensus in the crash–recovery model. *Distributed Computing 13*(2), 99–125.

Alpern, B. and F. B. Schneider (1985). Defining liveness. *Information Processing Letters 21*(4), 181–185.

Amir, Y., C. Danilov, and J. Stanton (2000). A low latency, loss tolerant architecture and protocol for wide area group communication. In *Dependable Systems and Networks (DSN 2000, formerly FTCS-30 and DCCA-8)*, pp. 327–336.

Amir, Y., D. Dolev, S. Kramer, and D. Malki (1992). Transis: A communication sub-system for high availability. In *Fault-Tolerant Computing (FTCS-22)*, pp. 76–84.

Amir, Y., L. E. Moser, P. M. Melliar-Smith, D. A. Agarwal, and P. Ciarfella (1995). The Totem single-ring ordering and membership protocol. *ACM Transactions on Computer Systems 13*(4), 311–342.

Attiya, H., A. Bar-Noy, and D. Dolev (1995). Sharing memory robustly in message-passing systems. *Journal of the ACM 1*(42), 124–142.

Attiya, H. and J. Welch (2004). *Distributed Computing: Fundamentals, Simulations and Advanced Topics* (Second ed.). Wiley.

Babaoglu, Ö., A. Bartoli, and G. Dini (1997). Enriched view synchrony: A programming paradigm for partitionable asynchronous distributed systems. *IEEE Transactions on Computers 46*(6), 642–658.

Ban, B. (2002–2010). JGroups, a toolkit for reliable multicast communication. http://www.jgroups.org.

Ben-Or, M. (1983). Another advantage of free choice: Completely asynchonous agreement protocols. In *Principles of Distributed Computing (PODC 1983)*, pp. 27–30.

Ben-Or, M. and R. El-Yaniv (2003). Resilient-optimal interactive consistency in constant time. *Distributed Computing 16*, 249–262.

Berman, P. and J. A. Garay (1989). Asymptotically optimal distributed consensus (extended abstract). In G. Ausiello, M. Dezani-Ciancaglini, and S. R. D. Rocca (Eds.), *Automata, Languages and Programming (ICALP 1989)*, Volume 372 of *Lecture Notes in Computer Science*, pp. 80–94.

Bessani, A. and P. Sousa (2009–2010). SMaRt — High-performance Byzantine-fault-tolerant state machine replication. http://code.google.com/p/bft-smart/.

Bhatti, N., M. Hiltunen, R. Schlichting, and W. Chiu (1998). Coyote: A system for constructing fine-grain configurable communication services. *ACM Transactions on Computer Systems 16*(4), 321–366.

C. Cachin et al., *Introduction to Reliable and Secure Distributed Programming*,
DOI: 10.1007/978-3-642-15260-3,
© Springer-VerlagBerlin Heidelberg 2011

Birman, K. (1999). A review of experiences with reliable multicast. *Software – Practice and Experience 29*(9), 741–774.

Birman, K. (2005). *Reliable Distributed Systems*. Springer.

Birman, K., M. Hayden, O. Ozkasap, Z. Xiao, M. Budiu, and Y. Minsky (1999). Bimodal multicast. *ACM Transactions on Computer Systems 17*(2), 41–88.

Birman, K. and T. Joseph (1987). Reliable communication in the presence of failures. *ACM Transactions on Computer Systems 1*(5), 47–76.

Birman, K. and R. van Renesse (1993). *Reliable Distributed Programming with the Isis Toolkit*. IEEE Computer Society Press.

Birman, K., R. van Renesse, and W. Vogels (2001). Spinglass: Secure and scalable communications tools for mission-critical computing. In *Survivability Conference and Exposition (DISCEX 2001)*.

Boichat, R., P. Dutta, S. Frølund, and R. Guerraoui (2003a). Deconstructing Paxos. *SIGACT News 34*(1), 47–67.

Boichat, R., P. Dutta, S. Frølund, and R. Guerraoui (2003b). Reconstructing Paxos. *SIGACT News 34*(2), 42–57.

Boichat, R. and R. Guerraoui (2005). Reliable and total order broadcast in a crash–recovery model. *Journal of Parallel and Distributed Computing 65*(4), 397–413.

Bracha, G. (1987). Asynchronous Byzantine agreement protocols. *Information and Computation 75*, 130–143.

Bracha, G. and S. Toueg (1985). Asynchronous consensus and broadcast protocols. *Journal of the ACM 32*(4), 824–840.

Brasileiro, F. V., F. Greve, A. Mostéfaoui, and M. Raynal (2001). Consensus in one communication step. In V. E. Malyshkin (Ed.), *Parallel Computing Technologies (PaCT 2001)*, Volume 2127 of *Lecture Notes in Computer Science*, pp. 42–50.

Cachin, C. (2009). Yet another visit to Paxos. Research Report RZ 3754, IBM Research.

Cachin, C., K. Kursawe, F. Petzold, and V. Shoup (2001). Secure and efficient asynchronous broadcast protocols (extended abstract). In J. Kilian (Ed.), *Advances in Cryptology – CRYPTO 2001*, Volume 2139 of *Lecture Notes in Computer Science*, pp. 524–541.

Cachin, C., K. Kursawe, and V. Shoup (2005). Random oracles in Constantinople: Practical asynchronous Byzantine agreement using cryptography. *Journal of Cryptology 18*(3), 219–246.

Cachin, C. and J. A. Poritz (2002). Secure intrusion-tolerant replication on the Internet. In *Dependable Systems and Networks (DSN 2002)*, pp. 167–176.

Canetti, R. and T. Rabin (1993). Fast asynchronous Byzantine agreement with optimal resilience. In *Symposium on the Theory of Computing (STOC 1993)*, pp. 42–51.

Castro, M. and B. Liskov (2002). Practical Byzantine fault tolerance and proactive recovery. *ACM Transactions on Computer Systems 20*(4), 398–461.

Chandra, T., R. Griesemer, and J. Redstone (2007). Paxos made live – an engineering perspective. In *Principles of Distributed Computing (PODC 2007)*, pp. 398–407.

Chandra, T., V. Hadzilacos, and S. Toueg (1996). The weakest failure detector for solving consensus. *Journal of the ACM 43*(4), 685–722.

Chandra, T. and S. Toueg (1996). Unreliable failure detectors for reliable distributed systems. *Journal of the ACM 43*(2), 225–267.

Chang, J. and N. Maxemchuck (1984). Reliable broadcast protocols. *ACM Transactions on Computer Systems 2*(3), 251–273.

Charron-Bost, B., F. Pedone, and A. Schiper (Eds.) (2010). *Replication: Theory and Practice*, Volume 5959 of *Lecture Notes in Computer Science*. Springer.

Cheriton, D. and W. Zwaenepoel (1985). Distributed process groups in the V kernel. *ACM Transactions on Computer Systems 3*(2), 77–107.

Chockler, G., R. Guerraoui, and I. Keidar (2007). Amnesic distributed storage. In A. Pelc (Ed.), *Distributed Computing (DISC 2007)*, Volume 4731 of *Lecture Notes in Computer Science*, pp. 139–151.

Chockler, G., I. Keidar, and R. Vitenberg (2001). Group communication specifications: A comprehensive study. *ACM Computing Surveys 33*(4), 427–469.

Clement, A., M. Kapritsos, S. Lee, Y. Wang, L. Alvisi, M. Dahlin, and T. Riche (2009). UpRight cluster services. In *Symposium on Operating Systems Principles (SOSP 2009)*, pp. 277–290.

Cooper, E. (1984a). Replicated procedure call. In *Principles of Distributed Computing (PODC 1984)*, pp. 220–232.

Cooper, E. C. (1984b). Circus: A replicated procedure call facility. In *Reliability in Distributed Software and Database Systems (SRDS 1984)*, pp. 11–24.

Coulouris, G., J. Dollimore, and T. Kindberg (2005). *Distributed Systems: Concepts and Design* (4th ed.). Addison-Wesley/Pearson Education.

De Prisco, R., B. Lampson, and N. Lynch (2000). Revisiting the PAXOS algorithm. *Theoretical Computer Science 243*, 35–91.

Delporte-Gallet, C., H. Fauconnier, and R. Guerraoui (2002). Failure detection lower bounds on registers and consensus. In D. Malkhi (Ed.), *Distributed Computing (DISC 2002)*, Volume 2508 of *Lecture Notes in Computer Science*, pp. 237–251.

Delporte-Gallet, C., H. Fauconnier, and R. Guerraoui (2010). Tight failure detection bounds on atomic object implementations. *Journal of the ACM 57*(4).

Delporte-Gallet, C., H. Fauconnier, R. Guerraoui, V. Hadzilacos, P. Kouznetsov, and S. Toueg (2004). The weakest failure detectors to solve certain fundamental problems in distributed computing. In *Principles of Distributed Computing (PODC 2004)*, pp. 338–346.

Diffie, W. and M. E. Hellman (1976). New directions in cryptography. *IEEE Transactions on Information Theory 22*(6), 644–654.

Dolev, D. and H. R. Strong (1983). Authenticated algorithms for Byzantine agreement. *SIAM Journal on Computing 12*(4), 656–666.

Dolev, D. and A. C. Yao (1983). On the security of public key protocols. *IEEE Transactions on Information Theory 29*(2), 198–208.

Doudou, A., B. Garbinato, and R. Guerraoui (2005). Tolerating arbitrary failures with state machine replication. In H. B. Diab and A. Y. Zomaya (Eds.), *Dependable Computing Systems: Paradigms, Performance Issues, and Applications*. Wiley.

Dutta, P. and R. Guerraoui (2005). The inherent price of indulgence. *Distributed Computing 18*(1), 85–98.

Dwork, C., N. Lynch, and L. Stockmeyer (1988). Consensus in the presence of partial synchrony. *Journal of the ACM 35*(2), 288–323.

Eugster, P., R. Guerraoui, S. Handurukande, P. Kouznetsov, and A.-M. Kermarrec (2003). Lightweight probabilistic broadcast. *ACM Transactions on Computer Systems 21*(4), 341–374.

Eugster, P., R. Guerraoui, and P. Kouznetsov (2004). Delta-reliable broadcast: A probabilistic measure of broadcast reliability. In *International Conference on Distributed Computing Systems (ICDCS 2004)*, pp. 636–643.

Ezhilchelvan, P., A. Mostefaoui, and M. Raynal (2001). Randomized multivalued consensus. In *International Symposium on Object-Oriented Real-Time Distributed Computing (ISORC 2001)*, pp. 195–200.

Fekete, A., N. Lynch, and A. Shvartsman (2001). Specifying and using a partitionable group communication service. *ACM Transactions on Computer Systems 19*(2), 171–216.

Felber, P. and R. Guerraoui (2000). Programming with object groups in CORBA. *IEEE Concurrency 8*(1), 48–58.

Fidge, C. (1988). Timestamps in message-passing systems that preserve the partial ordering. In *11th Australian Computer Science Conference*.

Fischer, M., N. Lynch, and M. Paterson (1985). Impossibility of distributed consensus with one faulty process. *Journal of the ACM 32*(2), 374–382.

Friedman, R. and R. van Renesse (1996). Strong and weak virtual synchrony in Horus. In *Symposium on Reliable and Distributed Systems (SRDS 1996)*, pp. 140–149.

Garbinato, B., R. Guerraoui, and K. Mazouni (1995). Implementation of the GARF replicated objects platform. *Distributed Systems Engineering 2*(1), 14–27.

Garbinato, B., F. Pedone, and R. Schmidt (2004). An adaptive algorithm for efficient message diffusion in unreliable environments. In *Dependable Systems and Networks (DSN 2004)*, pp. 507–516.

Gifford, D. K. (1979). Weighted voting for replicated data. In *Symposium on Operating Systems Principles (SOSP 1979)*, pp. 150–162.

Golding, R. and D. Long (1992). Design choices for weak-consistency group communication. Technical Report UCSC-CRL-92-45, University of California Santa Cruz.

Goldreich, O. (2001–2004). *Foundations of Cryptography*, Volume I & II. Cambridge University Press.

Gray, C. and D. Cheriton (1989). Leases: An efficient fault-tolerant mechanism for distributed file cache consistency. In *Symposium on Operating Systems Principles (SOSP 1989)*, pp. 202–210.

Gray, J. (1978). Notes on database operating systems. In *Operating Systems: An Advanced Course*, Volume 60 of *Lecture Notes in Computer Science*, pp. 393–481.

Guerraoui, R. (2000). Indulgent algorithms. In *Principles of Distributed Computing (PODC 2000)*, pp. 289–297.

Guerraoui, R. (2002). Non-blocking atomic commit in asynchronous distributed systems with failure detectors. *Distributed Computing 15*(1), 17–25.

Guerraoui, R., P. Eugster, P. Felber, B. Garbinato, and K. Mazouni (2000). Experiences with object group systems. *Software – Practice and Experience 30*(12), 1375–1404.

Guerraoui, R., N. Knežević, V. Quéma, and M. Vukolić (2010). The next 700 BFT protocols. In *European Conference on Computer Systems (EuroSys 2010)*, pp. 363–376.

Guerraoui, R. and R. Levy (2004). Robust emulations of a shared memory in a crash–recovery model. In *International Conference on Distributed Computing Systems (ICDCS 2004)*, pp. 400–407.

Guerraoui, R., R. Oliveria, and A. Schiper (1998). Stubborn communication channels. Technical Report LSR-REPORT-1998-009, Ecole Polytechnique Fédérale de Lausanne (EPFL).

Guerraoui, R. and M. Raynal (2004). The information structure of indulgent consensus. *IEEE Transactions on Computers 53*(4), 453–466.

Guerraoui, R. and A. Schiper (2001). Genuine atomic multicast in asynchronous distributed systems. *Theoretical Computer Science 254*, 297–316.

Gupta, I., A.-M. Kermarrec, and A. Ganesh (2006). Efficient and adaptive epidemic-style protocols for reliable and scalable multicast. *IEEE Transactions on Parallel and Distributed Systems 17*(7), 593–605.

Hadzilacos, V. (1984). *Issues of Fault Tolerance in Concurrent Computations*. Ph. D. thesis, Harvard University.

Hadzilacos, V. and S. Toueg (1993). Fault-tolerant broadcasts and related problems. In S. J. Mullender (Ed.), *Distributed Systems*. New York: ACM Press & Addison-Wesley. Expanded version appears as Technical Report TR94-1425, Department of Computer Science, Cornell University, 1994.

Hayden, M. (1998). *The Ensemble System*. Ph. D. thesis, Cornell University, Computer Science Department.

Herlihy, M. and J. Wing (1990). Linearizability: A correctness condition for concurrent objects. *ACM Transactions on Programming Languages and Systems 3*(12), 463–492.

Israeli, A. and M. Li (1993). Bounded timestamps. *Distributed Computing 4*(6), 205–209.

Jelasity, M., R. Guerraoui, A.-M. Kermarrec, and M. van Steen (2004). The peer sampling service: Experimental evaluation of unstructured gossip-based implementations. In H.-A. Jacobsen (Ed.), *Middleware 2004*, Volume 3231 of *Lecture Notes in Computer Science*, pp. 79–98.

Kaashoek, F. and A. Tanenbaum (1991). Group communication in the Amoeba distributed operating system. In *International Conference on Distributed Computing Systems (ICDCS 1991)*, pp. 222–230.

Kaashoek, F., A. Tanenbaum, S. Hummel, and H. Bal (1989). An efficient reliable broadcast protocol. *Operating Systems Review 4*(23), 5–19.

Kermarrec, A.-M., L. Massoulié, and A. J. Ganesh (2003). Probabilistic reliable dissemination in large-scale systems. *IEEE Transactions on Parallel and Distributed Systems 14*(3), 248–258.

Koldehofe, B. (2003). Buffer management in probabilistic peer-to-peer communication protocols. In *Symposium on Reliable Distributed Systems (SRDS 2003)*, pp. 76–85.

Kotla, R., L. Alvisi, M. Dahlin, A. Clement, and E. L. Wong (2009). Zyzzyva: Speculative Byzantine fault tolerance. *ACM Transactions on Computer Systems 27*(4), 7:1–7:39.

Kouznetsov, P., R. Guerraoui, S. Handurukande, and A.-M. Kermarrec (2001). Reducing noise in gossip-based reliable broadcast. In *Symposium on Reliable Distributed Systems (SRDS 2001)*, pp. 186–189.

Kshemkalyani, A. D. and M. Singhal (2008). *Distributed Computing: Principles, Algorithms, and Systems*. Cambridge University Press.

Ladin, R., B. Liskov, and L. Shrira (1990). Lazy replication: Exploiting the semantics of distributed services. In *Principles of Distributed Computing (PODC 1990)*, pp. 43–57.

Lamport, L. (1977). Concurrent reading and writing. *Communications of the ACM 11*(20), 806–811.

Lamport, L. (1978). Time, clocks and the ordering of events in a distributed system. *Communications of the ACM 21*(7), 558–565.

Lamport, L. (1986a). On interprocess communication. Part I: Basic formalism. *Distributed Computing 2*(1), 75–85.

Lamport, L. (1986b). On interprocess communication. Part II: Algorithms. *Distributed Computing 2*(1), 86–101.

Lamport, L. (1998). The part-time parliament. *ACM Transactions on Computer Systems 16*(2), 133–169. Initially appeared as Technical Report 49, DEC Systems Research Center, 1989.

Lamport, L., R. Shostak, and M. Pease (1982). The Byzantine generals problem. *ACM Transactions on Programming Languages and Systems 4*(3), 382–401.

Lampson, B. (2001). The ABCD's of Paxos. In *Principles of Distributed Computing (PODC 2001)*.

Lesley, N. and A. Fekete (2003). Providing view synchrony for group communication services. *Acta Informatica 40*(3), 159–210.

Li, H. C., A. Clement, A. S. Aiyer, and L. Alvisi (2007). The Paxos register. In *Symposium on Reliable Distributed Systems (SRDS 2007)*, pp. 114–126.

Lin, M.-J. and K. Marzullo (1999). Directional gossip: Gossip in a wide area network. In J. Hlavicka, E. Maehle, and A. Pataricza (Eds.), *European Dependable Computing Conference (EDCC-3)*, Volume 1667 of *Lecture Notes in Computer Science*, pp. 364–379.

Liskov, B. (2010). From viewstamped replication to Byzantine fault tolerance. In B. Charron-Bost, F. Pedone, and A. Schiper (Eds.), *Replication: Theory and Practice*, Volume 5959 of *Lecture Notes in Computer Science*, pp. 121–149. Springer.

Lynch, N. (1996). *Distributed Algorithms*. Morgan Kaufmann.

Lynch, N. and A. Shvartsman (1997). Robust emulation of shared memory using dynamic quorum acknowledged broadcasts. In *Fault-Tolerant Computing Systems (FTCS 1997)*, pp. 272–281.

Lynch, N. and A. Shvartsman (2002). RAMBO: A reconfigurable atomic memory service for dynamic networks. In D. Malkhi (Ed.), *Distributed Computing (DISC 2002)*, Volume 2508 of *Lecture Notes in Computer Science*, pp. 173–190.

Lynch, N. A. (1989). A hundred impossibility proofs for distributed computing. In *Principles of Distributed Computing (PODC 1989)*, pp. 1–28.

Malkhi, D. and M. K. Reiter (1998). Byzantine quorum systems. *Distributed Computing 11*(4), 203–213.

Martin, J.-P. and L. Alvisi (2006). Fast Byzantine consensus. *IEEE Transactions on Dependable and Secure Computing 3*(3), 202–215.

Martin, J.-P., L. Alvisi, and M. Dahlin (2002). Minimal Byzantine storage. In D. Malkhi (Ed.), *Distributed Computing (DISC 2002)*, Volume 2508 of *Lecture Notes in Computer Science*, pp. 311–325.

Menezes, A. J., P. C. van Oorschot, and S. A. Vanstone (1997). *Handbook of Applied Cryptography*. CRC Press.

Milosevic, Z., M. Hutle, and A. Schiper (2009). Unifying Byzantine consensus algorithms with weak interactive consistency. In T. F. Abdelzaher, M. Raynal, and N. Santoro (Eds.), *Principles of Distributed Systems (OPODIS 2009)*, Volume 5923 of *Lecture Notes in Computer Science*, pp. 300–314.

Miranda, H., A. Pinto, and L. Rodrigues (2001). Appia, a flexible protocol kernel supporting multiple coordinated channels. In *International Conference on Distributed Computing Systems (ICDCS 2001)*, pp. 707–710.

Miranda, H., A. Pinto, L. Rodrigues, N. Carvalho, J. Mocito, and L. Rosa (2001–2009). Appia communication framework. http://appia.di.fc.ul.pt/ and http://sourceforge.net/projects/appia/.

Mishra, S., L. Peterson, and R. Schlichting (1993). Experience with modularity in Consul. *Software – Practice and Experience 23*(10), 1059–1075.

Moser, L. E., P. M. Melliar-Smith, and D. A. Agarwal (1995). The Totem system. In *Fault-Tolerant Computing Systems (FTCS 1995)*, pp. 61–66.

Naor, M. and A. Wool (1998). The load, capacity and availability of quorum systems. *SIAM Journal on Computing 27*(2), 423–447.

Neiger, G. and S. Toueg (1993). Simulating synchronized clocks and common knowledge in distributed systems. *Journal of the ACM 2*(40), 334–367.

Oki, B. M. and B. Liskov (1988). Viewstamped replication: A new primary copy method to support highly-available distributed systems. In *Principles of Distributed Computing (PODC 1988)*, pp. 8–17.

Parrington, G., S. Shrivastava, S. Wheater, and M. Little (1995). The design and implementation of Arjuna. *Computing Systems 8*(3), 255–308.

Pease, M., R. Shostak, and L. Lamport (1980). Reaching agreement in the presence of faults. *Journal of the ACM 27*(2), 228–234.

Pereira, J., L. Rodrigues, and R. Oliveira (2003). Semantically reliable multicast: Definition, implementation, and performance evaluation. *IEEE Transactions on Computers 52*(2), 150–165.

Peterson, G. (1983). Concurrent reading while writing. *ACM Transactions on Programming Languages and Systems 5*(1), 46–55.

Peterson, L., N. Bucholz, and R. Schlichting (1989). Preserving and using context information in interprocess communication. *ACM Transactions on Computer Systems 7*(3), 217–246.

Powell, D. (Ed.) (1991). *Delta Four: A Generic Architecture for Dependable Distributed Computing*. Springer.

Powell, D. (1994). Distributed fault tolerance: Lessons from Delta-4. *IEEE Micro 14*(1), 36–47.

Rabin, M. O. (1983). Randomized Byzantine generals. In *Foundations of Computer Science (FOCS 1983)*, pp. 403–409.

Raynal, M., A. Schiper, and S. Toueg (1991). The causal ordering abstraction and a simple way to implement it. *Information Processing Letters 39*(6), 343–350.

Reiter, M. K. (1994). Secure agreement protocols: Reliable and atomic group multicast in Rampart. In *Computer and Communications Security (CCS 1994)*, pp. 68–80.

Rivest, R. L., A. Shamir, and L. Adleman (1978). A method for obtaining digital signatures and public-key cryptosystems. *Communications of the ACM 21*(2), 120–126.

Rodrigues, L., H. Fonseca, and P. Veríssimo (1996). Totally ordered multicast in large-scale systems. In *International Conference on Distributed Computing Systems (ICDCS 1996)*, pp. 503–510.

Rodrigues, L., R. Guerraoui, and A. Schiper (1998). Scalable atomic multicast. In *International Conference on Computer Communications and Networks (ICCCN 1998)*, pp. 840–847.

Rodrigues, L., S. Handurukande, J. Pereira, R. Guerraoui, and A.-M. Kermarrec (2003). Adaptive gossip-based broadcast. In *Dependable Systems and Networks (DSN 2003)*, pp. 47–56.

Rodrigues, L. and M. Raynal (2003). Atomic broadcast in asynchronous crash–recovery distributed systems and its use in quorum-based replication. *IEEE Transactions on Knowledge and Data Engineering 15*(5), 1206–1217.

Rodrigues, L. and P. Veríssimo (1992). xAMp: A multi-primitive group communications service. In *Symposium on Reliable Distributed Systems (SRDS 1992)*, pp. 112–121.

Rufino, J., P. Veríssimo, G. Arroz, C. Almeida, and L. Rodrigues (1998). Fault-tolerant broadcasts in CAN. In *Fault-Tolerant Computing (FTCS 1998)*, pp. 150–159.

Saltzer, J. H., D. P. Reed, and D. D. Clark (1984). End-to-end arguments in system design. *ACM Transactions on Computer Systems 2*(4), 277–288.

Schneider, F., D. Gries, and R. Schlichting (1984). Fault-tolerant broadcasts. *Science of Computer Programming 4*(1), 1–15.

Schneider, F. B. (1990). Implementing fault-tolerant services using the state machine approach: A tutorial. *ACM Computing Surveys 22*(4), 299–319.

Schwarz, R. and F. Mattern (1994). Detecting causal relationships in distributed computations: In search of the holy grail. *Distributed Computing 7*(3), 149–174.

Shamir, A. (1979). How to share a secret. *Communications of the ACM 22*(11), 612–613.

Shao, C., E. Pierce, and J. Welch (2003). Multi-writer consistency conditions for shared memory objects. In F. E. Fich (Ed.), *Distributed Computing (DISC 2003)*, Volume 2848 of *Lecture Notes in Computer Science*, pp. 106–120.

Skeen, D. (1981). A decentralized termination protocol. In *IEEE Symposium on Reliability in Distributed Software and Database Systems*.

Song, Y. J. and R. van Renesse (2008). Bosco: One-step Byzantine asynchronous consensus amnesic distributed storage. In G. Taubenfeld (Ed.), *Distributed Computing (DISC 2008)*, Volume 5218 of *Lecture Notes in Computer Science*, pp. 438–450.

Spread Concepts LLC (2001–2010). The Spread toolkit. http://www.spread.org.

Srikanth, T. K. and S. Toueg (1987). Simulating authenticated broadcasts to derive simple fault-tolerant algorithms. *Distributed Computing 2*, 80–94.

Tanenbaum, A. and M. v. Steen (2002). *Distributed Systems: Principles and Paradigms*. Prentice Hall, Englewood Cliffs, NJ, USA.

Tel, G. (2000). *Introduction to Distributed Algorithms* (2nd ed.). Cambridge University Press, Cambridge.

Thomas, R. H. (1979). A majority consensus approach to concurrency control for multiple copy databases. *ACM Transactions on Database Systems 4*(2), 180–209.

Toueg, S. (1984). Randomized Byzantine agreements. In *Principles of Distributed Computing (PODC 1984)*, pp. 163–178.

van Renesse, R., K. Birman, and S. Maffeis (1996). Horus: A flexible group communication system. *Communications of the ACM 4*(39), 76–83.

Veríssimo, P. and L. Rodrigues (2001). *Distributed Systems for System Architects*. Kluwer Academic Publishers, Dordrecht (Hingham, MA).

Veríssimo, P., L. Rodrigues, and M. Baptista (1989). AMp: A highly parallel atomic multicast protocol. In *Communications Architectures & Protocols (SIGCOMM '89)*, pp. 83–93.

Vidyasankar, K. (1988). Converting Lamport's regular register to atomic register. *Information Processing Letters 28*(6), 287–290.

Vidyasankar, K. (1990). Concurrent reading while writing revisited. *Distributed Computing 2*(4), 81–85.

Vitányi, P. M. B. and B. Awerbuch (1986). Atomic shared register access by asynchronous hardware. In *Foundations of Computer Science (FOCS 1986)*, pp. 233–243.

Voulgaris, S., M. Jelasity, and M. van Steen (2003). A robust and scalable peer-to-peer gossiping protocol. In G. Moro, C. Sartori, and M. Singh (Eds.), *Agents and Peer-to-Peer Computing (AP2PC 2003)*, Volume 2872 of *Lecture Notes in Computer Science*.

Wensley, J., L. Lamport, J. Goldberg, M. Green, K. Levitt, P. Melliar-Smith, R. Shostak, and C. Weinstock (1978). SIFT: Design and analysis of a fault-tolerant computer for aircraft control. *Proceedings of the IEEE 10*(66), 1240–1255.

Xiao, Z., K. Birman, and R. van Renesse (2002). Optimizing buffer management for reliable multicast. In *Dependable Systems and Networks (DSN 2002)*, pp. 155–166.

List of Modules

List of Algorithms

Index